The Annals of Ballitore

Silhouette of Mary and William Leadbeater
Courtesy of the Friends' Historical Library, Dublin.

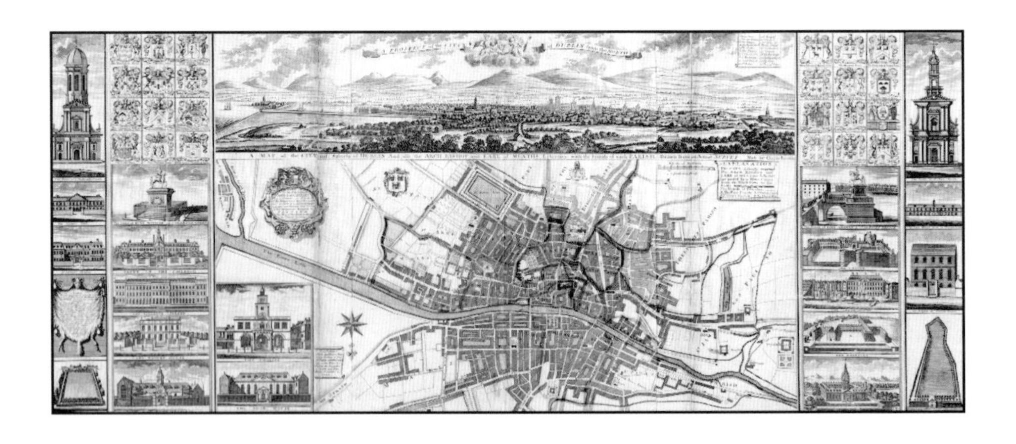

1728 Map of Dublin by Charles Brooking.
The original of this map was donated by the Chinn family in memory of
Kathleen Elizabeth Chinn (neé Shackleton) 1925-2000.
The map originally hung above the chimney-piece in Ballitore School *[see p.17]*
and is now on display in Ballitore Community Library and Quaker Museum.

The Annals of Ballitore

being a compilation of

Mary Leadbeater's,
'Annals of Ballitore,'

and

Betsy Shackleton's,
'Ballitore & Its Inhabitants Seventy Years Ago.'

Compiled and edited by
Mario Corrigan, Michael Kavanagh and Karel Kiely.

Printed by
Naas Printing Limited, Naas 2009

All profits from the sale of this publication will go to
Athy Town Heritage Centre and Museum.

DEDICATION

Eve Róisín Corrigan and Sarah Murnane
Colette, John and Ann who give us time to do what we do.

John MacKenna and for absent friends
Willie Kelly and Con Costello
who would not let us forget!

978-0-9561244-0-1 Paperback
978-0-9561244-1-8 Hardback

Published by Kildare Collections and Research Services,
The Local Studies, Genealogy and Archives Department,
Kildare County Library and Arts Services
in association with
Athy Town Heritage Centre and Museum

Cover design: Mario Corrigan
Illustrations – Kildare Collections and Research Services
Front Cover – reproduction from original book of illustrations drawn by
Mary Leadbeater's brother, Abraham, while she lay ill.
Rear Cover – Ballitore Village from 1st ed. 1837 OS Map – with kind permission

The added description of Ballitore from the microfilm copy of the
original manuscript is reproduced here by kind permission of the
National Library of Ireland.
The Frontispiece (silhouettes) by kind permission
of the Friends' Historical Library

Original drafts prepared with the help of the Nurney/Kildangan C.E.P.
and Cill Dara (Kildare Town) Historical Society.
Annals of Ballitore – Breid Kelly & Maria O'Reilly.
and Naas Computer Studies Course
Ballitore & Its Inhabitants Seventy Years Ago – Elizabeth Reilly

Printed by
Naas Printing Limited, Naas 2009

Table of Contents

INTRODUCTION.

Mary Leadbeater's 'Annals of Ballitore,' published in 1862 with a second edition appearing later that year is essentially a diary of people's lives and events in the vicinity of the village of Ballitore, Co. Kildare, from 1766 to 1824. 'The Annals,' with a Memoir of Mary Leadbeater and a list of the pupils of Ballitore School formed volume one of a two volume set entitled, 'The Leadbeater Papers.' Volume II (not reproduced here) consisted of correspondence including letters from Mary's father's great friend, Edmund Burke.

In 2004, Kildare Collections and Research Services, (Kildare Library and Arts Services) decided to make 'The Annals' more accessible to the public with the intention of publishing it on the internet. With the help of Joe Connelly and the FÁS funded Nurney–Kildangan C.E. Project and Cill Dara Historical Society (acting as sponsors), Breid Kelly and Maria O'Reilly typed the work over a period of months from 2006 to 2007. It soon became apparent that we might publish the work. We decided to do this in partnership with Athy Heritage Centre and Museum and also to include Betsy Shackleton's remarkable little volume.

This is the first hardcopy reprint of the original full–text of the Annals since 1862 although there was an excellent edited version published by John MacKenna in 1986 and the first edition has been reproduced on the internet. For those acquainted with the book it is indeed a welcome addition to the published sources for County Kildare and for those who have yet to acquaint themselves it will prove to be a unique discovery of 18th and 19th century life in this small village in Co. Kildare. The original manuscript description of Ballitore in 1766 was omitted from the 1862 publications but was uncovered for us by Christopher Moriarty, Archivist with the Society of Friends Historical Library. I would like to express our thanks to Colette O'Daly and the Board of the National Library for their kind permission to reproduce the 'missing' excerpt in this volume. Our thanks to Christopher for his efforts and his enthusiasm and indeed to the Society of Friends, who have always been great supporters of Kildare Library and Arts Services in relation to its commitment to Ballitore, Ballitore Library and the Mary Leadbeater Museum. I would also like to pay tribute to my friend and library co–worker, Mary Malone, curator at Ballitore who continues to preserve the legacy of Mary Leadbeater and the Quakers at Ballitore.

This project could not have been completed without the support of Kildare County Council, Co. Librarian, Breda Gleeson and Senior Executive

Librarians, Marian Higgins and Eimear McGinn, Genealogist Karel Kiely, Rose Sheridan, Mary O'Hara, the staff of Kildare Library and Arts Services and James Durney. Likewise it could not have been completed without the aid of Elizabeth Reilly, Joe Connelly, Breid Kelly and Maria O'Reilly who initially made it possible. The current volume has been edited and checked by myself, Karel Kiely and Michael Kavanagh the former Local Studies Librarian in Kildare County Library. Thanks also to James Durney for his efforts and expertise. We do hope that it is worthy of the original. For local historians, researchers, third level students, school children and anyone interested in the rich and varied history of the County of Kildare it will hopefully prove to be an invaluable resource.

It is made all the more so by the addition of the text of a lecture prepared and delivered by John MacKenna to the Historical Committee of the Society of Friends early in 2008 and at Athy Community Library for Heritage Week. John MacKenna's essay contextualises the work of Mary Leadbeater but as well as allowing us an insight into the development of the Quaker community of Ballitore he develops the historical figure of Mary Leadbeater into a living person; very much alive in her own environment – for it is Mary Leadbeater's vision of the world, her surroundings and the people that she encounters that truly make this a unique source.

We have taken the liberty of adding a second book to the current volume, the memoir of Mary Leadbeater's niece, Betsy Shackleton, also published in 1862, 'Ballitore & Its Inhabitants Seventy Years Ago.' A little known work, this charming recollection of the village and its inhabitants adds to the description drawn so forthrightly in the Annals and helps develop the writer's stories even further. There is a danger that we might concentrate on their Quakerism and certainly we cannot hope to understand the diarists unless we understand that above all they were women and they were Quakers. If we quantify this as but an intrinsic element of the story we realise that these remarkable women recorded and captured the lives of people who would have been lost to us through time – the lives of the Finns, the Murrays, the Websters; of Dr. Johnson – of ordinary folk about their business and the effect on a small village of a revolution thrust upon it – recorded from the inside out, not through research or revisionism but through the eyes of those who lived through it.

The publication is part of the process of making primary and secondary material more available through the Internet (www.kildare.ie/library) or in hardcopy which has been undertaken by Kildare Collections and Research Services, to encourage people to engage in local history and genealogy as well as increasing accessibility to the fabulous Irish, Local and Archival collections in Kildare County Library. Some spellings and misspellings are retained and identified in the endnotes as they appeared in the original. The practice of leaving a space before a colon, semi–colon etc. has been abandoned. The original footnotes are replaced by endnotes and those of the original editors are in bold. The poem on Ballitore which was included in the 1862 editions of the 'Annals' has been reproduced as an Appendix to 'The Annals of Ballitore'.

The front cover is obviously a child's drawing and may seem a strange choice as an illustration but when Mary Leadbeater was recovering from an illness, she thought of her recently deceased brother, Abraham (Betsy Shackleton's father) and remarked, "Never can I forget the time when, at ten years old, I had the ague, nor his visits every evening to draw a picture for me in a little book which he had made for the purpose. That book, preserved with care and often looked at with great enjoyment, I am now afraid to open." The drawing is taken, I believe, from this book of illustrations, now in the Archives of Kildare Library and Arts Services. I would also like to thank Dan O'Connell and the Ordnance Survey of Ireland for their kind permission to reproduce the map of Ballitore on the rear cover.

The book is published in association with Athy Heritage Centre and Museum. This partnership approach will hopefully serve once again as a model for future projects. We are lucky in County Kildare to have so many Local History Groups, the Federation of Local History Groups, the County Kildare Archaeological Society and numerous talented individuals who continually research and publish new material. But there is also a need to highlight the resources we already which are no longer available except in libraries and private collections. This publication will hopefully serve to illustrate the importance of such material and to promote the history and heritage of the county.

The Athy Heritage Centre and Museum was delighted to be associated with the project and any revenue collected will help preserve both the building and the service. I would like to thank the Athy Heritage Company, particularly its Chairperson, Frank Taaffe, and Centre manager, Margaret Walsh, who have been tremendously supportive from the outset.

Mario Corrigan
Executive Librarian
Kildare Collections and Research Services
1 March 2009

FOREWORD.

It is a great pleasure to welcome this new edition of The Annals of Ballitore. For a number of reasons, Athy Heritage Centre is proud to be associated with the republication of the Annals.

Mary Shackleton–Leadbeater is one of the great figures in the history of south Kildare and her Annals are an important part of the social fabric of the area. Mary was also an antecedent of Ernest Shackleton and Athy Heritage Centre has a particular affinity with Ernest, through our permanent exhibition of his memorabilia and through the annual Shackleton Autumn School.

But, most importantly, the republication of the complete Annals, after a century and a half, brings one of the most important social documents of late eighteenth and early nineteenth century life in Ireland back where it belongs – on the bookshelves of readers.

Frank Taaffe
Chairperson
Athy Heritage Company

NOTE ON RESTORED PAGES.

Shortly before this edition of The Annals of Ballitore was completed, the editor Mario Corrigan contacted the Friends Historical Library in Dublin in search of some pages which were not included in the 1862 edition of Mary Leadbeater's great work. The editor of that printing felt that, *'The general description of the village of Ballitore as it appeared in the year 1766 ... is now so inapplicable that it is thought best to omit the few pages it occupies in the 'Annals,' and to substitute, with some omissions, a poem written by her in the year 1778 ...'*

Times and interests have changed and a description of a mid-18th century village is now seen as a matter of exceptional interest. There was no trace of an earlier edition in the Friends Historical Library, nor of the original manuscript. By chance, the Quaker historian Richard Harrison was working in the reading room and was able to tell us that the manuscript was held in Dublin in the National Library. There was no problem in making a transcript from the microfilm of the original work and restore the section to its rightful place – making the present edition the first complete printed version of the 'Annals' ever to be published.

In these few pages Mary Leadbeater takes the reader on a tour of Ballitore, giving a description of its woodlands and gardens, of its houses great and small, together with asides on some of the residents. While many of the great houses and gardens of 18th century Ireland have been described in considerable detail, similar treatment of an entire village is very much rarer. Although the text appears under the heading '1766' neither the handwriting nor the style are those of an eight–year–old and the description of the village probably refers to a considerably later date. But the absence of any mention of the damage done in 1798 implies that the observations were made prior to the Rising.

In this version we follow the author's distinctly personal use of punctuation which, amongst other foibles, includes an unhappy lack of enthusiasm for dividing her text into paragraphs.

In spite of this, her prose remains highly readable and entertaining. Quaker historians – among many others – are delighted, first to see this remarkable personal account of 18th century life made available once more and, secondly, to see the missing pages in print after more than two centuries in hiding.

Christopher Moriarty
Clerk,
Historical Committee of the Religious Society of Friends in Ireland.

Lecture delivered to the Historical Committee of the Society of Friends and as part of the Heritage Week programme for Co. Kildare at Athy Community Library 2008:

MARY LEADBEATER

AND THE QUAKER INFLUENCE IN BALLITORE.

JOHN MACKENNA

The subjects of this lecture are Mary Leadbeater and the Quaker influence on the village of Ballitore in Co. Kildare, so it seems right to begin by putting the record straight.

Ballitore is not a Quaker village, in the sense that it is not a village and community founded by Friends. The very name Ballitore (Baile an Tobar – the town of the well or the marshy place) predates the English speaking Quakers who arrived there in the early eighteenth century. That it became a village dominated by Quakers is a fact but there was a community there with its own language, social construct, religion and life before the Quakers arrived.

In fact there were two communities living in the area. The landowning class of, mainly, Church of Ireland families who lived, literally, in the big houses, owned the best land, held the best positions and were part of the ruling elite. These were English speaking and wealthy and had, for the most part, little or no connection with the peasant class who were Catholic, mostly labourers or craftspeople, and who lived, literally, in the valley of the marsh on smallholdings of poor land or in cramped, overcrowded and often destitute conditions.

Into this divided society came the newly arrived Quakers with their dissenting religious beliefs and practices, with their strong North of England accents, with their distrust of the established Protestant church and all it stood for and with a commitment to buying and improving the poor land of the area or establishing business, particularly in mills and shops. These Quakers were the newly emerging middle class but they differed from other bourgeois groups in that they had no aspirations to become a part of the ruling class, they refused to serve as jurymen, refused to take oaths and refused to join the army and they might have been viewed as suspiciously as the local Catholics had it not been for their avowed pacifism

One of those who arrived from Yorkshire was Abraham Shackleton who had come to Ireland, initially, as a tutor to the Duckett and Cooper families of Co. Carlow. Abraham became, in time, a part of the newly established Quaker community in Ballitore and, with his background in education, he established a school in the village in 1720. In 1756 his son, Richard, took over as headmaster of the now successful school, which had grown in numbers and had up to sixty boarders as well as day pupils at its peak. The day pupils were almost exclusively local Quaker children – girls as well as boys – but the boarders were drawn from as far away as Norway and France and also from wealthy Irish families, not all of them Quaker.

Among the pupils were Edmund Burke, Napper Tandy who was to become one of the founders of the United Irishmen and Paul Cullen who was to become Cardinal Cullen, Catholic Primate of Ireland. This cosmopolitan collection of young men and women brought a great vibrancy to the village. Many lodged in local houses and the existence of the school was a boon to the local economy.

There was, of course a darker side. Many of the young boys who came at the age of three or four to Ballitore and remained there until their education was complete at eighteen or nineteen did not see their parents more than once or twice in the intervening years. This was particularly true of the young boys who had come from abroad. For a number the story was even darker, they contracted smallpox or chickenpox and died. Mary Leadbeater (or Shackleton as she was then) recounts in her diary the death of one young French boy who had been at the school less than a year and who spoke little English. He was nursed by Mary's mother and appeared to be recovering but died, leaving the students traumatised.

Mary had been born to Richard Shackleton and his second wife Elizabeth Carleton in 1758. By then the Quaker community was thriving. As well as its involvement in the school in Ballitore, the Shackleton family was involved in milling and farming. Indeed, the Quakers in the fifty years since their arrival had transformed Ballitore and its surroundings. The marshy land had been drained, fields had been made and hedged, orchards and native trees had been planted. New houses, solidly built, lined the streets of the village. The school building was a central part of the local architecture and the Meeting House was the only place of worship in the community – no Catholic church having been built because of the Penal Laws and no Church of Ireland church having been built because the local landlord class worshipped in the nearby village of Timolin.

It's worth mentioning here, as we move towards 1798 and the central role the Quaker community played in the events of that summer's rebellion, that the Penal laws were intended to cripple the Catholic population of Ireland. Take as an example the penal code introduced under William III in 1697:

An Act for banishing all papists exercising any ecclesiastical jurisdiction and all regulars of the popish clergy...Sec. 1. Whereas it is notoriously known, that the late rebellions in this kingdom have been promoted by popish bishops and other ecclesiastical persons of the popish religion.....all popish archbishops, bishops, vicars–general, deans, Jesuits, monks, friars, and all other regular popish clergy shall depart out of this kingdom before the 1st day of May, 1698, and if any of said ecclesiastical persons shall after that day be in this kingdom, they shall suffer imprisonment, and remain in prison until transported out of his Majesty's dominions, wherever his Majesty or the chief governors of this kingdom shall see fit, and if any person so transported shall return, he shall be guilty of high treason.

But as Mary Shackleton grew through childhood into adolescence life in the community of Ballitore remained, for the most part, calm. There were incidents and accidents, personality clashes and confrontations but, in general, life was peaceful. In the valley of Ballitore, on the bank of the River Griese, the Quaker and Catholic populations lived amicably side–by–side. On the hillsides overlooking the valley the landed gentry got on with their lives. The one thorn in the side of peace was the constant presence of both British soldiers and militiamen in the village. Arrests, punishment beatings, floggings and imprisonment were regular occurrences in the Catholic community. In many cases poverty bred the need for crime and pilfering and robbery were dealt with severely and swiftly. The sword of justice might not always fall equitably but it always fell.

One of the very positive influences of the Quaker school in Ballitore was on Mary Shackleton. Her father insisted she receive an education that matched those of her male relatives and friends. The curriculum in the school included reading, writing, Latin, mathematics, geography and science. It was this liberal curriculum and a commitment to an holistic education which drew children from far and wide. It should be said, however, that for most of the children of Ballitore, education was to be found in the penny–schools and hedge schools run by individuals in the area. Yet again, the long–term intention of the Penal laws was to insure that the Catholic population remained uneducated. Those with money could send their children to schools like Ballitore or to schools in Europe but for the peasant class the little education that was available could be found in the kitchens of houses or the shelter of hedges. It was a rough and ready education but it was the only one available.

In 1791, Mary Shackleton married William Leadbeater. William had come as a pupil to Ballitore and had returned as a qualified teacher to work in his alma mater. He had joined the Religious Society of Friends as a young man and now he and the thirty–three year old Mary were married. They renovated and extended a house on the Square in the village and, when it was ready, they moved in, sub–letting part of the house as a shop and living quarters to two local Catholic sisters, Mary and Anne Doyle. William had by then decided on a career change and moved out of teaching and into farming, house–building and trading. Mary had become the local Post–mistress, the first in Ballitore, opening the post office in their home.

The defining event in the history of Ballitore was the rebellion of 1798 and the defining occurrence in the history of Quakerism in the village was that same event. In order to understand why the rebellion took place and why the Quaker community in general, and Mary Leadbeater in particular, were so sympathetic to the rebels it is necessary to step back a moment and look at the socio–political background of Friends in the village in the decade before the rebellion.

Women in late eighteenth century Ballitore were of three distinct classes. The Anglo–Irish, upper–class Protestant women of the ascendancy were reasonably well educated but not politically involved. They belonged to a stratum which had not come under any political pressure in a hundred years. They were comfortable, politically and economically self–centred and disinterested in their peasant neighbours.

Irish peasant–class Catholic women were badly educated, ground down by poverty and too busy trying to keep body and soul together to become involved in the politics of the secret societies, particularly those of the United Irishmen. They were also members of a faith which saw women in a subservient light.

Irish Quaker women were part of a religious group which had a much more enlightened attitude to women. Friends believed in the equality of all in the sight of God – and not just in the equality of all men. They also had an economic security which allowed them the privileges of education.

Perhaps most importantly of all, Ballitore Quaker women were at the centre of a community where the constant coming and going of Friends (with and without the capital F) insured a steady stream of news, opinions, experiences and political attitudes from across Europe. Past pupils, parents and friends of current pupils, travelling Quaker preachers, returned non–Quaker students – all brought their opinions to the community table.

Mary Leadbeater, herself an inveterate letter writer, was constantly debating the issues of the day, both in her own home and in correspondence. She had friends on all sides of the political and social divide. Some, like a number of United Irishmen, she had grown up with and played with and remained friends with into adulthood. Others, from the big houses, had come to know her through the publication of her verses (not very good verses it should be said) and through her nose for news and gossip. Mary was a warm woman and she never allowed class, creed or politics to come between her and a good story.

Her study window overlooked the Square in Ballitore and the arrival of the Bianconi coaches, disgorging passengers, delivering letters, bringing news, was a source of not only information but also of pleasure to the local post–mistress. Had she had the added benefit of manning the local telephone exchange, a hundred and fifty years later, she would have been in the seventh heaven!

On a more serious level, the distribution, reading and discussion of political pamphlets was common among Quakers in Ballitore in the 1780's. Direct political involvement might have been frowned upon by the Elders and some of the more conservative elements in the community but among more liberal Friends (including William and Mary Leadbeater) the social implications of politics were a topic of constant discussion.

This is hardly surprising, given the militant nature of George Fox's socio–religious activities. Quakerism grew out of an uncompromising stance. Liberal Friends a hundred years later would have seen themselves as following in his radical if not revolutionary footsteps.

One of those whose work was read widely by certain Ballitore Friends was Theobald McKenna, a radical Catholic pamphleteer who was also strongly critical of the United Irishmen. He wrote:

"The Republican's desire for equality seldom reaches lower than his own rank. His reluctance to acknowledge a superior is sometimes rather inconsistently combined with a repugnance to denounce his own pre–eminence."

Mary described McKenna as a "genius" and when he visited Ballitore, in the company of William Lecky in September 1797 she struck up a friendship with him.

Edmund Burke had of course been educated at Ballitore and remained a firm friend of Mary Leadbeater. However his trenchant views on the French Revolution were not shared by her. Instead, she was quite sympathetic to the ideas of William Godwin, one of the first philosophical anarchists. Godwin argued that the state lacked moral legitimacy though he did not advocate revolution. Rather he claimed that individuals had no obligation or duty to obey the State.

Another figure whose work was read and admired by Mary Leadbeater was Mary Woolstonecroft. Woolstonecroft, in her book 'A Vindication of the Rights of Women' argued that women are not naturally inferior to men, but appeared to be so only because they lacked education. She made the then radical suggestion that men and women should be treated as rational beings and she promoted a social order founded on reason rather than history, wealth or gender.

It's interesting to consider for a moment the amount of discussion, information and political debate that went on at these talks in Ballitore. While the United Irishmen were organising in secret in and around the village and while the ruling elite were using the army and militia to protect their interests, the pacifist non–political Quaker community was a hotbed of political, social, religious and humanist debate on the rights of men and women, the rights of the poor and the wealthy and, most importantly, the duties of Christians towards their fellow man and woman.

There were others whose influences were more immediate upon Mary and her friends in Ballitore.

There was Thomas Bewley whose interest in all things French earned him the nickname "Citizen" Bewley in the wake of the French Revolution.

There was Job Scott the American Quaker whose Republican sympathies and electric style of preaching earned him admiration and suspicion among Quakers. Scott was virulently anti–Catholic hierarchy and it's interesting to note that many Attenders at Ballitore meeting, who were themselves Catholics, left the meeting because of his preaching on this subject. Undeterred Scott went on preaching at Meeting Houses and in private dwellings.

In November of 1793, while in Ballitore, he contracted small pox and wrote on the 14th of that month:

"Dearly beloved parents, brothers and sisters, relations and friends,

I am now at Ballitore, twenty–eight Irish miles from Dublin, and I suppose undoubtedly entered five days into the small–pox; the eruption began yesterday, and is very greatly increased to–day. I am very agreeably attended by physicians and the kindest of friends. I believe this is, on several accounts, one of the most favourable situations for having this disorder, in the nation, but my physicians are apprehensive that it will not prove the most favourable kind, nor perhaps of the most unfavourable. My distress of body, through extreme difficulty of breathing, &c. has, for a short space of time, been almost equal to any thing I can suppose human nature capable of, but, (it is now half–past nine at night,) this has been a very comfortable day; and just now, and for several hours past, I have been almost as easy as at any time in my life; I think certainly never more so in mind. I feel no kind of alarm."

A week later Scott was dead.

Another huge influence on Mary and her circle was Robert Grubb, a cousin of hers.

Grubb was a constant visitor to France and an extremely active anti–slavery campaigner. Indeed, under his influence many Friends undertook a boycott of sugar produced using slave labour. Pamphlets advocating an end to slavery were widely circulated by Friends, both among themselves and through travelling peddlers. Taking the boycott even further, there was a move to boycott slave picked cotton. Some women Friends, like Sarah Newland, found the sugar and cotton boycotts too political for their liking and advised against them but, as a statement and a practical act of support for the slaves, it was an effective and useful stance.

Robert Grubb's other passion was France and he was a frequent visitor in the wake of the French Revolution. Indeed, he developed a plan and founded a group which had as its aim the establishment of a Technical College in France. One of the Directors of the group was William Leadbeater, Mary's husband. William and Mary considered the possibility of moving themselves and their children to France, to become involved in the project. Grubb had received the support of the revolutionary government in France and their agreement that students at the college would not be liable for military service.

The plan never came to fruition but the fact that the Leadbeaters were prepared to consider leaving Ballitore and travelling to a country newly emerged from a revolutionary war, a country where the ideas of liberty, equality and fraternity were the maxim shows a very definite and positive commitment to the living of the Quaker ethos and also a commitment to the ideals of a classless society.

But there were, equally, negative influences at work in the Leadbeater minds. Not only were they enthused by the possibilities of life in France, with all it offered in the way of social, educational, religious and political freedom, but they were also depressed by the lack of peace and safety in the daily life of Ballitore.

The emergence of the United Irishmen as a force, albeit a secret one, had drawn the ire of the political and military authorities who knew something was going on, though not exactly what. Through the middle years of the 1790's there was a feeling in the air that Ireland would follow the French example. Not only that but it was obvious, too, that the revolutionary government in France would actively support a rebellion in Ireland.

Ballitore was one of the hotbeds of United Irishmen support and recruitment and it's not difficult to understand why. The growth of radical, revolutionary republicanism was a direct result of a century of repression under the Penal Laws. A number of local uprisings across the country in that period had amounted to nothing. The mood of disillusion with the status–quo which was sweeping Europe, however, had found homes in France with the successful revolution of 1789 and had, equally, found an organised home among the membership of the United Irishmen.

During the 1780s, a number of liberal Protestants had suggesed the broadening of the franchise and increasing Catholic and Presbyterian rights in Ireland. These people were also concerned that the Protestant Ascendancy as a body was pro–British and not interested in the promotion of Ireland, politically or economically.

Thomas Paine and his book 'The Rights of Man' were influential on these people and in 1791, Theobald Wolfe Tone published 'An Argument on Behalf of the Catholics of Ireland' which maintained that religious division was a tool of the elite and put forward the case for unity between Catholic, Protestant and Dissenter. Nine Belfast Presbyterians interested in reforming the Irish Parliament read Tone's pamphlet and liked his ideas. They invited Tone to Belfast where the group met in October 1791. At this first meeting, the group, which became known as the United Irishmen, passed the following three resolutions:

"That the weight of English influence in the Government of this country is so great as to require a cordial union among all the people of Ireland, to maintain that balance which is essential to the preservation of our liberties and the extension of our commerce.

That the sole constitutional mode by which this influence can be opposed is by a complete and radical reform of the people in Parliament.

That no reform is just which does not include Irishmen of every religious persuasion."

On a more local level, the membership of the United Irishmen in Ballitore was drawn from a class of people who had been denied education; denied land rights; denied the right to a language; denied the right to openly practice their religion; denied access to positions within the education, legal and electoral systems and treated as some kind of sub–human group, unworthy of even basic rights.

If news and opinion travelled fast within the Quaker community to Ballitore, equally it travelled among the landless, penniless, oppressed majority that was the Catholic population. The success of the French revolution heartened the United Irishmen and their supporters and while members of the Society of Friends may have winced at the summary execution of King and nobles in France the feeling among the peasant class was much less sympathetic. They believed that what had happened in France needed to happen in Ireland and they knew exactly who they would bring first to the metaphorical guillotine of their imagination.

Ballitore was a small village and a tightly knit community. For the landed class living on the higher and better ground it hardly existed, other than as a cauldron of possible trouble. But for the people living in the village friendship was more important than politics or religion. As a child Mary had grown up in the company of Quaker and Catholic children and through her adulthood she continued those friendships. Business was conducted on a daily and hourly basis between Quakers and Catholics, each group viewed the other primarily as neighbours and friends. Among the people Mary had grown up with were the Delany brothers, Peter and Malachi.

Malachi was a leading light in the United Irishmen, one of the main recruiters and organisers in the South Kildare and West Wicklow areas. He was also a constant visitor and a close personal friend of Mary and William Leadbeater. Mary describes him as: *"a great talker and qualified to handle var-*

ious subjects, though he confined himself to two – religion and politics. His mode of treating the first was of ranting at the clergy and the last in abusing the government." But, she adds: *"he was not a secret enemy and he had at least the merit of sincerity."*

Between 1793 and 1795 he came and went between Ballitore and Dublin but in 1796 he returned to live in Ballitore and to prepare for the imminent rebellion. Knowing the radical nature of his politics, the Leadbeaters, nevertheless, continued their intense friendship with him.

One of the personal effects of these troubled times on Mary Leadbeater, the inveterate letter writer, was, as Kevin O Neill has noted in his studies of the period, the absence of letters to or from Mary. Committing thoughts to paper had become a dangerous occupation. Houses were regularly raided by the military, pamphlets or letters expressing political opinions would be seen immediately as criminal and revolutionary and their possession was punishable by imprisonment or worse. And so letters remained unwritten or were destroyed once read.

The attempted landing of French forces in Ireland in 1797 further fuelled the rumour mill and brought the military regime down even more heavily across the country. Forced billeting of soldiers in local houses – including Quaker households; constant raids at all hours of the day and night; regular searches of people and property; arrests; torture and threats became part of the daily lives of those living in Ballitore. If the idea was to frighten the local people it succeeded to an extent. But behind the fear there was a growing and inevitable resentment that would find its expression in the summer of 1798.

Such was the feeling of imminent violence that Friends were ordered by the Society to destroy all arms held for personal use. The guns, they were told, could not be sold or given away. They must be destroyed.

The Spring and early Summer of 1798 brought events to a head in Ballitore as elsewhere. The arrival of the Orange band of soldiers, the Tyrone Militia in the village in April brought Wiliam Leadbeater, literally, to tears. They came with a terrible reputation and immediately set about seizing food from the local people, interrogating local men and generally causing mayhem for Catholics and Quakers alike. Those who were not with them were seen as being against them.

In May two local blacksmiths, also friends of Mary Leadbeater, Owen Finn and Tom Murray, were arrested and taken to Athy prison. Their tools were seized and destroyed. They were suspected of making pikes for the United Irishmen. A week later the Suffolk Fencibles set fire to much of the village and carried out public floggings in an attempt to terrify the locals into identifying United Irishmen in the community.

On May 24th Ballitore was taken by 200 rebels, led by Malachi Delany.

For three days the village remained under their control and raiding parties were sent out to attack loyalists in the nearby villages of Narraghmore and Castledermot. On May 27th – known as Bloody Firstday or Bloody Sunday by Ballitore Quakers of the time – the army retook the village, burned houses, looted and immediately executed suspected United Irishmen, though, of course, the United Irishmen had fled once the army took control of the village. So the havoc was wreaked on mostly innocent people.

Mary Leadbeater is a unique witness to these events, recording in her diaries and later in her published work, *The Annals of Ballitore,* the terrible events of that time. Her house and the part of it let to the Doyle sisters was, like all the houses in the village, constantly invaded and searched by the army. There are closely observed and sometimes light–hearted moments in the midst of this mayhem. Mary bemoans the removal of her best green tablecloth to make a rebel flag; she comments on the good looks of a young British soldier who threatened to shoot her; she expresses disgust at a militiaman whom she describes as "a fat tobacconist from Carlow lolling in a chair, telling me how he burned a man in a barrel of tar."

But these moments were fleeting. In the streets outside houses were ablaze; men were being shot; others – less fortunate – were put in barrels of tar and burned alive. Mary's lifelong friend Frank Johnson, the local Doctor, who had ministered to all who were wounded on both sides was arrested by the Suffolk Fencibles and shot, without trial, outside Mary's door. His body was thrown over a low wall and the local people were ordered not to remove it. As Mary notes, all they could do for the days it was left lying in the street was to keep the pigs away so that it wasn't devoured.

The failure of the rebellion of 1798 was not immediate. Skirmishes continued over a number of weeks but the subsequent arrest and execution of many leading members of the United Irishmen meant that the organised revolutionary movement had been smashed. What remained were small groups of men, hiding out in the countryside, who constantly raided villages like Ballitore for food, drink, arms and clothes.

In the wake of the rebellion, the army withdrew from Ballitore, leaving it as a series of burnt shells, with the occasional house still intact. The village was of no further use to the Crown forces.

As a result, through the late summer and autumn of 1798, the Leadbeaters and others were constantly being woken in the night, their doors and windows smashed, their money, watches, clothes and food stolen and their children frightened by bands of armed men, the remnants of the United Irishmen. Some were local men, known to the family. When they came, they came with a mixture of threats and promises.

Having been robbed once, the Leadbeaters found themselves the victims of another raid just two nights later:

"I was knitting in the parlour when I heard them demand William's watch which he gave them. They desired him not to be afraid, he told them he was not. I desired that they not disturb the children, they did not. Then one of them put fire in the alcove to extort more money but soon let Wm take it away and behaving with more civility than might be expected went away leaving us very calm."

In raids on Quaker homes virtually no personal violence was directed against the Quaker families. Others, mainly the gentry, Protestant farmers and supporters of the Crown were often less fortunate and a series of murders was carried out through the late summer and autumn in and around Ballitore by the remnants of the United Irishmen.

One such attack, on September 24th 1798, is described by Mary:

"A fine moonlight night but marked with death and destruction. Hannah Manders (a widow) had her house burned tonight, herself, two sisters and a nephew and another woman killed."

In another raid, on Boakefield, one of the local "big houses," the rebels were held at bay and a servant escaped and went to the nearby village of Timolin to alert the army garrison there. The soldiers refused to come to Ballitore, telling the man who had alerted them that they had been ordered to "leave the devoted hole to itself."

In spite of all of this and on a more humane note, William and Mary Leadbeater and other local Quakers sent letters of commendation on behalf of local men who had been imprisoned as suspected United Irishmen and William made a number of journeys to Naas to visit local men in the prison there. More than once, these letters proved crucial in gaining men's freedom or saving them from execution.

I've spent a lot of time in talking about the lead up to the rebellion of 1798 and about the liberal background from which Mary came because, not surprisingly, the events of that summer of 1798 are pivotal in altering both Mary as a person and the Quaker community in Ballitore as a group.

For the Quakers as a community, 1798 was a torment witnessed. True there were robberies, there were night raids by soldiers and United Irishmen, there was damage to property, there were arrests and threats of violence but, amazingly, – and this a credit to the Quakers of that time – apart from some instances of manhandling, there was no direct personal violence against members of the Society of Friends.

What there was, however, was a life–altering witnessing of the torture, psychological and physical and the butchering of many of their neighbours. Most of those who died during the summer and into the autumn and winter of 1798 into 1799 were Catholics, some were members of the Church of Ireland.

No one who lived in Ballitore at the time would come through the experience unscathed.

There was also an enormous social and economic fallout from the rebellion. The village was virtually razed to the ground, industry came to a halt, farming was disrupted, trade and travel were impossible and, though the Quaker school remained open through the rebellion period, once an uneasy peace had settled in the autumn and winter of 1798, parents began to withdraw their children from the school.

This was inevitable. The threat of a further outbreak of organised rebellion remained a real possibility, low–level violence from the army and the armed gangs hiding in the foothills of the nearby Wicklow Mountains was a weekly if not daily occurrence and the country was in a state of real unrest and unease. Stage coaches were being stopped and robbed; murders were still happening; the Crown forces seemed unwilling or unable to guarantee the safety of those who had not taken sides in the rebellion and there was a very real fear that the militiamen might, at any time and without provocation, wreak revenge for imagined wrongs on the community in Ballitore.

For these reasons, many parents travelled, as soon as it was safe, to Ballitore and took their children home. Local children and some boarders continued to attend but the loss of numbers meant the school was quickly becoming nonviable as a commercial enterprise and, eventually, in 1802 the school closed due to lack of numbers. Four years later it reopened and remained open until 1836 but it never achieved the numbers – or the reputation – it had formerly had.

Much of the Quaker involvement in business in Ballitore was based on the milling industry – that, too, was damaged by the rebellion and its aftermath. But most of all the lifeblood had been drained, literally and metaphorically, from the heart of the community. There was an atmosphere of constant distrust in the village and its surrounding area; there was the continuing threat of violence; there was the tightening noose of the Act of Union in 1801 which operated as a seal of victory by the Loyalist population and stamped out, for almost fifty years, even the energy for rebellion; there was economic stagnation; there was architectural dereliction; there was ravaging poverty and there was a deep, though undefined, collective post–traumatic stress. Mary's response to it was one that spoke of war–weariness. She wrote

"I long only for peace and quiet."

Not only had there been a rebellion but there had been beatings, shootings, imprisonment, torture, burnings and public executions. Many people had simply disappeared. Some were on the run but others had been killed and their bodies dumped in bog–holes and ditches. Children had been orphaned, families broken and a community traumatised. Little wonder, then, that as a society Ballitore would never fully recover from the events of that year.

There is one other seemingly unimportant incident, in the immediate aftermath of the 1798 rebellion to which I want to refer. When peace – or a kind of peace – settled on the village in the late summer and autumn of that year, one of the first tasks that faced most of the population was the rebuilding of houses. To rebuild, people needed timber and the most obvious source of timber was the trees that lined the streets of the village. William Leadbeater bought quite a number of these trees – to preserve them from being felled. This seems to me to be an extraordinary step by a man whose neighbours were, literally, living without roofs over their heads. As I said, it's a detail but an important one in terms of William's priorities.

On a more personal level, it was to be for Mary and William Leadbeater an even more painful period. Living with the uncertainty that others shared; having their house used as a billet and then having it raided and burgled was bad enough. Seeing neighbours arrested; having close friends disappear; watching companions since childhood executed in the streets was worse. But the shadow of the final family tragedy of that dark year was yet to fall inside the Leadbeater house.

Mary's mother had come to live with her daughter and son–in–law. She was suffering from dementia and needed constant attention. The events of the summer had not been helpful to her mental state.

On the 29th of November 1798, Mary was not only looking after her mother but also nursing her daughter Deborah, who was suffering from smallpox. Her other daughters, Elizabeth and Jane, who was four, were in the house with her.

Mary writes in her diary:

"Just then my sweet Jane told me she wanted to go upstairs and I most unfortunately, stupidly and carelessly trusted the wax taper with her, though I thought me not, and then again she was so steady, and though I am mostly attentive to danger of fire she went not into mother's room but into the one over the parlour and setting down the candle on the floor I suppose when she rose from the pot it caught her. I heard her cries and immediately apprehended the cause. We found Molly Webster (her mother's nurse) attempting to put out the fire. I lay with her...she was fine and cheery and desired I would buy a coach for Deborah at the fair..."

Jane died of her burns the following day.

Mary's heartbreak is palpable in this excerpt from her diary:

"My lovely child; her round blue eyes, her dented nose, her rosy cheeks and white teeth all rise to my idea and I feel inexpressibly my loss. I was vain of her I believe and cherished hopes from her stability and affection to me more I think than from the rest..."

There is no doubt but that the brutal events which Mary Leadbeater witnessed in 1798 made her reconsider her position on politics and revolution.

What she had read in pamphlets regarding the French Revolution had been theoretical, the bloody and squalid reality of revolution was another matter. The murder of her close friend Frank Johnson outside her door had been a particularly harrowing experience. But the death of her daughter, though not directly related to the revolution was, by association, a continuation of the loss of that summer and cut her to the heart, changing her life forever.

Where Mary had been enthusiastic about the political policy of liberty, equality and fraternity and had thought seriously about moving to France and helping to establish a school there she now turned her energy towards working with the likes of Maria Edgeworth in establishing associations for the improvement of the peasantry.

Gone was the rebel, the revolutionary sympathiser, the secretly–political empathiser. In her place was the liberal theoretician, writing pamphlets about self–improvement, encouraging – in books like *Cottage Dialogues* – a more sober way of life; suggesting cottage industry as the best way in which people might improve their lot. It was as if Mary had been to the barricades and had withdrawn to work behind them, finding what was on the other side unacceptable.

There is a striking parallel between the position of the Ballitore Quakers in the period 1798–1801 and Catholic worker–priests in south America in the wake of Vatican II. In each case you have a community faced with barbarous and inhumane treatment of those about them. In each case there is a decision to be made. With the Ballitore Quakers there was an inevitable return to peace. In South America there was the development of Liberation theology, which saw poverty as the root of evil and thus of sin and the decision was that the response required was political activism. The Catholic priest Philip Berryman argued that liberation theology is:

"an interpretation of Christian faith through the poor's suffering, their struggle and hope, and a critique of society and the Catholic faith and Christianity through the eyes of the poor."

For Mary Leadbeater this too was, in many ways, the case but her experience of where political and then military action took her community caused her to reconsider. The death of her daughter, however, was the factor which sent her in a different direction.

Nor should we find this surprising. Mary was, first and last, a Quaker. Seventy–five years later, Marx would write:

"From each according to his ability, to each according to his need"

and, to a great extent, this was a philosophy with which Quaker's could agree. Not that they were Pre–Marx Marxists, rather that they took the teaching Christ and passages like this, from the Acts of the Apostles seriously:

"Neither was there any among them that lacked: for as many as were posses-

sors of lands or houses sold them, and brought the prices of the things that were sold, and laid them down at the apostles' feet: and distribution was made unto every man according as he had need" (Acts 4:34–35).

Which makes William Leadbeater's decision to preserve the village trees all the more difficult to understand.

It seems to me that the work in which Mary and some of her friends became involved after 1798 was trite, ineffective and condescending. It was part of a philosophy which dismissed the ability of the poor to be their own people. Yes, it sometimes gave them a small income. Yes, it sometimes gave them an aim in life. Yes, it encouraged sobriety and responsibility. But it also limited the potential of that income and it limited the aim to which they might aspire and it set the limits of the responsibility they were given. It was a watered down version of everything Mary had empathised with in the 1780's and 1790's.

It was an acceptance of something rather than a pursuit of everything and, worst of all, it was the making of an assumption about what was best for the majority, based on the notions of a few well–heeled, well–placed and well–meaning people who had chosen to ignore the root causes of the poverty among the Irish peasant class and concern themselves, instead, with the symptoms of that poverty. It was, in other words, a stop–gap system which was bound to fail. Emmet's rebellion of 1803; the Famine of the 1840's; the Young Ireland rebellion of 1848; the Fenian Rebellion of 1867 were all proof, if proof were needed, that the real causes of what happened in 1798 had never been dealt with.

For Mary, the remaining years of her life were given over to caring for her family, running the post–office in Ballitore, supporting William in his work as a farmer, builder and merchant. Her writing continued and she went on producing pamphlets, composing verse, keeping her journals and corresponding with friends far and wide. She also remained at the centre of life in the village, recording the births, marriages, affairs, and deaths. There are intriguing pictures in her writings of the visit of the first camel to Ballitore; of the tragic deaths of young women in childbirth; of lost loves; of old people living out their days; of children's dreams; of goings–on in the big houses and the cottages and of the changing lives of her family and friends.

It's as an annalist that Mary is at her best. She loved a good story and the more salacious the better. She regularly turned up at the scenes of mayhem in the area – firstly to help but also to see what was happening at first hand.

But while Mary was a driving force in Quaker life in Ballitore, she was only one member of that community. By the time she died, in 1826, that community was in decline. Ten years after her death, the Quaker school closed for the final time.

The great famine of the 1840's still lay twenty years ahead but already social, religious, political and economic forces were undermining the survival of the community.

Economically the school's closure was a blow but not a huge one. Pupil numbers had never regained the heights of the 1790's. However, there were other factors at play. Taxes in Ireland were higher than in Britain, making the survival of any industry difficult. The woollen industry was in steep decline and, from 1815 onwards there was a post–war recession and, as a result, the milling industry was struggling.

Politically, Catholic Emancipation had become the rallying cause for Irish Catholics and Daniel O Connell's monster meetings were drawing attention and enthusiasm. One of them was held at the Rath of Mullaghmast, close to Ballitore. But politically, too, the folk–memory of 1798 was still alive and a deep–seated resentment burned in the local people. Indeed, interestingly, you only have to talk, even today in Ballitore, to descendants of those involved as participants or victims of the rebellion to discover how close to the surface that folk memory and that anger sits.

From a religious and social point of view, I would suggest that the central issue in the decline of Quaker involvement in the community was the inability of Friends to "marry out." Quakers who married outside the membership of the Society were, at that time, disbarred from continuing that membership. In a small community, this policy leads inevitably to decline. If Friends married out they were forced out of the Society. If they didn't marry out they had a choice of looking locally for a partner, a difficulty in an area where intermarriage had been happening for generations, or of leaving the community in search of a partner elsewhere. Either way the numbers of Quakers declined rapidly.

In 1837 the population of Ballitore was 933. Then came the famine. By 2002 that figure had fallen to 338, though the building of new housing in the area is bringing this up, but mainly as a potential dormitory town.

By the end of the nineteenth century, the Quaker population had died out and the Meeting House closed and remained closed for seventy–five years.

In many ways the arrival of Barcroft and Strettel, the first Quakers to buy land and settle in Ballitore was a blessing. It brought a regeneration and a new community to the area but, in the longer term, Quakerism, in its economic entities, may have proven a castle of sand for the community. The Quaker millers, merchants, farmers, builders and shopkeepers were the emerging and then successful middle–class of the late seventeenth, eighteenth and early–nineteenth centuries in Ballitore. Despite their sympathy for their Catholic neighbours they did not radically alter the social strata of the community. Instead of simply having a landed oligarchy and a peasant class, you had a middle class pushing itself between the two and acting, to a great extent, as an employer for the peasant class but not as a political force in village life.

Inevitably, with the decline in Quaker numbers, the collapse of the economy and the departure, through death or economics, of many of the Quaker business and farm owners the community collapsed as an economic and social entity. There was no emerging group of leaders in the peasant/working class community. Many of those who might have taken that role in the early years of the nineteenth century had been imprisoned or killed or deported in the wake of the 1798 rebellion.

Ballitore remains a depressed community, even at this remove. Unemployment is high, facilities are few, self–belief is a commodity in short supply. The population will, inevitably, grow. There's a rash of new housing in the area but, like so much of the house–building of recent years it comes without any social infrastructure. Ballitore has one building available for young people's activities, the downstairs room of the Meeting House. In this more that a hundred young people gather weekly as part of a youth theatre project run, in the main, by one woman. Mary Leadbeater's old home is now a library and museum. But a walk through the streets of the village is a sobering experience. It lacks heart, literally and metaphorically. It is strewn with derelict buildings.

Inevitably, one wonders how it would have fared had the Quaker community not arrived there in the early years of the eighteenth century. Physically what they have left is an architectural heritage and little else. The landed gentry have gone but they have been replaced by a central and local government that is doing nothing for the community.

When Mary Leadbeater wrote these lines in her diary in 1794, she might well have been writing about life in her beloved village two hundred and fourteen years thence:

"What can be more injurious than the accumulating upon a few, every means of superfluity and luxury to the total destruction of the ease and plain but plentiful subsistence of the many?...Is it well that so large a part of the community should be kept in abject penury, goaded to the commission of crimes and made victims of the merciless laws which the rich have instituted to oppress them."

We live in more subtle times but walking through Ballitore in 2008, one can see that we do not necessarily live in better times. It's important that we value and respond to the other legacy left by Mary Leadbeater, that of righteous anger in the face of exploitation.

John MacKenna

[Some of the references quoted above are taken from Mary Leadbeater's diary and differ from the text of the printed editons of 1862 and consequently the text of the current volume]

NOTE ON THE 1st & 2nd EDITIONS OF THE ANNALS, 1862.

I have examined the two 1862 printed editions letter by letter and line by line. There are many small differences such as words being italicised in one and not in the other, words hyphenated or not, commas and semi–colons in one edition and in a different position or not included in the other etc. To be honest there is virtually no loss of emphasis for the modern reader and while I have made notes of the changes for future researchers to view in Kildare Library if they wish I do not feel the need to include a note for every tiny discrepancy, and it would make the volume extremely cumbersome. Various spellings of the same word e.g. favourite and favorite are retained.

If a different term/word was used, or a line was inverted or significantly altered it has been referenced in the notes. We originally chose to reproduce the Second Edition as this was the copy we had to hand in the library but in fact this proved to be a good choice as it contains quite a lot of extra material not contained in the original edition (for example see Chapter IV which has almost 5 extra pages of material not in the 1st ed.). There are however, a couple of occasions where a significant difference is notable and this is referenced. Where material is included in the 1st Edition but not the 2nd Edition, it has been added. So while essentially this modern edition is a re–production of the Second Edition published in 1862 it now includes the previously omitted manuscript description of the Village in 1766 and some material that had appeared in the First Edition but was left out by the editor from the Second Edition.

To help differentiate between the editorial comments we have included the original notes from both 1862 editions in bold. The appendices appear after the 'Annals' as they relate to the original publication.

There is an overall discrepancy of about 13 or so pages in total, between the two 1862 editions, mostly due to material not included in one volume or the other but also simply due to the actual formatting of the type on the page.

According to her obituary in the Irish Times of 1884, Lydia Jane Fisher, last surviving child of Mary Leadbeater, had edited 'The Leadbeater Papers,' in 1858. It appears from the Preface to 'Ballitore & Its Inhabitants Seventy Years Ago,' that the editor of this work may have been Richard Davis Webb. Webb may have edited the 2nd edition of the 'Annals,' possibly with the knowledge and help of Lydia Fisher, or she may have edited both editions of the 'Annals' and simply removed what she saw as unwieldy from the first edition.

Mario Corrigan

GLOSSARY.

Ague	Shivering fit or fever with hot and cold stages
Apoplexy	Stroke
Barm	Kind of yeast; foam or scum from fermenting process used to leaven or lighten and soften bread/dough
Bleachgreen	Area for spreading cloth or fabrics for bleaching
Bleeding	Act of drawing blood
Bolting mill	Mill where the flour was sifted
Bonds of Hymen	Marriage vows
Camera obscura	Latin for dark room – a portable optical device whereby light from a scene or images are projected through a pinhole, appearing upside down. Helped pave the way for modern photography
Columbine, statue of	Mistress of Harlequin – short skirted dancer; dramatic figure
Comfits	Sugar coated dried fruits, spices or nuts – sweets
Confabulations	Gatherings where people talked openly
Cotemporary	Contemporary
Crom–a–boo	Fitzgerald war–cry and motto – Victory to Croom
Cupping	Bleeding by using a glass in which partial vacuum is formed by heating
Cwt.	Hundred weight
Deprecating	Pleading earnestly against
Digitalis	Drug from dried foxgloves leaves – to stimulate the heart
Disaffected	Disloyal
Disowned	Renounced or repudiated – Quakers disowned by the Society could still attend worship but not partake in normal business of the Society
Distemper	Illness – disturbance of the 'humour' or temper
Elder	Leaders of the community
Epicure	Person with refined tastes in eating and drinking
Equipages	Horse drawn carriage with attendants – also mentioned in connection with tea–set!
Faustus, Doctor, statue of	German astronomer and necromancer reputed to have sold his sold to the devil; dramatic figure

Fencibles	Scottish and English troops sent to Ireland when regular troops were withdrawn. Recruited only within the British Isles
Fetch	Spirit
Feu-de-joie	Salute by firing guns on a ceremonial occasion or a bonfire lit in a public place as a token of joy
First Day	Sunday; Second Day – Monday and so on
First Month	January; Second Month – February and so on
Free-quarters	Forcible billeting of military troops on the local population
Flagger boats	Unsure – may mean signal boats
Gruel	Liquid food of oatmeal etc. boiled in milk or water
Guinea	Sum of 21 shillings – gold coin
Harebine	A thin, rather stiff woolen material for women's wear now no longer manufactured
Harlequin, statue of	Pantomime character; jester-like
Height	Meaning in this volume – pride
Lancasterian School	Founded by Joseph Lancaster in 1798 – The Lancasterian system (or monitorial system) used older children who had already been given some education to teach the younger children. It was designed to provided a cheap basic education with limited resources and numbers of teachers
Laudanum	Narcotic painkiller; solution containing morphine produced from opium
Listings	Wiry, plain weave, coarse carpets, made of cotton with narrow coloured stripes – made of selvedges/ selvages or lists cut from other fabrics
Magic Lantern	The ancestor of modern slide projectors – whereby the image from a glass slide can be projected and in some cases manipulated to simulate movement
Malapropos	Inopportune or inappropriate
Marshalsea	Means the seat or court of a marshall or keeper; in this case prison or debtor's prison
Mignonette	Plant (Resada) with spikes of grey-green flowers
Militia	Compulsory service; barred from serving in their own county; to police local districts for national defence in lieu of local troops
Ne plus ultra	The ultimate – achievement or excellence; furthest attainable point
Oielet holes	Oielet or in modern terms eyelet – a small hole, usually round and finished along the edge, for the passage of a lace or cord or for ornamental effect

Orrery	Clockwork model of the solar system
Pattens	Shoe or clog with raised sole or set on iron ring; for walking in mud etc.
Pestalozzi	General and technical education method – learning by doing; school set up in Abbeyleix in 1818
Pikelets	Little treats which look like scones but in terms of texture and ingredients are very much like pancakes
Porringer	Small dish with flat (ornamented) handle on one end – often used to eat gruel or porridge; often from pewter and sometimes with a lid
Postillion	Person who rides the near horse of the lead pair of the team and guides the coach
Protection	Paper guaranteeing safe passage or the protection of the military
Quondam	That once was – former
Salop	Or salep – starch from tubers of various orchids; mostly as a yellow powder administered in milk, water, broth or jelly; insipid taste; often sweetened
Simples	Medicine – herbal remedies
Solar microscope	The solar microscope is in reality a magic lantern illuminated by the sun's rays; it serves to produce highly magnified images of very small objects
Spring-pottage	A type of stew
Tabinet	Strong fabric, originally with a warp of silk and a weft of worsted, but now usually made from cotton, in a plain weave with a finely ribbed surface – POPLIN
Tansy	Aromatic herb, yellow flowers – leaves sometimes used medicinally; steeped in buttermilk for nine days supposed to whiten skin; seen by some as a weed
Thrum	Little bits of waste yarn from looms often knitted into objects for added warmth; a fringe or tuft of yarns left on looms after cloth removed
Whey	Watery liquid left when milk forms curds
Worsted	Coarse cloth – yarn made from straight fibres in parallel to each other; wool
Yeomen	Initially a part-time locally raised force designed to assist with policing the country – served in the locality in which it was raised.

THE LEADBEATER PAPERS.

THE ANNALS OF BALLITORE,

BY MARY LEADBEATER,

WITH A MEMOIR OF THE AUTHOR:

LETTERS FROM EDMUND BURKE

HERETOFORE UNPUBLISHED:

AND THE CORRESPONDENCE OF

MRS. R. TRENCH AND REV. GEORGE CRABBE

WITH MARY LEADBEATER.

VOLUME I.

LONDON:

BELL AND DALDY, 186, FLEET STREET.

1862.

Title page of first edition

CONTENTS OF VOL. I.

A MEMOIR OF MARY LEADBEATER

THE ANNNALS OF BALLITORE, VIZ.:-

A MEMOIR

OF

MARY LEADBEATER.

MARY SHACKLETON, afterwards Leadbeater, was born in Ballitore in the county of Kildare, in the year 1758. Her father, Richard Shackleton, kept a boarding–school, which had been established in that village in the year 1726 by his father Abraham Shackleton, a native of Yorkshire, and a member of the Society of Friends. Abraham was a learned and good man, straightforward in all his dealings, and sincere in his converse with God and man. Such is the character handed down of the first of the Shackletons who settled in Ireland. His son Richard equalled him in wisdom, integrity, and learning, whilst his abilities were more highly cultivated, every advantage having been bestowed upon him which was attainable at that period. Although the son of a strict Quaker, he completed his education at Trinity College, Dublin, at that time a very unusual step for one of that persuasion. His temper was lively, he had a ready wit, and he wrote with facility in several languages besides his own.

Mary Shackleton inherited a large portion of her father's genius, and she evinced a turn for poetical composition at such an early age, that she might have been injured by the flattering attention paid to her on that account, had it not been for the extraordinary modesty and sweetness of her disposition, which were yet more remarkable than her many intellectual endowments.

The high character which her father held in society for his learning and worth introduced her at a very early age to the notice of his friends, some of whom ranked high in the literary and political world. She easily won their friendship by her talents and amiability, and she never lost a friend except by death. Edmund Burke, whose first letter to Richard Shackleton was dated from his entrance at college, and who afterwards kept up with his old schoolfellow and friend a regular and most affectionate correspondence, dictated his last farewell to the daughter when he was sinking under bodily and mental afflictions, and could no longer guide the pen.

In the year 1791 she was married to William Leadbeater, a descendant of the Huguenot families of Le Batre and Gilliard, which were compelled to fly from France by the revocation of the Edict of Nantes. Being left an orphan when very young, he was placed at Ballitore school. Having completed his education there, although he had been destined by his father's will to be brought up for the bar, his guardian, who proved unfaithful to his trust in this as well as in other respects, bound him to Mr. Roger North, a respectable attorney in Dublin, with a view to his following that profession. In the office of that gentleman he remained for the full term of his apprenticeship; but having at the end of his time become convinced of the principles of Quakerism, and at the same time being perhaps unconsciously attracted by an attachment he had formed while at school to the youthful subject of this memoir, he threw up his profession, sought and obtained admission into the Society of Friends, removed to Ballitore, and after some years obtained the hand of Mary Shackleton. In her society he spent thirty–five years of happiness, uninterrupted, we believe save by those casualties which are the lot of the most fortunate, and by the calamities of war, followed by disease and famine, which in 1798 and the few following years so fearfully distracted and afflicted his native country. Having a turn for agricultural pursuits, he became an extensive farmer of large tracts of land in his own neighbourhood, and managed them so successfully that he realized a modest competence. He died about a year after his wife, to whom he was devotedly attached.[1]

Her first essay at authorship was in the year 1794, when she published anonymously a small volume of "Extracts and Original Anecdotes for the Improvement of Youth." This little work attained considerable popularity: it was probably one of the first attempts to introduce literature of a lightsome and interesting yet instructive character into the juvenile libraries of "Friends," from which works of an entertaining kind had been heretofore somewhat rigidly excluded. Like all her little books for children, it contains many of those beautiful touches which proceed only from a tender and benevolent heart.

Her name first came before the public in 1808, when a selection from her poems was published by subscription. With the exception of a "Translation of Maffeus's Continuation of the Æneid," these were all written on domestic occasions, and were addressed to the members of her own family, or to some of her most intimate friends; and, although perhaps now forgotten by the public, they are still precious to those who knew the writer, and the circumstances that called into action the susceptible feelings of her heart. They all breathe an innocent enjoyment of the pleasures of domestic affection, and of a retired and rural life; they are the unpretending effusions of a mind alive to the beauties of nature, overflowing with love to those around her, with charity to all men, and with gratitude to the Giver of those simple joys which made the happiness of her life.

The first series of her "Cottage Dialogues of the Irish Peasantry" appeared in the year 1811, and was followed by a second series in 1813. In these Dialogues, with a felicity of language rarely equalled by any writer previous to her time, she has painted the virtues and the failings, the joys and the sorrows, the feelings and the prejudices of our impulsive and quick–witted countrymen. This is the work by which Mary Leadbeater is chiefly known, and its utility has been fully proved by the approbation of all who were at that time interested in the welfare of the Irish poor, and by their efforts to circulate them as widely as possible among the class for which they were intended. They were subsequently published in a larger form for the English public, and were enriched with notes illustrative of the character, manners, &c. of the Irish peasantry by the author's friend Mr. W. P. Lefanu, the founder and proprietor of the "Farmer's Journal," and by Miss Edgeworth, who interested herself warmly in the success of the work, and addressed several letters to Mary Leadbeater expressive of her esteem, and of her desire to do everything in her power to promote her benevolent views. A third series of the "Cottage Dialogues," which remained in manuscript at the time of the author's death, was published in a duodecimo volume along with the earlier series, and has been pronounced by competent judges to be even superior to them in interest and simple pathos.[2] In the "Dialogues," we may observe that Rose, who is a model of excellence, always imparts advice or information to her idle neighbour with a mildness and diffidence far removed from the loquacious, self–important manner in which some of the perfect characters held up to our view are made to dictate to their misguided companions, and which almost disgusts the reader with perfection. They also afford an example of that lambent wit and humour which made the author's conversation and correspondence so attractive.

The publication of the "Cottage Dialogues" was followed by the "Landlord's Friend," "Cottage Biography," "Biographical Notices of Irish Friends," and "Memoirs of Richard and Elizabeth Shackleton;" besides which she wrote poems, essays, characters, and tales, some of which have found their way to various periodical publications.

The last work she lived to publish was a little book called "The Pedlars," written for the Kildare–Street Education Society, consisting of dialogues descriptive of the natural and artificial curiosities of various parts of Ireland, and of what was always her favourite theme – the character of the Irish poor, their virtues, their sufferings, and the best mode of improving their condition.

All these works, different as they are in subject and style, bear the stamp of a mind ever disposed to look at the favourable side of things and characters, to receive the good thankfully, and bear the evil with cheerful resignation.

Amongst her literary performances may be reckoned a very extensive correspondence with people of different ranks and situations in life. She excelled in this department. She expressed herself with ease and conciseness, and related little domestic occurrences with spirit, accompanied by touches of the most gentle wit, which gave a charm to the merest trifle. If she were the messenger of sorrowful intelligence, it was delivered with tenderness and caution, accompanied by the balm of comfort which almost deprived the unwelcome tidings of their sting. Being known to hold the pen of a ready writer, she was frequently solicited to write letters on intricate subjects, where judgement and delicacy were required.

Her power of turning in a moment from one occupation to another was amazing. In the midst of her long accounts, if she were asked to write a letter of kindness, a petition, or a recommendation, she immediately gave her thoughts to it, and put it into execution.

Exposed to continual interruptions from friends, who found her always ready to sympathize in their tastes and pursuits, be they ever so different from her own; from visitors, whom her fame often brought from a distance to enjoy conversation; from the poor, who daily came to her for advice or help; she never seemed in a hurry, and with perfect regularity carried on her various occupations. She began to keep a diary in her eleventh year, and continued it till within a week of her death. She also kept a private journal of her own life, and compiled "The Annals of Ballitore," extending from the year 1766 down to 1824, two years before her death. These two last works are interesting not only from the number and variety of characters, ludicrous or pathetic incidents, and anecdotes of celebrated individuals whom she met with in her travels or who visited Ballitore, but also on account of the faithful and lively picture which they present of her own home, and of the small but cultivated circle of which she was the ornament. In these volumes she lays open her whole heart, whose every thought seems to have been pure and dictated by love, and upon whose warmth years had no other effect than that of adding to it wisdom and experience. She was to the last youthful in her affections, of an open and unsuspicious disposition, and ready to hail with enthusiasm every improvement of later times.

She was for many years instrumental in assisting the enlightened efforts of the late Mrs. Richard Trench, mother of the present Dean of Westminster, to reclaim a numerous body of tenantry on one of her estates from misery and degradation to comfort and industry; and the inhabitants of the neat cottages of Ballybarney, a few miles from Ballitore, regarded Mary Leadbeater as a friend, a governor, and a judge, kind–hearted and beneficent in all these various capacities. Happy were the days when, accompanied by some of her friends, she visited the estate to decide on the merits of the tenants, and to distribute the premiums granted by the generous proprietress.

She was always warmly received, and her companions partook of the unstudied welcome and the homely cheer which were so cordially offered. The cottagers familiarly recounted their successes, their misfortunes, and their future plans; and, when disputes arose among them, she calmly heard both sides, and neither party was afraid to lay the whole matter before her. She knew each one by name and character, and remembered from one year to another how they prospered. She admonished some, encouraged others; and her sympathy was often awakened by the lamentations of these warm–hearted people for their relatives who had died or emigrated. An expedition to Ballybarney in her company had the charm of a party of pleasure.

In the course of her life she had many afflictions to endure. She was deprived by death of many relations and friends. She saw her native village almost destroyed by the calamities of civil war, and she was witness to the succeeding horrors of nightly robberies. No one felt these distresses more keenly than she did; but when she was deprived of one enjoyment, she clung the more closely to those which remained.

She was of a most unsuspicious nature, and was thus delivered from a host of distressing thoughts and conjectures; and jealousy, that fatal enemy to peace and friendship, found no place in her mind. She knew and felt that she was beloved.

Her friends were numerous, and many of them, with whom she corresponded, were scattered over the face of the earth; but her extended friendships or extended usefulness did not deprive her family of her society or prevent the fulfilment of her domestic duties. She wrote a great deal while her friends were conversing around her, and sometimes joined in the conversation. One of her daughters generally read to her while she was transcribing, Her industry, perseverance, and energy were so remarkable, that her domestic performances exceeded those of many more active women. She had a familiar, persuasive manner about her household affairs, which induced her servants to enter into her views, and delight in doing what would please her.

Many strangers who came to Ballitore wished to see her, either from admiration of her character and writings, or from mere curiosity. While she sat to be looked at by such people, the smile of politeness lighted up her countenance; yet her eyes were cast down, and she was generally more silent than usual on such occasions, and seemed merely an attentive listener to what the strangers had to say. If they praised her writings, she looked pleased, and perhaps thanked them for their approbation, with a modesty and simplicity seldom equalled. She spoke to her familiar friends of her own writings with as much ease and freedom as if they belonged to another person, and received their approbation or censure with equanimity.

Although she looked back upon the days and the friends and the customs of her youth with tender regret, with love and veneration, she delighted to contemplate the improvements of modern society, the prison discipline, the schools, the savings' banks, and the other means of bettering the condition of the poor. She used to speak of Dublin with enthusiasm. She admired its public buildings, its squares, its quays, and the surrounding scenery; but, above all, its charitable institutions. She never gave up the hope that the punishment of death would be abolished. Her horror at the idea of a human creature being led out to execution, for any crime whatever, was often expressed in conversation and in her writings.

In her character she exemplified St. Paul's inimitable definition of charity: "Charity suffereth long, and is kind; charity envieth not; charity vaunteth not itself, is not puffed up, doth not behave itself unseemly, seeketh not her own, is not easily provoked, thinketh no evil; rejoiceth not in iniquity, but rejoiceth in the truth; beareth all things, believeth all things, hopeth all things, endureth all things. Charity never faileth."

Her humility rendered her averse to speaking of her religious experience, but her care to impress the hearts of her children with a feeling of reverend dependence on their heavenly Father, and the many expressions of her own trust in divine aid which her diary contains, show that she was favoured with a deep feeling of religious fear and love.

About a year before her death she began to be afflicted with dropsy, which, in defiance of medical skill and the tender cares of her anxious family, gradually increased till she was confined to her chamber. Yet even there her mind seemed unchanged. She manifested the same anxiety for the welfare of all around her; and she was equally accessible to the many who came to consult her, or to enjoy her company once more. She continued her literary occupations to the very last week, preparing a volume of Essays, Tales, and Anecdotes for the Kildare Place Education Society.[3]

During the few last days she became rapidly worse. Her sufferings were great, and she feared that her patience would not hold out to the end, and that she could not part with perfect resignation from those blessings to which her heart clung with increased affection. But she was supported by Divine help through the trying close, and her death was indeed that of the just. She died on the 27th June, 1826.

THE ANNALS OF BALLITORE.[4]

Chapter I.
1766.

Preliminary Reflections. – Description of Ballitore in prose and verse. – The first Abraham Shackleton. – His ancient mansion in Ballitore. – The forge, Mick Murray, and his dentistry. – Reminiscences of Peter Widdows. – The widow Taylor and her daughter Polly, Sarah Braddock, the widow Jackson and her daughter Julia, Joseph Wills, Jonathan Haughton, and Lee Masters.

12 to 21

WHY do we not better remember that truth which we know so well, that we are not sensible of the value of our blessings till we lose them? In sickness the comfort of health is painfully recollected, though apparently in little esteem when possessed. When death has deprived us of our tender parents, affectionate friends, or engaging children, – sensible that we are cut off from every hope of again enjoying their society, how is every endearing circumstance of the past revived, and every omission on our part towards them roused to anguish!

When a state of disturbance pervades a nation, when the horrors of war have been felt or threatened, how do we cast a retrospective view to the days of tranquillity, when we sat as it were under our own vines and fig-trees, and none made us afraid – astonished that any are willing to relinquish the sweets of peace. The situation of outward alarm and the prospect of unsettlement ought to loosen the mind from those terrene things in which it was wont to delight.

It has not had that effect upon me. My heart swells with tender recollections of the past, and though prompt to enjoy the present, feels a regret at the memory of what I have lost, mixed with a pensive satisfaction that I have enjoyed those quiet pleasures. My native village was never so dear to me; and though the vernal time of childhood and the glowing sensations of youth are past, the autumn of life is not destitute of its tranquil enjoyments. This season of the year I am partial to; I admire the rich and varied prospects of the autumnal season, the employments by which it is enlivened, and the awakened remembrance of the year nearly gone.[5] Thus, in the autumn of life, I feel my early sensations revived in the children and youth of our family, and I am led to look back, and, with the partiality which I feel to Ballitore, desire to retrace for their amusement and for my own those scenes, indifferent to other eyes, which have passed before mine not unnoticed. My abilities are limited; my sphere is limited also to the "sweet spot of the world" where my days have been spent, and where I desire to end them.

Ballitore, in the county of Kildare, twenty–eight Irish miles from Dublin, is a village a little off the high road from Dublin to Cork. It is situated in a valley encompassed by gently rising hills, except where the river Griese takes its meandering course of about fourteen miles from its spring at Tubber, in the county of Wicklow, to its union with the Barrow near Jerusalem, a little hamlet in the county of Kildare. Ballitore derives its name from its former marshy condition (*bally* in Irish signifying a town or village, and *togher* a bog), from which it was reclaimed by drainage and careful cultivation. This fertile portion of land was purchased about the end of the seventeenth century by John Barcroft and Abel Strettel, respectable members of the Society of Friends. It is reported to have been very bare of wood till the new proprietors began to plant, which they did abundantly, and groves, orchards, and thick hedge–rows soon adorned the valley. In a work published in 1792, it is thus described:– "Within a mile of Timolin on the right, our eyes were enraptured with the most delicious situation, when through the lofty trees we beheld a variety of neat dwellings. Through a road that looked like a fine terrace–walk we hastened to this lovely spot, where nature assisted by art gave us the most perfect gratification. It is a colony of Quakers, called by the name of Ballitore. The river Griese winds its stream very near the houses; and the buildings, orchards, and gardens show an elegant simplicity peculiar to this people. Their burying–ground near the road is surrounded with different trees, whose verdure made us imagine it a well–planted garden, till we were informed otherwise. The hedges that enclose the meadows and fields are quickset, kept of an equal height, and about every ten yards trees regularly pierce through them, forming beautiful groves of a large extent. Industry reigns amongst this happy society; all their works are executed with taste corrected by judgment, and seem to prosper as if Heaven smiled on their honest labours."

I was born in the last month of the year 1758. I suppose when about seven years of age I began to remark the familiar shades under which I grew. I shall attempt a description as I first remember them.[6] The circuit of the village, including the Mill, as my Mother got it measured, is a mile. The high road near it had then but few houses on it. At a little distance from the road, on the gentle slope down to the village, was a grove of fir trees planted, so as to meet the eye in every direction with a straight lined avenue to the centre, where was enclosed the place of interment belonging to Friends. We entered the Grove at a large door, from which an avenue led to the Grave–yard, both avenue and enclosure were ditched in. The gloom of the surrounding trees so perfectly according with the place, had a very striking effect. Fir trees grew on the side of the road next the Grove. The high road had formerly run at the foot of the hill from which we entered Ballitore, & the trees on each side the descent, were of a later growth than those which continued from thence, which formed an arching shade over head, till on our right hand the ancient habitation of old Abraham Shackleton, encompassed by his own hand, arrested the traveller's attention. The trees continued on the left hand till this house was a little past, there was a shaft open to the bridge which was narrow and the battlements much broken. At either end of the bridge at the right hand, the river extended considerably past its limits. When we cross the bridge, on the left hand was a handsome field, with fish ponds round it, enclosed next to the road with a double ditch, & double hedgerow to the corner where the road or street turned nearly opposite the Burrow gate; There was a large Elm; whose branches overhung the bridge. On the bank of the river, at the lower end of this field was a walk short and sweet, between a double row of Elms. This field, on our left, & the water on our right hand, we reached the Burrow, a knot of old, & for the most part mean houses, chiefly inhabited by artificers. The most respectable were the old mansion of the Strettels & next in neighbourhood & esteem Edward Miles. A pair of ruined piers, probably once the entrance into Abel Strettel's concerns, were called the Burrow gate. If we proceeded right onwards the trees enclosing Taylor's orchard, the School, Andrew Nelson's & a little space to a thatched low stone house with the end to the road, the widow Jackson's on the right: on the left a pond, or rather ditch, tall ivied trees fronting the school & enclosing Joseph Wills's orchard, the round–topped, nailed, iron–spiked gate into it seemed to terminate the village, though the road continued on to Narraghmore and Athy. We return to the Burrow Gate, & take our way upstreet, as this principal part of Ballitore is called. A dead wall on the right where Edmund Burke told me there had been a pond & indented hedge enclosed part of Joseph Wills' concerns; his slated offices without windows or doors to the street, continued the enclosure to his house, which was long and low being but two stories high, the upper windows dormant. A flight of handsome steps with battlements, forming a sweep at each side, topped with nice flags & making agreeable seats, led to his Hall door, which was ornamented by a brass knocker, two round panes of glass and a pent house, still more by his friends from Dublin, who seated on these battlements, in a fine summer evening, displayed their gay apparel to the admiring eyes of the Villagers. Onward from the house was the garden wall, with a flight of steps sideways to the red door, the wall soon turning up enclosed the garden. Fronting the hall door, a low gate painted green entered the field mentioned before, surrounded with fish ponds. I do not think the hedge row was continued, or it was for a very short way, at this end of the field: but there was a low, neat, white wall at each side the gate. Next this field were the ruins of an unfinished building, & amongst them was Frank Malone's slaughter house, from which was a pretty space and hedge–row to his house which was snug, low & thatched. On the other side was a little open leading to the fields, between Joseph Wills's garden wall & the school house, to which adjoined a long, slated house where Abraham Shackleton first lived in Ballitore. The garden & orchard belonging to this house were enclosed with very tall Ash trees, & in the orchard were some fine walnuts. A gate into a field was between this hedge–row and the Meeting–house grove, & here a stream ran, under the road, & sometimes overflowed it, called the runner, convenient for scouring pails, churns &c. The grove was on each side of the meeting–house, there were some fine Beeches, & various kinds of trees on it, a little stream ran through it, & it was a situation capable of high improvement, yet though it joined the garden of Abel Strettel ju[r], this seems not to have occurred to him, as his father planted them the trees grew, & the stream flowed as Nature directed it. The meeting–house had a double roof, the gable ends in front, a court before it. The roof supported within by a wooden pillar with two branches (Charles Coote says when he was a little boy; he thought this was meant to represent the Trinity). From Frank Malone's a row of trees, & a row of cabins, mostly inhabited by Jonathan Haughton's combers stretched on to his yard gate, in at which we entered to reach his hall–door, gardens, offices, & the pretty walk between two Privet hedges, which led to the River, beside which stood the Buck house, a building belonging to a Bleach–green which had formerly been here. It served Jonathan for washing his wool, & his daughters undressed here for bathing. There was a little descent from the street to Jonathan's shop, which was on the other side of his house to that on which we entered by the hall door. His garden hedge row was continued to Fuller's Court, till the trees fronting the great house had been felled to accommodate a gentleman of the name of Toler, who lived there with the fair prospect of the river, hill & Graveyard Grove. The neat hedges which enclosed Jonathan Haughton's fields compensated for this loss. Opposite to JH's house was the short terrace walk overlooking the road in the garden belonging to the great house, a garden not planned by taste. This house, built by the son of the worthy purchaser, was like the dwellings in Yorkshire villages called Halls, undoubtedly in the first consideration in the place, & old Margaret Shackleton told, with pleasure of her little grandson Abraham, that he said he would not like to live in such a proud house. The stately dwelling withdrew a pretty space from the road, with a large court before the door, the entrance into which was near the house, a passage between the court & orchard led to that, & to the offices which retired from sight. The blooming orchards on our right continued till we turned to a neat cottage, its end to the road, its back to the orchard, a yard & garden before it, where James & Nancey McConnaughty resided. On either side from hence to the termination of the street, the full–grown, thickly–planted trees, meeting at top, formed a sweet retired walk while leading to the enjoyment of society. A field planted with firs, forming a very thin grove, was on the right, fields & hedge–rows on the left, & a large gate before us led into Fuller's Court; at the foot of one of the piers was a seat covered with a flag which I think was rather famous for the meeting of lovers. In this court lived Sarah Fuller, a widow, & in an adjoining house her tenants Rachel & Deborah Carleton, the rest of the square was composed of offices, chiefly belonging to the Wool–combing business, which the late John Fuller had carried on. Through this court was a passage, open by day but locked by night. Then we pass through a place called the Bawn & turning to the left over a stile in to the Mill–field, which had a gentle rise & descent, commanding a rich prospect of the Mill–pond, grave–yard–grove &c, & in the Spring was yellow with cowslips. A row of trees beside the path–way, were at this time just felled, a garden & orchard were at the other side of the path. Crossing a ditch over a bridge with a hand rail which was often torn down, we turned on the road into a smooth gravel walk beside the fair Mill–pond, at the rear end of which were little islands planted with willows, & near it a chalybeate spa. When we come to the end of this smooth expanse, if we turn to look back, the view of the village is beautiful. On the right, a little retired, was the dwelling house then inhabited by Ephraim Burke. At the other side of the pond was an uneven road between that & the river, over a part of which the superfluous water emptied itself into the river & formed a pretty cascade called the Slip. The kilns were built hereabout. The mill fronted the pond, & the river was crossed by a board, placed I think at an unsteady height, a pathway through fields led to the high road; the horse way was over the Slip, & a little bridge.

Such was the appearance of this sequestered spot which, though very little removed from the great road between Dublin and Cork, seemed desirous to escape observation by hiding its dwellings in its shades. The modest merit of many of its inhabitants bore in this respect, a resemblance to the place.[7]

The first abode on entering the village was that of old Abraham Shackleton, a man whose memory was long held in veneration. His exterior bespoke his character; his countenance expressed the sweetness and humility of his mind, mixed with a gravity sometimes bordering on austerity. Being the youngest of six orphans, and his habit of body not being robust enough for labour, he betook himself to letters, and though twenty years of age when he began to learn Latin, he succeeded so perfectly as to write that language not only with correctness but with elegance. He was a native of Yorkshire, and became an assistant in the school of David Hall of Skipton, in whose family his future wife, Margaret Wilkinson, David Hall's near relation, was also an inmate. Having removed to Ireland, he was engaged by William Cooper of Cooper–hill, and John Duckett of Duckett's–grove, who were both country–gentlemen and Quakers, as private tutor to their children. Sensible of his talents and worth, they encouraged him to open a boarding–school, which he did in Ballitore on the first of the Third–month, 1726, having previously prevailed on his beloved Margaret to become his wife and accompany him to a strange land. Under the auspices of piety and honesty the school prospered beyond their humble hopes. To them were born a son, Richard, and a daughter, Elizabeth; the latter wounded her parents' hearts by a clandestine marriage with Maurice Raynor, a young man who was usher to her father. She died early in life, leaving one son, William, who was taken by his grand–parents, and whom Margaret Shackleton, (who was somewhat of a wit) used to call "a twig of the rod." Behold the venerable Abraham, in the first place devoting his time to the duties of religion and the services of his society, then indulging his taste for cultivating his lands and planting, having resigned the school to his son Richard. His wife, who was some years older than he, and debilitated by rheumatic pains, sate by her fireside, her countenance innocently sweet, her conversation innocently cheerful, and her heart truly humble. Her sister, Mary Barnard, a widow, was stout and active on her limbs, but being deprived of sight, she went about the house, felt the under parts of the furniture to try whether all was clean; examined closely the bottom of her petticoat lest a jag had been worn; made spring–pottage and sour–cake, of which her friends partook; was led among her poor neighbours, to whom she made little presents of a halfpenny lace, a row of pins, or gifts of equal value, which were kindly accepted from the simple, honest–hearted donor.

I hardly recollect the ancient mansion; the large room like that apartment which in similar residences in Yorkshire is called "the hoose" (neither parlour nor kitchen) in which was a closet, and in that closet an owl; the parlour where the afternoon meeting was held, with its sashdoor opening into the garden, and the map of Dublin, ornamented by pictures of its remarkable buildings, &c. over the chimney–piece.[8] But "the Friends' room," so named from its being appropriated to the use of strangers, impressed my young fancy with an idea of superior elegance of which I can scarce divest myself even now. Perhaps some peacock's feathers about the chimney–piece caused this childish error of judgement. The ceiling was actually supported by props to prevent it from falling in, and the crazy state of the house occasioned no little uneasiness in stormy weather to the friends of the occupants, though I believe not to themselves. At length the old man was prevailed upon to rebuild; he finished the kitchen end, but was by that time so thoroughly tired of artificers, that he resigned the completion of the job to his daughter-in-law. Their grandsons Abraham Shackleton and William Raynor resided with them; the latter was a child, the former a stripling just bursting out into that brilliancy of talent for which he became distinguished, and which was veiled by amiable modesty and softened by good nature; he was pronounced by Mary Barnard a child who could not be spoiled, and was the pride and darling of the venerable trio.

The forge next presents itself, at the extremity of a little row of cabins. Although a shattered-looking place, it was well frequented, both on account of business and news; nor have the genteeler sort disdained to sit on the stone bench at the door. Adjoining thereto was the dwelling of the proprietor, Mick Murray, an old man who was not only skilled in shoeing horses and prescribing for their distempers, but occasionally drew teeth with his pincers. He is reported to have once lifted my mother three times from the floor, in his fruitless attempts to extract a tooth; and that good woman, who always strove to be relieved of pain of body or mind as speedily as possible, sate with heroic resolution while he went home and sharpened his vile instrument to complete the operation.

The abode of Peter Widdows adjoined the forge. He was by trade a tailor, and by religion a Quaker, though he had been disowned for marrying his maid servant, who was not a member of the Society. He had several children. Age and infirmity had overtaken him; and when bed-ridden he kept a little school, sometimes calling his son Joseph off his tailor's board to correct untoward pupils. The last days of the old man were favoured with peace. He once proposed to apprentice his son Joseph to Richard Shackleton to fit him to be a schoolmaster; and, being asked why he did not teach him his own trade, replied that his son had not capacity for it. The son did not, however, coincide in his father's choice; for, after running away (the knight-errantry of schoolboys), and mistaking Kilcullen for Dublin, "because the Liffey ran through it," he settled down to the trade of his father, at whose death he became master of the cottage. Having a prospect of a comfortable livelihood, he obtained the hand of Abigail Pope, a young woman of high spirit, who had been upper servant with the Pims of Tullalost, and therefore regarded herself as allied "to some of the top families."[9]

The ancient mansion of the Strettels commanded, from the casement windows in an upper room, a view of the street, though further from it than most of the other houses. Here lived the widow Taylor and her daughter, with frugal neatness and exemplary industry. The widow was tall and thin, and had the remains of beauty. She was a chatty woman, skilful in the complaints of children, and kind in assisting by advice and attendance. Her name was Bridget, but she generally bore the appellation of "aunt." About this time, while going to Abraham Shackleton's one windy evening, wrapped in her camlet riding–hood, which gathered the wind, she, being very light, was blown into the river, and was in danger of perishing before the accident was discovered. The inflated riding–hood bore her up along the stream. Her daughter Polly, a fine tall blooming young woman, appeared to me, especially when adorned with a stay–hook set with shining stones, a beauty so resplendent that I gazed in silent admiration. She was prevailed upon by my mother to take my younger sister and me as day–scholars, before we went to my father's school. We were very carefully taught by our fair instructress, and were great favourites with her and her mother. Polly Taylor afterwards married Joshua Haughton, and was known as Molly Haughton.

Most awkwardly in the way of the entrance to this mansion was the end of Edward Miles's, some of the apartments of which being quite dark gave rise to stories that the house was haunted.

The buildings which joined and darkened this house were partly inhabited by journeymen shoemakers. One of them was called the Ball–room, and there the school boys sometimes footed it to the scrape of old Bowden's fiddle, which disgusted my ears with its discordant sounds, when, in passing to school, I sometimes stole a peep at what went on.

Over this room was an apartment which belonged to Sarah Braddock, who would not resign it, though offered a bed at Richard Shackleton's house, where she lived in the day–time, and where, seated in a low armchair in the nursery, she was constantly employed in mending the boy's stockings. We youngsters deemed her of a peevish temper because she could ill bear with our childish tricks, for which some of us wept with remorse at her burial. A young lad having accidentally broken her pipe, and being unwilling to encounter her resentment, professed ignorance of the matter; but this did not avail him, for Sarah declared "there was not a Christian in the nursery but himself and the cat." Cats, geese, and sparrows were high in her favour, and manifested reciprocal attachment. As our family were always uneasy when she became unwell at her lodging, she was at length prevailed upon to stay at our house, where she would be properly attended to. The day before her death, my father sat by her bed–side, and spoke of the peaceful end of his father. "My old Master!" said Sarah, in a shrill and angry tone; "don't tell me of my old master. If I was as good as him, I would not be afraid to die to–night, before to–morrow;" which she accordingly did. She died in 1773.

The last habitation at this end of the village belonged to the widow Jackson, who was remarkable for speaking ill of nobody, though ever so bad.

She was the daughter of a clergyman, and was left by an extravagant husband in reduced circumstances. She valued her descent from Bernard Gilpin, the apostle of the North, whose life she was pleased to find in a biographical dictionary. Her genteel deportment and blameless life interested her neighbours. Joseph Wills gave her a spot of ground, others I suppose assisted her in building a comfortable cottage; her daughter Julia it is said made some of the inner partitions with her own hands. This was a fine young woman, industrious and ingenious, full of health and vivacity, but she fell a victim to the small pox. Her mother's sorrows were soothed by the worthy rector of Narraghmore, Richard Beauchamp, and his benevolent Julia (one of the Keatinge family), who took her into their house, and treated her with that respect and affection which her character deserved, and which they were wont to bestow. Her house was now occasionally inhabited by persons who took care of it for her, and kept her furniture, &c. locked up in the parlour. The display of this room, with which I was sometimes indulged, excited sensations of admiration and pleasure, not exceeded when the wonderful productions of the first masters, exhibited in the gallery of Sir Joshua Reynolds or at Somerset House, burst on my view. The screen on which "The Harlot's Progress" was depicted, and the family pictures disposed about the walls, especially one into which a little boy was introduced (rendered more interesting by hearing he had been killed by a fall from a castle), were devoured by my greedy eyes "with ever new delight."

But I leave this enchanting scene, and return upon my steps to the Burrow–gate, proceeding thence up the main street of the village, where the habitation of Joseph Wills first attracts us. Joseph was a man retired from business, who lived upon his income in a genteel, comfortable style, keeping what is called good company and a good table, and attentive to the cultivation of his land and garden, and to the provision of his household. He was elderly, rather low in stature, somewhat corpulent, and his nose large and carbuncled; he wore a gold–laced hat and waistcoat, and moved along the street with slow and stately pace, smoking out of a long, clean pipe. Thus arrayed, he frequently walked into his neighbours' houses, which opened with latches, and enquired what they had for dinner, at the same time poking his staff into the pot, for they mostly sat in their kitchens in the forenoons. This familiarity was of course not always acceptable. Sarah Fuller's servant ran in to warn her mistress of his approach: "Here's Mr. Wills, here's Mr. Wills!" but she was not quick enough. "Noble intelligence!" retorted Joseph, gravely, as he followed her. He had his singularities, but he was "respectable," and Elizabeth Shackleton piqued herself on being always on good terms with him. He encouraged and assisted her taste for gardening; he delighted in dandling her sweet little Rachael and receiving her caresses, and avoided the house for some time after death had taken from thence his little favourite: this trait of tenderness the mother remembered with gratitude. His parlour was wainscotted and hung round with engraved portraits, but what I best remember was a closet beside the parlour fire, from which Joseph failed not to bring comfits, which he dispensed to his little guests. The back window faced the principal walk of the flower–garden; the borders on either hand were decorated with sweet peas climbing up painted sticks. From this garden moss–rose trees were first introduced amongst us.

We now reach Jonathan Haughton's. It was about this time that worthy man was deprived of the society of a valuable and amiable wife. The care of the household and younger children devolved upon Hannah, then about thirteen, and admirably did she perform those duties with prudence, economy, and affection; but care early furrowed her youthful brow and damped the vivacity of her age. The other children were John, Debby, Sally, and little Joe. Debby was two months elder than I, Sally six months younger than my sister Sally, so that nature seemed to present to each of us a chosen friend. The tie was early formed, and, like ties formed at that age, peculiarly tender and peculiarly strong. Ye sweet companions of my childhood, whose loss I have never ceased to regret; although surrounded by dear friends and dear relations, death has not been able to loosen that tie! The father of this family was one of the most amiable of men. Possessed of no shining abilities, he possessed what was of more value – a heart moulded by benevolence, which impressed his countenance. A husband and father tender to a great degree, a kind master, a true friend, and one of the best of neighbours, his affectionate attentions extended to children. I remember the resolutions I have made not to approach his knees when he came to sit a while with my grandmother and aunt, because I was sensible that I could not keep within bounds when Jonathan began to play with me, which he surely would, – but the temptation always proved too strong for my resistance.

The Great House was at this time inhabited by Lee Masters, an English gentleman of fortune, whimsical, and who frequently changed the place of his residence. His wife seems to have partaken of his whims, for we heard of her having drank tea one evening on the bridge, a freak which might have been attended with inconvenience, if the bridge had been half so much of a thoroughfare as it is now, for it was then but half its present width.

Chapter II.
1766.

Sketch of the Annalist's parents, Richard and Elizabeth Shackleton. – The school–house and garden. – Elizabeth Haughton, William Gill, and John Buckley. – Ballitore School. – French and Norwegian pupils. – Story of Aldborough Wrightson. – Edmund Burke an "old Ballitore boy." – Anecdotes of his childhood and boyhood. – His subsequent visits to Ballitore. – Fuller's Court, its inhabitants and its early attractions. – Notices of George Rooke, one of the early Quaker patriarchs. – His daughter Rachael, and granddaughter Deborah Carleton. – Tom and Sam Eyre. 22 to 38

BALLITORE SCHOOL, at the earliest period to which my memory extends, was kept by my father Richard Shackleton, who was then in the prime of life. He was carefully educated by his parents, according to the system prevailing in the time of his childhood, which occasioned greater restraint and awe of parental authority than that which he adopted in the education of his own children. In early life, although, from the liveliness of his disposition, exposed to temptation, he turned his back upon the allurements of the world, and embraced religion with a heart sincerely devoted to it. He married Elizabeth Fuller, an amiable and worthy young woman, to whom he had been long attached, and who left him at the age of twenty–eight a sorrowful widower with four young children; the last of whom, a son, was born shortly before the death of his mother, and survived her only two years. Shortly after the death of this child, Richard Shackleton married Elizabeth Carleton. She lived in Dublin with her mother and sister, and their little property was managed with respectable economy. In her youth she indulged in dress as far as possible, she had a musical ear, she sang, and had an uncommon taste for drawing.[10] Before the season of youth was past she renounced those delights, and was faithful and diligent in doing what she believed to be her duty. Her adopted children witnessed this, and they repaid her kindness with filial affection. Lads have been educated in the family, and were surprised to hear afterwards that my father's children were born of different mothers. The worthy pair were desirous above all things to promote the cause of truth and righteousness, and were anxiously concerned faithfully to discharge the arduous occupation in which they were engaged. Richard Shackleton was a man of wit and learning, he had a genius for poetry, and was conversant with the classics. Superior to these was his deep and solid understanding, and, far excelling all, an honest and benevolent heart; these he possessed. His conversation was delightful, for he was unassuming and condescending; it was instructive, for amid the blaze of superior talents humility shone unrivalled. He was the gentleman, the scholar, and the Christian. His cheerful temper caused him to enjoy every good, while his pious resignation taught him to bear what is called evil with quiet submission. His temper was naturally quick, but his generous mind was ever ready to atone. His wife had not his liveliness of disposition; she was grave, circumspect, and cautious, perhaps to an extreme. She took upon herself the care of all within and without, and entered into the affairs of her poor neighbours, not from curiosity but kindness. The multiplicity of her cares at times caused her much anxiety, yet, being regular in her habits, she probably got through them with more ease than if she had more quickness of action and disposition. Her relaxation consisted in the cultivation of her garden, from which she extracted much pleasure, and she was curious in her collection of flowers. With an improved and solid understanding she had much simplicity of character, and it was not difficult to impose upon her; but I believe few had the heart to injure her materially, she was so much beloved. It not unfrequently happens that the simple and artless penetrate into the characters and motives of others more readily than those do who are busy concealing their own. This good woman possessed great tenderness of heart, and was a cordial sympathiser with the sick and afflicted.

Casting their cares upon Providence, this exemplary couple felt the shackles of the world hang loose about them. Their duties to the children intrusted to their care were conscientiously fulfilled, and the grateful love which their pupils retained for them was a convincing proof of it. They were useful members of their religious society, and, with clean hands and in the meekness of wisdom, were qualified to take an active part in conducting the affairs of the church. They attended the general meetings very constantly, and Richard Shackleton took a method with his pupils which was well calculated to maintain order in his absence. He gave in charge to the eldest boy, or to him whom he suspected of being most likely to give trouble, a portion of care over the rest; he arranged matters to the best of his knowledge; he addressed the boys in general; and, above all, he openly committed them to the care of Providence.

The house which contained the family was large; and, though old and inelegant, was comfortable, and became by dint of improvement convenient. Between the house and garden was a large yard, with two squares of grass for the boys to play on. The piers of the garden gate were covered with ivy, the berries of which had been sown by James Mc Connaughty the day my sister Sally was born, the 6th of Sixth-month, 1760. A broad walk reached from the garden–gate to the old arbour of yew at the upper end of the kitchen–garden, in which were planted several apple-trees. So far as the walk continued through the flower–garden, it was gravelled; thence it became a grass walk, and had at each side thick yew hedges, in the ends of which, as they were intersected by cross–walks, chairs were cut. In the flower–garden were two large yew–trees, all of which my mother used to have trimmed with care, except the tops, which she hoped in time to form into an arch. The tardy branches were at length extending to meet her hopes, when, in luckless hour, Fardy the gardener, either ignorant or forgetful of the wishes of his mistress, rounded off the tops with great dexterity and ill–timed officiousness. I need not add what vexation and disappointment ensued.

At the head of the household was placed Elizabeth Haughton, a near relation of Richard Shackleton's first wife, who, being left a widow in narrow circumstances, accepted of this charge, her two children being taken in also. She was a religious woman, of an excellent disposition, kind and humane; and "cousin Betty" was universally respected and beloved.

The steward was William Gill, a man of strict and approved fidelity. He was advanced in years, of a portly person and comely countenance. He had served Abraham Shackleton in the days when Edmund Burke went to school to him, and was attached to that great and amiable man by those ties of affection and admiration which bound all who knew him.

There also lived in the family, at this time, an old man named John Buckley, son of Allan Buckley, a shoe–maker, to whom Richard Shackleton and Edmund Burke resorted when they were boys, when Edmund used to amuse himself making mathematical figures out of Allan's wax. I suppose Allan was a Quaker, for his remains were laid in our graveyard; and his son with pious attention dressed his grave, a mark of filial affection which reflected more honour than the headstone placed at the grave of Abel Strettel. John continued this affectionate office while he was able. He had been a soldier, was tall, thin, and upright, and much older than he appeared to be, cheerful, lively, and quick in temper; yet during his occasional fits of illness he felt much distress of mind, approaching to despair. His duties were to assist in cleaning the shoes and knives, to cut the bread, attend the boys' table, and announce at the schoolroom door when the meals were ready. His age was considered with tenderness; indeed no burdens were laid upon any; and I believe it was thought Elizabeth Shackleton was too indulgent a mistress. When Johnny grew very old and feeble, she thought proper to make him a bowl of salop every evening, which at first was grateful to his failing appetite; but I was once greatly surprised when I brought him the well–seasoned draught, that he took it from me in a pet, and hastened to the scullery. I followed, enquiring what he meant to do with it. "To throw it down the sink," said Johnny, "for I am tired of it." Of course no more salop was made; but the peevishness of age and infirmity was passed by without exciting resentment.

The inferior servants, who were generally Roman Catholics, often lived in the house until they were married, when they were treated to a wedding supper, and continued to be friends after they ceased to be servants.

The school mostly consisted of fifty, and sometimes sixty boarders, besides day–scholars. There were generally a few parlour–boarders, who were, for the most part, grown young men. Several French men and boys came here in the time of my grandfather, to learn English, and they left the name of "the French room" to a large apartment in which they slept.

Two Norwegians were also sent to this school, the only natives of that country who were ever at it. They were both from Drontheim, perfect strangers to one another, and each was sent to Ballitore in order to be entirely out of the way of meeting with a fellow countryman. They came much about the same time. The elder was Svend Peter Stuberg; the other Laurence Nicholas Zelius, a beautiful gentle youth. He did not appear so quick in capacity as Stuberg, who was older and rougher, and quite baffled Zelius by speaking his own language to him; so that he could make no progress in English, and was obliged to quit the school, more regretted by others than by his countryman, who, it was thought, looked upon him as a rival in the affections of the family and neighbours. Peter then had the field to himself; he soon spoke and wrote English with facility; and amazed the villagers with his wonderful stories of northern superstition. After he left, he for several years kept up a correspondence with the family; presents were interchanged of the produce of the two countries; and once he paid us a visit, at which time I remember him playing on a German flute at the lime–kiln in the Mill–avenue, and remarking the effect of the echo. He told us he was about to marry a fine young woman of his own country, who was "very like Betsy Pim."

Aldborough Wrightson, whose short but eventful history makes no uninteresting part of the village annals, was born in 1746; and, with his elder brother Thomas, was sent to Ballitore school in 1754. He was a beautiful sprightly child. Aldborough went to college, but on his brother's death, his father, a wealthy alderman, wished him to supply the vacant place in his counting–house; and his mother would have desired him to go of her errands to her milliner and manteau–maker, and to attend her in that round of diversions which, in one of his last letters, he said "had frittered away her understanding." His high spirit and taste for letters not corresponding with their views, he became irregular in his habits; which would have been freely pardoned by his parents had he entered into their plans, but as he did not, these irregularities served as a pretext for holding him at a distance, though once their beloved, and now their only son. It is just within the compass of my memory his being taken dangerously ill, either with a spitting of blood which brought him very low, or with a mortification in his thumb which was afterwards amputated, and for which operation he strove to prepare himself by the Stoic philosophy that pain was no evil. At one of those times his father and mother came down for him; not so soon as he expected, it seems, for the idea presents itself to my memory of the languishing youth reclined in a straw arm–chair, and his mother rushing into the parlour with maternal haste, wringing her hands, and exclaiming, "Did you not think we were brutes?" Her heart was not callous then: how it afterwards became so I cannot explain.[11] It was thought that interest fomented family dissensions.[12] When Aldborough was displeased or displeasing at home, he was sent to Ballitore, an exile from his father's house; and he always found a father in his old master, although not by any means dependant on him, for his father made him an allowance for his ordinary wants. If Wrightson had been irregular in his habits, nothing of this appeared in his conduct in Ballitore. He was to his master's children as an elder brother; he encouraged in young Abraham Shackleton the love of literature, and I believe by example and precept counselled him well. The elder girls were driven by him with some harshness into the parlour, if he found them associating with servants or other company which he disapproved of. With the younger ones he often joined in their childish plays, from which he appeared to extract as much delight as they did. I have some pride in saying I was a peculiar favourite of his; he quarrelled with my mother for not getting me inoculated for the small–pox: some silly rhymes I made at about seven years of age he seemed delighted with, and insisted upon my being taught Latin, which my mother and aunt unfortunately prevented, from a mistaken notion that it would increase an impediment in my speech. He taught me some Greek verses and some beautiful lines of Cowley; strove to correct my walk and carriage; now commended, and then scolded me; and, fearing him more than either, I loved him next to my father and James Mc Connaughty. He did not attend school, for he was fully supplied with the treasures of learning, and his conversation, abounding in good sense, was enlivened by sallies of wit expressed with such elegant simplicity, that even I, a child, understood and admired them. I cannot but think that in his vigorous turn of mind and extent of genius he strongly resembled the great Burke. His letters at the same age are fully equal, and very similar in style, to those of our dear honoured Edmund. But Wrightson was early crushed into the grave. Burke grew and flourished, the ornament of an admiring world! Let us hope that their spirits have met in that kingdom where human policy and human acquirements are no more.

Richard Shackleton's intimacy with Edmund Burke commenced when

Edmund was the pupil of old Abraham Shackleton, from whose school he entered Trinity College in the year 1744. He came to Ballitore with his elder brother Garrett, and his younger brother Richard, on the 26th of Fifth–month, 1741. They had been when very young at school with an old woman who was so cross, and they resented her crossness so much, that one holiday the three little fellows set out for her cabin with intent to kill her. As her good genius would have it, she happened to be from home, and their fit of fury evaporated before the next opportunity. Garrett Burke, who had a great turn for humour, was an eminent lawyer, and died before my time. His brother Richard could not be excelled by him in the talent for drollery, and it is well known that Edmund also had his share.

Burke's friendship with Richard Shackleton grew with their growth and strengthened with their strength, and lasted to the end of their lives. My mother cordially entered into the attachment of her husband. She had first seen Edmund when, on a journey before her marriage, she called at Ballitore. Both he and his friend were remarkably short–sighted, and they were trying which could read best by twilight. I cannot forget the first visit which occurred in my time of this illustrious man to Ballitore. Edmund Burke was expected; we naturally loved every friend of our parents, but to these predilections were superadded sentiments of respect and admiration in the present instance, which caused his visit to be expected with impatient wonder. The chaise stopped at the big gate, which unfolded wide, and my imagination still presents the graceful form of Edmund, as I beheld him from the nursery window, leading in his wife, a pretty little woman, with no covering on her head but her beautiful unadorned auburn tresses. On Elizabeth Shackleton expressing surprise that she wore no cap, in which respect she was singular at that time, she said that she dressed conformably to her husband's taste; however, she promised to put on one, and next morning appeared in the first French night–cap that was ever seen in Ballitore. The plain dress of Edmund disappointed my expectation, and I thought the postillion's habit, daubed with livery lace, much more elegant: the sight of our guest's laced waistcoat, however, a little reconciled me. Yet, when, in taking a survey of the family of his friend, he stood over me as I sat in a little chair and viewed me through the glass which assisted his short sight, I felt so abashed and confused that I directly annexed the idea of austerity to his countenance; nor could the testimony of many witnesses efface that idea, till I afterwards saw him in London in the year 1784, when with a very uncommon sensation of pleasure and surprise it was at once put to flight; for never did I see so much benignity and intelligence united, as in the manly beauty of that countenance, in which were blended the expressions of every superior quality of the head and of the heart. This visit was previous to the purchase of Beaconsfield, and to his "taking root in England," as he expressed it.

He was frequently in Ireland, and of course often in Ballitore. At one time my mother, while walking in the fields at the foot of the Nine–tree–hill, was surprised to hear a familiar voice behind her; she turned and beheld Edmund Burke, who was going in search of her, and having just arrived, took some path remembered by him which she did not know of, and had got behind her. Their little son sometimes accompanied them in their visits, in one of which he was in disgrace with his mother, and she kept him at a distance; but the fond father was solicitous to put up a bit of bread for him when they were setting out. He was now the only child, for they had buried another son. My father and mother went once to visit Edmund at Dublin Castle, where he had apartments, and found him seated on the floor playing with his two little boys. Edmund brought a painter with him at one time, Richard Sesson, a man of talent, and prevailed on my dear father to sit for his picture; he consented, though it was against his judgment, as not consonant to the practice of our Society. Probably for this reason an expression of uneasiness appears on the portrait, although it is otherwise a good likeness. The portrait of his old master, Abraham Shackleton, was also longed for by his illustrious pupil; but he durst not request it. To the conversation of the two accomplished friends, which was indeed "a feast of reason and a flow of soul," young Wrightson listened with delight, but with that silent modesty which is often the companion and ornament of exalted minds, especially in youth. Richard Shackleton, suddenly turning to his pupil, enquired, with that liveliness peculiar to him, why he did not speak, assuring his friend that he could speak, and to the purpose. The youth blushed. Edmund grew angry, and retorted fiercely, "You insult his modesty."

My father used to delight in detailing instances of Burkes singular aptitude, and how soon he attained a superior station amongst his schoolfellows, many of whom he readily assisted in their exercises. He showed thus early his capacity for exerting his abilities on a sudden emergency, and of turning the ideas of others to useful account. Burke and his schoolfellows were permitted one day to go and see the procession of the judges into the county town of Athy, on condition that each of the senior lads should write a description of the spectacle in Latin verse. When Burke finished his own task, he was earnestly solicited by another lad to assist him, the poor fellow declaring that he had laboured in vain for hours to knock something out of his brains, and that rather than try again he would walk barefooted to the top of Lugnaquilla, which is the loftiest of the Wicklow mountains, about twelve Irish miles from Ballitore. He reminded his schoolfellow how often he had helped him before, and said that this was the hardest task he ever got. Burke was for the moment somewhat puzzled how he could compose a second paper on the same subject; and, hoping to obtain some hint for the composition, he asked the applicant what had struck him as most remarkable in the procession. The lad replied that he had noticed nothing in particular, except a fat piper in a brown coat. Furnished with this hint, Burke immediately commenced and in a very short time completed a humorous poem in doggrel Latin; the first line of which was as follows:–

"Piper erat fattus, qui brownum tegmen habebat."

He loved humour, and my father was very witty. The two friends sharpened their intellect and sported their wit till peals of laughter in the schoolroom often caused the reverend and grave master to implore them, with suppressed smiles, to desist, or he should have to turn them both out, as their example might be followed where folly and uproar would take the place of humour and wisdom. Burke's heart was tender, too, and my father was wont to relate a circumstance which proved that in boyhood, as well as in riper years, he felt an invincible hatred to oppression. A poor man having been compelled to pull down his cabin, because the surveyor of roads declared that it stood too near the highway, Burke, who saw the reluctant owner perform his melancholy task, observed with great indignation, that if he were in authority such tyranny should never be exercised with impunity over the defenceless; and he urged his schoolfellows to join in rebuilding the cottage. My grandfather, however, would not permit this to be done.

The mansion–house in Fuller's Court was inhabited by the widow Sarah Fuller. Her family consisted of her three daughters and three sons; Deborah Watson, mother of her late husband, and Mary Pim, who were boarders; and occasionally boys who boarded there to attend the school. She was of the Duckett family; a very clever, domestic character, kind and goodnatured, rather high, yet not very polite in her manners. Although her kitchen inspired a laudable ambition in the neighbourhood, it ever retained its pre–eminence, unrivalled in cleanliness. The dresser shone with pewter bright as silver, and brass and copper–pots shining like gold. I do suspect that some of these were kept chiefly for ornament, and that Aunt Fuller was not without some vanity in the display. A little book–closet beside the kitchen fire often attracted my observation: it was also attracted by the china cupboard behind it, which opened into the parlour, into which I seized every opportunity of getting a peep. The parlours were nicely kept; a sash–door opened into the garden, well kept also and well cultivated, quite in the antique taste, with large yew and holly trees, and a bower of yew, which at my request, many years after this period, was rescued from the axe, – for, though whatever beauty it had possessed was gone, my father had courted his first wife in that bower, and therefore it remained an object of veneration. A jessamine tree not only surrounded the parlour window, but made its way inside. How I have delighted to pass and repass the dairy window, which also looked into the garden, inhaling the sweetness and freshness from within, mingled with the fragrance of the woodbine from without. Beyond the garden was an orchard, where the ground was white with snowdrops in spring. Here was the bleachgreen for the clothes, the large stone to beetle them on, and a hole cut through a tree for a cider–press, and steps down to the water which ran between two hedge–rows at one side of the garden; the banks were high and narrow, and, for what reason I know not, it was called "the Sconce." At the termination of a walk which led through the orchard was a red door, which I often contemplated with a wish to pass this *ne plus ultra*. Seldom was it opened; but when it was, some lofty trees, and a bubbling stream, which I supposed to be a fountain, and, above all, the charm of novelty made that appear a delightful spot into which the red door admitted us.

Deborah Watson, the mother of my father's first wife, was possessed of considerable intellectual endowments, and amiable, engaging manners, and was dearly loved by my father. She had married a second husband, worthy Samuel Watson of Kilconnor, when both were advanced in age, and she survived him. She was a woman of a meek and quiet spirit, daughter of John Barcroft of truly honourable memory, a man of liberal mind, universal benevolence, cultivated understanding, and deep humility; thus have I heard my father describe him. He had but two children who survived him, both daughters, one of whom married John Pim of Edenderry, and left a large family of daughters and one son. This son had several daughters, most of whom were married – one of them to Thomas Bewley. The eldest, Mary, remained single, was now elderly, and boarded at Aunt Fuller's. She had a strong and well–cultivated understanding, was much attached to her relations, and was the most eminent knitter of her time.

Forming an angle with Sarah Fuller's house was the abode of my grandmother Rachael Carleton and her daughter Deborah. Rachael Carleton was daughter of the venerable George Rooke, a man whose sweet and gentle disposition made him as much beloved as his piety commanded respect. He was a native of Cumberland; he joined the Society of Friends when a youth, and became a public preacher amongst them, in which capacity he frequently travelled from home. In one of his journeys to Ireland he became acquainted with Joan, daughter of John Cook of Limerick. She had married early in life a person of the name of Clarke, who afterwards went abroad, and was reported to have died. Many lovers then made suit to Joan, who besides being very beautiful, was a wealthy heiress. Her mother, a widow, had suitors of her own, but on assuring them she would on a second marriage make over her property to her daughter, she was freed from further importunity. The lovely Joan would hearken to no addresses till she was better assured of her husband's death, of which doubts hung about her mind, though letters were brought to her naming the exact time when the event took place. At length, however, return he did, but in ill-health, and lived but a few days, leaving his widow at liberty to form a connection with one more deserving of her than he had been.

Her beauty and her wealth were not the charms which secured the affections of George Rooke; he met in her a kindred mind, and her virtue and piety determined his choice. As he rode to Limerick with intent to make the tender of his hand, he was joined by another young man, who opened his heart to him, and told him he was on his way to address the fair widow, requesting his interest on the occasion. George's alarm at finding he had a rival was great, and his emotions occasioned such agitation, that one after another the buttons of his waistcoat burst open. However, he proved the successful candidate, and was married to Joan in 1686. They were accounted the handsomest pair that had been married in the meeting-house for a long time, and they lived in comfort and plenty in Limerick, till the horrors of war broke in upon their domestic quiet.

When Limerick was besieged by William the Third, officers and soldiers of the Irish army were lodged in their house, and cannon-balls passed through every room but one. On one occasion Joan Rooke sate on her chimney-hob, watching the pot in which her dinner was boiling, lest the Irish soldiers should make a prey of it. The pot was removed, and she had left her seat when a cannon-ball dashed through the hob where she had sat. We had also a family tradition that she had stooped her head to let a ball pass over it. That she was a woman of courage was evident from her having threatened the soldiers who were quartered in her house, to complain to their officers of the ruffianly conduct which they declared their intention to pursue. They had spoken in Irish before her, believing her ignorant of the language; she understood it, but heard them out before she let them know that she did so, and then awed them into good behaviour.

After the first siege of Limerick, George and Joan Rooke thought it would be presumptuous to await the issue of the second. My great-grandmother quilted some of her broad pieces of gold into the tucks of her under petticoats, and filled false heels in her shoes with the remainder. They melted their plate into wedges, and abandoned their comfortable house and costly furniture, which had once been the objects of Joan's nice housewifely care; and ever after she was perfectly indifferent how simple her furniture was, if it were only kept whole and clean. They hired a guard to convey them to Dublin, and it was uncertain what might have been their fate had he not been faithful to them. This man, when old and poor, was tenderly cared for by George Rooke, so true is it that "honesty is the best policy." They lay the first night in a place surrounded by Rapparees. My careful great-grandmother lay awake watching their property. Her husband forgot all care in a sleep so refreshing that in the morning he congratulated his wife with, "My dear, we have had a fine night;" she had not found it so, and notwithstanding all her care had lost her riding–hood. After a short stay in Dublin they embarked for England with their three little children. My grandmother, who was then about three years old, never forgot her great affliction at letting her doll fall out of the cabin-window, and seeing her treasure swallowed by the waves. They staid till this land was freed from disturbance, sold their estate in Limerick, and then settled in Dublin.

George Rooke dealt in timber, and kept a timber–yard in Earl–street. He outlived his wife, who was eighty–four at the time of her death. The old man possessed remarkable sweetness of temper. He often smiled, but never laughed, and though a friend to innocent cheerfulness was wounded by noisy mirth. He rose early, as all long–livers, I believe, do, and was often in his timber–yard at four o'clock. Little children flocked around him, and called him "daddy," and he was seldom unprovided with good things for them. His neighbours called him "the bishop." A collegian seeing him among his timber called out, "See the priest in the wood!" "It is better," answered the pleasant old man, "than to be a wooden priest!" Although universally beloved, he unintentionally gave offence to one family by some familiar chat. His daughter Carleton, who lived with him after she became a widow, resented their touchiness, and wished him not to call at the house; but her sweet–spirited father could not harbour resentment, he visited there as usual, and when his daughter enquired where he had been, he used to reply with a smile, "In a house." William Penn, grandson to the great legislator, had George Rooke's likeness taken by stealth, my aunt assisting. This picture is now in my possession, with a lock of the beautiful silver hair that curled naturally around a face which extreme old age could not deform. He loved to have the Scriptures read to him, especially "the Little Prophets," as he was wont to call the books at the end of the Old Testament. He died of a pleurisy at the age of ninety.

Rachael Carleton was the remains of a fine old gentle–woman, who had lived long in the city, and "knew what was what." Her stately reserve was censured as "height" (the softened term for pride), but she was a worthy character, and had in her past life encountered keen misfortunes, I believe with patience and resignation. Desirous of being near her married daughter – for of a large family but two remained – she and her daughter Deborah came to reside in Ballitore about the year 1759.

My aunt Carleton was fourteen years older than my mother, of a very lively, cheerful temper. In her youth she had been much admired, though her nose had a flatness at the upper part. Some of her neighbours being inclined to criticise, remarked that "Debby Carleton would be a very pretty girl, but for her nose." She happened to overhear them, and bolted upon them with the retort, "She would be much worse without it." The voice of envy unjustly accused her of sleeping in iron stays; for her figure was taper and shapely – "fine by degrees and beautifully less." The remains of her fine figure and her blooming complexion were still visible as I first remember her, and time could not destroy the animation, benevolence, and sensibility of her countenance. From early youth she was subject to ill-health, and to a nervous headache which often attacked her, confining her one day to her bed, or two if she struggled against it. When more dangerous illnesses visited her, we welcomed this headache as a sign of her recovery to usual health. But no interruption of this kind could lessen her filial attention to her aged mother. Her life had been much devoted to the care of the aged and infirm, and she frequently remarked that it seemed to be prolonged for that purpose.

She also enjoyed the happiness of saving several persons from impending death. One of these was a woman whose brutal husband in a fit of drunkenness and rage held a razor to her throat. My aunt heard her cries as she lay in bed; she ran to the window, and so effectually employed that power of persuasion which she eminently possessed, as to save the life of the unfortunate woman. Subsequently, as she was walking in Dublin, she was advised to turn back, as there was in her way a drunken woman, maddened by the insults of the rabble, and throwing dirt and stones at all who came near her. My aunt, however, went on, and quickly perceived that this wretched woman was the same whom she had rescued from the fury of her husband. Calling to her by her name, she reproved her conduct, and commanded her instantly to return home. Gratitude overpowered every other emotion in the distracted creature; she dropped on her knees in the channel, imploring a blessing on her benefactress; then, rising, directly obeyed her. She saved another life by thrusting her hand into the mouth of an enraged mastiff who had seized a boy by the throat. The animal, knowing and loving her, quitted his grasp of his victim in order to avoid hurting her.

If her cares were precious to the aged, they were more so to the youth. In the science of education I never saw her surpassed. She had the happy art of inspiring confidence without forfeiting respect.[13] She won our hearts and they were laid open to her. She made every proper allowance, granted every proper indulgence, yet she possessed much penetration, would quickly discern danger, and vigilantly guard against it. Her company and converse were as pleasing as profitable, and it is a proof of this that the young men who boarded at my father's, and who generally called her "aunt," used to prefer sitting with her on First-day evenings while we were at meeting, which her poor health seldom permitted her to attend, to amusing themselves in other ways at a time when they were free from observation. After one of these visits I remember my aunt remarking the emotion with which Henry Leslie read to her the lamentation of Esau on being supplanted by Jacob. Henry wept and sobbed, and I'll warrant my aunt did so too, for seldom has there throbbed a more sympathizing heart.

Her limited circumstances, it would appear, forbade her indulging her natural benevolence, but she contrived to unite the pious offices of humanity with that strict economy which it behoved her to practise. She seemed to possess the gift of healing. The country resorted to her for advice. She kept a large assortment of drugs, she distilled simples, she sold to those who could afford to pay, and dispensed gratis to those who could not. In her rides she called to see or enquire for her patients. She was firm as well as tender, resisted imposition, and her foresight and presence of mind seldom deserted her. When a young woman, while out walking in Dublin with a friend of her own age, they were surprised by the appearance of a wild tumultuous mob, which they found it impossible to avoid. Her companion was ready to faint, and my aunt's terrors were perhaps little less, but she exerted herself to suppress them, and in a loud and animated tone encouraged her friend to come on; "for," added she, "they are our own Liberty boys, and will not hurt us!" A huzza instantly followed this expression of confidence from the pleased multitude, who made a lane for the fortunate damsels to pass through.

My aunt got little out to religious meetings, or to meetings for discipline; her ill health and her care of the aged and youth might plead an excuse, but I never heard her plead any. Religion assumes not the same form in every character; some are called upon to fulfil its more active duties; others in retirement fulfil what is required of them. "Let her alone," said Elizabeth Robinson, in a meeting held in my aunt's house, "she hath done what she could." She commended and recommended decent pride, by which she meant abstaining from low or mean actions or company. She was not so strict in matters of dress as my mother, though she carefully avoided counteracting her plans.

My worthy mother, cautious not to grant more liberty to her own children than to those of her husband's first wife, really granted us less; for at the time when particular distinguishing marks of plainness were put upon them, they were also put upon us, though we were several years younger than they were; and our youth rendered these distinctions much more remarkable. Our sisters as well as our aunt wished our mother to relax a little towards us in this respect, but this was a point not to be disputed, and whether it was that our situation was secluded so much from the world, or that our tastes did not yet lie in that direction, her intent was accomplished, and the fondness for dress so natural to youth was pretty much starved; nay, it became, perhaps, a matter of too much indifference to my sister and me.

Yet to Friends, who profess simplicity, certainly simplicity in dress ought to belong; it is a kind of fence, and where a manifest disregard of our customs in this respect is evinced, it invites to associations inconsistent with our education, and betrays an attachment to an object unworthy to engross a rational mind.

In reading, also, my aunt was less severe than my mother. There were few if any books at that time calculated for children which combined entertainment with instruction, and there was great danger of our flying to stolen gratifications in this way without judgment or discrimination, had not my mother possessed a fondness for history, which she encouraged in us, and had not my aunt indulged us now and then with books of entertainment. The worst of this was, that the book was clapped under the cushion of her chair when my mother appeared. I had, by my aunt's permission, a collection of ballads containing "The Babes in the Wood," "Chevy Chase," "Pennyworth of Wit," and others of equal respectability – but the very word ballad was a word of disgrace. At one time I stood at my aunt Fuller's gate with this favorite volume in my hand, when I saw my mother approaching; I ran in, terrified, to hide my book, and my mother rebuked me afterwards for not running to meet her.

My aunt kept her house neat, and was active in her domestic concerns. Being well skilled in the science of cookery, her little dinners were very comfortable. She perfectly understood the roasting of a pig or a hare. My father was always invited on these occasions (my mother made it a point not to dine abroad), and his conviviality and enjoyment of the little repast heightened the general satisfaction. My aunt's patients frequently brought her a present of a hare; this she concealed lest they should incur the aspersion of poaching, and it became a standing joke that my father asked who was the donor, and my aunt refused to tell. On one of these occasions my sister Margaret, his eldest daughter, delighted him by a remark which was frequently quoted afterwards, "Here are the hare and many friends."

Two little boarders, illegitimate sons of Stratford Eyre, the warden of Galway, made part of my aunt's family about this time. When their foster–father brought them to school, Tom Eyre was not long out of petticoats, and Sam still wore them. My mother was fearful lest they should be hurt in so large a school of bigger boys, and she prevailed upon my aunt to take charge of them. It was easy for children to win my aunt's love; and these were peculiarly engaging and interesting. If any one was born to be a soldier, I often thought it was Tom Eyre. His undaunted, open countenance, and the spirit of his fine black eyes announced a disposition full of courage. Poor Sam and I found that this disposition was apt to degenerate into tyranny, for Tom, on his return from school, sometimes dashed our playthings about the room, despising our tears as well as our amusements. Yet Tom was truly goodnatured when not under the influence of an impetuosity of temper which required the able hand of my aunt to restrain. Her calm reasoning allayed the tempest of his passion, and melted him into tears of contrition. With all his failings, Tom was a universal favourite, whilst Sam possessed sweetness of temper, an early sense of rectitude, and a superior degree of understanding. He was more grave than his brother, and less apt to speak at random. His countenance was like our idea of that of an angel, and his mind did not belie his countenance. Sometimes he gently rebuked his brother: Tom bore this with impatience, and when he knew he had deserved a lecture, and thought Sam was preparing one for him, he tried to ward it off by exclaiming, "Now, Sam, none of your philosophy, or I'll lick you!" Tom, however, had his own philosophy, and thus he reasoned: "I think I love another boy better than Sam, but if that boy and Sam were falling from a house, I would run to catch Sam."

We all took small–pox at the same time. My attack was the lightest, and I was first able to leave my room to visit the Eyres. Great as was our joy at meeting, we did not part without a quarrel. But they suffered no one else to affront me or displease me, reserving to themselves the exclusive right. When we were some years older, the schoolboys, taking advantage of my simplicity, enclosed me in a tub without a bottom, and declared that they would not set me free unless on condition that I should ask the evening's play for them.[14] I was too much chagrined to consent, and my situation was mortifying indeed, when Sam came up, and, insisting upon my unconditional enlargement, his command was instantly obeyed, though he was but a little boy. We were much of one age, and we dearly loved one another. Ah! why, then, was that sweet age clouded with quarrels? And why must I remember with regret that Sam and I pulled each other's hair behind my grandmother's screen, in a contest for the possession of a hole in it, which we called a window? And why did we all three regularly fight when the showman came with his box, because one of the glasses was cracked, and none of us would willingly consent to look through that one?

When these boys had been two years at school, their father came to see them, and he liked their situation so well that he sent for two older boys whom he had at school in England, where they were taught, boarded, and clothed for £10 a year each. Accordingly Edward and Robert were added to my aunt's household. They were fine boys, but, unlike their younger brothers, were not at all remarkable. Time rolled on. Their father, while on a visit to Dublin, was seized with an apoplectic fit, and dropped dead. His widow, while she lived, continued the attention to his children (they were not hers) which he had bestowed on them; but she did not long survive her husband, and then their orphan state was manifest. Their uncle, who strove to withhold from them the provision their father had bequeathed them, died in a similar manner to his brother, in the Parliament house. Whether the unfortunate circumstances of their birth made it difficult to secure their property, or from whatever cause, certain it was their guardians could do nothing for them; and my father, seeing that if he deserted them they had no earthly friend, would not abandon the orphans to an unpitying world, but kept them till they were fit to go to business; and thus, for education, board, and clothing, a debt of £800 was incurred. Children though they were, they understood and felt this kindness; and I remember one evening when we swam our flagger boats down the river, and talked of hidden treasures found under stones in fairy streams, that Edward Eyre breathed his wish to find a pot of gold: "And then," said he, "I would pay the master."

Poor Edward! Very soon after, he took measles, which fell upon his lungs, and carried him off. Tom wept bitterly over the breathless corpse, till he declared his fountain of tears was quite dry. Edward was particularly attached to him, although they were only half-brothers, being children of different mothers. On his death-bed he recommended Tom seriously to my mother's care, as he said that he feared most for him, he was so "arch." And thus was this youth mercifully taken, in his fourteenth year, from a world through which his brothers had to struggle with various fortunes. Tom, after all this trouble, said he could not bear to hear of death, for he dreaded dying before he saw Dublin. Little did he then dream of his future wanderings. In course of time Robert was placed with an attorney, and Tom and Sam were apprenticed to apothecaries, who took advantage of their unprotected state to treat them harshly. When their old master visited Dublin, they poured out their complaints as into a paternal bosom. Once, as Sam told his artless tale, he saw that his sufferings touched the good man's heart. He thought they touched it too deeply, and, looking up in his face with one of his inexpressibly sweet smiles, he added, "Oh! master, I shall do very well." But my father had them removed to other situations in the same business.

On the breaking out of the American war, the soldier broke out in Tom Eyre, and he went as a volunteer at the age of sixteen, to seek his fortune beyond the Atlantic. Sam accompanied his brother three miles on his march, weeping bitterly, for it was their first, and, alas! it proved their final separation. Not all the charms of novelty nor all the allurements of military glory could suppress the pangs felt at this solemn parting; and Tom's heart felt heavy indeed when he passed by Ballitore, and saw no old acquaintance at the top of the avenue leading down to the village. This cruel disappointment added weight to his knapsack and weariness to the fatigue of his long march on foot from Dublin to Cork. He embarked at Cove, and landed on the American shore, young, unprotected, inexperienced, but full of health, spirits and courage.

About two years after Tom's embarkation, Sam entered the navy. He became a midshipman in the Foudroyant, under Captain Jervis, now Earl St. Vincent, of whom he spoke most warmly in his letters to his old master – letters worthy of the master and the pupil. The last of these was dated from on board the Superbe, which was destined for the East Indies. He sailed full of the sanguine hopes and ambition which animate a young, ardent, and generous mind.

Thus were the early companions of my childhood borne away on the waves of ambition or enterprise, while my own youth glided gently down the quiet current of my uneventful life.

CHAPTER III.
1769.

ON my father's succeeding to a small estate in which the Mill now stands, my Aunt Carleton removed to Griesebank, and we bade adieu to the old habitation of Fuller's Court, and to the field where the little cow Tidy grazed, and where Tom Eyre, Sam, and I planted our teeth when they dropped out, in the fond hope of some marvellous growth, such as had resulted from the successful experiment of Cadmus. Indeed so little idea had I of the nature of vegetation, that I applauded my sagacity in secretly laying seeds of sweet–pea in a hole in the floor by the parlour hearthstone, anticipating my mother's agreeable surprise when she should see the flowers in bloom by her fireside. To Griesebank we went, followed by Tidy and the pig. I cannot say whether it was that very pig which I once saw stand on his hind legs, and with his nose lift the knocker of the hall–door to gain admittance into the house. All my aunt's domestics and domestic animals were somewhat extraordinary in my eyes, and the care of them constituted no inconsiderable part of her happiness; indeed the kind attention which her leisure and her humanity led her to pay might very well produce peculiar effects. At one time, when her health was ailing, and her lively spirits were depressed by confinement to a sick chamber, a cousin to amuse her brought her three eggs which the parent hen had deserted after bringing forth a clutch. The invalid placed these eggs in a basket of wool close to her hearthstone, and her care was soon rewarded by the appearance of three little chickens, which she cherished and fed with such watchful attention that they attached themselves to her as to a parent hen. They grew into two beautiful pullets and a cock. Their mutual attachment continued, and the hens were wont to lay their eggs on a cushion under their mistress's chair. It was told of her well–trained dog, that, though accustomed to attend his mistress wherever she went, he never attempted to accompany her when she had on her green apron and long black hood. At that time a bright light green silk apron was worn by the female Friend when going to meeting; also a black silk hood with long ends or lappets, and no bonnet. She had also a tame stare which spoke pretty distinctly, and whistled "High Barnaby" to admiration, turning the tune accurately. "Jacob," for that was his name, was very particularly attended to, and the servant often said he would be in his *warm* grave but for the mistress. Poor Jacob died very soon after her, at the age of fourteen.

The Great House of the village was inhabited by the widow and family of the elder Maurice Keatinge. She was a woman of great respect and worth, and was allied to the poet Waller. Her second son Cadogan and her four unmarried daughters cheered her declining age with exemplary affection. They were somewhat advanced in years, which they took no pains to disguise. Though of the first family in the country, their attention to their neighbours of every description bespoke their humility as well as their benevolence; their manners were soft and polite as well as kind and good–natured.[15] Their simplicity and affability of demeanor in no wise abated the deep respect which was ever paid them. The poor beheld them with reverence, and no class esteemed it an honour conferred upon "Madam Keatinge" when the Duke of Leinster's equipage with outriders rolled into the village, bringing the duke and duchess to dine with her, though the inhabitants pressed forward with eager eyes to catch a glimpse of a "real live duke." The old lady never visited; she spent her day in devotion and reading, and closed the evening with cards, at which she played for amusement only.

Except at the Great House, my aunt's, and Joseph Wills's, all the parlours had earthen floors; the hall doors opened with iron latches, and were without knockers; and most of the windows were casements. In process of time, as a taste for elegance arose, the earthen floors were found to be damp and liable to break, and then it was impossible to repair them; so they were replaced by boards and listing carpets; the casement windows gave place to sashes; and grinning lions' heads guarded and ornamented the hall doors. Elizabeth Shackleton, though she endured the demolition of her floor, thought the washing of the boards of such a large room would be a job of too great magnitude; so she procured flags from Rosenallis for her parlour. However, as taste gained ground, even that room was submitted to timber flooring, and the pickaxe at length invaded the Meeting–house, where the old-fashioned flooring, with loose boards laid under the feet of the women Friends, had remained time out of mind. There was no place of worship in

Ballitore except the Friends' meeting-house. To Crookstown, about half-a-mile distant, resorted the inhabitants who were of the Romish persuasion, and those of the Established Church attended service at Timolin. An usher of that profession was always employed at the school, who accompanied the boys to this place of worship, and heard them their catechism.

My father used to entertain us by anecdotes of the school as it was in his boyhood, some of which I shall introduce here. The lively spirits of the schoolboys often led to mischievous tricks, to the annoyance of the neighbours, especially of those who complained of them. My grandfather, wishing to examine into some offences of this nature, and to exercise justice on the delinquents, requested the attendance of some of the neighbours; Charles Braddock was one of the number. They took their seats, the venerable Abraham took his, and the boys, overwhelmed with the consciousness of their misdeeds, awaited in fearful expectation. A pause preceded the enquiry, when, on a sudden, the awful silence was broken by Charles Braddock roaring forth,

> The charge is prepared, and the judges are met:
> The lawyers all ranged – a terrible show.

The solemnity of the scene in a moment vanished, and even the grave countenance of the master relaxed. Charley was a rattle; he continued to rattle away in prose, to show the impossibility of detecting the chief offender, as all had such a propensity to transgress; "For," said he, "as my turkeys stood on the wall by the pond, one of the mischievous little fellows, as he ran past, could not resist the temptation of knocking a turkey into the water!" My father's heart died within him, for it was he had done the deed. But his fears were needless; Charley would not tell who was the culprit, and the court of justice was broken up with a general admonition.

In those early times there was a lad at school, Henry Graham by name. He was in the army, and received pay; his manners and air were military. A "barring-out" took place, and Abraham Shackleton, after having tried other methods in vain, forced the door with a sledge-hammer. While this was being done, the garrison strove to capitulate. They asked for "a week's play." – "No." "A day's play." – "No." "An evening's play." – "No." "Pardon for their fault." – "No." Graham snapped a pistol, which missed fire. The offenders were led to punishment: those who expressed sorrow for what they had done escaped the dreaded whipping. Graham would not, and was whipped. He was then asked was he sorry now?– "No" He was whipped again. Was he sorry? – "No." He was whipped again. Was he sorry? – "Yes; he was sorry that the pistol had missed fire!" Though his master could not overcome his inflexibility, he won his affections, and an attachment was formed between them which continued while Graham lived. He corresponded with his master when he went abroad, and sent him the plan of the English camp. At the battle of Fontenoy, when leading on his men, he called out to them with gay humour, "A ducat to any man who will make a pun." In the retreat of the English at this battle, the officers kept at the rear of their men to be ready to head them if they returned to the charge. This was Graham's situation when a spent cannon–ball struck him between the shoulders, and his men ran to support him. "Lay me down, my lads," said he, "and let me die easy." They did so, and he expired.

When the venerable Abraham Shackleton had resigned into the hands of his son his post of usefulness to the rising generation, he employed his time either in religious visits, or in cultivating his land at home; for he was active for his years, and, delighting in agriculture, was wont to work with his own men in summer–time with his coat stripped off, and labouring as hard as they did.[16] A poor man who saw him assisting in shaking his orchard vigorously in his seventy–second year, enumerated the perfections which were apparent even then in his frame, and concluded with, "It would be a murder you should ever die!" My little sister and I were sometimes indulged in being permitted to accompany him to his meadows, to toss the hay with small pitchforks which he had got made for us. He was kind to us, but was never pleased when he saw us playing with our dolls. His general deportment was very grave, yet we loved and venerated without fearing him. I remember one evening, when he had been describing to us Shackleton House, the family mansion near Bingley in Yorkshire, of which I now only recollect its being built of hewn stone, that I thought within myself, "How can I ever survive my dear grandfather?" The stars which he pointed out to me from the hall-door at Griesebank are the only ones with which I am acquainted, although long afterwards I studied astronomy; and I never look up at the belt of Orion (which in our childish glee we used to call "the Irish gentleman, O'Ryan,") the polar star, and Ursa Major, without fondly recalling the good old man.

In 1769 he went to the yearly meeting of London for the last time, and took my brother with him. His illustrious pupil Edmund Burke prevailed on him to pay him a visit at Beaconsfield, and sent his coach to convey him thither. My grandfather shrank from the idea of riding in such a grand coach, and offered Burke's servant half-a-guinea to permit him to travel on his own horse, but the servant firmly refused; and, however reluctant, the humble man had to consent to be conveyed in unwelcome pomp to the arms of his pupil, who treated him with that hospitality, kindness, and respect which his sincere affection dictated. In the following winter the candles suddenly went out in our meeting–house without any apparent cause, and the subsequent illness of "the old master" interpreted this into an omen of his death. His spirit, disengaged from the world, awaited in calm acquiescence the Divine will, and often overflowed in sweet counsels to those who visited him, although through his long life he had been always "swift to hear, slow to speak."

Amongst his visitors at this time was Mary Watson, niece to Dr. Fothergill. She had been lately married to Robert Watson, and was on her way to his home in Waterford. The degree of éclat which attended her arrival in Ireland was surprising. Her dress, which was remarkable for Quaker elegance, came directly into fashion. The gifts of Nature and fortune, the adoration of a doating husband, and the general admiration she excited might naturally exalt the mind of a young woman of one and twenty years of age; but no consciousness of any merit of her own appeared in her. Methinks I still behold the interesting picture, and I remember the very spot where I sat, a little silent, observant child, and looked on the decaying form of the patriarchal Abraham Shackleton on his dying-bed, his emaciated hand stretched forth, while beside him knelt the lovely creature in the bloom of youth and beauty, heightened by her elegance of apparel, bending her head, raising her white hands to her eyes, and, all dissolved in tears, listening with the deepest attention to the impressive words of the expiring saint as she received his blessing, "Do thou worthily in Ephratah and be famous in Bethlehem."[17]

On midsummer-day, 1771, our venerable grandfather expired. His family, assembled around his death-bed, witnessed the humble resignation with which the purified spirit took its flight. He had led a righteous life, and was blessed in the reward of a tranquil, hopeful, trusting death-bed; for "Blessed are the dead that die in the Lord!"

A great concourse of Friends came from distant parts to attend the funeral. Although it was a fine summer's day, it thundered while Elizabeth Hutchinson appeared in testimony, in the course of which she quoted, "O Death, where is thy sting? O grave, where is thy victory?" The deep, awful voice of nature added to the solemnity of that scene in the graveyard, embosomed in the dark grove of fir-trees. My father long bewailed the death of his worthy parent. I remember his bursting into tears at his own table; and he was in the habit of retiring to the room where his father died to give vent to his sorrow in silence and solitude. It was remarkable to see a cheerful, happily circumstanced man, in the prime of life, lament with such prolonged affliction the loss of an aged parent.

On this occasion Edmund Burke thus expressed himself to my father: "I am heartily affected with the subject of your last letter. I had a true honour and affection for that excellent man. I feel something like a satisfaction in the midst of my concern which I had not in the same degree before, that I was fortunate enough to have him once more under my roof before his departure. He was indeed a man of singular piety, rectitude, and virtue, and he had along with these qualities a native elegance of manners which nothing but genuine good-nature and unaffected simplicity of heart can give, and which they will give infallibly, be the exterior forms what they will."

In speaking of my early days, I must not omit to mention James and Nanny Mc Connaughty. Who that knew us has not known James and Nanny? Their honesty, their neatness, their simplicity, and even their singularities claimed affection and respect. Nanny had been servant to my father, and her integrity and diligence, and above all her piety, gained her universal esteem. An old man sometimes frequented Ballitore, by name John Mc Connaughty, famous for having made a perfect pun. It was thus: John, having joined the Society of Friends, entered into a religious disputation with a clergyman, who threatened, at length, that he would cane him. "I believe," said John, "thou hast more of the spirit of Cain [cane] than of Abel [able] in thee." Old John was charmed with the good qualities of Nanny Waring, and destined her for wife to his son James, whom, on his return home, he sent to visit her.[18] One *bon mot* amongst others is recorded of James during his courtship. While arguing on one occasion with his beloved upon some indifferent matter, she said, by way of reproving his positiveness, that she believed he wanted to persuade her out of her name. "It is the very thing I wish most to do," replied the brisk bachelor. His wish was accomplished; and as they were returning from having presented their marriage, while James rode attentively beside his intended bride, a person remarked, not very kindly, on his complaisance, and added, "But when poverty comes in at the door, love will fly out at the window."[19] Nanny never forgot this sarcasm. She often repeated it, and always with this observation: "No, no! though poverty came in at the door, love *never* flew out at the window."

They lived at my father's, James as steward, and Nanny as children's maid. If a boy ran away from school, James was despatched after him, and such was his success that the boys gave him the name of "the blood-hound." They loved him heartily notwithstanding. He was well esteemed, cheerful, and so religiously disposed, that he sometimes spoke as a minister in our religious meetings. On one of these occasions his text was concerning the elect lady and her children. I perplexed him by running to him after meeting, to ask what lady he had been telling us of – "Was it Lady Burrows?" who sometimes called to see him, for he had been a steward to her father. He frequently introduced extempore rhymes into his conversation, which entertained his hearers, and delighted us little ones.

When he afterwards left my father's service, and took the grist-mill on the river, his integrity procured him the title of "the honest miller." But his simplicity was often imposed upon, and he extended hospitality to those who brought their corn to be ground oftener than was consistent with economy, or with poor Nanny's ease of body or mind. Having met with some offence in the market of Athy, James posted on his mill–door a written invitation to the neighbouring farmers to bring their corn and commodities to Ballitore on the second day of the week. The invitation was accepted, and thus a market was established. A few years after this, a weekly market and three fairs were established at Ballitore. If a market afforded a scene delightful for its novelty and bustle, how much more delightful was a fair! Ale–houses were increased, which did not add to the happiness of the inhabitants. Law was called in to preserve order, and those who lost any of their goods went stoutly to search suspected houses, having previously borrowed Ephraim Boake's search–warrant, which, though long very much the worse for wear, continued in use and esteem for a good share of thirty years.

During the absence of our parents at the yearly meeting in Dublin, my aunt always removed to the school, to see that all went right in the house–keeping, and she took my sister and me with her. The large family – the days – the bustle – so different from our usual retirement! – it was the world, and the world has its charms![20] On these occasions my aunt always gave us one day to spend to our heart's content. This day, devoted to pleasure, I knew not what to compare it to. Our little companions came to us with their dolls newly dressed as were ours. A feast was prepared, in which a pudding and decanters filled with wine were conspicuous. It is true these decanters were only two ends of an hour–glass, but they contained sufficient to afford each a taste. Yet such is the nature of pleasure, that our spirits generally flagged towards evening, and the day seldom ended as it began. I am ready to conclude that had the yearly meeting held longer than a week, we should have tired of the world, and sighed for our quiet abode, where a race up the Mill-avenue, when a carriage passed along the high road, to get a peep at the fine folk it might chance to contain, made one of our chief amusements.

Even into our quiet abode trouble and temptation sometimes intruded. Well do I remember that evening when, with no intention of breaking our prescribed bounds, we stretched our necks over the orchard hedge to procure a sight of feats of horsemanship which were being exhibited in a neighbouring field; but Tom Wray and John Elsey, who saw our situation, prompted by good–nature or politeness, approached and prevailed upon us to descend the ditch. We went with the timidity of conscious misdoing, and, mixing with the crowd of spectators, did not lose this uneasy sense in the entertainment which so new a scene afforded. Yet amusement was beginning to be the predominant sensation, when, to our utter dismay and confusion, James Mc Connaughty made his appearance! I do not think he spoke one word, but we followed him from the place of diversion with countenances glowing with shame, and hearts smitten with remorse. Thus were we introduced into the presence of our aunt and our sister Margaret. My discerning aunt saw we were already punished, and added little to our punishment; but my sister had become "serious," and had sincerely embraced religion.[21] Affrighted at the slippery paths of youth, she regarded our error with more severity than did our more experienced aunt. Her lecture was very grave on our having clandestinely stolen away to partake of amusements which we knew would not be approved of, and she inquired how the query periodically asked in our meetings of discipline, concerning attendance at "vain sports and places of diversion," could be answered.[22] At this climax we verily believed we were in imminent danger of being disowned by the Society. We burst into tears, which ceased not to flow till we lost the sense of our guilt and sorrow in the sweet oblivion of sleep.

Though our general conduct was, I suppose, not more correct than that of other children of our age who had like advantages, we had great awe, not to say terror, on our minds of committing offences against religion. For this reason we thought we must not speak to transgressors; and I remember an incident, singular enough, which befel me when very young. I was engaged in working a pair of pockets for myself in a shell pattern with green worsted. My brother called in; I showed him my pocket; and, willing to exhibit my dexterity, began to work at it, when on a sudden I recollected it was First–day.[23] Alarmed at what I had done, I laid my work down in dismay, and went to my favourite window in the garret, which commanded a pretty view. While I was thus solacing my eyes and comforting my heart, the window–sash fell on my neck, and made me a prisoner. I roared with all my might. My aunt heard the cries, which being outside the house, she feared one of us had fallen into "the Sconce," and ran about greatly terrified, to search for us, whilst the continued wailings resounded in her ears. At length, finding that no one came to the rescue, I made a desperate effort, and disengaged myself, having escaped with a bruised neck and scratched face; but I firmly believed that this accident befell me because I had broken the sabbath.

As I could read when four years old, I was able to peruse Stephen Crisp's "Short History of a Long Travel from Babylon to Bethel," an allegory I by no means understood. Believing the whole to be literally true, I was wonderfully desirous to see that house which was the end and reward of so wearisome a journey. I frequently ascended a sloping flower–bank in the garden, to gaze with awe–struck admiration on the house now much enlarged and called Willowbrook, which, as children measure everything by their own size, I thought at such a distance must be the object of my ardent desires. How I was undeceived I know not, but undeceived I was; and, on my grandfather's return from a London yearly meeting, thinking that Bethel was surely the object of so long a journey, I approached him with the enquiry if he had seen "God's house."

Griesebank was indeed a delightful residence, and continues to be so, though the neatly clipped hedges which ran through the middle of the orchard, and were terminated by "Peggy's arbour," are now entirely gone. My partiality for orchards may arise from having spent so much time in this one, where I often roamed for hours alone; for my young mind was rather of a contemplative turn, and the impediment in my speech made me avoid company in which I was not perfectly at my ease. This retired spot permitted me to indulge my little reveries, sometimes sitting on the mount, and gazing with delight on the surrounding scenery; which was not the less admired because it was familiar, for I ever had a passionate love for the beauties of nature. At other times I amused myself with carving on the bark of the trees; and, when the red sap followed the incision, I thought of Ovid's legends of mortals transformed into trees, and queried, could such things be? Was this blood, and had I inflicted a wound?

At the close of the year, or rather the beginning of the new one, the mummers paraded the village. These were two men wearing shirts adorned with ribbons over their clothes, and attended by a frightful mask, which they called a "pickle–herring." My horror of them was beyond telling. Indeed they were a general terror to children; but they afforded so much amusement to the people, that the wiser part of our community were unable to suppress them. In after years the Whiteboy Act frightened the mummers as much as they had frightened others, and put a stop to their proceedings.

There lived at the foot of the Nine–tree–hill, about this time, a comfortable farmer named Loughlin Duffy. His son Thomas, when nine years old, while returning from the funeral of a brother, was suddenly taken ill, and lost his speech and the power of walking. Continuing in this state, he permitted no one to see him eat, but took what was left for him, taught his brothers and sisters to read and write, wrote a good hand himself, and performed several works of ingenuity, such as making a fiddle, a wooden lock, &c., under the bedclothes. There was, of course, but one cause assigned for this marvellous dispensation: Tom was fairy–struck. The fairies visited and instructed him in the solitude of his confinement; he was serving his apprenticeship to them, and at the end of seven years he would come forth a great doctor. The term, however, continued two years longer, and on his recovery Tom became a schoolmaster, which occupation he filled with credit among the lower ranks for the remainder of his life. He seemed to enjoy good health, his constitution when he arrived at maturity having probably overcome those nervous affections which were the cause of his strange condition; but he was ever small in size, and had a dwindled, pale appearance. After his neighbours had looked for a while for something extraordinary from him, the fairy theory seemed forgotten. To visit him in his confinement made a favourite walk for our visitors. Not far distant from his habitation was the Rath of Mullaghmast, the chief abode of fairies in this country, and the place where they held their court. Tradition also reported it to have been a Danish fort; and the hole in the centre, which was bare of grass, was asserted to have been made to contain the blood of their prisoners of war, for no grass ever grew where human blood had been shed. As another proof of this assertion, a bare spot on the Nine–tree–hill was shown as that where a gentleman named Dillon had been shot in a duel.

All the learning and piety in our village could not conquer the superstition of the age. A neighbour died of a malignant fever; he had a thrice repeated dream before he took ill, in which a voice called to him three times, "Prepare!" It seems as if intimations of no common import have been occasionally thus conveyed, and that some attention is due to them; but, as all good things are subject to abuse, superstition has made of dreams instruments of torture to weak and susceptible minds; and, alas! superstition was one of the sins of Ballitore. The death of one of the Fuller family was said to be announced by the melodious wailing of the Banshee, who, when visible, appeared in the form of a beautiful woman combing her hair. For the rest of the neighbours the croaking of a raven sufficed on these solemn occasions. The spirits of the departed were said to be seen gliding through the meeting–house grove; and "the Runner," a stream flowing through the heart of the village, could not be crossed after midnight without fear and trembling. The candles going out suddenly during an evening meeting foretold the death of the venerable Abraham Shackleton; previous to which candles went out several times in the chamber of a little pupil, and even my sensible mother deemed it a warning that her father–in–law would shortly expire – which he did.

Amongst the pupils at this period was a young Quaker from Jamaica, Jesse Balrieves. On rising one morning and beholding the ground covered with snow, a sight he never had seen before, he called out in astonishment, "O boys! see all the sugar!" Many West Indians were sent to this school. Two of these, Newman and Sam Curtin, were so small and so lively, that, fearing harm should come to them in their wanderings, my mother kept them pinned, literally *pinned*, to her apron. She had them to sleep in her room, and watched them with a mother's care. Poor little Newman strayed from her once, to his cost, for one of his schoolfellows, in attempting to mow, grievously wounded him with the scythe. My mother needed all her fortitude, tenderness and skill, and all these she possessed in no common degree. Edward Miles, the village shoemaker, was immediately summoned, he closed the wound, which was in the calf of the leg, with two stitches; my mother applied her favourite styptic – "the liquid balsam," (made of Solomon's seal and white sugar pounded together) – the child was kept on low diet, no fever came on, and a cure was speedily effected. The lad who wielded the scythe was compelled to sit by while Newman's wound was dressing, and this was punishment enough.[24]

The high–spirited lads of this time generally manifested an ambition for the army. It was so with young Black. Immediately on leaving school, he resigned the luxuries of his paternal home for the hardships of the camp in the war with America. He served with Lord Cornwallis, who noticed him, encouraged his abilities, and employed him in drawing maps and taking observations. This unfortunate youth was wounded, made captive, and confined in a crowded prison, without sufficient bedding, proper food, or any of the comforts which might alleviate his distressing fate. Thus he died, and dying remembered Ballitore, saying just at the close, "Ah! If I were in Ballitore, I should not be thus." This intelligence came from a brother officer, who was a complete stranger to us.

Soon after Tom Eyre had left us, William Cornwallis Hall came to school. The striking likeness which he bore to our beloved Tom impressed us in his favour. At sixteen he was sent, a lovely victim to war, to America. He and Tom Eyre afterwards met in the West Indies; they quickly found they were both "Ballitore boys," and soon loved each other. William told Tom we had called him "Second Tom Eyre." When peace was proclaimed, the remains of the army returned, and with them William Hall, then a captain of distinguished merit.

A Bourdeaux merchant named Skinner sent a son about eight years old to Ballitore school, and, having paid him a visit, was so pleased with his situation that he determined on sending his second son, little David, though the child's mother was reluctant to part him at so early an age as five years and a half. It was no wonder he should have fast hold of a mother's affections, for he quickly seized upon ours. His tender age, his foreign language, his extraordinary beauty, and artless affection, interested the whole family in his favour. His sister could scarce have loved him better than I did; he was my joy, my pride, and my delight. By this time his brother had forgotten his French, and little David could not speak English. "I know not what you say," replied James to the prattle of his brother. *"Je ne sais pas ce que vous dites,"* answered David. Embraces were a language they both well understood, and David enquired the English of *"mon cher frere."* He found little difficulty in making us comprehend his meaning, his countenance and gestures were so expressive. He learned our names, picked up English words, and was the plaything of the whole house.

When the measles again visited Ballitore, and our darling David, amongst others, was attacked, my distress was excessive. All the invalids recovered except our little foreigner, whose tender age, conspiring with the change of climate, probably caused the rapid decline and hectic fever which immediately succeeded the attack of disease. His uncle was written for, and so was

Dr. Gervase of Portarlington, who spoke French fluently, and was thus the better able to understand the child's complaints. We beheld with inexpressible concern his decaying state, his fading bloom, his wasting flesh, the lustre of his fine black eyes extinguished, and the peevishness of sickness taking the place of the vivacity of his age and country. Yet hope was beginning to revive, the summer was advancing, our little patient was able to take the air, carried by my brother on a pillow before him on horseback, and we thought his spirits and appetite were reviving; when one evening a carriage arrived with a messenger sent by his uncle to convey him to Dublin, whence, as soon as his strength permitted, he was to return to Bourdeaux. To part with our lovely David, perhaps never to see him more – to resign him, doubly endeared as he was by his sufferings – to give him up to the arms of a stranger – oppressed the whole family with grief; but mine was immoderate. Every post brought us an account of him, and I awaited the news with distressing agitation. Exactly a month after he left us the fatal letter came. I dreaded the account, and walked into the garden to avoid it. When I returned, my cousin, with trembling voice, said, "The little boy is dead." I am a mother, and I have lost by an untimely death a lovely and engaging child; yet, to this hour, I cannot speak or think of little David Skinner without emotion.

CHAPTER IV.
1772.

Last days of Aldborough Wrightson. – The first Jew visits Ballitore. – He exhibits a mandrake. – Story of Lady Cathcart. – A mail coach accident. – A father's blessing. – A relic of the penal laws. – The "honourable" George. – A *mauvais sujet*. – William Leadbeater. – Aldworth Phaire – Marriage of Margaret Shackleton. – Death of Aunt Carleton. – Aldborough Wrightson's grave. – Heroism of Arabella Forbes. – Tom Eyre rebuked by a blockhead. – Richard and Elizabeth Shackleton remove to the Retreat. – Marriage of the second Abraham Shackleton to Lydia Mellor. – Sketch of the bride. – Death of a "convinced Friend." – Birth of the second Richard Shackleton. – Lines addressed to the infant by his grandfather. – Molly Hudson begins a twenty years' visit to the Retreat. – A convict rescued from "the Duke of the World." – A tender-hearted Judge. – Reminescences and anecdotes of the Author's parents.[25] 51 to 71

ALDBOROUGH WRIGHTSON had quitted Ballitore in a pique with my mother, who had discovered that he had joined the Freemasons. She much disapproved of this mysterious society, and their oaths of secresy; and, believing that he had violated his conscience by taking an oath, she told him her mind plainly. But when she found that, notwithstanding her remonstrances, he was resolved upon leaving Ballitore, she told him that when the hour of adversity had arrived, which she foresaw would come upon him, he should be welcome back. That hour came. His engaging society was sought for by the dissipated, and he was led astray by the example of people in every way unworthy of him. The consequence was that, in broken health, and oppressed with debt, he came back a penitent to his old master, determined to atone for past offences by returning to his father, and offering any terms for a reunion with his family. In this resolution his Ballitore friends encouraged him, and he left us, with mutual anxiety for the result.

We were astonished to hear no account of him for some weeks. At length he came again to Ballitore, so altered, so pale, emaciated, and melancholy, that he appeared but the shadow of his former self. "Mistress," said he as he entered, "I am come to you as my last resource." He accounted for our not having heard from him by informing us that, on going to Dublin, he stopped at the house of a friend, and from thence sent a message to his father, entreating permission to wait on him; but the only reply he received was that the house was full of company, and there was no room for him. That hope thus cruelly cut off, he sank into despair. He dreaded being arrested for debt, went on board a ship bound for Whitehaven, and had nearly perished in a storm. He found the air of the north too keen, and returned, as he said, "to die with his old master." The warm heart of friendship was open to him; he found himself where everyone loved him; he was cheered, and his engaging vivacity returned. But the vital principle was wounded, the noble spirit was broken, the stamina was destroyed, and a fixed consumption became daily more and more evident. His friends, grieved and indignant, exerted all their influence with his parents, and prevailed so far as to get an increase of allowance, to enable him to go elsewhere in search of health. But they still refused to see him. He went to Mallow, and appeared to be getting better; being ordered horse exercise, his parents were in vain solicited to provide him with the means. Even his mother's feelings were not touched by the representation of his condition, though we heard that at that very time she paid a hundred guineas for a pair of diamond ear–rings. She wrote indeed to him, and told him that in so doing she broke a vow. "Alas!" wrote the dejected, dying son to his friend Richard Shackleton, "tell me, for you know, ought parents to make vows against their children?" He, however, got the use of a horse, and he found such benefit from the exercise, the mild air, and the waters, that if he had been fostered by parental love, he might have recovered.

His allowance, ample as his father deemed it, was not adequate to meet the calls of illness and infirmity at a watering–place; and he had therefore to leave Mallow. For some time after his return, the improvement of his health supported his spirits under the pressure of unkindness, and his conversation continued to afford us ever new delight. Some of his remarks I still remember, and often perceived their truth. One of these was that the books we see in a man's house generally denote his character; another, that ailing people did not like to be told they looked well. The "Elegy on an Unfortunate Young Lady" he said was Pope's best production; his "Messiah" was a paraphrase of Isaiah, but that beautiful poem was all his own. He was provoked at Purver's translation of the Bible.[26] "This," said he, taking an old tattered Bible in his hand, and looking with disdain on Purver's two volumes in folio, "this book, which one would think scarce worth taking out of the gutter, is worth a dozen of that."

The cold of the following winter and the sharp winds of spring proved too much for his delicate frame; we noticed with deep regret the return of every fatal symptom, and he felt himself that this world would soon know him no more. One day his hair was being thinned, and my little sister and

I eagerly asked for some of those beautiful locks to adorn the heads of our dolls. "You may have it all by-and-by," said our dear Wrightson in a melancholy tone, and our hearts were smitten with sorrow at the idea that he was gliding away from us. The hair was then worn long and loose, save that it was confined near the head with a string; and this fashion admirably displayed the grace and beauty of those shining auburn curls which Aldborough used gaily to call his "thrum." "And, mistress," he would say, "when I become a Friend, won't you let me keep my thrum?"

Whilst his Ballitore friends watched his looks, anticipated his wishes, and strove to alleviate his distress of body and mind, – for he often said, "I am sick of many griefs," – his parents inflexibly maintained their cruel reserve, though frequently remonstrated with by letter and in person by those who loved and pitied him; and, when asked where they would have their son buried, they coldly replied, "In the nearest church-yard." One who chanced to be in his room while he slept heard him on waking, when he believed himself to be alone, break forth with this complaint, "Can the annals of any history furnish an example of cruelty like my mother's?" Cadogan Keatinge often came to see him, and offered him any service which lay in his power, as a gentleman, a clergyman, or a friend. Aldborough requested him to write to his father – once more to appeal to him. In consequence he received a visit from his brother–in–law Nesbitt, who was on his way to the races at the Curragh. He assured Aldborough that his parents had no idea he was so ill. My mother, who was present, indignantly told him that her husband, who was known to be a man of veracity, had often informed them of his state. The visitor was very polite, and declared that everything should now be done for him. The dying victim, turning his expressive eyes upon him, replied, "It is too late; all is over; my heart is broken; and I am murdered." His own good sense and skill in medical science taught him the nature of his complaint too well to allow him to entertain those hopes of recovery with which consumptive patients are so apt to flatter themselves. Yet the love of life, even embittered as his had been, and the benefit he had before derived from the waters of Mallow, induced him again to undertake a journey thither. On parting from my mother, being too weak to rise from his chair, he took off his hat, and, taking a last and solemn farewell, said, "I die with more love to you, than to any other woman in the world; and you are more my mother than she who bore me."

The evening of the day he left Ballitore his mother stopped at my father's gate; but, on hearing he had left, she would not come in. She was told that her son was so weak he could not get beyond Carlow, and that she could readily overtake him. "No; he had treated Mr. Nesbitt very ill." She was invited to take some refreshment, but she excused herself lest her horses might take cold; and, turning about, drove away, leaving us full of surprise and indignation at the tenderness shown to brute animals by a mother who refused it to her dying son, one of the loveliest and most accomplished men of his day. This forsaken, dying son was enabled by easy stages to reach Clonmel, but found himself totally unable to proceed further, and expired there in the arms of his nurse, who had accompanied him from Ballitore. Thus died, at the age of twenty-four, far from the friends who truly loved him, one who had promised to be one of the brightest ornaments of the age.

The summer of 1775 was remarkably fine, and amidst the variety which marked it was the appearance of a Jew, the first of that nation who had ever entered our village. He called himself Emanuel Jacob, and carried about as a show, enclosed in a glass case, that plant of ancient memory, the mandrake. It appeared to combine the animal and vegetable in its formation, and this was really the case; for my father's house-keeper, when she had the show-man safely occupied with his breakfast, impelled by curiosity, opened the case, and found the wondrous plant to be composed of the skeleton of a frog and fibres of the root of a plant. However, as it was not her wish to deprive the man of his livelihood, she carefully closed the case, and permitted Emanuel to proceed on his way, unconscious of detection.

Robert Baxter, from Monaghan, was a parlour boarder at my father's at this time. He was but sixteen, yet was six feet high, and lusty in proportion. His understanding seemed mature also; it was improved by classical learning, by refined society, and by the conversation of an excellent mother. He was affectionate, artless, and unassuming, and we soon loved him. He delighted in visiting my Aunt Carleton, and they entertained one another with tales of former times, hers drawn from her own experience, his from tradition. One of his anecdotes was concerning the imprisonment of Lady Cathcart by her husband, (afterwards wrought by the able pen of Maria Edgeworth into her tale of "Castle Rackrent").[27] He said that it was stipulated by that lady on her marriage, that she should never be required to leave England as a residence; but, by pretending that he was only taking her out in a pleasure–boat for a trip, her husband conveyed her to Ireland and confined her in his castle, where he seldom visited her except to force her property from her by cruel and unmanly treatment. She managed, however, to conceal jewels to the amount of several thousand pounds, which her brutal tyrant could not obtain. She entrusted this treasure to her attendant, Kitty Armstrong, to carry to a person of the name of Johnson. The death of her husband at length emancipated her, after years of barbarous usage, during which she was almost starved, and clothed in filthy tattered rags. She rewarded her faithful friends by a gift to Johnson of £2,000, and 500 guineas to her trusty Kate, and left Ireland for ever. Poor Kitty, it would appear, was not so careful of her own property as of that of her lady; for, after Lady Cathcart's death, she became a dependent in the house of Robert Baxter's father; and her character, dress, and deportment made a great impression on the little boy, especially as she used to chastise him freely. Kitty wore a scarlet riding dress, a man's hat and wig, and had a cat which used to catch snipes for her

One violently tempestuous night, in the winter of this year, the stage–coach from Dublin to Cork was overturned at the Sandy–hill, and two of the passengers were killed. One of these was a young woman who was engaged to be married to a gentleman in Waterford. He was lying ill of fever, and requested to see her, and she was hastening to him when arrested by the hand of death. Her intended husband, from whom the event was concealed, expected her coming with great anxiety, and wondered at her delay. He died of the fever; let us hope they were united in Heaven. I did not see the body – I could not bear it – but I heard of her beauty, her elegant dress, her slender form, and her long fair hair, so lovely in death.

Samuel Hudson, another pupil of my father's, was the only surviving child of a family of twenty–five. This boy, who was weak in body and mind, was exceedingly dear to his parents; but, alas! they outlived him also. When his father, a rich Connaught gentleman of rough manners, came to see him at school, the boy ran blubbering into his presence, dropped on his knees, and cried out, "Your blessing father!" The father, struggling with fond paternal emotion, replied, "You have it, you dog." When my parents were travelling in Connaught they accepted an invitation to Hudson's Bay, the residence of this family. They were welcomed with the greatest kindness, and entertained with the utmost profusion. The fond mother, when walking with Elizabeth Shackleton in a retired part of the demesne, suddenly knelt down, and audibly poured forth her thanks to that gracious Providence who had put it into her heart to place her child under such care.

Charles Coote, when about eight years old, was sent to Ballitore school by his father, Lord Bellamont, whose natural son he was reputed to be; the fact was that he was the offspring of a marriage with a Roman Catholic young woman, which Lord Bellamont did not look upon as legal, he being a Protestant. But the lady being able to show that she had privately read her recantation previous to the marriage, it was proved to be binding, and a noble alliance which he was on the point of forming was thus prevented. In revenge he chased from him his beautiful wife, whose reason was subverted by the shock, and she died miserably in Clonmel.

The father of George Massey, another of the pupils, was created a peer, and as in his letters to his son he addressed the little boy with the title of "Honourable," it afforded to the lad's schoolfellows a source of diversion so vexatious to George, that often, in bitterness of heart, he lamented the day that his father became a lord. However, he had a companion in his misfortune when the young baronet, Sir Richard Eyre Cox, came to school. He was nephew to the Honourable George, though much older; and his life came to a melancholy conclusion after he left school. While rowing on one of his own ponds at Dunmanway, in 1783, his oar broke, and he fell into the water and was drowned. Though not quite of age, he left a widow and an infant daughter.

There was also a boy at school, mean in sentiments, person, and manners, who had been an indulged child, and was possessed of a good fortune. One of his tricks was feigning to have the ague, in order that he might partake of the indulgences provided for some of the boys who really had it. But by overacting his part he incurred suspicion, for his shaking fits were so violent as to affect the whole room, and led the nurse–tender to endeavour to examine his nails for the blackness which precedes the shaking fit; but he firmly opposed her attempt. However, as deception could not be positively proved, his desire to partake of the comforts of the nursery was answered, and he might have fully enjoyed his success, had not the arrival of "Molly Ass" been announced. Molly was a hawker, and she possessed an ass which the boys hired of her to ride whenever she came; and this lad took particular pleasure in the amusement. On hearing the unexpected news, the gratification of his present situation faded before the recollection of the active enjoyment he should have had if it had not been for his deceitful conduct, and he exclaimed in pathetic accents, "Oh! murder! and I sick!" "Molly Ass" afforded us another joke. When addressing my sister Sally and me one day, she made use of the pronoun "thee" to one of us. Now Sally was a very well-disposed child, and laid great stress on adhering to the plain language; therefore, calling me aside, she whispered, "Molly Ass is convinced" [i.e. of Friends' principles.][28]

To return to the delinquent of the nursery: a fall from an apple–tree, while robbing Taylor's orchard, dislocated his shoulder, and the bone–setter was sent for. During the operation my sister and I, though at the most remote part of that large house, thrust our heads up the chimney to avoid hearing the cries of the sufferer, and the equally loud sympathetic cries of Tom Eyre, who sat by during the operation. A second confinement to the nursery was the consequence, where if he endured more suffering than during his former one, he also received more compassion. Ere his hurt had perfectly healed, he again dislocated his shoulder, whilst breaking open the box of one of his schoolfellows to steal a crown out of it. This was not his first robbery, for on a former occasion he stole sixpence out of the pocket of our blind cousin, Joseph Thompson, while he slept. He was finally expelled from the school, and finished his career in a state of abject beggary.[29]

But the darling of the house was Aldworth Phaire, whom his father, Colonel Phaire, brought hither at five years of age. My sister received him in my mother's absence, and, surprised at his youth, unthinkingly asked was his mother dead. "She is dead to him," said the distressed father. Soon afterwards we heard that his mother, a woman of rank and beauty, the wife of an affectionate husband and the mother of a lovely family, had basely deserted them. The little creature wound himself into our hearts in such a manner, and became such a plaything, that when his father removed him it was a serious affliction to us. The usher met him afterwards, and Aldworth clung about his knees, and could hardly be separated from him, and, showing his old hat, said with a mixture of shyness and regret, "I got this in Ballitore." Years rolled on. Our darling boy entered the army, and at length we received word from his brother, Colonel Phaire, that he had died in the West Indies.

In 1776, my sister Margaret was united in marriage to Samuel Grubb of Clonmel. A wedding was a novel scene to us, and the preparations occasioned no small bustle. Our lovely sister was removed from us to a great distance, and we sadly missed her engaging society; but the happiness of her situation and the acquisition of many valuable connections compensated for the separation. Other weddings followed, and many events occurred full of importance at the time, but now too trivial to record. My happy and careless childhood had advanced into gentle and timid girlhood, and I felt as if I could not proceed much further on my path through life without being aroused from my peaceful dreams by some stroke of fate.

On the 7th of Fifth–month, 1777, William Leadbeater came to school. His brother–in–law and guardian, an episcopal clergyman, and his neighbour, a clergyman of the Church of Rome, accompanied him hither. That these men lived not only in good neighbourhood but in sincere friendship was matter of wonder to some; while others saw no reason why a difference of religious sentiments should prevent liberal minds from assimilating. The orphan boy whom they introduced possessed dispositions calculated to gain the good–will of that family of which he now forms a part. Charles Rawdon came at the same time, and they early became close companions. Both were amiable, and virtue perhaps appeared more engaging in their beautiful forms, for both were remarkably handsome.[30]

Early in the year 1778, there was a tremendous thunder storm. It came in the dead time of a long, dark night; and I, who was awakened by one terrible clap of thunder, fully expected that the next would destroy me. The school–boys all got up to pray. The storm subsided at length; but the whole of the next day our agitated spirits dwelt in the midst of trembling alarm. Alas! before the close of the year came another storm of a different nature, the effects of which were far more lasting and far more distressing. My beloved Aunt Carleton died. I cannot describe the anguish of that separation. My friends pitied me, and strove to console me by suggesting the aids of good sense and philosophy; but, alas, had I possessed either of these resources, they would have been of no avail, for my whole soul was overwhelmed with affliction. My only comforts were the conviction that I had never knowingly given her pain, and the certainty that for her awaited the blessed welcome, "Well done, thou good and faithful servant; enter thou into the joy of thy Lord;" for I believe her "prayers and her alms–deeds had risen up for a memorial before her." But she had left me for ever in this world – my dearest parent; for was I not to her a child, a darling child?

My deep dejection affected my health so seriously, that it was feared I might go into a decline and quickly follow her. I was ordered to ride on horseback, and was afterwards sent on a visit to my sister in Clonmel. There I visited the churchyard where lay the partial and faithful friend of my childhood, Aldborough Wrightson. No stone marked the spot where he lay, and when a grave was pointed out to me as his, I stood beside it without emotion. The sexton now came up, and telling us our guide had made a mistake, took us to another grave, which I felt certain contained the beloved remains, for my heart suddenly swelled, and my tears began to overflow. Tears which did more honour to his memory than mine have been shed there. His old master has wept and sobbed in unavailing sorrow over this interesting spot, where, at my entreaties, a weeping willow was planted.[31]

Our neighbour, John Forbes, a clergyman, after a residence of about two years in our village, took ill of a fever in Dublin. His wife attended him with anxious care, but he died. She remained in Ballitore only long enough to settle his affairs, and then took her two little girls, Arabella and Emily, with her to Dublin, where Arabella and I sometimes met with mutual delight, and continued a correspondence for many years. Emily was advantageously married at the age of eighteen to a young clergyman in the county of Tyrone. Arabella lived with her mother, who died in the year 1786. I then saw my friend in her mourning attire, and I never saw her since. About two years afterwards our correspondence dropped, yet I trust we still loved each other, and I heard with pleasure of her marriage with a gentleman named Harman. In 1795 her husband was attacked in his house by armed robbers, against whom he made a resolute resistance, his wife standing by his side charging his pistols; but the banditti succeeded in robbing and mortally wounding him. On their quitting the house, his wife laid him on a bed, and ran across fields and over hedges to alarm the neighbours, for their servants did not act so as to inspire confidence. When she returned she found her husband making his will, by which he left her an ample fortune. He died in a few days. My heart yearned towards the afflicted widow, when I learned that she was my early friend Arabella. However, as she then moved in a higher sphere of life than when our correspondence ceased, I was obliged to suppress my feelings, which would have led me to endeavour to express to her my sympathy for her loss.

Our landlord, John Bayley, who became possessed of Abel Strettell's part of Ballitore on marrying the heiress, and whose three sons, as well as himself, had been educated here, now sent the youngest as a parlour boarder, to gain a little more learning. He was a tall, comely lad of seventeen, very goodnatured, and sensible of the slowness of his capacity. He requested that my sister Margaret would allow him to read Leland's History of Ireland to her in the winter evenings, and that she would set him right when he miscalled any of the words; "for," said he, "I believe I coin more words than Johnson." However, at the Mill–house he was sure of not being laughed at, and many a cold winter's night he undertook that long walk and hopeless labour. Though sometimes stung by the derogatory remarks of his schoolfellows, he did not deserve their contempt. As Tom Eyre (who was much his inferior in age and size), Bob Bayley, and I were walking through the Mill–field, a dispute arose between the lads. "As for you," said Tom, in wrath, "you are a blockhead." "I know I am," replied Bob, "but it does not become you to tell me so."[32]

On the 22nd of Twelfth–month, 1778, in anticipation of my brother's marriage, my father, mother, and I left the house which they had occupied above twenty years, to sleep at the Retreat, still to diet at the school. That night, when the master and mistress left their old habitation, afforded a scene of mourning. The servants were bathed in tears. Sally Wood locked herself up in the pantry, and Moll Whelan's noisy lamentations were heard all over the house. Poor Moll soon after this grew extremely ill, and every evening lost the use of her limbs. At length she seemed to be expiring; she had the family about her, sent her love to my father who was then from home, asked forgiveness of those whom she had offended, and declared to my mother that she had never wronged her, but of her time. She, however, recovered, went to her sister's to recruit her strength, and lived to become Moll Casey, a well-known retailer of apples, gingerbread, and similar delicacies to the schoolboys.

The 23rd of Second–month, 1779, Abraham Shackleton and Lydia Mellor were married in Meath–street meeting–house, Dublin; the house of her friend Mary Pemberton being the temporary home of the bride. Our new sister, now the young mistress, graced the old mansion; the lightness of her form and the beauty of her "mind–illumined face" attracted universal admiration, and her unwearied and animated benevolence excited proportionate affection. The filial love and respect with which she treated her husband's parents, her kind attention to all his relations, her sedulous and conscientious care of his pupils, her excellent example as a wife and mother, could not have been so uniformly sustained merely by her strict sense of propriety; her integrity of heart and strong religious feeling were surer guides. Her manners were a style above village simplicity, although perfectly easy and natural; and her native dignity caused her in some degree to incur the censure of "height," which had been attached to my grandmother Carleton. Bred in the town of Manchester, accustomed from infancy to the refinements of good breeding, trained by a mother as accomplished as she was amiable, our sister was born a gentlewoman, and the neighbours were willing, on these considerations, to excuse the young mistress; especially as no consequential airs, no consciousness of superiority, or any want of consideration to inferiors marked her conduct, and she was of all people one of the most free from detraction, or making lessening remarks upon others. Though ever perfectly neat, her dress by degrees became more conformed to our ideas of simplicity. An anecdote presents itself as not quite malapropos. I dyed a cloak for sister Lydia, and, to my no small mortification, completely spoiled it. I was certain of receiving no rebuke, but was greatly surprised the next meeting–day to see her walk into meeting with this cloak on her shoulders. Concerned as I was to see her dressed so unbecomingly, I felt the delicacy of the compliment to my good intentions, and her endeavour to reconcile me to my blunder.

Her sister, Mary Mellor, was a very acceptable addition to our little circle. She was lively, well–informed, clever, good–humoured, and handsome. We rejoiced in our acquisitions, and our late sore affliction was softened into a tender regret. Our time was now for a while devoted to paying and receiving visits, and it was in the midst of this blameless festivity that an express arrived from Kilkenny, with the tidings of William Colles's death. This amiable and worthy young man had been educated at Ballitore school; he was much attached to the family, and to our society, and, by little and little, had assumed the garb and manners of a Quaker. "How does thy wife take it?" enquired my father. "Very badly, master," said he; "she weeps." This touched his heart more than complaints or reproaches would have done. His unexpected death by fever in the prime of life was a great shock to his family and friends, and was rendered still more touching to us by his request to be interred in our graveyard in our manner. Thither his remains were brought from Kilkenny, and his sorrowing master and mistress, whom he loved so well, attended them to the grave.[33]

My parents and their three daughters were now settled at the Retreat, a pleasant mansion. My mother delighted in her garden, which she kept in neat order. Her collection of exotics was curious and afforded much variety. She had no greenhouse, but kept those tender plants in the house, and the soft perfume of some of them was very grateful. My father, released from the cares he had so long felt, yet still active in body and mind, employed himself in writing, and walking about the village on visits to his neighbours, especially when leaving home or returning to it. In his absence they felt a want, and the old master's return was welcomed by all ranks. He now devoted more of his time than he had yet done to the service of his own religious society, in which his zeal to support good order was strengthened by that love which unites in the bond of peace. His true helpmate, when not engaged – as she often was – in like labours of love, managed their temporal affairs with that prudence, forecast, and liberality for which she was remarkable.

On the 28th of Eleventh-month, 1779, young Richard Shackleton was born. The delighted grandfather welcomed the arrival of the little stranger by exercising on the occasion his poetical talent. Of this he had a considerable share, but he did not make it his study; he devoted his care to the higher endowments of the mind, and kept poetry in that subordinate station, befitting those relaxations which it is allowable occasionally to indulge in. When I have heard the muse's lyre condemned as vain and idle, I have thought of the gentle remonstrance of Paris to Hector, when upbraided by him with setting too much value on external accomplishments. The polite Phrygian acknowledges the superior qualifications of his brother, yet entreats him not to despise the softer graces, for

"No gifts can gain them, but the gods bestow!"

The following are the lines which my father penned on the birth of his grandson and namesake: –

Welcome be the lovely boy,
His fond parents' hope and joy!
By thy birth what tender ties
All in social order rise!
To the names of husband, wife,
Dearest in domestic life,
Thou hast added all these other
Names of grandsire, father, mother,
Aunts and nephews – ties that bind
In close union humankind.
Welcome, beauteous babe! For thee
Hath old age, with tott'ring knee,
Wand'ring in the muse's bowers,
Stooped to cull the fairest flowers,
And, with trembling hand, e'en now
Weaves a garland for thy brow.

Welcome thrice, my darling child!
Sure propitious Heaven has smiled

On thy birth; for ev'ry grace
Marks the features of thy face,
Where we both thy parents find –
Ease and dignity combin'd.

Sweetest infant, since thou art
Sent to act in life a part,
While of yet unconscious age,
Ere thou tread the public stage,
Sunk in balmy slumbers, rest
On thy mother's fragrant breast,
While thy grandsire comes to shed
His best blessings on thy head!

God – before whose awful sight
Thy forefathers walk'd aright,
By His hand all–powerful led,
By His gracious bounty fed,
And His guardian angel still
Watching to preserve from ill –
Bless the lad! And may the name,
Better than all worldly fame,
Sacred name, which qualifies
For admission to the skies,
That new name, O Richard, be
Namèd evermore on thee![34]

Molly Hudson, having lost some property in her brother's house, which was destroyed by an accidental fire, was invited to my father's till the house should be rebuilt, and she spent twenty years in the family, endearing herself by her inoffensive manners, and particularly to me by her kind attention to me in a dangerous fever which I had in Dublin. My mother came to me there, as did my sister Debby, whom of all the family I longed most to see, and of whose tenderness I partook largely, for she was one of the most affectionate of nurses. I was treated by our valued friends, Joseph and Elizabeth Pike, at whose house I was, in such a manner as claimed and excited strong emotions of gratitude. Though from home, the news of our own neighbourhood reached me, and an adventure which happened in Athy gave me much satisfaction. A young man was sentenced to die, for being an accomplice in a crime. His mother implored the Duke of Leinster, and in the simple eloquence of despair, gave him titles enough – "Duke of Leinster, Duke of Ireland, Duke of the World, save my son!" In vain did a mother's pleadings attempt to stay the iron hand of justice: the day appointed for the execution arrived, and the duke, at the head of his corps of volunteers, escorted the convict towards the gallows; but just as they drew near the turnpike–gate, a number of men who had mingled with the crowd, disguised in women's clothes, attacked the duke's martial party with a volley of stones, and discomfited them. The brother of the condemned man, then taking him in his arms, threw the trembling culprit over the wall on the right hand side within the gate, and effected his escape – an event which it is probable the many–titled duke, who possessed great goodnature, did not regret. It must be a severe trial to a feeling mind to take an active part on those occasions which doom the life of a fellow–creature to be sacrificed.

The son of Lord Chancellor Hewit had to pass sentence of death at the assizes of Maryborough. Thomas Chandlee was present; he heard the judge, with a faltering voice, announce to the prisoner, also a man gifted by the Creator of man with health and strength and life, the day on which he was to be deprived of these by the laws of his fellow–men. Justice or law demanded this: humanity claimed her right also. After he had pronounced the fatal sentence, the judge covered his face with his hands, and, leaning on the table, burst into such a passion of tears as obliged him to retire, and incapacitated him from attending to any more business for that day. It is probable that he also, when this felon escaped by breaking his chains, felt his mind relieved; yet justice and humanity must unite in lamenting that there is so seldom an alternative between the punishment of death and liberty for the disturbance of peaceful society. Why are not our laws improved by enacting such chastisements as man has a right to inflict? for certain it is, *he has not a right to inflict death.* This day may come, for I hope the world in general is not growing worse, and humanity follows the footsteps of civilization.[35]

The 26th of the Tenth–month, 1780, was the wedding–day of Thomas Chandlee and our sister Deborah Shackleton, and on the next day they went home to Athy. Although united to one so much beloved and esteemed by us, we felt the loss of our dear, kind–hearted sister. Our domestic circle had also another loss to regret. William Rayner left Ballitore on the 2nd of Tenth–month for Waterford, where he became clerk to George and William Penrose. It was to me like parting a brother of whom I might say with perfect truth, –[36]

In infancy our hopes and fears
Were to each other known,
And friendship in our riper years
Combined our hearts in one.

I followed and he returned several times to repeat the last farewell. I think we neither spoke nor wept, but our hearts were full.

My brother's young family were now rising around him, and formed one of the delights of their grandfather. Frequent during the day were his visits to the little flock who gathered round his knees, while he often held the youngest before him in the reading–chair which he sat in, repeating Greek verses, whose sonorous musical sound seemed very grateful to the infant ear. He often read to us while we sat at our work, especially when a new poem was presented to the public; his remarks heightened the interest of what he read, and formed our tastes and judgment.

Pleasant and engaging as was my father to young and old, cordial and sympathising as was my mother, their truly religious characters inspired a sentiment approaching to awe, though they were beloved more than feared. Those who were so much in the habit of swearing as to swear almost involuntarily, restrained themselves in their presence, and others who were sensible of deserving their reproof shunned it. They governed their household with firm yet gentle sway, and around the supper–table the housekeeper, the ushers and other assistants in the school, enjoyed their society with confidence in their paternal kindness. My mother spoke of her deceased children with an expression of satisfaction at their early escape from a world of danger; my father did not like to mention them, and seemed smarting with the pain of regret when the subject was introduced; yet both were equally tender parents. If either of them remarked the absence of any of our members from meeting, a visit of inquiry was pretty certain to follow, on the supposition that illness must have been the cause, for no other pretext was regarded as a sufficient excuse for neglecting this duty.

Those who live in the country and go little from home are apt to be tenaciously attached to their own opinions. The humility of our parents preserved them from this error, their intercourse with polished and literary society tending to enlarge the mind. Still there was a degree of singularity in our education, in consequence of our ignorance of the manners of the world, the simplicity of our profession, and our situation in a retired village; for though our parents encouraged no confined ideas in us, and taught us a courteous demeanor by example and precept, yet in the cautious observance of truth we forbore to disguise our sentiments of any kind, and I think were too little skilled in the rules of good–breeding, that charming accomplishment, which, whilst compatible with sincerity, teaches young people, I will not say to disguise, but to suppress their sentiments, and is in fact a virtuous self–denial; for if the expression of one's opinions will do no good, but, on the contrary, inflict pain, they should be suppressed, be they ever so blameless.

It was not while in the circles of his distant friends or acquaintances, engaging their admiration, love, and esteem by his superior talents, fascinating manners, delightful converse, and exalted virtue, that my dear father shone most; it was by his own fireside that his sweetness of temper, his vivacity, and his unaffected piety beamed brightest. He loved to take us to ride or walk with him, he made his children his companions and his confidants; he generally showed us the letters he wrote and received, and he expected the like confidence from us. This gave him an opportunity to correct our style and handwriting, to judge of the characters of our correspondents, and to encourage or discourage the friendships we were about to form. He disliked the canting manner of some young persons in dealing with religious subjects, of which he suspected they knew little; and though he was a nursing father to what was good, he desired not to hear the awful theme of religion introduced without a deep sense of its importance.

As long as I can remember, it was my father's practice to retire, at the close of the day, either to his garden or to his chamber, where I have no doubt he wrestled for a blessing, his countenance when he returned to his family betraying with whom he had been. He lay down to rest sweetly, and if he was in any difficulty, the first thoughts which occurred in the morning were generally those to which he took heed, and by which he was delivered from what annoyed him. Indeed he was remarkable for casting his care upon Providence, even in cases which might be accounted trivial. Few had a higher relish for polished and literary society; yet, being as humble as he was accomplished, he enjoyed with equal relish the society of those who, though neither polished nor literary, were ennobled by virtue. He had the manners of a gentleman without departing from the strictness of his own profession, and these manners were marked by a degree of simplicity which derogated nothing from the dignity of his character. I have frequently applied to him the following lines:-[37]

> And such a man was he
> As Heaven just gives to human sight,
> To show what man should be.

On the publication of Leland's History of Ireland, my father received a letter as if from the author, requesting his opinion of the work, but written in a style which conveyed no high opinion of the abilities of the historian. It was, however, politely answered; he disclaimed any pretensions to critical judgment; he said he was no prophet, nor a prophet's son, but if the author wished for his opinion he was willing to give it. Dr. Leland promptly answered this letter, assuring my father that he knew nothing of that which had been written in his name, nor could he imagine who it was that had been guilty of offering this unprovoked insult to them both; but, whoever he was, he held himself under an obligation to him, as having been the means of introducing him to such an acquaintance. The letter concluded with repeating a wish for my father's opinion of his work, and requesting that if he thought it worth his acceptance, he would not return the volumes he sent him. Thus a wanton joke upon two respectable men ended in creating mutual esteem. My father attentively read the work, and candidly gave his opinion, which was very favourable, though he censured some misrepresentations of our Society which it contained. Dr. Leland took his remarks and suggestions in good part, and promised to attend to them in a future edition.

My mother had some years previously written to David Hume, who calls Friends "deists" in his Essays, and "enthusiasts" in his History of England. She received a reply from him, which though polite was not satisfactory, as he seemed to think he had complimented us by the former appellation, as classing us with those who had shaken off the dominion of priests.

My mother with her excellent understanding had an innocence and simplicity in her mind and manners which softened the awe inspired by her gravity. It was very pleasant to read history to her; her memory was very good, she did not lose the thread of the narrative, nor did she suffer us to lose it. She entered into the characters which the historian introduced, and almost detested Augustus Caesar. She could not think otherwise of Caligula, than that the fever he had before he came to the throne had affected his brain, and had caused the great alteration in his conduct. She said Seneca had acted unfaithfully in not having restrained the excesses of Nero's youth; the consequences were Nero's vileness and the murder of his tutor. She liked to read only what was true; and her faith in the story that Captain Donnellan had poisoned his brother–in–law, Sir Theodosius Boughton, cost us all our laurel–water. I beheld my mother quietly emptying bottle after bottle into a ditch, nor were we again permitted any more of that culinary ingredient once held in such high estimation.

My father was generally an accurate judge of poetry; although his partiality led him to value mine, especially when I was a child. Of his own talents and accomplishments he had too much good sense to be vain, and yet I do think he was vain of the rhymes of his little daughter. My mother, ever watchful and careful, often expressed her justly grounded fear that my mind was too much engrossed by this propensity; but my respect for her prevented me from reminding her of the engrossing delight she took in cultivating her flowers. My father met with a book called "Emma Corbett, or the Miseries of Civil War." As the American war was then raging, he thought the book treated on this subject, and brought it home to his wife.[38] He read to us several passages containing good sentiments, pretty sentiments, but little or no information, and very soon got tired of it. Having resigned the volume to me, I read on, knowing well the kind of book I was reading, and secretly enjoying the future joke. At length the story began to grow a little more romantic, and my mother asked if I believed it to be true. "Oh, no, mother, we do not expect truth in a novel." My mother's astonishment at this discovery increased our mirth at the idea of my father's having borrowed a novel to read to her.

It was a custom with my mother to go into the hall when the boys were preparing for their place of worship, and to examine their dress and their hands, and see that all were clean and in order. When a boy was leaving school, she seldom or never failed to give him advice as to his future conduct in life. These lectures, "warm from the heart, and to the heart addressed," often made a deep and with some a lasting impression. She often had harder tasks to perform. If the misdeeds of her neighbours came to her knowledge, she spoke not of them to others, but to themselves; and if unguarded words and actions fell under her observation, however hard to her timid mind, how little soever she was acquainted with the transgressors, or whatever their rank, she must relieve her mind by informing them of her sense of their errors; and this was done in such a spirit and in such terms as rarely, if ever, gave offence. One incident of this kind I must record. My father and mother, with others of their family, were by special invitation at the house of their landlord, Clayton Bayley, at Gowran, when Beauchamp Bagnell and a young man of the Butler family, who had dined at Lord Clifden's, came in a state of intoxication to the house. Clayton Bayley was very unwilling to be intruded upon while enjoying the company of his former preceptor; and his wife was greatly distressed, for she was certain that "that wicked Bagnell would insist that her husband must drink with him all night, or else fight him." It was in vain our host insisted that he was "not at home," which he firmly maintained malgré the lectures of his old mistress; he was at length obliged to appear, and, as an apology for not receiving them, to inform Bagnell that he had Quaker guests in his house. This Bagnell declared was an additional inducement to him to desire admission, for of all things he loved Quakers. He entered on crutches, having been lately hurt in a duel; and, though disfigured by lameness, and obscured by intoxication, the grace of his form and the beauty of his countenance were so conspicuous, as to excite in no small degree the mingled sensations of admiration, pity, and regret. He had entered into the world with splendid gifts of fortune and still more splendid gifts of nature, and possessed a mind not unworthy of them, till, drawn into the vortex of dissipation, his mind debased, his constitution shattered, his fortune impaired, he became the wreck which now appeared before us. It was to my mother that Bagnell addressed his conversation. He repeated his declaration of affection to the Society of Friends, and assured her that he agreed with them in sentiments, and wished to belong to their body, "only that he could not in that case retain his corps of volunteers." My mother made little reply, but he, rising soon after to leave the room, expressed much unwillingness to lose her company, and at length left the house, much to the relief of all who remained in it except my mother. Her mind was so impressed with sadness in contemplating the situation of this man, that she believed it her duty to inform him of it. In the course of a few months she heard he had come to visit his sister Keatinge; she went to Narraghmore, and had a conference with him, honestly laying before him the injury he did himself and others by his conduct and example. He heard her not only with polite but with serious attention, acknowledged the truth of her remarks, and lamented his inability to keep those good resolutions which he had often made. He assured her that he approved and esteemed the principles of her Society, and that the sentiments he expressed in his state of intoxication were sincere. He thanked her cordially, and at parting kissed her hand.

Another incident of a similar kind was as follows. John St. Leger, a gentleman of unhappy notoriety for extravagant dissipation, was reduced by his vices to a languishing condition, and no one about him had the courage to tell him of his danger. My mother was greatly concerned to hear this, and she imparted to him by letter her feelings on his account, urging him to review his past life, and to prepare for the life to come. I was told he was much affected by this letter; that he caused it to be read to him several times as he lay on his death bed; and recommended it to be sent to another gentleman, who, he said, wanted such advice as much as he did.[39]

My mother often spoke of the death of two of the boys in a very touching manner. The first of these was Chaworth Brabazon Hallowes, who came to school in 1756. His father was an officer in foreign service; he was an only child about nine years old. His mother had been consumptive till his birth, after which she was free from the disease, which seemed to be transferred to her child. The physicians told the mother that if her son was attacked by measles or small–pox he would be in great danger. She was immediately informed when the small–pox came into the school, but she did not remove the child. In a little time she had to attend the summons to see him on his death–bed. "Oh mama! I am dying!" was the salute she received from the poor little victim of disease. "My dear, I know you are," she replied, and the person with whom she lodged in Dublin, and who accompanied her on this journey, immediately took her out to walk. I have been often surprised that my mother did not seem to accuse her of want of maternal tenderness, but merely pitied her as a timid woman under the influence of a blustering landlady, who made her do as she pleased, and who actually gave orders that if the child died in the night they should not be disturbed. Her orders were obeyed, and before morning the mother was childless. My mother's distress at this event was great.

The other boy was John Eyre, a lad of fifteen, from the county of Galway.

My mother heard a sudden shriek of pain; she quickly enquired the reason, and was told that Jack Eyre was seized with a pain in his heel, which continued with unabated violence, and resisted all the means which were tried for relief. He even compelled his attendants to press his heel so as almost to bruise it, thinking it afforded temporary ease. As he sat opposite to my mother at the other side of the fireplace, she looked at him, and, shocked at the expression of death which she saw in his face, she sent immediately for my father and requested he would lose no time in sending for the boy's parents. The express was despatched, and they arrived. The character of the father was such that my mother felt a kind of dread, but nothing of turbulence appeared in his demeanour. Softened by sorrow, his manners were remarkably gentle, and he performed the offices of a nurse for his languishing son with feminine tenderness. The boy's mother witnessed his sufferings with all a mother's sensations, and from the time she ascended the stairs to his chamber, never came down till she followed the corpse of her son. Although the intense pain was not to be relieved, the poor lad tried to bear it with patience, and was very loving and tender to those about him. The gloom became deeper the patient's strength was exhausted by pain and fever, and the candles went out suddenly in his chamber without any apparent cause; superstition was aroused by this circumstance; and even my sensible mother remarked it, and gave directions that if the youth should suddenly expire, great care should be taken to preserve quietude. His mother, on closely questioning him, found that he had cut an issue in his leg, and had dried it again; for he was addicted to trying experiments, and had at one time inoculated himself with small–pox. This she thought might have caused the malady. The lad perceived his dissolution approaching, and solemnly said, "None know this road but they that go it," and not long after, having just spoken in a voice as strong as usual, expired as suddenly as the candles went out. My mother, who was not present at the time, was terrified by a most violent and lamentable shriek; she feared it was either the boy's last agony, or that his departing spirit was disturbed by the outbreak. Neither was the case, for his mother had been taken out of the room before her grief had thus found utterance, and my mother found her seated on the bedside in another apartment, wringing her hands, and in the agony of grief incessantly repeating, "O death! death! death! Jack! Jack! Jack!" Lord Baltinglass, who was related to the family, sent his coach to convey the parents home. As the mother followed the remains of her beloved child out of the house, she turned back, "And now," said she, "had I twenty sons I would send them all to you." Her nephew, Poyntz Willington, came in a short time after.

James Forbes, the only child of his father, had a wooden leg, yet his activity was surprising. My mother was once much alarmed by being told that one of the boys had broken his leg, and was greatly relieved when she found it was Forbes' wooden leg. He always took care to have a ready–made limb lying by to season.[40]

My mother often had the journals of Friends read in the winter evenings by Friends' children. She entertained a few rather singular scruples, one of which was her objection to images, even in china, on which we sometimes amused ourselves with finding an almost imperceptible man or bird. To gratify this scruple, the parent of one of the pupils procured for her a tea service from China without any images. Her consideration for her fellow-creatures would not permit her to cover her floor with what might cover the poor, and, being remarkable for neatness, it was a difficulty to contrive what should at once keep her apartments clean and her mind easy. Haircloth was a bad substitute for carpets, but when listings were introduced, the discovery was welcomed by my mother as a valuable one; industry and dexterity were soon exercised, and the rooms were presently furnished to her satisfaction. She was remarkable for freely taking advice and trying the methods of others, yet not unfrequently it proved that her own mode was preferable; as Edmund Burke once remarked in reference to experiments in farming, that the advantage in trying them often consisted in proving that the old way was the best. The butchers were of all tradesmen the chief annoyance to my mother, as they frequently intruded on her while at breakfast, exhibiting their wares, and praising "the colour and fat." On seeing them approach, my father was wont to call out, "Mistress, fortify, or, if possible, *fiftify* thyself against the butchers."

She was very strict in inculcating good manners; we were early taught to pay deference to old age and courtesy to strangers; and were not allowed to call poor old people by the abbreviations of "Bet," "Moll," &c., which were more in use at that time than at present. I remember being sent back to a shop to make acknowledgments for some sugar–candy which I had been given, and which I had accepted without saying that "I was obliged." So strict was her adherence to truth that she scarcely allowed herself to assert anything positively, nor would she permit us to do so; and so accustomed have I been to this habitual caution, that even to this day, if I hear an extravagant expression, I examine it involuntarily in my mind before I perceive the exaggeration. I think a ready method of discouraging that false wit which consists in telling lies would be – never to laugh at it.

My mother was by no means insensible to the charms of taste, but as they had too much influence on her youthful mind, she feared to yield to their attractions. To her the sick resorted for medicine, the poor for relief, the afflicted for comfort, and the perplexed for advice. We were not insensible to the happiness we enjoyed in being favoured with such excellent and amiable parents, whose youth had been spent in the pursuit of virtue, and who now reaped the reward when age was deadening the natural faculties, and enforcing the warning that "we have no abiding city here." Their future prospects were not overwhelmed by gloom; they looked forward steadily and humbly to "the recompence of reward," while they enjoyed their outward blessings with a sweeter relish than those do who place their chief happiness in them. It was not their fault if all within their influence were not made better by their example, and happier by their society. The wish often arises that I may make the youth of my children pass as comfortably as they did mine, and thus repay part of the debt I owe them. And while I exult in the honour of being descended from progenitors whose virtues confer a dignity to which titles, wealth, and rank alone can never aspire, I say with Cowper:-

> My boast is not that I deduce my birth
> From loins enthroned and rulers of the earth,
> But higher far my proud pretensions rise,
> The child of parents passed into the skies!

CHAPTER V.
1782.

Anna Taverner settles in Ballitore. – The wet summer of 1782. – A fickle fair one. – The mysterious Welsh clergyman. – How Wentworth Mansergh dreaded coming to school – and how he changed his mind. – A cautious swain and a terrible widow. – Major Dunbar. – "Gazetteer" Walker invades Friends' burial ground. – The author and her father visit Beaconsfield. – Her poem on the occasion, and Burke's reply. – Primitive "coosins" in Selby. – Return of Tom Eyre from the war. Death of his brother Sam. – Travellers' tales. – His ideas on the management of the war – and on the march of improvement in Ballitore. – He marries, and becomes a captain. – The story of Captain St. Clair.

THE beginning of 1782 brought a new inhabitant to Ballitore – Anna Taverner, a young Londoner, whose father was nevertheless a native and inhabitant of the city of Limerick. She had, like me, been educated by an affectionate aunt, and, like me, had lost her, and suffered in health from the shock. Were the old meeting–house in Sycamore–alley now standing, I think I could point out the very spot where I first beheld this delightful vision brightening the gloomy aisle. Her stature was rather tall, her form elegant, her carriage inclining a little forward, yet far removed from an awkward stoop; her complexion was delicately blooming, her eyes a dark hazel, her teeth white and even, her hair shining amber, her looks intelligent and expressive, and peculiarly marked with sweetness. Critical judges might not pronounce her to be beautiful, but all hearts acknowledged her to be lovely. Her manners and conversation were as captivating as her person; an excellent understanding and a still more excellent heart beamed through her transparent countenance, even when the purple light of youth and the rosy bloom of health were almost annihilated by years of sickness and sorrow. My heart expanded to meet her, and, without many professions of friendship, we have continued to love each other with steady affection. An orphan now, she came to Ballitore, which seems to attract with a kind of fascination those who remain long in its quiet shades. Though the wind sweeps through our valley, and makes the difference between summer and winter more observable than in many other places, yet pleasant faces and cheerful firesides more than compensate this disadvantage, and the summer and the winter evenings have each their peculiar charms in Ballitore.

We welcomed our dear Anna Taverner with joy; but our enjoyment of her society was soon marred, for she was prostrated by a lingering and painful illness. Her sufferings were dreadful; her nerves were racked by convulsions, and at length her tongue lost the power of articulation. Copious bleedings appeared to be the only means of preserving her life, though it was believed they increased her complaints by the weakness they produced. Her kind-hearted physician, beholding her suffer agonies which all his skill could not relieve, cried out in accents of distress, "The Lord help you! You have nothing but religion to support you." He spoke truly. Nothing short of this support could give that patience which equalled her sufferings. For four months she continued deprived of speech, except that once during that time her mouth was opened in prayer. When her speech was fully restored, her first use of it was to utter the sentence, "Great and marvellous are thy works, Lord God Almighty! Just and true are all thy ways, thou King of saints."

The year 1782 was remarkable for its wet summer and late scanty harvest. It was said that Sir Isaac Newton had predicted that in this year there would be little difference between summer and winter weather. It was so; and in 1783 the distresses of the poor were great, and it was said there were instances of some having perished of want. No such misfortune occurred in our village.

About this time there came to our neighbour Susy Bayly's a handsome young man, Jack Cooper, a relation of the family. It was natural that, what with walking and riding together, the beauty of the youth's person and the melody of his voice, young Susan felt that "friendship in woman is sister to love," and that, on the other hand, her affability and independent fortune won his heart. Her mother disapproved of this attachment, and Jack was sent home. His fair one continued to correspond with him by the assistance of Dr. Johnson, which of course led to an acquaintance with "the elegant doctor," as he was frequently called, and poor Susan's susceptible heart again experienced the danger of this kind of friendship. The doctor was surprised when he perceived his good fortune, and finding the same attractions in the damsel which his rival had found, was disposed to possess himself of the prize. However, though her fortune was at her own disposal, he had too much honour and delicacy to take her without the consent of her family. Her brother encouraged his hopes of success, and the doctor went to Dublin for the license and ring. Her mother disapproving of this connection also, the daughter was confined to her room and roughly treated; her former lover returned her letters, but soon followed them, accompanied by a relative, to excuse this conduct. On seeing her first love, young Susan's first flame revived, the mother now consented, and next morning, when the carriage conveyed the young couple to Cooper's Hill to be married, the whole village was in a ferment of wonder and mirth. This was followed by serious alarm, on Dr. Johnson's return with the license and ring, for the consequences of a meeting between Bob Bayly and him. That alarm was dispelled by another surprise – a bonfire blazed in the street, and noisy acclamations congratulated the doctor on his escape from becoming the spouse of such a fickle fair one!

A Welsh clergyman named John Roberts was an inmate with Abby Widdows for about a year. He said he had come to Ireland on the invitation of Lord Aldborough, and he frequently visited at Belan, the seat of that nobleman. He was an elderly, portly, well-looking man, very communicative of his stock of knowledge, which consisted chiefly of hymns and receipts in physic and cookery. I had the misfortune to stand pretty high in his favour. I say, misfortune, for one evening when Abby Widdows had assembled in her parlour a pleasant party of her young friends, Doctor Roberts, as we called him, seated me beside him, and, producing a newspaper, read aloud to me the debates of the Irish parliament, which covered one page. Now politics are my aversion; and though I have often been ashamed of my ignorance, I have thought it unnecessary for me to endeavour after such knowledge, and to affect it would have been a dangerous experiment. I practised no little self–denial in sitting out the tedious detail, and rejoiced in my heart when I saw land. But when the courteous doctor turned to the next page, covered in like manner with the English parliamentary proceedings, I cast a despairing glance at my companions, whose arch looks and suppressed smiles showed how little they envied me the partiality of the old gentleman.

As something mysterious hung about this man, Molly Webster firmly believed that he was Doctor Dodd in disguise. The unfortunate Doctor Dodd had suffered death for forgery a short time before, and Molly had either heard, or imagined she had heard that means had been privately and successfully used to restore him to life. Molly stood alone in her conjecture, but it was evident that Doctor Roberts did not desire to be fully known. Abby Widdows, when travelling from Dublin one day in the stage–coach, met a gentleman who knew her lodger, and gave her a card to present to him. The doctor, on receiving it, discovered symptoms of embarrassment, and soon afterwards left Ballitore. Hearing some time after that he was living at Whitehaven, I wrote to him, but received no answer. In the course of years I heard that he was in Cumberland, lodging near my friend Thomas Wilkinson, through whom I sent another letter for him; but he took no notice of that letter either, nor did he ever mention having been in Ireland. He soon afterwards left that neighbourhood also; but I made no further enquiry, and left him to enjoy his obscurity in peace

There was at school at this time a youth named Wentworth Mansergh, youngest brother to a gentleman of fortune near Cashel. His brother George had been at Ballitore school, and cruelly told the child that at the Quaker school he should be flogged without mercy; and inspired him with such horror, that when they proposed sending him to Ballitore, he eloped from his brother's house and took shelter with his grandfather, till his terror abated and he ventured to return. This occurred several times; at length the reluctant boy was captured, and his elder brother set out with him for school. On the way he got at his brother's pistols, turned the horses about, and threatened to shoot his brother if he did not go back. This desperate effort proved ineffectual, and poor Mansergh was brought in triumph to Ballitore. His anxious eyes were soon fastened on the handles suspended from a loft for the pump–churn; this he believed was a machine to which the boys were fastened to undergo flagellation. The grave looks of the master and mistress filled him with dread; however, he kept his mind to himself, and in a few days took an opportunity of setting out on a pilgrimage to his beloved home. When he got to the end of the village the cross roads puzzled him, and he could not recollect the name of the last town he had come through while on his way to Ballitore; he therefore returned, expecting shortly to learn it without incurring suspicion. But long before he did so, his desire to leave the school had subsided, and he found that an evil report had been given of the good land. He remained here for six years, greatly beloved, for he was the soul of good nature and kindness –

> He had a heart for pity, and a hand
> Open as day to melting charity.

As he spent much of his leisure time with us at the Retreat, we were surprised that some days had passed without a visit from Mansergh, although we had seen him apparently very much occupied; sometimes carrying bread from the baker's, sometimes frequenting other shops, whilst a stranger of reduced appearance was now and then seen with him. When this stranger had departed and Mansergh reappeared in our circle, we learned after repeated inquiries concerning his late guest, that this poor man had been a tutor in his brother's family, but was now in great poverty. We already knew he had supported him here, and had shared his pocket–money with him; but the generous youth was more willing to tell us that when he parted from his guest, having walked with him some miles, and pressed upon him the remainder of his cash, the poor fellow with tears firmly refused the gift, declaring he had given him too much already. "I know not what was the matter with me," continued Mansergh. As he spoke, his colour heightened, his lip quivered, his eyes filled fast with tears, and we changed the conversation.

Though he was so full of drollery that we were often weary with the fits of laughter he caused, yet when a tale of sorrow was introduced in the height of his mirth, I have seen his countenance fall in a moment, and all sensations vanish but anxiety to relieve the distressed. This tenderness of disposition extended even to the brute creation. He and I once met accidentally in Youghal; he was truly glad to see me, yet he presently started away, with eagerness and displeasure in his looks, to pursue a crowd of idle boys, and rescue from them a dog to whose tail they had tied a kettle.

Our sequestered shades were frequently sought by those who wished to conceal themselves from the world. A young gentleman came to my father's school, yet not regularly to school. He said he wished to improve himself in the classics, but he attended school too little to reap any benefit from the instruction given there, nor did he appear to study in his chamber. He preferred the amusements of drawing and poetry, and wandering about in the rural scenery; especially when squire to the maids of the valley, who were pleased with his gentle manners, intelligent conversation, and handsome face, all made more interesting by that air of dejection which seemed to cloud the morning of his day. He appeared to possess a mind too ingenuous and innocent to be the prey of guilt, nor were we troubled with an inquisitive spirit. Once, on lending me a book, he requested me not to let it go into other hands, and, showing me a name written in it different from that which he then bore, gave that as the reason, and offered to tell me the circumstances which had induced him to conceal himself under a feigned name. Far from being flattered at the prospect of obtaining the stranger's confidence, or curious to develop the mystery, I was alarmed for what might be the consequence of knowing his secret, with which I told him I had no wish to be made acquainted. However, to ease his mind, he communicated the cause of his depression.

He had finished his studies in Edinburgh, taken out his diploma, and returned to his parents in the north of Ireland, when it was proposed to him to marry a handsome and rich young widow, who on her part had no objection to the union, while his own family were anxiously solicitous to settle him in such an apparently comfortable situation. But the youth, having had much opportunity of observing the lady's temper during the life of her first husband, recollected that it was too violent for his taste, and rejected the proposal. This continued, notwithstanding, to be vehemently urged, and the consequent annoyance had such an effect on his health that a journey to the south of France was judged necessary, and his friends believed him to be at Montpelier, while he was inhaling the temperate breezes of Ballitore, and recovering his health and serenity. The cause of his concealment being removed by the fair widow's making another choice, he remained here only three months, and we expected he would soon dismiss us from his memory. But not so: he had a warm sincere heart, and occasionally corresponded with us; and in about two years I had a kind of farewell letter from him, previous to his departure for Canada, as surgeon to the 5th regiment of foot. My brother, some years after this, had an affectionate letter from him from Quebec, and another written in England at the time of the rebellion in Ireland, making most anxious enquiries after our welfare. Touched at his continued remembrance, I begged to be permitted to answer this letter, and soon had a reply in the style of old cordial friendship. He told me he had married into one of the first families in Canada, had five fine children, and was in very good circumstances, being surgeon to the forces in the Lower Province.

Griesebank was taken by George Dunbar, commonly called Major Dunbar. I never could learn that he had ever been in the army, but he seemed to inherit the title from his father, who left him an inheritance more substantial – some good estates. He was a small, active, elderly man, on whose education I doubt not much expense had been bestowed, – for he had been taught fencing and dancing and the French language. His first wife had been a widow Agar, mother to Lord Clifden. He kept fine company, wore fine clothes, visited in fine equipages, but while he basked in the sunshine of grandeur his patrimony melted before it. He was married to a second wife, and they had one son. He filled Griesebank with excellent furniture; many prints of Hogarth, and some family pictures ornamented the walls of the parlours and bed–chambers, and he laid out the garden with taste. He was a member of Parliament, and very obliging in giving franks. We liked our lively neighbour, though we saw that vanity was a predominant feature in his character, and thought his manners were too gay for his age and for our taste. In 1787 he again became a widower. My mother and I visited him on the occasion, and when I went to look on the lifeless body, he accompanied me, though I begged he would not. "There she is," he exclaimed as we entered, waving his hand to the walls, "surrounded by her relations." Not knowing but that some of her relatives had come on the occasion, I looked around, but saw only some of my own lowly neighbours. Possibly he perceived my surprise, for he pointed directly to the family pictures, repeating their titles with no small emphasis; and, concluding with his own, "And there is unfortunate George!" he darted out of the room. The nominal major and his son soon afterwards left Ballitore.

We received a visit of a few days from John Walker, the author of the Geography and Gazetteer. His simplicity and good sense recommended him to us, as they did to others; and he seemed much pleased with us, our school, our village, and our gardens, remarking that my bower reminded him of Rowe's Letters. I suppose he was not so well pleased with our place of interment, for the stone which marked the grave of Abel Strettel appeared to him inconsistent with our principles as a religious society; and on the night before his leaving Ballitore, he got into the graveyard, and, alone and unassisted, completely buried the stone. This was discovered a few days afterwards, and Robert Bayly, displeased at the indignity offered to the bones of his grandfather, desired leave of my father to re–establish the stone. My father assured him of his ignorance of the transaction, but thought that, since it had been removed, it would be as well not to restore it, seeing that such records were contrary to the practice of Friends. Robert departed in great wrath, which, however, he forebore venting on his respected master; and, even when he had scaled the walls of the graveyard, armed with guns and attended by men with digging implements, his forbearance continued, and he judiciously determined, "Though I am in a passion, I will make no noise here." The hiding-place of the famous stone was soon discovered, and Robert and the monument of his ancestor upreared their heads in triumph once more. This was a very rare instance of a gravestone in one of our burying grounds.

In the year 1784 my father took me to London, to attend the yearly meeting of Friends. While there we frequently visited Edmund Burke, and at his house we met some distinguished characters. Amongst these were Sir Joshua Reynolds and the poet Crabbe, whom their illustrious host had purposely invited to introduce to them his old companion and highly esteemed friend. It was his practice to invite some of the superior minds of the day when Richard Shackleton was in London, knowing how pleasant would be such communion to one buried in a secluded village, while endowed with a refined and accomplished taste. Crabbe's "Village" had just then been published, and won my father's warm admiration. Well do I recollect the modest deprecating manner of the gentle poet, when my father in complimenting him said, "Goldsmith's would *now* indeed be the Deserted Village." From London we went by earnest invitation to Beaconsfield, which seemed to me a paradise on earth. I shall here insert part of a poem written after my return home.

BEACONSFIELD.

All hail, ye woods in deepest gloom arrayed!
Admit a stranger through your reverend shade,
With timid step to seek the fair retreat
Where virtue and where genius fix their seat:
In vain retiring from the public gaze,
Not deepest shades can veil so bright a blaze.
Lo! there the mansion stands in princely pride;
The beauteous wings extend on either side:
Unsocial pomp flies from the cheerful gate,
Where hospitality delights to wait;
A brighter grace her candid smile bestows

Than the majestic pillars' comely rows.
Enter these ever open doors, and find
All that can strike the eye or charm the mind;
Painting and sculpture there their pride display,
And splendid chambers decked in rich array.
But these are not the honours of the dome
Where Burke resides and strangers find a home,
To whose glad hearth the social virtues move,
Paternal fondness and connubial love,
Benevolence unwearied, friendship true,
And wit unforced, and converse ever new.
Ye cultured walks where grace and beauty dwell,
Ye humbler scenes of rural life, farewell!
Mourn not your shades dishonoured by my praise,
Your shades which whilom learned far other lays;
For here of old, yon waving woods among,
With Waller's strains the joyful valleys rung.
Methinks his tuneful sprite still lingers here,
Still loves these scenes to all the muses dear;
Still the dear name charms with delightful sound,
And "Edmund! Edmund!" echoes all around.
  And thou, the master of this fair domain,
Vouchsafe t' accept this tributary strain.
To thee the muse her artless song commends,
Nor fears the fate of what thy smile defends:
She to thy friendship dares aspire, 'tis true,
And claims it as hereditary due;
Deem not base flattery framed the simple lay,
Nor turn thy disapproving ears away:
Parental cares watched o'er my growing youth,
And early stamped it with the love of truth;
But while they bade my words and thoughts agree,
They bade my heart to love and honour *thee!*

The following is the letter of thanks which Edmund Burke kindly addressed to me in response to my poetical tribute:–

EDMUND BURKE TO MARY SHACKLETON.

"My dear Miss Shackleton,

I ought not to have suffered myself to remain so long at a disadvantage in your mind. My fault is considerable: but not quite so great as it appears; for your letter went round by the way of Carlisle, and it was a good while before it came to my hands. It ought indeed to have been my care to have made the earliest possible acknowledgment, where nothing more was required; and in a case where indeed there was little more in my power to do than to tell you, in a few plain and sincere words, how extremely sensible I was of the honour you have done me, by making this family and this place the subject of some of the most beautiful and most original verses that have for many years been made upon any place or any persons. They make us all a little the more fond of ourselves and of our situation. For my part I will not complain, that when you have drawn a beautiful landscape, you have put an old friend of your father's as a figure in the foreground; nor shall I pretend that I am not pleased even with the excess of partiality which has made him an object worthy of appearing in such a scene. The scene itself, fine as it is, owes much to the imagination and skill of the painter; but the figure owes all to it. You great artists never draw what is before you, but improve it up to the standard of perfection in your own minds. In this description I know nothing of myself; but what is better, and may be of more use, I know what a good judge thinks I ought to be. As to your picture of this part of the country, I cannot help observing that there is not the least of commonplace in it. One cannot apply it equally to every country, as most things of this kind may be turned. It is particular and appropriate, and that without being minute or tedious in the detail. Indeed it is a sweet poem; and shows a mind full of observation, and retentive of images in the highest degree. Some of the lines are not quite so finished as to match the rest, and some time or other I may take the liberty of pointing them out to you; and some of the rhymes hitch upon words to which nothing, not even you, can give grace. But these are lesser blemishes, and easily effaced, either by omission, or a trivial change. You will excuse this freedom. But in so fine a poem, in which your kindness for an old friend of your father has given me so great an interest, you will naturally expect that I should wish for the perfection which I know you can give *your* work with a little more of *your* care.

Pray excuse this very late and very imperfect acknowledgment of the great favour you have done me. I cannot plead business in favour of my delay. I have had a great deal of leisure time. At the moment I write this, I never was more busy in my life; and indeed thus much is in favour of activity and occupation, that the more one has to do, the more one is capable of doing, even beyond our direct task.

I am ever, with Mrs. Burke's, my brother's, and my son's most affectionate regards to you, and to all Ballitore, which we love with great sincerity,

My dear Miss Shackleton,

your most faithful

and most obliged and obedient

humble servant,

EDMUND BURKE.

Beaconsfield, Dec. 13th, 1784."

On receiving the above letter, I penned the following stanza: –

> If I am vain, this letter read,
> And let it for my pardon plead.
>   When he whom listening courts admire,
> A senate's boast, a nation's pride,
>   When Burke commends my artless lyre,
> I care not who commends beside;
> And his reproof I value more
> Than ere I valued praise before!

After leaving Beaconsfield, my father and I went to a far different scene, and amongst singularly different people – to a little village in Yorkshire, and on a visit to some very primitive relatives, amongst whom my father left me for a while. Many amusing passages occurred during my stay. Quite regardless of my blushing shamefacedness, my relations invariably introduced me to their friends as "Our coosin frae Ireland that maks the bonnie verses;" which was frequently followed by the entreaty, "Say some of them, wilt thoo?" The place was remarkably secluded, and shut out from the world. Retired as was my native place, this was still more so; and primitive as were the inhabitants of Ballitore, they were fashionable people of the world compared with those of Selby. The "great hoose," where the squire resided, was the object of their exceeding admiration, and my relatives were most anxious that I should obtain an entrance, yet dubious whether I should be esteemed worthy of an invitation, although the owner graciously permitted his silver coffee–pot to be sent to every house in the village where I was entertained, to do me due honour as a visitor.

At length the much–coveted invitation came, and, dressed in their "best bra's," my cousins went with me to the great house. There I saw the coffee–pot at home, with its grand adjuncts in all their splendour. After tea was over, the company were invited to ascend to the roof of the house. Upon scrambling out upon the leads, we found chairs placed for our accommodation, and refreshments were handed round. Beneath a broiling sun I strove to admire the surrounding landscape, which was not at all worth the toil and trouble we endured. At length the silent, stately visit was concluded, and we were permitted to descend and return home; but all through the remainder of my stay this evening was descanted upon by my cousins with delight, and every acquaintance was saluted with, "Dost know our coosin was at the great hoose to tak tea?" As is usual in that part of England, there was in the dwelling of my friends one large apartment, neither parlour nor kitchen, called "the hoose," in which the family usually sat, but they insisted on my sitting in solitary state in the parlour. On First–days, after meeting, the old folk sat in "the hoose," each with a Bible in hand, reading aloud from it, while the daughter read in her Bible, also aloud; and, peering over my shoulder, stood the son behind my chair, reading aloud from the Bible which I was silently studying. No two of the readers, except myself and my companion, were perusing the same part of the sacred volume. Yet, notwithstanding their peculiarities, I was happy in the warm affection of these simple people, and always remembered this visit to England as some of the golden days of my youth: Beaconsfield and Selby were both so interesting and so different.

During the winter of 1784 a frost set in, and continued so hard for some weeks, that an American visitor said it equalled the cold of his native country. One night my mother heard a crackling noise in her room, and in the morning found her water–jugs fallen to pieces, but their shape remaining in solid ice. We were in the midst of this frost and snow, when a young stranger hastily entered the parlour; he looked round – fastened his ardent black eyes first upon one, then on another, with a mingled expression of anxiety and pleasure, as he exclaimed, "Don't you know me? – Don't you know me? – Don't you know Tom Eyre?" The exclamations and warm welcomes which succeeded soon convinced him that he had found again the same friends he had left. Ten years had made much alteration in his person, and the deep tinge which his face and hands had acquired from foreign suns and foreign gales, formed a striking contrast with the original whiteness of his skin when he drew up his shirt sleeve to display it. He had indeed grown a fine young man, and his manners without having lost their originality had received from intercourse with the world a pleasing polish. When the first ferment of our joy at seeing our friend had in some degree subsided, it was but natural to look for another. "Where is Sam? – shall we not see him also?" Then it was that a cloud passed over his countenance, and his trembling accents became full of sorrow as he said, "I expected to have met Sam in Ireland – but Sam is dead – and all the world is now alike to me." "Sam dead! Our dear Sam; so good, so beautiful, so beloved. When, where, and how did he die?" "He died as he was just about to return home, and he died of a broken heart!"

Then followed the sad story. Sam was running on fast in the career of naval glory – had attained, by his dauntless bravery, the rank of first lieutenant of a man–of–war, and with a handful of men had taken possession of a fortified place of strength, the name of which has escaped my memory. The governor requested some indulgence, which the generous and unsuspicious young warrior, incapable himself of treachery, readily granted, – but he had not to do with such a mind as his own. The governor availed himself of this indulgence, and secretly delivered up the place to the East India Company. The gallant youth, thus traitorously robbed of fame and fortune, when he was on the point of returning home, crowned with both, to the embraces of his brother, sunk beneath the cruel blow and the weight of disappointment. A burning fever seized him, he struggled against it, held to his post on ship–board, and died in his clothes. He died at Calcutta, at the age of twenty–two! "If amongst the many officers who laid down their lives in this war," said poor Tom, "there are any who have gone to heaven, surely my brother Sam is one of them!" In every turn of events, great or small, the idea of his darling Sam seemed to pervade his brother's mind. While he was with us, a child died in the village. I asked Tom, whose medical skill was considerable, to accompany me to see the infant, hoping that the vital faculties were but suspended. He went with me, and I asked him could he do anything for it. "No," he replied, "unless I can bring the dead to life, and if I could do that, I would fly to the East Indies to restore my poor Sam!"

He dwelt much on the subject of his brother's valour, and this dear brother had by letter informed me of Tom's, particularly at the battle of Long Island. Tom, whose courage was sincere, and therefore unsullied by boasting, made little account of his own exploits, but declared his forlorn situation was the cause of his promotion; for having neither money, friends, nor interest, he could not, as the other volunteers did, go into winter quarters, and as he continually followed the army, his name was returned every month to General Howe amongst the men fit for duty. He endured all the hardships of a common soldier, and without pay, which he would not accept until he earned a commission; he was therefore not so much under the control of the officers, and was at liberty, as a volunteer, to change from one corps to another if he deemed himself badly treated, for his high spirit could not brook an affront. After escaping many dangers he was taken prisoner by the Americans, and hurried from place to place, worn out by fatigue, and by the dispiriting thought that he was now forgotten by the British general, forlorn, friendless, a prisoner! In this situation he learned by accident that fortune and his general had remembered him, and that he was appointed second lieutenant in the 23rd regiment. Soon after, the general sent him thirty guineas, he bought a horse, and made his escape to the English army then quartered at Philadelphia; but was not permitted to join his regiment until his general received assurance from the enemy that he had not broken his parol.[41] I believe Tom Eyre would have found it a far easier thing to die than to break his word of honour.

He served four months in the fleet and obtained prize money, which enabled him to purchase a first lieutenancy in the 35th regiment. After the conquest of St. Lucia, which he represented as an extraordinary feat of valour, he was stationed there. He called it "a dungeon in hell," and said the plagues of Egypt were not to be compared to the sufferings they endured there. His health, which had supported him under all his toils and hardships, forsook him. He saw his brother soldiers droop and die around him, victims to the fatal climate, and amongst them Rupert Preston Vallancey, his quondam schoolfellow, who however did not appear to recollect him; "But," said he, "the land–crabs soon had him." "Land–crabs!" we asked, "what are they?" "Crabs which burrow in deep holes in the earth and feed on the dead; they fattened prodigiously after we were stationed at St. Lucia." "This remark implies that you have been reduced to eat them! Can it be possible?" Alas, it was possible, for the evils of pestilence were aggravated by those of famine. The large and poisonous reptiles which infested this marshy, woody island were another source of dismay, especially as the dog–headed snake, twenty–two feet long, had caused the death of two of the soldiers by its venomous bite. Alligators eighteen feet long, and bats whose spread wings were as wide as his extended arms, made a dreadful variety. A hurricane came, of which he could find no words to give us an adequate idea, but after its fearful violence had subsided the air was clearer and the island more healthful. While at St. Lucia he chanced to meet with several Ballitore boys, and although they had not been cotemporaries, they hailed one another as brothers. He endured this dreadful climate for five years, and was sick for ten months, when at length he got leave of absence. The island of Barbadoes he called "divine," being beautifully planted with cocoa trees, and the scenery diversified with hills, viewed from which the surrounding sea enriched the landscape. But England was more congenial to his heart, and Ireland was dearest of all. The temperate climate, the commodious dwellings, and the beauty of the rural damsels, whom he declared to be "fair and sweet as the daisy, and as innocent," refreshed his mind, wearied with the ardors of the torrid zone.[42]

The loss of America was a subject on which he could not speak with patience; he insisted that the British army were able to conquer the Americans, and they would have done so had not General Howe been restrained by orders from home, where they knew nothing about it. He was provoked beyond all patience at those fellows, "with their big wigs and enjoying their ease," presuming to direct the brave soldiers. "America," said he, while indignation flashed from his eyes, "America is manured with the blood of our noble fellows, and we have lost it!" His description of the wasting march of their army, plundering the houses, dislodging the families, and then burning the dwellings, was heart–rending. Then he told of the excitement which urges on the heat of the battle; how rage subsides when the fight is over, and both parties engage indiscriminately in rendering the offices of humanity to the wounded: how treacherous and vindictive an enemy the Americans were, and how generous and gallant the French; how dreadful the taking of New York was made by the Americans setting it on fire, and what care the English took to protect the inhabitants and to prevent plunder in a captured town. All these topics were as interesting as they were terrible. Poor Tom Eyre did not pause to consider that the Americans were the party aggrieved, and that the French were not fighting for their own freedom.

But it was not without much effort and dexterous management that I could prevail upon Tom to give anything like a regular series of his adventures, for every now and then the recollection of some old acquaintance would dart across his mind, and break the thread of his narrative – a narrative rendered intensely fascinating by the enthusiasm and glowing warmth with which he identified himself with the details, by the simplicity of his manner, and the total absence of self-praise. Once, when he had my whole soul thrilling with interest, he suddenly stopped, and then uttered a passionate wish to see the old stone which stood at the corner of our Burrow gate. The famous treaty–stone in the city of Limerick could not have created a keener interest in the lovers of historical relics, than did this unrecorded one in the affectionate memory of Tom Eyre.

Several alterations and improvements had been made in the old mansion and grounds since he left Ballitore. The vest of winter was at this time spread over the fields; had they been decked in the pride of summer, they could not have found favour in his eyes. He bitterly regretted the changes in the house, declaring they made no improvement. Every thing in Ballitore appeared to him to be on a smaller scale than formerly. This natural sensation is easily explained. Children measure objects by their own size and experience, which increase with years, while the objects remain the same.

He told us he had written several letters to us from America: these had never come to hand. He brought one which he had written to his friend "Peggy," and which he had not been able to forward. Tom had brought a dog with him from the West Indies, for he must have something to love and to be kind to; he called him "Choque." We had a black cat, which would have been accused of witchcraft had she lived in the last century, for she knew how to open the doors, and would enter the parlour with demure pace when least expected. She kept entirely out of the place whenever a friend of ours who had an antipathy to cats visited us; she murdered one rival, and, on the introduction of another, finally disappeared. This black cat and Choque engaged in a furious combat. They were with difficulty separated, and the cat vanished. A year afterwards Choque attended his master again to Ballitore; immediately on entering the parlour, the battle was recommenced with as much spirit as though they had been parted but a moment before; and again the poor cat vanished during the stay of the obnoxious visitors.

When Tom Eyre took his leave he brought me two letters, which were all that the vicissitudes of war had permitted him to receive from his brother

Sam. "Take these," said he impressively; "these are all of Sam which remains to me. In the hurricane of St. Lucia I preserved these, my commission, and my letters to Peggy. I preserved nothing else – nothing in the world. Take these letters; keep them safe for me; I am afraid I cannot take proper care of them!" I received the precious deposit, and seven years afterwards I resigned the packet to Tom's wife, Theodosia Eyre. With Tom's permission I made extracts from those letters, for I feared too frequent handling of them would injure them. At the close of one he transmits to his brother the salutary counsel which he had received from their old master, desirous that he too should reap advantage from it. "A military person ought above all to be distinguished for his piety. Marshal Turenne of France and Colonel Gardiner of England were as famous for their attention to the duties of their church and their duty to their Creator, as they were renowned for their courage in the service of their King and country. Keep such bright models of imitation before thy eyes, and never be ashamed to be religious." Sam's second letter concludes thus: "Success and happiness attend the British arms! From my heart I pray it; but with greater fervency, I must confess, I earnestly beseech the Giver of all good things to heap his blessings on you in particular. Farewell, my dearest brother, and if this should be the last letter you receive from me, don't be afraid; if you should never see me here again, do not grieve for me, but hope with me that once more we may meet from whence we shall never part. And, dear, dear Tom, do, and I hope I shall, endeavour that our meeting shall be as happy a one as it will be perpetual. Farewell, dear Tom; once more farewell, my brother! May God bless you, is the sincere prayer of your truly loving brother." This was indeed the last letter Tom received from his beloved brother, nor did they ever meet again in this world. O war! relentless and destructive! How many noble victims have been sacrificed at thy shrine!

Tom Eyre never seemed able to comprehend the science of etiquette. On meeting an old acquaintance in one of the busiest streets of Dublin, he flung decorum to the winds, and, yielding to his emotions of delight, he folded his friend in his arms, repeatedly kissing him, and uttering exclamations of joy, to the no small amusement of the passers-by. Meeting my mother and another equally "plain" friend walking together in Dublin, he requested that they would each take an arm, and permit him to escort them. My mother declined his assistance, explaining to him that the striking contrast between their singular attire and simple appearance and those of a young officer dressed in his full regimentals would expose them to ridicule. Tom complained loudly and bitterly that his regimental coat should be the means of preventing him from walking with his "old mistress," and declared he would never wear it again in her company.

Peace was now proclaimed (1784), and the many young officers with their sunburnt complexions and foreign accents whom we continually saw in the streets of the metropolis, formed an interesting spectacle. Our poor Tom had only got leave of absence on account of his health, and was to rejoin his regiment at Grenada, where he expected to fall a victim to the sultry clime. The pleasure of preventing such a disaster was reserved for his old friend. When I accompanied my father to visit Edmund Burke, I mentioned the circumstance to him. His brother, Richard Burke, who had once been Governor of Grenada, got a memorandum from me of the name, rank, and regiment of Tom Eyre, and promised to try if he had interest sufficient to procure for him a longer furlough. I did not know how far my application had succeeded, but heard that my friend was still in Ireland. When I next saw him he told me his pay had been stopped for four months, and he had received orders to join his regiment without delay, when all of a sudden, to his great surprise, those orders were revoked, his pay restored, and a furlough for six months longer granted, at which time his regiment was expected to return. He could not tell by what means this favor had been granted, and, when I told him, it did not lessen his satisfaction, nor did I think him less grateful because he expressed no surprise, but appeared to consider it as a service which a sister might and ought to render to a brother.

Shortly after having become a captain, he introduced his wife to us, on their way to their quarters at Clonmel, where he rejoiced in the society of his old friend, my sister Grubb, and her family. His wife was a very little woman, a native of England; he told us she was very amiable, but she had little opportunity of display, for her husband scarce ceased talking of old adventures, admiring old scenes, and reprobating new. He sought his brother Ned's grave in our little enclosure. He kissed little George Shackleton, and declared he had his brother Sam's innocent smile; and he confessed that he had wept for his favourite dog Choque, whose attachment to his master, whom he followed to too great a distance, caused his death.

John St. Clair was amongst those who returned home at the end of the war. As we had heard he was dead, my father was pleasantly surprised by meeting his old pupil. Some months afterwards, my father, sister, and I being in Mountmellick, and learning that St. Clair was lying very ill at the lodgings of his father, whose regiment was stationed in that town, we called to enquire for him. His father received us affectionately, and, telling us we should grieve to see his son's situation, led us to him. The physician of the town and the surgeon of his father's regiment were in the sick room, his sister was there also, and in an easy chair sat our poor St. Clair, far gone in consumption, and exceedingly weak. He was unable to rise to meet us, but, while he gave us his poor emaciated trembling hand, his sunken eye became enlivened, and his wan, hollow cheek displayed the dimples which used to adorn it when it was plump and ruddy. His voice was very low, yet he talked a good deal. He praised America, its climate, and the situation of the inhabitants before the war; he lamented the measures, which had been pursued, but did not inveigh against the Americans as Tom Eyre had done. He had not smarted like poor Tom under the sufferings of war; his hardships were caused by returning home in a leaky vessel, in which he was near suffering shipwreck, and wet and fatigue laid the foundation of his present illness. He informed us that he was a captain of foot in a new regiment, which, being reduced, he was then on half–pay.[43] But his favorite topic was Ballitore, every stick and stone about which he seemed to remember. Many a juvenile adventure he recalled; his flute, his schoolfellows, our favorite walks were all talked of, and sickness and dejection were forgotten. The army surgeon said jocosely he now saw the reason of St. Clair's attachment to the Quakers; but this was no time for jocularity. The distressed father cast mournful looks alternately upon his son and upon us; he covered his face with his hand, and his tears fell upon the table on which he leaned. Several times he left the room, being unable to remain and witness his dying son's delight in recalling the days of his childhood; and when, at parting, my father expressed his wishes for his son's restoration, he could not utter a word. His sister took less pains to conceal her feelings; her apron was sprinkled with the tears which streamed down her face. Ours we suppressed, though it would have been luxury to indulge them, for I thought I never had witnessed a scene so affecting. This interview so revived poor St. Clair's spirits, that he seemed much better, and declared his hope of perfect recovery if he were once more under his old mistress's care. Accordingly it was so arranged, and he cherished the hope of coming to us; and even his ravings were of Ballitore. Soon – ah! very soon – a letter reached me from his father informing me of his death. He added: "the principles established under your good father give me every reason to hope he has exchanged for the better; but it requires more fortitude than I am possessed of to stand this shock as I ought to do."

Poor young St. Clair had told me he did not prefer a military life, but his father, thinking, I suppose, that his advancement in the world would be more speedy by placing him in the army, procured him a commission, and sent him to join the troops in America. I am inclined to believe that his being thus the remote cause of his son's death preyed upon the poor man's heart, and urged him to commit the deed of desperation by which he put a period to his own existence about six months after the death of his son.

Meeting thus with my old schoolfellows after long separation aroused new sensations in my heart. There was a satisfaction mingled with the pain of beholding poor St.Clair; and the lively pleasure which Tom Eyre's return occasioned was tinged with a pensive shadow; for, besides his being unaccompanied by our precious Sam, there were many sad ideas awakened, – of the memory of departed friends, of terror at the dangers he had escaped, and apprehension of those which still awaited him. We might almost literally say,

We twa hae paidlet i' the burn
Frae mornin' sun 'till dine,
But seas between us braid hae roar'd
Sin auld lang syne!

CHAPTER VI.
1784.

THIS year the small–pox deprived my brother and sister Chandlee of their fine little Betsy. My mother, who seemed born to sympathise and to comfort, was not absent from her daughter at this trying time. She was awakened at seven one morning by the sound of sweet soft music. She knew it was no mortal harmony and it seemed to her the song of an ascending spirit. Perhaps it was so, for her little grand–daughter expired at that moment. My mother was very free from belief in preternatural occurrences, yet this and the following circumstances of a similar character made an impression upon her mind which no reasoning from natural causes could remove.

Death now prepared an arrow destined deeply to wound all our hearts, and to sever the endearing tie which bound Jonathan Haughton to his family. He took ill of a low fever, and the symptoms soon became alarming. O, how loth were we to resign our kind–hearted neighbour, our dear, engaging friend! And with what horror and anguish did his children anticipate the loss of such a father! All Ballitore was sad; the hours, dark with the gloom of suspense, rolled on, and the eleventh day of the fever arrived. It was a dreadful crisis, and nature sank. His daughters Hannah and Sally were beside him, watching and endeavouring to alleviate the last struggles, when a solemn sound of exquisite sweetness suspended their agonies and repressed their tears, and the gentle spirit then departed. Whether this seemingly preternatural circumstance was permitted in order to console the survivors is a mystery into which I may not pry.

Jonathan Haughton died the 25th of the Eighth month, 1785, the day twelvemonth that Anna Taverner's return to it as an inmate had diffused such joy through that house, now the house of mourning. The sweet sympathy of such a friend was felt to be a blessing; and time, which could never obliterate the image of their dying father, assuaged those feelings whose violence would otherwise have destroyed those who possessed them.

One of the tenderest of fathers to all his children, they believed without jealousy that Debby had the strongest hold on his affections. Her health had begun to fluctuate before this event; from this time it evidently declined, and the loss of her father seemed to sink deeper and deeper. Her dreams presented his gracious form coming to relieve her from distress; and often, her waking thoughts representing his death as an illusion, she fancied he was only from home, and thought of preparing for his return. The tenderness of her sisters spared her much exertion, and the languor of declining health disposed her yet more to indulge in melancholy reflections.

Their aunt Elizabeth Haughton, after having assisted a while in the care of my brother's family, much beloved and respected by the master and mistress and their household, retired from the bustling scene to the family of Jonathan Haughton. Here a consumptive disorder, which she imputed to cold caught in a summer shower, seized upon her, and its slow and certain progress baffled the affectionate, attentive care of the family. Her last exertion was to repay the kindness of her brother-in-law by her offices of love and assistance in his last illness. She was remarkable for her tenderness to the sick or distressed, and she experienced on her own dying bed those kind attentions which she was wont to administer. She mentioned to my mother her belief that she had worn out her constitution by using more exertion than she was equal to, or than was required of her; which she acknowledged to be wrong. She was often tried with great poverty and depression of spirit; but at the last was favoured with a sweet peaceful calm for which she expressed her thankfulness, as also her admiration that it should be granted to her mind, which was wont to be so tossed. But the sincerity of her heart was known to Him who rewarded it.

We were surprised by a visit from Murray Kathrens, one of my father's former pupils. As it was not unusual for him to call to see us, our surprise was occasioned only by the great alteration which appeared in his countenance. He who always looked as if he was stifling a laugh, and seldom spoke but to excite one, now exhibited a picture of deep melancholy. An unfortunate change in his circumstances had taken place; but it is likely his exertions would have restored them to a prosperous condition, had not his mental faculties fallen a sacrifice to his misfortunes. We were soon sensible that the noble and most sovereign reason was dethroned and deeply lamented that grievous calamity. Our poor friend now talked of becoming a Quaker; now believed it his duty to inspect prisons as Howard was doing; and now, in agony of distress, and with a flood of tears, exclaimed, "O, the feelings of a husband and a father!" Goodnature survived the wreck of intellect; hearing that Abby Widdows' affairs were embarrassed, and her spirits depressed, he paid her a visit, and endeavoured to comfort and advise her. The conversation of my mother had a soothing effect upon him, and now and then through the gloom of his mind some flashes of his native humour appeared; he recalled some of his early adventures, and reminded my mother of her vain attempts to improve his brown complexion by washing him with tansy and buttermilk. Again the clouds gathered and all was dark. His friends placed him in Swift's hospital for lunatics, where he lived several years, but never recovered his reason.

A few months after this visit from poor Murray, his cousin, George Kathrens, who had also received his education here, surprised us as much as Murray had done. We knew him to have been a respectable citizen, and were shocked to hear him asking pecuniary relief; but these feelings were changed to others not less painful, when we found that embarrassed circumstances had subverted *his* reason also, and that he had just escaped from a place of confinement. His insanity was of a different kind from his cousin's; he was merry, exulted in his escape, made verses, and said he was taught this art by the fairies, who cheered him with their songs, and in whose society he was very happy. He was brought back to Dublin, but soon broke loose from confinement, and his heart, true to the remembrance of his happy childhood, again impelled him to Ballitore, where, complaining bitterly to his old friends of the harsh treatment he had met with, he showed them with great indignation the marks which cords had left on his legs. His family found means to restrain his wanderings, but I believe his mind never was restored to sanity.

My father corresponded regularly with Edmund Burke, who sent all his publications to Ballitore. In a copy of the first edition of his "essay on the Sublime and Beautiful," printed in 1757, and presented by him to the friend of his youth, is written by his hand,[44]

To Mr. Richard Shackleton from the Author.

–

> "Accipe et haec, manuum tibi quae monumenta mearum
> Sint; et longum testentur amorem."[45]

Although not politicians, we read with avidity the speeches of Burke as they appeared in the newspapers, and felt interested in the fate of every measure seconded by him. My father and mother loved him as their steady and sincere friend, and perhaps we young folks extracted some gratification of our vanity from so illustrious an aquaintance. We certainly listened with pleasure to my mother's anecdotes of his assisting her to pick bogberries, and remarking how well they might be chosen by feeling, without the help of the eyes; how kindly he settled her on a car, when setting out to a meeting, and, pondering on what carriage she could travel in with most ease, recommended the bolted-down chair; how impressively he remarked that humility was what was wanting in the world, and how much his unassuming manners set an example of that virtue. Again, my father told of the pursuits of their youth, when they climbed the heights of learning and plucked the flowers of poetry together. He regretted the loss of his poem in praise of the Blackwater, and of a translation from Theocritus in competition with which my father attempted one of his own. He remembered that in Burke's version of the passage in which Venus despatches her Loves in search of the boar which had wounded Adonis, were the following lines, containing an idea not to be found in the original: –

Him the Love who rules the strong
With his bow–string dragged along;
While the Love who rules the slow
Lashed him onward with his bow!

A paragraph in a newspaper in 1785 alarmed us extremely. It ran thus: – "Mr. Burke lies dangerously ill. The news of his son's having been lost a few days since in his passage from Harwich to Holland has had such an effect on his health that his recovery is now very doubtful." Very soon after, "the death of Mr. Burke" was announced, accompanied by the following sketch of his character:– "By the death of the late Mr. Burke the world has lost an ornament, society a pleasing member, the poor a patron, and mankind a friend. As it would be impossible to do justice to his real worth within the limits prescribed by custom for that purpose, let it suffice to say that, in the several duties of husband, father, master, and benefactor, he acquitted himself in a manner which did honour to human nature, and in the fifty–seventh year of his age he died as much lamented as he had lived beloved." "Nothing more," said a friend, when he pointed out this character to me, "could be said." My heart was too full to contradict this assertion, which was meant good–naturedly as a ground for consolation; but I thought much more might be said. True, the most valuable part of his character was there; the duties of the private walks of life had been eminently well filled; yet must the splendid gifts bestowed by an all–wise Giver pass unnoticed? Where is the statesman whose mind comprehended such an extent of knowledge? – the orator whose irresistible eloquence poured conviction like a flood? – the luminary on whom the eyes of Europe were turned? Were these to glide from the world unattended by the voice of public regret? Yet the previous reports we had heard of the death of young Richard Burke, and the distress which we knew must overwhelm the heart of his father, the fact that his illness had been mentioned, and that his age agreed with the account in the newspaper, called forth our most painful apprehensions.

My father disbelieved these reports, yet, I thought, felt a secret dread; he wrote to his friend, and while we waited for a deliverance from this bondage of suspense, many who could not know more than ourselves thought, I suppose, that it added to their consequence to speak decisively upon it, and they teazed us with conjectures which were mostly unfounded. However, the clouds began to break; the silence of succeeding newspapers encouraged hope; and I thought the person of our neighbour the Rev. Thomas St. Lawrence never appeared more elegant, his countenance more intelligent, his manner more engaging, nor his conversation more interesting, than when he assured me that the character I had read referred to Dominick Burke, the agent of the public charities in Dublin; and thus the news of the death of a gentleman of worth, benevolence, and public usefulness conveyed to my heart a sensation of joy with which death had never inspired it before. Our illustrious friend had replied immediately to my father's inquiry. The welcome day arrived which brought the welcome letter to "his oldest friend," as the generous Edmund styled my father. His son was then safe and well at Paris, the vessel in which he crossed having narrowly escaped being overtaken in a dreadful hurricane which had done much mischief on the coast of Holland. The distress of mind which his parents suffered while ignorant of their son's fate furnished the ground of this report. That silent and grateful joy which is peculiar to relief from suspense now diffused itself over our hearts, and I felt that this was indeed one of the white days of my life.

In the following year, 1786, Edmund Burke paid his last visit to Ballitore; he was accompanied by his son, and on the 23rd of Tenth–month they gave us a most pleasant surprise. The great man could not, I think, possibly have appeared to more advantage than while he again reviewed the scenes of his youth. He remembered where the trees had stood which stood no longer, and greeted those which remained as old acquaintances; the alterations in the buildings were not unnoticed, and with peculiar delight he went through the apartments of the school–house, and walked in the Four–tree–field. He called to see all those with whose families he had formerly been acquainted; and his finished politeness was mingled with so much good–nature and simplicity that they delighted while they flattered his friends. The village was all agape while the distinguished strangers made the tour of it, attended by the old master and most of his family; and the patriotic comber, Ames May, declared he would see the great Burke, suppose he lost his day's work by it. "Hast thou ever heard of Edmund Burke?"

queried my father of Joshua Webster, who had just handed to the graceful stranger a bowl of the cider which he was making in Aunt Fuller's orchard. "He is now drinking your health," said Edmund, raising the bowl to his lips, and Joshua long remembered the friendly greeting. How pleasant was the evening he spent amongst us! My brother's family having joined ours, he expressed with much cordiality his pleasure in so comfortable a *Retreat* being afforded to the age of his friends, whose situation he reckoned enviable; and in our family harmony, with which, he said, "we were happy in being so near each other; but, were it otherwise, it would be well to have a kingdom between us."[46] Old William Gill, who had been servant to my grandfather when Edmund Burke was his pupil, and who loved him sincerely, and had been celebrated in his and my father's juvenile verses by the name of "Hobbes," came to behold this great and beloved man once more. With all his native suavity, our illustrious guest shook his humble friend by the hand often and cordially; while his son, who had shortly before been particularly noticed at the court of France, rose with graceful courtesy and came to his father's side to be introduced to poor old William, as to a venerable friend whose gray hairs demanded respectful attention. The old man's heart was full; he bowed, and bowed; told Edmund (I believe it was literally the case) that he was proud to see him, and added, "You have a great many friends in Ireland, sir!" "I am happy, Mr. Gill, that you are one of them," said Burke, and then congratulated Gill on wearing his age so well. He asked Gill if he thought him much altered, and, on William's replying he could not well see, he took up a candle and let his benevolent countenance beam on the delighted old man. I think no one could have beheld this action without admiring it. It was a subject worthy of the pencil of Burke's friend, Sir Joshua Reynolds. Next day they left us; my father, mother, and I escorted them part of the way, and, as if waking from a delicious dream, my mother and I took a last leave of father and son. I should not omit to say that the schoolboys were delighted with the sight of Edmund Burke, whom they declared to be "the cleverest fellow they had ever seen." My father, who generally attended the yearly meetings of London, had on these occasions frequent interviews with his friend, which were very pleasant to them both. At the time of the yearly meeting following my beloved father's death, I wrote a particular account of his illness and death to Edmund Burke, who soon after the sad event had written a very kind letter to me. I gave my letter to the care of my friend James Abell, who at my request took it himself to the house of Edmund Burke. John Pim accompanied him; the footman accosted them as his master's friends, and introduced them to the sitting-room without any previous enquiry, where Edmund and his wife received them with their accustomed kindness. Edmund opened my letter, looked at it, and, putting it by, said that was what he wanted. We had from henceforward few opportunities of intercourse with our illustrious friend, but he failed not, when opportunities did occur, to evince his continued regard for the family of him who had been so dear to him.

Our great neighbour Lord Aldborough cultivated a friendly intercourse with our family. His talents had been made the most of by a literary education, on which he seemed to value himself; his early education it is probable had not been equally attended to. His lady was an English woman of high rank; she was friendly, too, but she spent most of her time in her native land, and at those periods Lady Hannah Stratford presided at Belan. John Pemberton and Thomas Cash, ministers of our Society from England travelling on a religious visit, having appointed a public meeting in Ballitore, Lord Aldborough was amongst those invited, and he pressed so hard that these friends, with my father's and brother's families, should dine with him next day, that the invitation was accepted. Lady Aldborough was at home, the entertainment was suited to the rank of the entertainers, and to the marked respect and attention they destined to pay their guests. A year later, Lady Aldborough died suddenly at an inn in England, while on a journey with her lord; who, in a note to my brother, made affectionate mention of her worth and his regret. In 1787 he married a young Englishwoman, daughter to Sir John Henneker, and niece to the Duchess of Chandos, who accompanied her to Belan, and regaled Ballitore with the novel sight of a duchess.

Squire Keatinge now settled on his estate, and showed great kindness to his tenantry. People of all ranks respected him, and rejoiced to see in the representative of this ancient family a person of so much worth. In 1790 he married Lady Martha Brabazon, sister to the Earl of Meath. Of her it might truly be said,

> Her wit and beauty for a court were made;
> But truth and virtue fit her for the shade.

The old mansion–house at Narraghmore had been thrown down, and, till he had built a house fit to receive his bride, Squire Keatinge proposed taking one near her brother's seat at Kilruddery. He had previously occupied Battlemount, a genteel but small house, and she declared against his taking a new residence, saying if Battlemount suited him it would suit her also. They came home in a private manner, yet the tenants had heard of it, and lighted a bonfire. The bridegroom, on observing it, gave a crown to a man to put it out. Lady Martha soon became the delight of the neighbourhood, and the worthy pair took the lead not only in rank but in virtue. It was easy to perceive who were the Squire's tenants by the comforts around their cottages.

Ephraim Boake's daughter Abby, a beautiful girl of seventeen, was married to William Carter, a person of much respectability, advancing to the middle term of life. But his happiness was soon overcast. She came to her father's house at Boakefield to be confined, and gave birth to a son, but died two weeks after his birth. No danger was apprehended till very near the close of her life. She died in her father's arms; and in a few hours the father had to encounter a trial scarcely less severe; for he had to meet her husband, who came, filled with delight, on a second visit to his son, hoping to meet his darling wife in the parlour. Ephraim met him as he entered the gate; his looks announced the sad tidings, and the distracted husband fell to the ground like one shot. It was a most affecting sight to see him silently gazing upon the cold remains – a wife, a mother, and a corpse before her eighteenth year was completed. To the transports of his piercing grief the calm dignity of enduring sorrow succeeded. He had tenderly loved his wife, and he never entered into another matrimonial engagement.

The oldest man in the village at this time was Finlay McClane, a native of the Highlands of Scotland, who, to those who understood his native Gaelic, could relate the account of many a battle in which he had been engaged, including disastrous Fontenoy. He told us, and we all believed he told the truth, that he was born in the year 1689.[47] He was an out–pensioner of the Royal Hospital. His wife Mary was a very industrious body. One dark evening their chimney was perceived to be on fire. The neighbours ran thither affrighted, and Hannah Haughton put the jar of gunpowder which she kept for sale, out of the house. Mary McClane, a little, blunt, consequential woman, stood with her arms a–kimbo, and thus addressed the affrighted crowd: "Have you any thing to do at home? If you have, I advise you to go home and do it, for if I had fifteen chimneys I would clean them in no other way." Fortunately the house was slated, so the danger was the less. The old man at one time lay very ill in consequence of a fall which injured his hip and occasioned incurable lameness. "There he lies," said his sympathising helpmate, "and off that bed he will never rise." The poor man looked sorrowful at this denunciation, and turned his eyes wistfully, in silence, upon us; we blamed Mary for her apprehensions, at least for expressing them in this uncomfortable manner; and we encouraged Finlay, and soon had the pleasure of witnessing his recovery to health, though not to activity. He survived his matter–of–fact spouse, and his great age had not deprived him of sensibility, for he mourned her with many tears, as he attended her to her last home. In his hundred–and–tenth year, 1798, the old Highlander once more heard the sound of war, and saw the weapon of destruction aimed at his breast by a soldier; another soldier arrested the stroke, telling his comrade that he would never serve the king as long as that old man had done.

This year Robert Bayly purchased the Mill–field and the other parks belonging to that quarter from the representatives of John Boake.[48] He cut down the orchard, levelled the ditch, and threw it into the Mill–field. Joshua and Mary Haughton removed to the little thatched house where James and Nanny once lived. Robert Bayly gave it to them during their lives, as a testimony of his mother's and his own friendship for their relation Mary Haughton, who had lived there when a child; and now the cottage resumed its long forgotten neatness.[49]

William and John White had been a little more than a year at the school, when John, who was about eight years old, was removed by death from inflammation of the lungs. His sufferings were very great, though every means of alleviation were tried. The little creature wished to live, for life was in its delightful spring, yet he also said he would like to go to heaven, if he were sure of meeting his father and mother there.[50] His artless, endearing expressions, full of love to those around him, his entreaties for his brother not to cry, his grateful affection to his master and mistress, who he said were like a father and mother to him, added to the distress we felt in witnessing those pains which we could not relieve.

William Gill died this year, very far advanced in life, but having had a strong constitution, nature struggled against death, and the last morning of his life, when my sister Lydia went to visit him, she found he had got out of bed. She called assistance, and they had just got him into bed when he expired. He died in my brother's house, and was tenderly cared for to the last, as his faithful services well deserved. He had seen the fourth generation of the family he served, and his favourite little Ebenezer sat by his dying bed, and shook hands with him when near the close. He wished we might all be happy, and that heaven "might direct the navigation into the right port." Most of the family attended his funeral. This was a mark of respect my parents were accustomed to pay to their neighbours.

My brother's family were visited with the small–pox, and little Ebenezer was in great extremity. The child's mother left him that she might not see the last struggles, endeavouring to resign him, and to put from her mind the remembrance of his little virtues and his winning ways, dreaded the opening of the door, and the words which should announce that all was over. But the door was opened to relieve her agonizing suspense, and the child recovered.

This year my sister Sally appeared in the ministry, with humility and fear, and I believe she was universally approved, for her conduct was consistent with her office: the vessel was clean, and its contents were pure.

Our dear Sally Haughton's decline now became more rapid. She lost her voice, yet loved to hear us converse beside her. On First–day morning, the 15th of Third–month, 1789, she evidently changed for death; but when my mother tenderly bade her farewell, wishing for herself as peaceful a close, and retired in tears from her bedside, the invalid expressed her belief that her time was not quite so near, and so it proved. My sister Sally devoted herself night and day to her early friend, and to relieve and support her afflicted sister Hannah. It was a pitiful sight when our dying friend looked round upon us, and then at her mourning sister, and the happy scenes of childhood recurred to the mind, as if to increase the darkness of the present hour. Some days rolled heavily away, and still our dear sufferer felt the clogs of mortality. She could say but little, but she had not now to make her soul's peace, and what little she said manifested this. She acknowledged her sister's tenderness as a mercy granted to her; she loved to have her dear Sally Shackleton in her sight, and her last intelligible words were to her. She called for her brother John and spoke to him, but her words were now unintelligible; she could not make herself understood. She strove to write, but could not: this was very distressing. Next morning, the 20th, the last agonies came on; I could hear her heavy breathing as soon as I entered the house. The parlour was darkened, and John sat beside the fire, pale and sad. In the chamber of death sat poor Hannah, trembling and silent, shaded by the curtains from the view of her sister, not being able to bear the sight, yet afraid to leave the room lest she could not return. My sister Sally sat at the foot of the bed, watching the changes of the pale countenance. Oh, it was a solemn and impressive scene! And while we sat in mournful silence, I thought of those who perish on the field of battle, and that while we strove to fan the last spark of life, in how many is it suddenly and violently extinguished! But "the heart knoweth its own bitterness," and every thought still returned to the beloved object. It was nine o'clock in the evening when the painful breathing ceased, and the dear remains lay as in peaceful slumber. I had never before been present at the separation between soul and body. I took the intelligence to her brother; he had several times come into the room through this long dreary day, but could not remain there. When I told him that the struggle was ended, he rose, and walked backwards and forwards in agitation. I said I thought we should be thankful for her release. "It is hard to part," he said, and I forbore to urge those motives for consolation which reason in her own time offers, and which are too often urged upon the unattending ear of grief. The afflicted sister, worn with sorrow and fatigue, found in my sister a friend who could assist as well as sympathize, who performed the last offices for her lost companion, dressed the dear head, and cut the beautiful hair. Thus died our beloved Sally Haughton, having just completed her twenty–eight year. Her sister found some little token of remembrance for my sister Sally laid by, to be delivered after her decease, accompanied by the following note:– "And now, my darling friend, after struggling with my cough and shifting from side to side for an easy position, I have ventured to take my pen to request thou mayest accept this little token of my last remembrance. I know thou wilt think of me now and then, without any outward incentive thereto. Ah, why shouldst thou not? thou art and wilt be dearer to me than life. The boundless prospect of permanent felicity seems to assume new glories. Oh! may gracious Providence grant me a participation in those joys which at present I have but a slight foretaste of! Methinks I feel animated since I began to address thee; yet, notwithstanding, I must bid thee farewell. Oh, farewell! May kind Providence protect thee in all thy steppings! Remember and be as often as thou canst with the last surviving sister. Words could not express my love for thee!"

Old Edward Miles, the shoemaker, so long famed in the village for his surgical as well as his shoemaking skill, died very suddenly. He was regretted, being an ingenious, industrious man.

We lost our agreeable neighbour Joseph Haughton, who we hoped would have remained in his paternal mansion, but he thought it more eligible to engage in the cotton business in Dublin. In about two years he married Mary Wright, and settled in Ferns. He let his land to William Leadbeater.

My brother about this time declined taking any boys but those of our Society; and, in order to partake of the advantages of his school, several parents permitted their sons to conform in dress and language to the simplicity of our profession, and to attend our religious meetings.

Joshua and Mary (more commonly called Molly) Webster came to reside in Ballitore. They were members of our Society and were in low circumstances, but had seen better days. Their first dwelling here was on the turnpike road, as tenants to John Gavin, who was born a Quaker, but had long since forfeited his membership, and had married a very pretty woman outside our pale. John still esteemed himself a Friend, and had a particular seat in the meeting-house, on which if any one intruded it was on pain of his displeasure. He argued stiffly on points of doctrine, and quoted Scripture so well and so often, that his neighbours said it would be of little consequence if the Bible were lost, as Johnny Gavin had it by heart. Fronting the avenue which led to the village he had built himself a comfortable cabin, whose white walls, exalted situation, and supercilious master obtained for it the title of "Castle Gavin." One son was born to inherit his castle, his trade, and his assumed consequence.

Joshua Webster followed his business of wool-combing, and his wife Mary opened a school, a dame-school; and truly did she resemble Shenstone's exquisite description of a village schoolmistress. She had adopted this means of livelihood some years before, when her husband became unprosperous in his affairs. Poverty had not deprived them of the spirit of independence, and they struggled to preserve themselves from becoming burdensome to their friends. Joshua was a rough County Wexford man, good–natured, honest, and industrious. Mary's manners were accounted more polite. She had kept some genteel company in Athy in her youth, and was fraught with a variety of anecdotes. Her school was esteemed, and her pupils loved her. That she was in most things too superstitious was a shade in her character, yet her elder friends excused it, and her pupils having wondered at some of her tales, soon learned to laugh at them, yet without losing their respect for her. She had some skill in physic, and still more in surgery.

I must not omit to mention my "cousin Sam." Samuel Carleton, first cousin to my mother, had lately retired from business in Dublin, on a comfortable competency, and come to reside with my Aunt Carleton. He had several years before this time buried his wife, and all his children except an only son, who was universally beloved and esteemed, and whose good qualities consoled his father for all his losses. This young man married a pleasing young woman, and his father seemed to have nearly reached the summit of temporal happiness, especially when the prospect of a grandchild appeared. To the mansion house was added another parlour, pieces of plate decorated the sideboard, business throve, and everything wore the appearance of comfort. The first cloud over this cheerful scene was the premature birth and death of the expected heir, owing to a fright which the young mother met with. This disappointment was scarcely surmounted when Samuel's son was torn from his disconsolate father and afflicted wife by a fever. Universal regret prevailed on this occasion, and while Samuel followed the remains of all his earthly hopes to the grave, the spectators mournfully observed to one another, "There goes the poor father!" The young widow fell into consumption. The father–in–law spared no paternal care, soothed the rapid decline of the sufferer, and received her last sigh.

Having now no inducement to continue in business, he quitted the solitude of Dublin for the pleasing society of Ballitore. He was at this time nearly sixty years of age, of a portly person, and a benevolent countenance. He was exceedingly pleasant, cheerful, and conversable; and who so well qualified to chase *ennui* as cousin Samuel? He had a store of diverting anecdotes, which he related with a good grace, and joined heartily in the laugh, which they produced. I remember he was not quite so well pleased when a laugh was once raised at his own expense, particularly as he was never satirical himself, and his jokes wounded no one. He had the Carleton arms on the lid of his silver snuff–box; and in adding the motto, the correct words, "*Quondam his vicimus armis,*"– "With these arms we have conquered," – had been altered (through ignorance of Latin on the part of my cousin and his engraver) to "*Quondam his visimus armis.*" My father, for the life of him, could not restrain his wit on this occasion. He thought, "With these arms we have visited" extremely apropos to the snuff–box, and he said so. But though his wit was thus sportive, his good nature could repair its transgressions.[51] He loved the worthy relative of his beloved wife, and respected his age and his afflictions. They were frequently companions in travelling and in visiting, and when his friend Richard Beauchamp invited my father to the Glebe, he generally added, "Bring Carleton; everybody loves Carleton." Notwithstanding the flow of spirits which my cousin Sam possessed, it was often evident that he had received a deep and lasting wound. One evening, Hervey's Meditations being read aloud, the description of the death of a young man deeply affected the father's feelings; he wept, sobbed, and groaned without uttering a word. We were all full of sympathy; but he wished not to sadden any one, and, rapidly conquering his emotions, his cheerfulness returned. He died after eight years residence amongst us, regretted by all who had enjoyed his friendship.[52] He breathed his last in First–month, 1780, in the sixty–sixth year of his age.

Poor James Mc Connaughty, notwithstanding his industry and his integrity, was unfortunate in business. In 1778 his factor in Dublin failed, and James, on the following market day, shut the doors of his mill, and declared himself a bankrupt. The distress of himself and his wife was such as worthy, undesigning hearts must feel when conscious of having unwittingly injured others. They came to meeting as usual, for there they sought comfort and strength; but they took the lowest seats, and after meeting shrank away reluctant to be seen. The first private interview I had with my ever–dear "dada," he unfolded his sorrows to me in this moving couplet: –

> I who have been zealous in Zion's cause
> Am now become a transgressor of her laws!

As I wept bitterly at this self–accusation, accompanied as it was by the sorrowing looks and tears of my old friend, I was as much hurt as surprised at my father's hearty laugh when I repeated it to him. I knew him to be one of the last men in the world to laugh at misfortune; but he was conscious of his intention to succour, and therefore suffered himself to be amused by the combination of religion and poetry which expressed and soothed the distress of "honest James." That title his patron resolved he should maintain, though the voices of his creditors strove to deprive him of it. The debts amounted to about one hundred pounds; my father discharged them, took the mill into his own hands, and gave James a salary as overseer. As he was one of those who do better for others than for themselves, he was thus enabled to exchange the load of perplexity under which he had long groaned for the sweet burden of gratitude. Nanny was relieved from her cares and apprehensions; their appropriate seats in the meeting–house were resumed, and perhaps they never were more happily situated. And thus the even tenor of their humble life rolled on for some time longer.

As Nanny Mc Connaughty sat one day beside a sick and dying friend, she looked out of the window, and thought she saw her husband coming towards the house. She went down to meet him, he was not there, and when she went home she found he had not been out. She was shocked at the time, and was still more alarmed when James took ill of a pleuritic fever the very next day, for she believed that she had seen his fetch, as a forerunner of his death; and, trembling, she told my mother of the apparition. Now, whether Nanny was mistaken, or whether this warning was permitted to prepare her for the event, is still a doubt with some. The event was, however, fatal; in one week from this time Nanny became a widow. When James was ill, Nanny was also often ill from grief and terror, and I found her echoing his dying groans when I went to take a last leave of my dear old friend. I could not command myself to speak to him, for I was greatly distressed. My mother soothed his mind by promising to take care of his dear Nanny, and when the conflict was ended and the spirit was released, the poor widow was brought to our house in a state which seemed to promise her a speedy re–union with him to whom she had been twenty–four years joined in the bands of happy conjugal love. My mother desired James's grave to be made large enough to lay Nanny therein, it not being unlikely that in a few days it might be opened to admit her; for my dear mother was remarkable for forecast. At the time of her husband's funeral, Nanny, while lying on her sick bed, was comforted by the sweetness which clothed her mind. By degrees she recovered her health, but her sadness was long in wearing off, and might have sunk her into a settled melancholy had she not taken an active part in the domestic concerns for which she was most qualified, and she said that James came to her in a vision and charged her to be sure and take care of the mistress. Whenever she related this vision, my father's pretended jealousy that *he* had not been mentioned used to amuse us in spite of our regret.

Our dear old Nanny McConnaughty exerted her feeble frame in the management of our domestic concerns more than, on account of her health, we desired; but it was in vain we attempted to relieve her. It was with great reluctance she sometimes resigned the key of the pantry; for the key of the dairy a solicitation would be fruitless, her strict integrity not permitting her to hazard the chance of any thing been wasted under her care. She asked my mother's leave to give away broken meat at her own discretion, as she was unwilling to trouble her by frequent applications, and was not easy in her mind to give what was not her own, without this permission. We, who knew the sincerity and simplicity of her character, knew that this was no parade of virtue; her gratitude to her protectors was a predominant feeling at all times, for when she dreamed that the doctor who attended her in a fever was about to bleed her to death, she desired him to hold his hand till she had given up her accounts to the mistress. And when a fall down a flight of stairs called forth the exclamation from a servant, "O Nanny, you're kilt!" her reply was, "Hush, hush, don't waken the mistress!" Though the memory of her dear James was ever accompanied by deep regret, she had recovered by degrees her spirits and her innocent cheerfulness, and the anecdotes which she told of her early life amused and instructed us.

In 1790 Nanny attended the funeral of my brother Abraham's eldest little girl, the first time of her entering the graveyard since her husband's remains were laid there. Probably she now felt that the time of her rejoining him was not far distant, for our dear old friend's life was gliding away more swiftly and yet more swiftly as it approached the ocean of eternity. A short time before her death she asked my sister Sally what she thought of her spiritual safety; my sister replied that she would gladly be in her case. My father was from home when she expired; he returned without having heard of the death of his friend, whose faithful services of forty years he fully appreciated. It was a great comfort to us to reflect that she had wanted for no care or attention in her pining illness; still greater consolation to reflect on her innocent and exemplary life! Such a life, such a death, outweigh all the dazzling accomplishments, all the brilliant talents which are too often the means of vanity and vexation of spirit. When I look back upon the life and death of this humble, simple woman, and others of like character, how does the wish arise to be enabled to live as useful a life and to meet a death as peaceful.

CHAPTER VII.
1791.

The author's marriage. – David and Winifred Doyle. – Thomas Wilkinson. – James White. – Death of Samuel Neale, and of Richard Shackleton. – Letters of condolence from Edmund Burke and Thomas Wilkinson. – Ballitore visited by a camel. – Prospect of emigration to France. – Ballitore Mill built. – Death of Job Scott. – Movement of troops, and illegal oaths. – Squire Keatinge a colonel. – Jack Moran's sick–bed repentance. – Death in the snow. – Dick Miles and Jacob Fuller. – Biddy Murray's prophecy. – Molly Haughton's fowling–piece. – Mary and Anne Doyle settle in Ballitore. – Tragical funeral of John Lecky. – Robbery of the mail. – A genteel begger. – Military intrusion. – Death of James Kathrens. – Visit to Ballitore of Benjamin Rotch, a native of Nantucket, New England. – Division among Friends. – Spread of Republican principles. – Death of Edmund Burke. – Letter from him to the author, dictated during his last illness. – Colonel Keatinge an M.P. – Sally Shackleton's travels in the ministry. – Robbery, arson, and other signs of civil war.[53]

105 to 119

IN 1791 I changed my name of Shackleton, and took that which belonged to my friend William Leadbeater. Our affection, which had for some years been reciprocal, was established on a solid foundation, and successive years have increased its stability, and have not decreased its tenderness. My husband now filled a different situation in life from that which had been marked out for him. The impressions he had received at Ballitore were not effaced by mixing with the world; the virtues of truth and simplicity, of which he had an example in his tutor, were not rivalled by the superficial graces of more fashionable life, which might have cast them into shade. He considered that, next to Divine assistance, which is ever near to the honest heart, his preservation from many snares was owing to the virtuous attachment he had formed in his early youth. He had joined the Society of Friends in 1786.

Some of our friends from Dublin attended our marriage. At the inn at Kilcullen where they lodged they met with a young woman whose tale of woe excited their compassion. She said she was an American; that her name was Matilda Brown; that she had spent four years in France for the purpose of education; that she was the only female passenger who escaped from the "Charlemount" packet, which was lost a little before this time; that as her trunk containing her money and clothes was in the ship, she was left destitute in a strange country; that the American vessel in which she had expected to return had sailed before she arrived; and that she was now journeying on foot to Kilkenny, having some knowledge of the Butler family. The hearts of these good people were moved; they paid her hotel bill, gave her money, and brought her to Ballitore, meaning to send her on her way; but her story gained her friends here, a subscription was raised for her, and she was kept as a guest at the bridal feast, where some pitied and some suspected her. I was of the pitying party, till she related to us after dinner the circumstances of the shipwreck and of her own escape, with a degree of composure which no one who had really witnessed such a scene could command. In a little time one of our friends made inquiry concerning those who were rescued from death at that awful time, and discovered that Matilda Brown was an arrant impostor, and he greatly lamented having brought a blot on our marriage feast by her presence. We respected his humanity, and were not disconcerted at the mistake he had made. A paragraph afterwards appeared in a newspaper, relating this circumstance, and relating it fairly.

My father's servant, David Doyle, from Rathangan side, married Winifred Byrne, my brother's cook. The young couple were a pattern to their poor neighbours. David was ingenious; he could read, and he made a bookcase for his little library; he also made for his cabin sash-windows which opened; and to this admission of fresh air we may in part impute his recovery from a long and dangerous fever. David had some propensity to drink; which perhaps his own good sense and care for his increasing family could scarcely have overcome, had he not possessed so excellent a wife. She managed his earnings with prudence, prepared his simple meals with neatness, indulged in no luxury but the cleanliness and regularity of her house, and received him ever with cheerful looks and a cheerful fire. I have been delighted with the scene which their cabin presented, when I have stepped in unexpectedly in the evening, and found the mother busy at her needle, the younger children asleep, and their father, after his days work, teaching his son to read. They were as poor as any of their neighbours when they began the world, and would have continued so had they sat smoking in the chimney corner, drunk tea and whiskey, and let their furniture rot with dirt. But they are now comfortable, have a cow, and have built an addition to their house – their children, as they grow up, bearing the stamp of a good education. Winny Doyle contrives to assist others, though she never sought for assistance for herself. Two of my daughters may boast that they were nursed by this good woman in her neat cottage.[54]

Anna Taverner attended the yearly meeting of London in 1791, and on the journey met Thomas Wilkinson, with whose native courtesy and simplicity of manners she was as much pleased as my brother had been with his hospitality and unaffected humility at his own house in Cumberland a few years before.[55]

James White, from Cork, a boy of fine disposition, possessed of an uncommon understanding and great thirst for learning, came to school this year.

In the spring of 1792 our long loved friend, Samuel Neale, of Springmount near Cork, died of a mortification in his foot. The last time he was at my father's house, a few months before his death, my father left his own bed, which we never before knew him to do, and slept in the room with Samuel, that he might attend to him in the night, his health being then somewhat interrupted. On his death-bed, Samuel said his thoughts day and night often turned upon his dear friend, my father, whom he called "a bright star." These two friends, "lovely and pleasant in their lives," were not long divided in their death.

And now I come to an event which it is most painful to record, my husband and I, with our little daughter had left my father's house for one of our own.[56] My father saw us but for a few days settled thus, and he took delight in visiting his daughter's new abode; in nursing his little granddaughter, whom he used to call Princess Elizabeth, and in contemplating our little circle; while we with reciprocal delight received his visits, and endeavoured to induce him to repeat them.

He left home to attend the Provincial School committee in Mountmellick, the 21st of Eighth-month, having bathed that morning, and set out in usual health and spirits. Before he reached Athy, he was seized with the symptoms of a putrid fever, which increased upon him after he got to Mountmellick, though he strove against it. The 24th his servant and horses returned and brought accounts of his illness from John Gatchell, at whose house my dear father lay as carefully attended as if by his own children. My brother and my sister Sally went to him; my heart seemed bursting, I longed so much to go; but it was thought best that I should stay with my dear mother till we should be sent for, in case it were necessary. A gleam of hope was succeeded by worse accounts; and on the 27th I went with Doctor Johnson to Mountmellick. I found the best of fathers dying, but heart-piercing as was the sight, my spirits were relieved, for I was with him. The disease had made rapid progress, yet my dear father's senses were for the most part preserved, and he was loving and even cheerful to those about him. When we arrived, he was just able to know us. Early on the morning of the 28th the last agonies came on. He had to endure not the pangs of a guilty conscience, but the struggles of death with an unbroken constitution, and his last words were, "The breasts of consolation!" Jonathan Pim had sent his carriage for my mother, and I thought it best to go in ours to meet her at Athy, so I left my dear, my honoured father before the conflict had ended. What were my sensations in this solitary journey, as I traced the ground I had often ridden over by my father's side! At Shane's Castle my mind suddenly became calm. I looked at my watch, it was eight o'clock, my imagination fancied it could hear whisperings in the sick chamber, and I thought perhaps the spirit was released. My mother had similar feelings at the same time, and we afterwards found that this was the moment of the departure. How melancholy was our meeting at Athy! "Am I a widow?" enquired our dear mother. "We shall have time enough to lament him all our lives!" said my deeply afflicted brother.

As we approached Ballitore on our return, I believe every person we met made enquiries of our servant, David Doyle. Many of the neighbours were standing at the doors of their houses watching for the intelligence, which was conveyed by the sad word, "Gone!" or a motion of the head, and was answered by some expression or gesture of sorrow. The dear remains, enclosed in a double–cased pitched coffin, were next day brought to Ballitore. It was feared that the disease had been communicated to him by the razor of the village barber, who had just before shaved a man that had died of putrid fever. The barber imprudently told my father of his having shaved the corpse, and it seemed to impress his mind. But if the very sparrows are cared for, how much reason have we to feel assured that such a life was under the Divine care, and would have been preserved by human means if unerring Wisdom had not made a better disposal. If the sympathy of kind friends could have healed our wound, it was not wanting. Our warm–hearted Samuel Haughton and his wife Jane – both dearly beloved by my father and dearly loving him – were amongst the foremost. When the account reached him in Carlow, he sent away all his workmen from their different employments, closed his place of business, and, resigning himself to grief, wept like a child. Several of our friends had dreams which seemed to portend this calamity; and my dear father had at different times before his death told us of having dreamed of his first wife, and of their sitting together in the yew bower, as in the days of their courtship; and frequently spoke of this companion of his youth, perhaps because the time of their re–union was so near.

My dear mother, who a little before my marriage had felt a numbness in her right hand, and for some time before an almost imperceptible decay of her mental powers, was so deeply penetrated by this affliction that the decline of her faculties was accelerated thereby. For some time we dreaded being bereft of her also; but her spirit was preserved from sinking amid those waves by that Hand on which alone she depended for consolation. Our dear sister Lydia, my brother Abraham's wife, bore a large share in this family grief. She was very dear to my father, and was strongly attached to him, and the poor little children wept sore. The vacuum his removal left was never filled up; but we have reason to confess that he was taken in the right time, and that the evening of his happy day, had it been protracted, would have been clouded with sorrow from various causes. It is a just and touching sentiment of my friend Thomas Wilkinson's: –

> Couldst thou thy part, as heaven the whole surveys,
> Perhaps thy sighs would change to songs of praise.

The testimony of his friend Edmund Burke, who could justly appreciate the character of him whom he had loved so long and so sincerely, ought, in justice to their mutual friendship, to find a place here: –

EDMUND BURKE TO MARY LEADBEATER.

"Beaconsfield, September 8th, 1792.

My dear Madam,

After some tears on the truly melancholy event, of which your letter gives me the first account, I sit down to thank you for your very kind attention to me, in a season of so much and so just sorrow to yourself. Certainly my loss is not so great as yours, who constantly enjoyed the advantage and satisfaction of the society of such a companion, such a friend, such an instructor, and such an example: yet I am penetrated with a very severe affliction, for my loss is great too. I am declining, or rather declined in life; and the loss of friends, at no time very reparable, is impossible to be repaired at all in this advanced period. His annual visit had been for some years a source of satisfaction that I cannot easily express. He had kept up the fervour of youthful affections; and his vivacity and cheerfulness, which made his early days so pleasant, continued the same to the last: the strictness of his virtue and piety had nothing in it of morose or austere; and surely no life was better, and, it is a comfort to us to add, more happily spent than his. I knew him from the boyish days in which we began to love each other: his talents were great, strong, and various; there was no art or science to which they were not sufficient in the contemplative life, nor any employment that they would not more than adequately fill in the active. Though his talents were not without that ambition which generally accompanies great natural endowments, it was kept under by great wisdom and temperance of mind; and though it was his opinion that the exercise of virtue was more easy, its nature more pure, and its means more certain in the walk he chose, yet in *that* the activity and energy which formed the character of his mind were very visible. Apparently in a private path of life, his spirit was public. You know how tender a father he was; to children worthy of him; yet he extended himself more widely, and devoted a great part of his time to the good of that Society, of no mean extent, of which the order of Divine Providence had made him a member. With a heart far from excluding others, he was entirely devoted to the benefit of that Society, and had a zeal very uncommon for everything which regarded its welfare and reputation; and when he retired, which he did wisely and in time, from the worthy occupation which he filled in a superior manner, his time and thoughts were given to that object. He sanctified his family benevolence, his benevolence to his Society, and to his friends, and to mankind, with that reverence in all things to the Supreme Being, without which the best dispositions and the best teaching will make virtue, if it can be at all attained, uncertain, poor, hard, dry, cold, and comfortless. Indeed we have had a loss. I console myself under it by going over the virtues of my old friend, of which I believe I am one of the earliest witnesses and the most warm admirers and lovers.

Believe me, this whole family, who have adopted my interest in my excellent departed friend, are deeply touched with our common loss, and sympathize with you most sincerely ...... I hope you will assure my dear friend, Mrs. Shackleton, the worthy wife of my late invaluable friend, that we sympathize cordially in all she feels; and join our entreaties to yours, that she will preserve to you as much as possible of the friend and parent you have lost.

EDMUND BURKE."

The following was subsequently received from Thomas Wilkinson:–

THOMAS WILKINSON TO MARY LEADBEATER.

"Yanwath, 28th of Tenth-month, 1792.

Dear Friend,

It is certainly more congenial to my disposition to visit the abodes of sorrow than the mansions of joy and festivity; not that I am insensible to the comfort and happiness of those I love, but if my friends are more near to me at one period than another, it is when they are under the pressure of affliction. Though I have deferred paying my visit of sympathy and affection in this way till now, it was not because you were not daily in my remembrance; but sorrow is not at all times communicative, and I reflected that numerous would be the tributes of condolence on the late mournful occasion: mine might, perhaps, have been spared. Of your loss I make estimation from what I have felt myself. I have but twice in my life had the satisfaction of any personal intercourse with the dear deceased, and these at six years' distance from each other; yet the lively impression of Richard Shackleton, left thereby on my mind, is equalled by few indeed. Few indeed possessed the powers of engaging and improving those around them, by their society, like him. His pleasant and communicative disposition opened his way with all ranks. It sometimes happens that the great and the good are encircled by a forbidding gravity, (I mean, something distinct from religious authority,) but in him the love of the Almighty was shown in kindness and good–will to those around him: this gave him place wherever he came, and his mind seemed equally fit for the vigour of reasoning, the capacious range of science, or to comfort and bring forward the hindmost of his brethren and sisters. To me he was kind indeed, and there is a sweetness accompanies his memory in my mind, hard to be described, which I believe will be the general feeling where he was known; so that his loss will be as extensive as his acquaintance, and lasting as the present generation. To you, dear friends, it must be peculiarly trying, – you who felt his paternal care, – you who felt the cheering influence of his daily conversation, and saw a thousand little acts of solicitude and kindness, unknown to the eyes of his more distant friends.

I need not, I cannot enlarge. Farewell: if the cloud of mourning o'ershadows your valley, extend your prospect to that bright region where your father, companion, and friend is, I believe, gathered to the just of all generations; and where a few more days, a few more tears, a few more struggles, and if we follow the light that guided him, we shall rejoin his released spirit, and be united to the redeemed and happy for ever and ever!

THOMAS WILKINSON."

In this year our friend Robert Grubb went to France, whither he had before accompanied his wife and some other friends on a religious visit to the few of our profession there. He now formed an acquaintance with Madame Roland and her husband, and received encouragement from them, from the Bishop of Blois, and some others, to make a purchase of lands with the view of establishing a school on an extensive plan. The place selected was Chambord, one of the palaces which the king had resigned. Several gave their names for shares if the purchase could be made. William Leadbeater was one – perhaps unconsciously impelled thereto by the mysterious influence of nature. He was not one who loved change, but his family had originally come from that fair land, and his thoughts dwelt much on removing thither. We had it in view to take part in the new establishment. Roland and his peerless Marie also spoke of settling themselves there. Robert Grubb described them as very amiable, worthy persons; but he regretted their having entered too much into the spirit of party. The breaking out of the war put a stop to this plan.

The villagers were astonished this summer by the first exhibition of a camel, which stalked about my brother's yard, while the walls were covered with spectators. Many events in after years were recalled by the date of the advent of this wonderful beast.

My brother built a large bolting mill upon the site of James McConnaughty's country mill; and the new building and business seemed to add to the respectability of our village. The little old kilns being pulled down, removed a rather unsightly object from the parlour windows of the dwelling house of the mill, or Griesebank, as it was now styled. In 1793 the mill was let to Peter Delany, the son of a rich neighbouring farmer. This young man was clever and enterprising. He built a wagon to convey his flour to the canal boat at Athy. His eldest brother, Malachi Delany, who spent much of his time with him, had been an officer in the service of the Emperor of Germany.[57] His figure was tall and striking, and his countenance strongly marked. Though a great talker, and qualified to handle various subjects, he confined himself to two – religion and politics. His mode of treating the first consisted in rating at the clergy, and the last in abusing the government. He had read his recantation from the Church of Rome, in which he had been educated, and he attached himself to no other. He had not served the government of his own country, nor did he pretend to wish to serve it; he was not a secret enemy, and he had at least the merit of sincerity.

In this year, 1793, we had many accounts of threatened disturbances in the County of Wexford and the Queen's County, occasioned by dissatisfaction at raising the militia; for now the flames of war between France and England blazed fiercely.

Our friend Job Scott from America, having in the course of his religious services arrived at Ballitore, was taken ill with the small–pox at my mother's house. He had dined at Robert Clibborn's in Dublin, and fondled his little daughter, who had the marks of that disease fresh upon her. The following day he came to Ballitore, and the day after he was taken ill. The pock appeared with unfavourable symptoms. Dr. Frank Johnson attended him, and also Dr. Paul, who was sent for to Dublin. Abraham Jackson, Joshua Beale, James Clibborn, Anne Tuke, and my sister Sally were his constant attendants, and the family and neighbours did what they could to alleviate his sufferings, and to prolong a life of such inestimable value to society in general, and to his six little motherless children in particular. All was in vain; he died on the thirteenth day of his illness, on the 22nd of Eleventh–month, 1793. Early in his illness he dictated a letter to his father and the parents of his wife, a precious testimony of the calmness and fortitude of his mind. His bodily sufferings were exquisite; his breathing was so extremely oppressed that his bed had to be drawn over to the window, and the sashes of both windows taken out to give him air. I lamented then the want of thorough air in any room in the Retreat house, and I believe that admitting its free circulation is very conducive to health. But though our friend's bodily sufferings were so severe, his spirit was preserved in that patience which nothing earthly could give, and ascended triumphantly to the rest prepared for the righteous. He had been much led to hold public meetings, and the testimonies which he undauntedly bore against superstition gave great offence, especially to those of the Romish persuasion. Anne Tuke, who had been his companion at some of those meetings, found it her place also to preach the gospel to the poor. She held a meeting in Haly's shattered house at Timolin, where she was listened to quietly. It was difficult to procure a meeting at Crookstown, till Bartle Toole (who reckoned his to be one of the best families there) lent his house, making a great merit of this condescension.

Soldiers were at this time marching in order to embark for France, and some of the artillery were billetted at my mother's house. They were fine looking men: many of them were serious, and seemed not to expect to return home. Great dissatisfaction now appeared on account of the embodying the militia. About a hundred men entered Ballitore early one morning, tendering an oath to all of their own class whom they met, that they should not join either militia or army, but be true to their own cause. Soon after this a party of soldiers were stationed here, – unusual inhabitants in Ballitore, which hitherto had only beheld the military *en passant*. The Kerry militia were first sent and billetted on the inhabitants. The villagers found they had nothing to dread from their armed guests, and great cordiality subsisted between them; so that when they were exchanged for the Longford militia, there was abundance of weeping and wailing; and, as "excessive sorrow is exceeding dry," some superfluous cups were drained on the occasion.

Squire Keatinge, having raised a regiment, now became a colonel.

Jack Moran, a butcher, a man whose looks and manner bespoke him not of the very lowest class, was seized with an alarming illness. It was reckoned a quinsey in the windpipe: his breathing could be heard at a great distance. My mother had once in private warned this man of the danger of drinking to excess, and now felt her mind drawn to pay him a religious visit, which was very satisfactory to both parties. The sick man acknowledged her kindness, saying that those who gave a cup of cold water should have a reward, and that she had done much more. He disclaimed all dependence on man, saying there was but one mediator between the Almighty and the soul. He recovered, and when able to get out paid my mother a visit, and appeared to have made good resolutions as to his future life. Alas! when the watch is not constantly kept up, of how little avail is mere resolve! This unfortunate man, by yielding to temptation, went astray by rapid steps: he became deeply engaged in the rebellion, and a few months after that event lost his life in a manner so mysterious, that it was imagined the report of his having been drowned was invented to conceal a more disgraceful fate.

A young officer of Colonel Keatinge's regiment, after dining at Power's Grove and leaving it at a late hour, or rather early next morning, was thrown from his horse in a state of intoxication, and lived but a few days. He was the second who lost his life by the mistaken hospitality of that house.

The year 1795 commenced with great inclemency. A breeches-maker left home in frosty, snowy weather. His wife anxiously expected his return, and was so unhappy at his delay, that her two brothers went to Dublin in search of him, but returned without any account. The melting of the snow in about two weeks revealed the dead body lying in a field beside the road to Dublin. Great were the horror and anguish of the widow; and her father, Daniel Scott, a respectable small farmer, took suddenly ill the same day, and died before morning.

Elizabeth Miles died at about eighty years of age. She continued her love of neatness and regularity when her strength did not permit her to do much more than issue her orders from her chair by the fireside, dressed in a clean cap and hood, and she maintained authority in her family, which consisted of her affectionate daughter Jane, her son Richard, and grandson Edward, a young man who wanted not understanding nor the advantages of education.[58] In his uncle Richard he had an example of the woful effects of intemperance, for no remonstrance could prevail upon unfortunate Dick to resign his habitual love of the bottle; and what mortified the Friends of the village was, that when in a state of inebriation Dick particularly chose to speak our plain language in its greatest purity, though not belonging to our Society. Poverty – the natural consequence of drinking habits – soon gave an altered appearance to the habitation, especially after the old woman's death.

Jacob Fuller, who had been born in our Society of one of its most respectable families, and had moreover served an apprenticeship to Abby Widdows, and learned the art of a tailor, contracted the destructive vice of drinking. He forfeited, of course, his membership with us; and, after having led a wandering life, professed reformation, and followed his trade at Ballitore. He was very desirous to be noticed, and valued himself upon his high birth.

A tolerable house had been built at the corner of the street where it turns to the school, by William Alcock, who married Sally, the only daughter of – Mooney, of Irishtown, and she bore him twenty children. This couple were the offspring of farmers accounted rather wealthy, and perhaps valued themselves too much upon this circumstance.[59] I suspect Sally had also the misfortune of aiming at gentility. But this did not protect her from Biddy Murray's anger when she heard her more polished neighbour, in a dispute between their husbands, begging her spouse not to meddle with such "inferior wretches." In the bitterness of indignation Biddy declared that her Tom had first lived in Ballitore, and foretold he should continue to do so when Bill should have left it. This proved true, for the Alcocks soon sought another abode.

About this time a visit was paid, by appointment of the monthly meeting, to recommend such of our Society as had fire–arms or other instruments for the destruction of man, to destroy them. The only person amongst us who was in possession of such an instrument was Molly Haughton, who resigned to destruction her husband's old fowling–piece, and joined in the laugh raised at her expense.

My husband having enlarged our new abode, it was now too large for our own family, and we proposed to Anne Doyle, who was about to join her sister Mary in opening a shop, that they should become our tenants for part of the house. On the 16th of Ninth–month, 1796, these dear friends came under our roof. The shop, and a front room which served them for kitchen and parlour, with a pantry and scullery adjoining, and a large bed–chamber upstairs, became theirs. We ascend to our chambers by the same staircase. It is but a step from our sitting–room to theirs, and we have this advantage over all our neighbours that no weather can prevent our visits to each other. I esteem it one of my blessings that those excellent young women have been brought so near us, and the unbroken harmony which has ever subsisted between us appears to me a proof that this step was favoured by Divine approbation. They have proved themselves faithful friends, sympathizing with us in our troubles and rejoicing in our joys; and, although they keep no servant, and their own engagements occupy them so much, they contrive often to render me material assistance in my domestic concerns, and in the care of my infant family. Anne Doyle I had long known, and admired her good sense, her taste, her modesty, and her gentleness. Mary was almost a stranger to me, and the fascinating cheerfulness of her conversation surprised and delighted me; while by her knowledge of the sick, especially children, I have been often comforted and assisted.

Robert Lecky, while at school here, was bereft by fever of his father, John Lecky of Ballykealy.[60] And what a father had he lost! – one who joined to that extraordinary tenderness which freed his children from restraint, the most watchful care of their conduct. John Lecky's cheerful, benevolent heart had made him the delight of his family and friends. Three days before his illness he read in the preparative meeting the query concerning wills, and remarked that his own was not to his mind, and that he meant to alter it, which he did, copying it neatly over when his death sickness was upon him. He also sent a clear message to the monthly meeting, concerning an appointment which he had fulfilled. His wife could scarcely believe he was no more; and her grief needed a higher consolation than her fellow mortals could afford. The poor almost idolized him. It was with difficulty their lamentations were suppressed on leaving the house with his funeral; but when out of hearing of the widow and children, they burst forth into loud wailings, which were, however, less affecting than the silent tears of the old men and children. Their friend, benefactor, and counsellor snatched suddenly from them in the prime of life, they resisted for a time the entrance of the body into the graveyard. But when the loved remains were about to be deposited in the earth, their grief passed all bounds, and they declared that he must not be laid in the dark and silent grave. In vain the gravediggers remonstrated. At length they laid down their spades, and joined in the lamentation; and for some time nothing could be done but to weep with them. Robert Lecky did not survive his father much more that two years. He died of fever at the school of Richard Roe in Waterford, and his mother's heart was again wrung by the loss of a son who promised to inherit his father's virtues.

Early in this year, the boy who brought down the postbags was knocked down and robbed of them. It was thought the plunderers had got a large booty: the boy declared his ignorance of their persons. A strong suspicion of one man so impressed my husband's mind, that he took him aside, and in privacy and with great gentleness told him his fears, advising him to restore what he had taken, and retain his peace of mind, in which case he had nothing to fear. The unfortunate man affected surprise and denied the fact, but without discovering anger at the suspicion. However, this man and his brother were believed to have been the robbers. No proof led to certainty, though it was said to have been nearly found out by a quarrel between their wives. Some years afterwards these men were detected robbing my brother's mill, yet they still continued in the village, till, on the execution of some mail–coach robbers, they took themselves away.

Trevor Fay came to Ballitore. He had left it in 1785 a young ensign; he returned in the character of a genteel begger, and in the dress of a sailor. His degradation excited much compassion here, where, though few are wealthy, the purse opens in unison with the heart. But when it appeared that their bounty helped to enrich the public–house, his acquaintances were ready to believe that Fay's degradation was the consequence and punishment of his vices, and became less willing to assist him with money.

Abigail Widdows left my brother's house, and went to my mother's as an assistant. She took part of what had been Taylor's orchard from William Leadbeater, who now rented the whole Burrow, on which he built a house for her.

Many of us were in Carlow, attending the quarterly meeting, when, on the morning of the 25th of Twelfth–month, the alarm came that the French fleet had been seen off Bantry. We saw the troopers march out of town to meet them. It was an awful sight, not knowing but that these, now in the pride of health, would be sacrificed to horrid war. The weather became very inclement, and the rigours of frost and snow were severely felt by the crowds of soldiers who were hastening to Bantry. Carlow was all in confusion; so was Ballitore, our houses being for a long time open to the military, going to and returning from Bantry. We were relieved from the present apprehension of invasion, but it had caused a ferment in the minds of the people. The inconvenience of having our houses thronged with soldiers we bore with becoming patience, but the idea that this might be the beginning of sorrows was distressing. Unused as we were to the military, some whimsical circumstances occurred. One evening our house being pretty much filled with soldiers, we retreated to Mary and Anne Doyle's parlour, and while we sat by the fireside, two tipsy soldiers, not of our party, entered and seated themselves also. We remonstrated gently against this intrusion, and he who appeared the most drunk of the two, told us that being informed that the master of the house loved a soldier as he loved his life, he came to visit him and to see the back apartments of his castle. William Leadbeater's love of soldiers being thus exaggerated, and our house really occupying much back space, made us ready to smile, though we shuddered at being exposed to such company, and at the oaths with which the chief speaker seasoned his discourse. His companion perceived this and desired him not to swear. "Me swear!" replied he, with seeming surprise, "I never swear in the greatest extremity."

James Kathrens had for the last two years found a considerable amendment in his health, and of course his prospects began to wear a brighter aspect, when, in the absence of the billet–master, being obliged as postmaster to stand out in the cold, giving billets to a party of the army, he was seized with an inflammation on his lungs and died in a few days. His mind, in this time of suffering, was preserved in a quiet state: he settled his outward affairs, and expressed his resignation and his good will to all. He was at his own desire buried in our graveyard. His afflicted widow, who might comfort herself with the thought of having so well performed her duties, remained in the same house, exerting herself for the sake of her two children, and by degrees the native content and cheerfulness of her happy disposition returned. She was sister to our sister–in–law Lydia Shackleton, and some years afterwards married a person named Chambers, with whom she removed to reside in Dublin.[61]

Benjamin Rotch, a native of Nantucket, son to the honourable William Rotch, stopped a day or two at Ballitore in making a tour through Ireland. Uniting as he did the Quaker and the gentleman, his conversation was very pleasant. In France he was acquainted with Thomas Paine, whom he described as a drunken, dissolute man, whose company was avoided by sober, well–bred persons. He also knew Mary Woolstoncraft, whom he liked, as she was candid and engaging.

Robinson, the minister of Bomba Hall, I suppose a curate for either Stratford or Dunlavin, an industrious, intelligent little man, sometimes called upon us. He expressed very liberal sentiments, and rather more in the *new way* than one should expect from his cloth.

Republicanism, both in church and state affairs, seemed now to be very prevalent; and serious divisions arose in our Society.

James White, in leaving Ballitore School, left behind him a tender remembrance of those virtues and talents which, already adorning the youth, promised to dignify the man.[62]

In 1797, our private sorrows were united with the public lamentation when the death of Edmund Burke was announced. A short time before, I had received the following kind answer to my enquiry after his health, dictated by him and signed by his own hand.[63]

EDMUND BURKE TO MARY LEADBEATER.

"Bath, 23rd May, 1797.

My dear Mrs. Leadbeater,

I feel, as I ought to do, your constant hereditary kindness to me and mine; what you have heard of my illness is far from exaggerated. I am, thank God, alive; and that is all. Hastening to my dissolution, I have to bless Providence that I do not suffer a great deal of pain.

I am very glad to hear that the vexatious dispute which has been raised against you about the few miserable trees, of which, if I do not mistake, I remember the planting, is likely to be settled to your satisfaction. I have never heard of anything so miserable as this attempt upon you.

Mrs. Burke has a tolerable share of health in every respect except much use of her limbs. She remembers your mother's most good–natured attentions, as I am sure I do, with much gratitude.

I have ever been an admirer of your talents and virtues; and shall ever wish most cordially for everything which can tend to your credit and satisfaction. I therefore congratulate you very heartily on the birth of your son; and pray remember me to the representative of your family, who, I hope, still keeps up the school of which I have so tender a remembrance; though, after so long an absence and so many important events of every kind that have distracted my thoughts, I hardly dare to ask for any one, not knowing whether they are living or dead, lest I should be the means of awakening unpleasant recollections.

Believe me to be, with the most respectful and affectionate regard,

My dear Mrs. Leadbeater,

your faithful friend,

and very humble servant,

EDMUND BURKE.

P.S. – Pray remember me to Mr. Leadbeater. I have been at Bath for these four months to no purpose; I am therefore to be removed to my own house at Beaconsfield to–morrow, to be nearer to a habitation more permanent, humbly and fearfully hoping that my better part may find a better mansion."

This summer a bonfire and the first illuminations ever seen in Ballitore testified the joy for Colonel Keatinge's having gained the election for the county of Kildare.[64] His amiable lady instituted an annual spinning match in the court of her own house, and distributed five prizes. This bid fair to awaken a spirit of industry; but the pleasant prospect was soon overcast.

Our valuable friend Sarah Talbot from America being here, my sister Sally felt it her duty to accompany her in a religious visit to England, Scotland, &c. My dear mother willingly resigned her, for, though her mental faculities were in a state of rapid decay, her religious sensibility still remained.

Soldiers now constituted a part of the inhabitants of Ballitore, and the Cork militia were stationed here.[65]

William Cooke, of Ballylea, about three miles hence, was attacked by a number of men, who set fire to his house and demanded his arms. The house was burned, the family went to Baltinglass, and we all saw with dread the approaching flames of discord.

CHAPTER VIII.
1798.

A rejoicing household. – Mysterious disappearances. – Popular militia replaced by Orangemen. – Free quarters. – Seditious papers. – Robbery by the yeomen. – Terms offered to the seditious. – Colonel Keatinge and his family leave Ireland. – Public whippings. – Six yeomen shot. – Alarming rumours. – The rebellion breaks forth. – Skirmish at Narraghmore. – The rebels enter Ballitore. – Murder of Richard Yeates of Moone. – Skirmish on the bog–road. – Abraham Shackleton and others taken prisoners by the rebels. – Courage and benevolence of young Betsy Shackleton. – Sad state of affairs in Ballitore. – Young girls in costume accompany the insurgents. – Merciless conduct of the military in Carlow. – John Bewley appeals to Colonel Campbell on behalf of the people. – His negociation fails. – The military destroy Colonel Keatinge's house, and murder his cousin. – Ballitore delivered up to rapine, fire, and slaughter for two hours. – Shocking incidents. – Cruel murder of Owen Finn, Tom Duffy, and Dr. Frank Johnson. – Friendly interference of Captain Palmer. – Escape of priest Cullen. – Visit to the bereaved widow of Dr. Johnson. – The doctor's funeral. – Timolin, Narraghmore, and Crookstown ravaged. – The insurgents send hostages, and deliver up their arms.

120 to 136

THIS year, 1798, which in its progress was clouded with so many horrors, opened upon me more delightfully than any former year had done; for on the morning of its first day my beloved husband's life, which for fourteen days was suspended in a very doubtful scale, rose up with hope, and the crisis of a dangerous fever was past.[66] It was like escaping from a prison–house, from torture, and from darkness, to breathe the free air, to shake off the painful shackles, and to gaze upon the sun, when this inestimable favour was granted. In this time of deep trial I received all the comfort and aid which friendship and sympathy could bestow. My husband *was to live*. When that was the case, all means co–operated to that end. The interest caused by the danger of one so much beloved and respected was exceeding and extensive, and among our immediate neighbours it was intense. It was touching to see one of his labourers, who would not be denied the privilege of seeing him, as he believed for the last time, approach his bed, take his fevered hand, and weeping, exclaim, "Oh, my dear master!" Even the great mastiff house–dog came pattering up stairs, laid his head on the bed, and looked at his master long and wistfully, with almost human affection in his eyes.[67] It was delightful when we could meet our friends at our fireside again, and receive their unaffected salutations, with smiles and tears which welcomed us once more to health and happiness.

The attack on Willowbrook alarmed Robert Bayly, who fled from Ballitore with his handsome wife in a fright, declaring that every man, woman and child in the village were "United Irishmen."[68] Now and then a person was missed, and this misfortune was unfeelingly accounted for by saying that "Brownie had eaten them." These mysterious disappearances were horrible, and no certainty of the fate of those victims of party rage was ever obtained. A time had come when nothing but what was honest, and fair, and "above board" could stand the test. Amongst other precautions, the names of the inhabitants were posted on the doors of each house, and the authorities had liberty to enter at any hour, night or day, to see whether they were within or not. This appeared a necessary precaution, yet it exposed the quiet of families to be sadly broken in upon.

Houses were now searched for fire–arms, proving the wisdom of our friends in banishing all such weapons from theirs. Notices were put up demanding the arms taken by the "United men" to be restored, on pain of allowing the military to live at free quarters, for many nightly incursions had been made by these robbers to plunder houses of whatever arms they contained. A detachment of the King's County militia was at this time sent here from Athy, where Sandford Palmer, an old Ballitore boy, was stationed as their captain. The men were very well liked; perhaps it was for that reason they were so soon removed, the villagers escorting them on their way with tears and lamentations; and when my husband, from his fields, saw them departing, he sent his workmen to join the procession. Perhaps these painful feelings sprung from an unconscious presentiment, for if those men had remained here, Ballitore might have escaped its subsequent distresses. They were replaced by the Tyrone militia, mostly composed of professed Orangemen, wearing the ribbon of their party.

Hitherto the soldiers were quartered in our houses, but found themselves in provisions; the threat respecting free quarters was now put into execution; foraging parties went into the country, shops and private houses were searched for whisky, which was ordered to be spilled; and seditious papers were sought for. On the day of this search I was not at home, else I suppose I should have opened my desk in the security of conscious innocence, quite forgetting that I had thrown into it one of the squibs then privately circulated, which in very tolerable poetry avowed disloyal sentiments. I started at the danger it was so near bringing upon us, and thankfully flung it into the fire. Account was taken of the stock and provisions in the village, that none should be sent away; and six cwt. of bacon which was being sent to Dublin by one of the villagers was seized by the yeomen. Robert Bayley was pursued because he attempted to take away one of his own horses; his horse was captured, and himself made a prisoner. Ephraim Boake's house was plundered, and he very narrowly escaped personal injury.

These attacks on the most loyal people amongst us were not to be borne. Some of the inhabitants went to Colonel Colin Campbell, who commanded the district, and got protections which stopped further depredations upon them, and procured the restoration of their property.[69] Colonel Campbell was willing to grant protections to all peaceable people, but none of the Friends applied for them, some doubt being entertained of its being consistent with our principles to apply for armed protection. We were thus exposed to the imputation of being disaffected, and the provision we had for our families was rudely taken out of our houses for the yeomen. This was an unpleasant sight to the soldiers who were with us on free quarters, and they hid our bacon for us and for themselves. Great waste was committed, and unchecked robbery. One hundred cars loaded with hay, potatoes, oats, etc. led by the poor owners, and guarded by soldiers, were in one day marched into Ballitore. Colonel Keatinge urged his yeomen to take with a sparing hand; to remember that this was the "scarce season," when the new food was not yet come in and the old was nearly exhausted, and not to bring famine upon the country. But he spoke to deaf ears, for pity seemed banished from the martial bosom. One exception I must record; one of those men quartered upon us refused to partake of the plunder upon which so many of his comrades riotously feasted, and appeared much dejected – yet he, as well as another of a very opposite cast of mind, fell by the insurgents when the burst came. Threats were multiplied, and the military poured in one day, so as to terrify the scared inhabitants with the prospect of immediate scarcity. Discontents arose between the army and yeomanry. Public notice was given that the nightly patrol should be withdrawn, to give opportunity for returning the arms of which the "United men" had possessed themselves, and that if not returned within a stated time, the whole neighbourhood should be burnt.

Colonel Keatinge went in person to the chapel, and with tears and fervent entreaties besought the misguided people to comply with these conditions: but he entreated in vain.[70] So when he saw that even his influence could not avail to preserve them, he and his lady left the country. They left their dear Narraghmore – left it never to return, and their loss has never ceased to be felt and deplored. A large quantity of arms was left as directed, but broken into pieces, and thus rendered useless. The clouds gathered darker and darker in our political horizon, though nothing could be sweeter, calmer, or brighter than our vernal sky and balmy gales. In the midst of these tumults a dear friend of ours died; we could not lament a tranquil escape to a world of eternal rest. My mind felt wearied with what appeared to me oppressive in the melancholy state of the times – rule and misrule fighting with each other, and the country torn to pieces with the strife.

To the Tyrone militia were now added the Suffolk fencibles; and the Ancient Britons, dressed in blue with much silver lace – a very pretty dress – came from Athy, seized the smiths' tools to prevent them from making pikes, and made prisoners of the smiths themselves. I could not see without emotion poor Owen Finn and his brother, handcuffed and weeping, as they walked after the car containing those implements of industry which had enabled them to provide comfortably for the family. Several of these were whipped publicly to extort confessions about the pikes. The torture was excessive, and the victims were long in recovering; and in almost every case it was applied fruitlessly. Guards were placed at every entrance into the village, to prevent people from entering or leaving it. The village once so peaceful exhibited a scene of tumult and dismay, and the air rang with the shrieks of the sufferers and the lamentations of those who beheld them suffer. These violent measures caused a great many pikes to be brought in: the street was lined with those who came to deliver up the instruments of death.

A party of military from Naas entered Ballitore, and took prisoners twelve of our neighbours, whom they removed to Naas gaol. Most of the villagers stood outside their doors to see them depart. They looked composed for the most part, though followed by their weeping wives and children. One child, with his cries of, "O father! father!" excited great compassion. Six yeomen were taken prisoners to Dunlavin. I was walking in our garden when they passed on a car, with their coats turned inside out, and one of their guards, a mere boy, cried out to me in a tone of insulting jocularity. We, who did not understand this case, were only qualified to see one side, and, though we forbore audibly expressing our disapprobation, our looks betrayed the depression of our minds. This excited jealousy of us.[71] How ill-founded! for who could expect us to rejoice at the misery and degradation of our fellow-creatures and neighbours, or even to behold them unmoved? These unfortunate yeomen were shot! There was too much exultation in the military; they were not aware, perhaps, how deeply an insult is felt and resented, and that an injury is sometimes more easily pardoned.

The morning of the 24th of the Fifth-month (May) orders came for the soldiers quartered here to march to Naas. A report was circulated that Naas gaol had been broken open, – that Dublin was in arms, and so forth. All was uncertainty, except that something serious had happened, as the mail-coach had been stopped. The insurrection was to begin in Dublin, and the mail-coach not being suffered to leave the city was the signal for general revolt. This purpose was defeated by the vigilance of government; the mail–coach had got to Naas before it was stopped, yet its detention here persuaded the people that the day was their own.[72] They threw off the appearance of loyalty, and rose in avowed rebellion. In the morning the Suffolk fencibles first marched out, nine men remaining to guard their baggage at the Mill, which was their barrack. The Tyrone militia followed, taking their baggage with them. All was hurry and confusion in the village. Several who had kept out of sight now appeared dressed in green, that colour so dear to United Irishmen, and proportionably abhorred by the loyal. The Suffolks went by the high road, the Tyrones through Narraghmore. As they marched out, a young woman privately and with tears told their lieutenant her apprehensions that their enemies lay in ambush in Narraghmore wood. He was therefore prepared to meet them, and sad havoc ensued; many on both sides fell, particularly among the undisciplined multitude. The courthouse at Narraghmore was attacked, and many met their death there. We heard the reports of firearms, and every hour the alarm increased.

Dr. Johnson had been sent for to Narraghmore to dress wounds; the rabble despoiled him of his horse and case of instruments, and sent him back jaded and worn out. About three o'clock in the afternoon John Dunne and many others came as far as the bridge with pikes, and Dr. Johnson turned them back; but not long after two or three hundred men, armed with pikes, knives, and pitchforks, and bearing sticks with green rags fluttering from them, came in at the western side, headed by Malachi Delany on a white horse, and took possession of the town; Dr. Johnson, as representative of the yeomanry–guard, having capitulated on condition of persons and property being safe. I saw from an upper window a crowd coming towards our kitchen–door; I went down and found many armed men, who desired to have refreshments, especially drink. I brought them milk, and was cutting a loaf of bread, when a little elderly man, called "the Canny," took it kindly out of my hand and divided it himself, saying, "Be decent, boys, be decent." Encouraged by having found a friend, I ventured to tell them that so many armed men in the room frightened me. The warriors condescended to my fears. "We'll be out in a shot," they replied, and in a minute the kitchen was empty.

Daniel Horan, a young farmer from the Long Avenue, was standing in our yard – a fine looking fellow. I had observed a dark cloud upon his countenance, when, a few days before, he was requesting a protection from the officers; that cloud was now gone, and joy and animation played on every feature, unaccompanied by any expression of malignity. A party of insurgents, as they went to the Mill, met some of the wives of the soldiers stationed there, whom they sent back to tell their husbands that if they surrendered they should not be injured. But the women, instead of delivering the message, ran shrieking to announce the approach of the rebels, and the soldiers prepared to stand on the defensive; but, when they saw such a multitude, fled. In the pursuit over Max's–hill a soldier turned, fired, and shot Paddy Dempsy dead. They were soon overpowered, and their lives were spared only on condition that he who had killed the insurgent should be pointed out; with this hard alternative his comrades reluctantly complied, and the soldier soon lay dead beside his victim. Another of the soldiers was killed by a shot from the Mill–field, which reached him about the middle of the avenue, and his remains were buried in the ditch just by the spot where he fell. Most of the others were wounded, but I believe none mortally.

Malachi Delany exerted himself to prevent bloodshed, and showed as much humanity as courage. He had thrown off no mask, for he never wore one, and he proved himself to be a generous enemy. A great number of strange faces surrounded us, and a message was brought to me to request any thing of a green colour. I told them we could not join any party. "What! not the strongest?" enquired one of the strangers. "None at all" – and though our parlour tables were covered with green cloth, they urged their request no further.

Richard Yeates, son to Squire Yeates of Moone, was brought in a prisoner, his yeomanry coat turned. A private of the yeomanry corps to which he belonged was also brought into our parlour, where my husband and I sat at tea. He was an old man; we made him sit down to tea, and invited also his captors, but they declined; one of them went to the table and helped himself to bread and butter, looked at himself in the mirror, and remarked it was "war time." The prisoner, with tears trickling down his cheeks, spoke sadly of his seven children; his guards strove to console him by telling him that "he was an honest Roman, and should not be hurt." Presently we heard a shot, and those strangers immediately said they "supposed Richard Yeates was shot." This was really the case. He was taken into a house, and in despite of his own entreaties, the endeavours of many others to save him, and even the efforts of Priest Cullen, who begged the life of the young man on his knees, – he was murdered, being piked and shot! That day his father had been requested, I suppose by one who knew what was intended, not to let his son leave the house; but he could not prevent him – he would join the corps. His brother–in–law, Norcott D'Esterre, narrowly escaped being taken a prisoner at the same time.

The insurgents at length left, first placing cars on the bridge as a barricade against the army. They took two of our horses. We saw several houses on fire northwards, and while standing gazing at them outside our door, bullets whizzed by our ears, and warned us to go in for safety. There had been an engagement on the Bog–road between the army and the insurgents; the latter were worsted, and Malachi Delany, finding his efforts to rally them were in vain, fled along with them. The soldiers retreating to Athy, had fired at random those shots which we had heard, and almost felt, and by which a poor woman was killed and her daughter's arm broken. They had also set the houses on fire; and one serjeant, one might think impelled by his fate, came into the village with a baggage car. It was thought he must have been in liquor, for had he his reason, he could not have thus exposed himself to his enemies in the height of their rage. He had just gone to bed in his lodgings when those enemies rushed in, and quickly put an end to his life.

The insurgents now returned from the Bog–road, and, having increased to an immense multitude, went to Castledermot late in the evening. Laying our beds on the floor, lest bullets should enter the windows to our destruction, we got some disturbed sleep. All became quiet, and in the morning messages came to us from our neighbours to tell us they were living. This was indeed good news, for we dreaded that many would never have seen the light of morning. The party who attacked Castledermot were repulsed by yeomanry who fired at them from the windows. The crowd dispersed, and did not assemble here in such numbers again.

As my friend and I walked out to see a sick neighbour, we looked with fearful curiosity over a wall, inside of which we saw lying the youthful form of the murdered Richard Yeates. There he had been thrown after his death, his clothes undisturbed, but his bosom all bloody. For many days after I thought my food tasted of blood, and at night I was frequently awakened by my feelings of horror, and stretched forth my hand to feel if my husband was safe at my side.

All the horses which could be got were taken by the insurgents. A man came to me with a drawn sword in his hand, demanding my own mare. I told him that one of the Tyrone officers had borrowed her, and fortunately another man who knew me bore testimony to my veracity, so that I was left unharmed. When I saw how the fine horses were abused and galloped without mercy by the insurgents, I rejoiced that my Nell was not in their hands.

A man afterwards came, with a horse–pistol in his hand, to take my husband. My brother had been previously taken, together with some of his guests. They were all to be brought to the camp in the hollow side of the hill at the east, and when the soldiers came, the insurgents said they should be placed in the front of the battle, to stop a bullet if they would not fire one.[74] This man, not finding my husband below, and thinking he was concealed, ran upstairs where our little children were in bed, with the huge pistol in his hand, swearing horribly that he would send the contents of it through his head if he did not go with him. I stood at the door, less terrified than I could have expected, and asked a young man who had accompanied the other if they meant to kill us. "To kill you?" he repeated, in a tone expressive of surprise and sorrow at such a supposition. At length he prevailed on his angry companion to go away, threatening as he went, that if the Quakers did not take up arms their houses should be in flames, "as Mr. Bayly's was."[75] I was sorry for the destruction of the Hall, but soon found that, though it had been attempted, the fire had been put out before much damage had been done. My husband, having gone to visit my mother, was not found, and did not know he had been sought for. Many came to us weeping and trembling for their friends; and to the doctor, who, having much influence with the people, exerted it to do them good. We could do nothing.

The cars laden with goods from Dublin, which the carriers were bringing to our shopkeepers, were plundered, and a barricade made of them across the road leading down to the village. The insurgents talked boldly of forming a camp on the Curragh. All who were missing were reported to have fallen in the ambush in the wood, or in the encounter at the Bog–road. At both places many did fall. The wife of one of my brother's labourers was told that he lay dead in the wood; she hastened thither; but when she reached the spot, she found the face so disfigured with wounds that she could not recognize it. She examined the linen – it was not his; even this melancholy satisfaction was denied her. But what a satisfaction was in store for her! She met her husband alive and well, and brought him in triumph to the house of their master, whose young daughter Betsy had participated in the anguish of the supposed widow, and now shared her joy with all the vivid warmth of her ardent nature. Though not more that fifteen years old, she was endued with uncommon courage and prudence in this time of trial.[76] Her bodily powers were exerted in paying attention to her father's numerous guests; for over a hundred people sought refuge under his roof; and the strength of her mind seemed to invigorate all around her. A soldier lay ill of a fever in a house in the garden. It would have been death to him if his asylum were known to the insurgents; so she carefully attended to all his wants herself. Such was Betsy Shackleton.

Everyone seemed to think that safety and security were to be found in my brother's house. Thither the insurgents brought their prisoners, and thither, also, their own wounded and suffering comrades. It was an awful sight to behold in that large parlour such a mingled assembly of throbbing, anxious hearts – my brother's own family, silent tears rolling down their faces, the wives of the loyal officers, the wives of the soldiers, the wives and daughters of the insurgents, the numerous guests, the prisoners, the trembling women – all dreading to see the door open, lest some new distress, some fresh announcement of horrors should enter. It was awful; but every scene was now awful, and we knew not what a day might bring forth.

All our houses were thronged with people seeking refreshment and repose, and threatening to take possession for the purpose of firing upon the soldiery when they should come. Ours seemed peculiarly adapted for such a purpose, being a corner house, and in a central situation; so, believing its destruction was inevitable, I packed up in a small trunk such portable articles as I esteemed of most value, amongst which were some of my dear friend's letters, and I made packages of clothes for my husband, myself, and the little ones. I wore two pair of pockets, wishing to preserve as much as I could; though in my heart I had not much fear of an engagement, believing that the spirit which had animated the insurgents had evaporated.

Young girls dressed in white, with green ribbons, and carrying pikes, accompanied the insurgents. They had patrols and a countersign, but it was long before they could decide upon the password. At length they fixed upon the word "Scourges." Sentinels were placed in various parts of the village. One day, as I went to my brother's, a sentinel called to a man who walked with me not to advance on pain of being shot. The sentinel was my former friend, "the Canny." I approached him and asked would he shoot me if I proceeded. "Shoot you!" exclaimed he, taking my hand and kissing it, adding a eulogium on the Quakers. I told him it would be well if they were all of our way of thinking, for then there would be no such work as the present. I thought I could comprehend "the Canny's" incoherent answer, "Aye, but you know our Saviour – the scourges, oh! the scourges!" With little exception, we were kindly treated, and the females amongst us were frequently encouraged to dismiss our fears, with hearty shakes of the hand, and assurances that they would "burn those who would burn us." We began to be familiarized with these dangers; and added our entreaties to the representations of our men that they should give up their arms, and resign the project which threatened them with destruction.

They had been mistaken as to their prospect of success. Dublin was safe, and at Naas and Kilcullen great slaughter of the insurgents had been made, though on Kilcullen-green many of the military had also fallen. An attack in the night had been made on Carlow, which was repulsed with slaughter, amounting almost to massacre. A row of cabins in which numbers of the defeated insurgents had taken shelter were set on fire, and the inmates burned to death. No quarter was given, – no mercy shown; and most of those who had escaped, burning with disappointment, rage, and revenge, joined the Wexford party. John Bewley, a man endued with wisdom, courage, and benevolence, exerted them all in behalf of the deluded people, along with my husband and brother; and as he was not exposed to the suspicion which attached to an inhabitant, he treated with Colonel Campbell on their behalf. The Colonel was willing to make favourable terms with the insurgents, most of whom were willing to come in to him, but a few still held out, and amongst these was a priest. John Bewley proposed to take another message to Colonel Campbell; the people at length consented; but so much time had been lost meanwhile that Colonel Campbell's terms were now less favourable. Six hostages were demanded to be sent before an appointed time, to guarantee the surrender of the arms before the noon of the next day. They could not decide upon the hostages, the hour passed by, and the fate of Ballitore was sealed!

We believed the hostages had been sent, for we perceived the people had begun to weary of ill–doing; and a stranger, who begged some refreshment wistfully, asked me when there would be peace. We got our beds replaced upon their steads, and sank into that quiet repose which for some nights we had not known, little imagining what the morrow was to bring forth. This eventful morrow was the 27th of Fifth–month (May). At three o'clock in the morning the intelligence that the army was near roused us from our beds. We saw the glitter of arms through the dust which the horses of the 9th Dragoons made, galloping along the high road from Carlow. We heard the shots repeatedly fired. We saw the military descend the hill, cross the bridge, and halt before our house, where some dismounted and entered, and asked for milk and water. As I handed it, I trembled; my spirits, which had risen superior to the danger till now, fell; the dragoon perceived my emotion, and kindly told me I need not fear, that they came to protect us, adding, "It is well you were not all murdered!" Thus assured, I recovered my composure. I should not have recovered it so easily had I known that my brother and his friends had walked forth to meet the troops, who were commanded by Major Dennis. John Bewley, holding up a paper from Colonel Campbell, said, "We are prisoners!" "It is well for you," said the Major, "that you are prisoners, else I should have shot you, every man." Then raising himself in his stirrups, he revoked the orders given to his men, to fire upon every man in coloured clothes. Oh, rash and cruel orders, which exposed to such danger lives of such value, which if thus sacrificed no regrets could have restored! Nothing can justify such commands.

I thought the bitterness of death was passed, but the work was not yet begun. Colonel Campbell's men, who had impatiently rested on their arms several hours, marched out of Athy. They took Narraghmore in their way, and directed their mistaken rage against the newly erected house of Colonel Keatinge, planting cannon to destroy the dwelling which so much worth had inhabited. They mortally wounded John Carroll, cousin to the Colonel. This party of soldiers entered Ballitore exhausted by rage and fatigue; they brought cannon. Cannon in Ballitore! The horse and foot had now met. Colonel Campbell was here in person and many other officers. The insurgents had fled on the first alarm, – the peaceable inhabitants remained. The trumpet was sounded, and the peaceable inhabitants were delivered up for two hours to the unbridled licence of a furious soldiery! How shall I continue the fearful narrative?

My mind never could arrange the transactions which were crowded into those two hours. Every house in the Burrow was in flames; a row of houses opposite to the School was also set on fire; none others were burnt immediately in the village, but a great many windows were broken, and when I heard this crash I thought it was cannon. We saw soldiers bending under loads of plunder. Captain Palmer came in to see me, and was truly solicitous about us, and insisted on giving us "a protection." Soldiers came in for milk; some of their countenances were pale with anger, and they grinned at me, calling me names which I had never heard before. They said I had poisoned the milk which I gave them, and desired me to drink some, which I did with much indignation. Others were civil, and one enquired if we had had any United Irishmen in the house. I told them we had. In that fearful time the least equivocation, the least deception appeared to me to be fraught with danger. The soldier continued his enquiry – "Had they plundered us?" "No, except of eating and drinking." "On free quarters," he replied, smiling, and went away.

A fine–looking man, a soldier, came in, in an extravagant passion; neither his rage nor my terror could prevent me from observing that this man was strikingly handsome; he asked me the same question in the same terms – and I made the same answer. He cursed me with great bitterness, and, raising his musket, presented it to my breast. I desired him not to shoot me. It seemed as if he had the will, but not the power to do so. He turned from me, dashed pans and jugs off the kitchen table with his musket, and shattered the kitchen window. Terrified almost out of my wits, I ran out of the house, followed by several women almost as much frightened as myself. When I fled, my fears gained strength, and I believed my enemy was pursuing; I thought of throwing myself into the river at the foot of the garden, thinking the bullet could not hurt me in the water. One of our servants ran into the street to call for help. William Richardson and Charles Coote, who kindly sat on their horses outside our windows, came in and turned the ruffian out of the house.

That danger passed, I beheld from the back window of our parlour the dark red flames of Gavin's house and others rising above the green of the trees. At the same time a fat tobacconist from Carlow lolled upon one of our chairs, and talked boastingly of the exploits performed by the military whom he had accompanied; how they had shot several, adding, "We burned one fellow in a barrel." I never in my life felt disgust so strongly; it even overpowered the horror due to the deed, which had been actually committed. The stupid cruelty of a man in civil life, which urged him voluntarily and without necessity to leave his home and bear a part in such scenes, was far more revolting than the fiery wrath of a soldier.

While Captain Palmer was with me, a soldier who had been previously quartered at my mother's came to him, to beg leave to go see "the old mistress." My dear mother, who was now in the stage of second childhood, in her unconsciousness of what was passing had lost the timidity of her nature, mingled and conversed freely in her simplicity with all parties, and was treated by all with the greatest respect and tenderness; for, amid the darkness of the tumult, some rays of light gleamed forth, some countenances expressed humanity and a weariness of the work of death.

I must be an egotist in these relations, for I can scarcely describe anything but what I saw and heard. I scarce had the guidance even of my own movements. Sometimes I found myself with my children, whom I had shut up in a back room; again I was below, enquiring for my husband. Our old gardener was discovered lying in the shrubbery, and the instrument of death which was aimed at his defenceless breast was arrested by his daughter, who, rushing forward, begged that her life might be taken instead. The soldier spared both, but poor Polly was ever after subject to fits, which reduced her to a deplorable situation, and by which she eventually lost her life, being seized with one as she crossed a stream. A carpenter in the village took his goods into the graveyard, and hid himself and his family there. But in vain – this solemn retreat was violated, their goods were plundered, and the poor old man was murdered in wanton cruelty.

Owen Finn, the smith, who had been imprisoned and liberated, felt himself secure because of his late acquittal, and could not be prevailed upon to conceal himself or leave his house. Alas! he was mistaken in expecting that rage reeking with blood would stop to discriminate. Owen was dragged out of his cottage; his pleadings were not listened to; his cottage, where industry had assembled many comforts, was pillaged and then set on fire. His wife ran through the crowd, to assure herself of her husband's safety. She beheld his bleeding and dead body: she threw herself with her infant upon the corpse, while those who had wrought her misery assaulted her with abusive language, and threatened to kill her also. "And I wished," said she, "that they would kill me!"

Tom Duffy, called "the Fairy," had come from Dublin that morning to the house of his sister, whose husband was a yeoman, and had fallen in the battle of Kilcullen. The widow, though agonized with sorrow, found some little comfort in assuring herself and her children of protection by reason of her husband having suffered on the side of government. Her grief was mingled with astonishment heightened to frenzy when she found she had deceived herself. Her brother, poor Fairy Tom, was murdered; her son was murdered; her servant–boy was murdered; her house was plundered; her little daughter, on seeing her brother's corpse, fell into fits which caused her death; and her own reason gave way. Such are the horrors of civil war.

Our poor Doctor Johnson had suffered much from fatigue and anxiety during those days of terror; he ate and slept but little; and on the 26th, coming into Mary and Anne Doyle's, he declared his firm belief that he should fall by one party or the other, adding he did not care how soon. They wanted him to lie down and get a little rest, but his agitated mind would not permit him to take any. Next morning he was made prisoner, not endeavouring to conceal himself. I saw him walking in his yeomanry dress with a crowd of soldiers, and thought he was in friendship with them. I did not know that they pressed the ends of their muskets on his feet as he walked, and, by thus tormenting him, showed how little mercy he had to expect from them. The crowd stopped before Mary and Anne Doyle's shop; the tumult was loud; I believe they called it a court martial. An officer asked my husband had the doctor been at the battle of Narraghmore. He assured him he had not. Charles Coote stood by him, and begged to have him taken to the colonel. What his friends said was disregarded. Some young men, prisoners, passed by; Doctor Johnson appealed to them, but they passed on in silence. He was alone and unarmed, and I believe had never raised his hand to injure any one. The dragoons hacked him with their swords.[77] Captain Sandys, who afterwards lost his life at Vinegar Hill, took the doctor's part in this business. So many swords and bayonets, and at length a musket, could not be long in taking the life of an unarmed man.

A short time before the end, a soldier came into our parlour, and, with a kind of bitter smile, told me they were going to hang the doctor. I said I hope not, and went up to my children, trembling. One of our servants entered the room, and said the doctor was shot. I started up and contradicted her; just then the trumpet sounded a retreat. The window near my bedside had for some time caused me a dread which I could not account for, save by having heard of persons being shot through windows. But to this window I now went mechanically, and saw stretched before it, lying on his back, the friend I had known from childhood – my neighbour, my physician. His arms were extended; there was a large wound in the lower part of his face; and his once graceful form and intelligent countenance were disfigured with more than the horrors of death. I took but one look; I cried aloud; and Anne Doyle led me away. We went to the back apartments; the glass of the windows was hot from the reflection of the burning houses, but I looked on them with a stupid composure. My only thought was, Is my husband safe? Had not our dwelling and offices been slated, we should have been probably houseless, for the unchecked flames rose in dreadful spires, and the crash of falling roofs caused a terrific sound. The morning was balmy, beautiful, and mild; bounteous Nature smiled sweetly upon us, rich with the treasures of a benign Creator. The unbridled passions of man alone deformed the scene!

Captain Palmer, naturally good-natured, was peculiarly desirous to preserve everybody and everything in the vale he loved so well. He learned the doctor's danger, and hastened from Athy to save him; but he came, alas! too late – too late for that purpose, but in time to rescue another who was in those hands reeking with blood, and ready to take his life, as, speechless with terror, he stood beholding the sad spectacle. Priest Cullen, justly apprehensive for his life, had applied to my brother for one of his coats wherewith to disguise himself, but dared not wait to put it on. He ran to Boakefield, and hid in one of the clumps of trees in the lawn, while several officers were refreshing themselves in the parlour, and soldiers were scattered about the house, who seemed to thirst for his blood.

After the trumpet had sounded a retreat, a soldier shot one of our pigs, for which he was tied to a car and lashed. Oh! how shocking that seemed to me! Commanded to take the precious human life – punished for taking that of a brute! The progress of the army on the way they now went was impeded by trees purposely felled by the insurgents a day or two before. Some of the soldiers availed themselves of this delay to return to Ballitore, and renew the work of plunder. This alarmed Charles Coote on our account, as he justly feared the protections previously granted would not again avail. The soldiers were overloaded with their spoils, and had to throw some away. A paper was discovered in a work-bag, containing a list of names which roused suspicion. Charles Coote, on the watch, claimed to look at the paper, and quickly convinced the soldiers that their suspicions were unfounded; yet his heart was wrung in secret, for this paper, in my handwriting, contained the charades and rebuses with which we had amused ourselves on one of our past happy evenings, with a list of explanations. He feared lest those who had returned might plunder and murder us; and the anguish of such an apprehension was quickened by the contrast with the convivial hour. Thus Homer heightens our interest in the fate of Hector, by pointing him to our view as flying from his destroyer by those fountains,

> Where Trojan dames, ere yet alarmed by Greece,
> Washed their fair garments in the days of peace.

Now the blast was over – all was silent and sad. Our houseless tenants were sheltered under our roof; we sat down with Mary and Anne, – the closed windows concealing our dead friend from us. Mary, pale as death, shook the table on which she leaned with her excessive trembling; and when Anne saw the body carried along and thrown over the little wall at the corner where the elm-tree once stood, her cry of grief was heart-piercing; – while I sate like a stone. The report of the soldiers intending to return made his neighbours afraid to shelter in their houses those dear remains. Here they were carefully watched, for the swine snuffing blood, were waiting to make a horrid repast. For several months there was no sale for bacon cured in

Ireland, from the well-founded dread of the hogs having fed upon the flesh of men.

The first use we made of our minds' returning strength was to visit Maria Johnson. She knew not that her husband was in the hands of his enemies, nor that they were his enemies, until one of the Tyrone militia came raging into the house, boasting that the doctor was shot, and calling for his wife that he might cut her head off. She sank down upon her knees in a state that baffles description; her sister was little better, and the lamentations of the children touched even the hearts of the soldiers – so that instead of doing farther injury they endeavoured to soothe their distress. I saw those mourners looking so sweet, so innocent, so sorrowful that I could not bear it, but hastened into the garden; thither their servant followed me to consult what should be done with her master's body. We concluded on having him buried in our graveyard without loss of time, in whatever clothes were left upon him, for alas! even his corpse was plundered. This needful conversation calmed my feelings, and I was able to return and sit with the widow.

There was no motive for consolation to be urged in this dreadful calamity; we could only weep abundantly with her. It was a comfort to us that she could weep. No harsher expression escaped her lips than, "Ah, it was a cruel enemy!" Her little Eliza sprang into the room, threw her arms about her mother's neck, and, in a tone which bespoke the anguish of her young heart, exclaimed, "What shall we do for my poor father!" He was one of the tenderest of fathers as well as of husbands; his little daughters were his pride and delight, and his family, including his sister-in-law, loved him with reciprocal affection. I caught myself saying, "Why are these things permitted?" And I thought that if the murderer were to see what I then saw, his conscience would compel him to cry out, "My punishment is greater than I can bear."

On the 29th, people ventured to seek for their friends, and to bury their dead. Whether it was that having so many companions in misfortune lightened the load, whether they considered those that had fallen as martyrs, or whether

> Vengeance, deep brooding o'er the slain,
> Had locked the source of softer woe,

there did not appear so much lamentation as one might have expected. The ruins of cars lay in some of the ditches at the entrance into Ballitore, and in another ditch lay the scull of the poor youth who had been burnt in the barrel where he sought refuge.

I saw moving along under the arching trees a few persons, chiefly women, bearing an empty coffin. I joined them in silence, and met in the graveyard my husband and two or three more, about to open the grave in which the poor doctor was laid, and at his widow's desire to re–inter him in a coffin. I saw the earth being removed; I wished, yet dreaded, to see the body. A shroud was wanted; I hastened back to Mary and Anne's for it; we hastily made it, and returning towards the graveyard, a boy met us who had been sent to fetch it; and before we got back to the grave, the body had been washed, wrapped in its shroud, and laid in the coffin.[78] I experienced strange and contradictory feelings while I stood at the graveyard gate, wishing and yet fearing to enter; Mary and Anne confessed to similar sensations, but we all regretted our irresolution when we heard the coffin lid screwed down. My husband, when he saw how it disturbed me, regretted that he had hastened to prevent our seeing so sad a sight, though the remains were little altered by having lain three days in the earth. The bloody waistcoat lay near, and the sight of it renewed our emotions of horror.

Timolin was attacked after Ballitore, and several houses in its suburbs burnt. Conway, a Protestant, was protected, or rather spared by one party of soldiers, but was cut down by another, and his house shared the fate of the other dwellings. The Dublin road for nearly four miles north of Ballitore exhibited a scene of desolation, few houses having escaped there; and about Narraghmore and Crookstown the same destruction was apparent. The street of Ballitore was strewed with broken glass and earthenware, ground by the trampling of the feet. We looked around at our altered village, and were ready to wonder that we yet lived. "Surely the wrath of man shall praise Thee, the remainder of wrath wilt Thou restrain." We were sensible that a preserving Providence had restrained that wrath which threatened general destruction.

Hostages having been sent, the insurgents prepared to deliver up their arms on the 30th. A little boy was the herald, who, with a bit of white paper stuck in his hat to announce his office and secure his person, passed safely between the opposite parties, and we respected the little fellow for his courage. The appointed spot for meeting was about half way between Ballitore and Athy, and there the insurgents learned that those who had assembled on the Curragh for a similar purpose had been, I suppose by some unfortunate mistake, fallen upon by a party commanded by Sir James Duff, and put to the sword.[79] Terrified by this intelligence, many returned at full speed; but by my brother's and Ephraim Boake's exertions, representations, and offers to accompany them, they were prevailed upon to go back and conclude this disastrous business, by delivering up their arms, and obtaining pardon for their offences against government, though not for those committed against the laws of their country. Ephraim Boake was a wise old man; he was truly loyal to his king, but he did not think loyalty incompatible with mercy. "Those who do not like this government," he was wont to say, "let them go and live under another; but while they are protected by this, let them not disturb it."

The prisoners had gone away under the protection of the army – some of the soldiers leaving money to relieve the present distresses of the poor. Indeed many characters were now developed; the sordid, the carnal, the selfish had gained opportunity of gratification; while brighter through the surrounding gloom beamed the candid, the liberal, the benevolent mind, and Captain Chenery and Captain Palmer will be long remembered and long beloved in Ballitore.

CHAPTER IX.
1798.

THAT pretty cottage built by poor Dr. Johnson, to which he had brought his bride, was now a blackened ruin. Many families sheltered themselves under hedges, or wherever they could thrust their heads; and some poor women brought forth their babes under these sorrowful circumstances. Yet the houseless wretches expressed thankfulness that their lives were spared, and a long period of remarkably fine weather was granted, as well as uncommon health, for we rarely heard of any sickness except that caused by wounds, and previously Ballitore had seldom passed through a summer without being visited by fever amongst the poor. Great was the terror in which the army were held. A soldier was an unwelcome sight, unconscious that the time was not far distant when they should be most welcome. And this dread was not without cause; we frequently saw the blaze of burning houses on the surrounding hills, and several men were shot by the military when going about their lawful business, so that people were afraid to cut their turf, save their hay and corn, or even to sleep in their own abodes.

When the corn had shot into ear, three months after her poor husband's death, Dolly Finn went to her little farm to look at her crop. She was alone; she entered among the black walls of her ruined cottage; her heart was oppressed with horror and grief, and she vented her anguish in tears and groans of despair, lamenting her deplorable condition. A soldier was passing at the time; he heard the sound of sorrow, and through the aperture which had once been a window he saw a lovely woman, whose appearance inspired his depraved heart with sentiments very different from compassion. He alighted from his horse, and, having questioned her closely, he showed her his pistols, and then attempted to seize her. She ran out of the walls, shrieking, believing his intent was to render her still more wretched; he followed, and compelled her to walk beside him. The trembling widow looked around and cried aloud for succour, in vain; the highroad was now solitary, war and terror had depopulated it. Some persons who had taken shelter in a deserted stable at length came out, when her enemy immediately assuming the character of a friend advised her not to frequent those ruins again, and departed. Her alarm was such that for a long time she feared to walk anywhere alone, and her fancy pictured every furzebush to be a soldier!

The garrisoned town of Athy was thronged with those who were afraid to remain in the country, – yet where was safety? Even in this garrison a man from Narraghmore was shot by a soldier – accidentally, they said.

When we went to the monthly meeting of Carlow we saw marks of dismay on all sides, especially in the pale and immoveable countenances of two women sitting before an open window. An attack from the insurgents was said to be expected that night, and yeomen hurried to and fro with weapons in their hands. The state of the times engrossed all conversation, till we longed to shut our ears from hearing of blood; and we scarcely dared to utter humane sentiments, the tide ran so strongly against those who had put the inhabitants in such jeopardy. All our friends rejoiced over us, as beings delivered from the jaws of danger and of death.

We hastened back to Ballitore, where, once more, all wore the appearance of peace and security; where we walked out in the delightful evenings, unmolested by those countersigns which had been so constantly called for during the last three months, – undisturbed by the sight of licensed or unlicensed instruments of destruction, – feeling for one another with that tender melancholy affection peculiar to fellow–sufferers. But all sensations of cheerfulness had fled, and our spirits wore a covering of sadness which forbade our enjoyment of the beauties of Nature. A retrospect of past events presented itself almost continually to the mind; and surely this state of humiliation was intended for our refinement by Him who afflicts not willingly.

Though the storm had spent its fury here, it raged elsewhere with redoubled violence. The reports from the county of Wexford were terrible – the hard–fought battle of Ross, the camp on Vinegar–hill, the horrible burning of the barn at Scullabogue, the slaughter on Wexford–bridge, and the dreadful retaliations. O how does the flame of party burn up all on whom it seizes! Do men forget that their common Father is a God of love, a God of mercy? Or must we say,

> There is no flesh in man's obdurate heart;
> It does not feel for man!

Some who had been witnesses to those shocks could palliate a little the excesses of the misguided multitude. They said the burning of the barn of Scullabogue was not the work of the whole body, but abhorred by them, and was done by a party maddened after the defeat of Ross. Women and children were spared, and Quakers in general escaped; but woe to the oppressor of the poor, the hard landlord, the severe master, or him who was looked upon as an enemy!

John Jeffers of Narraghmore, returning from Kilcullen to Athy, was waylaid near the ruins of his own house, which had been burned by the insurgents, and shot dead. His mother–in–law was within hearing of the shot; she got assistance to take away the body, and although most probably in the midst of enemies, was treated with kindness and compassion. Soon after this event three or four of our neighbours, young men, were made prisoners and suffered death in Athy. One young officer of dragoons, on his return to Dublin from Vinegar–hill, was heard to boast that he had cut off several croppies' heads; perhaps he might not be quite so brave in the day of battle. Most of our neighbours who had been prisioners at Naas, now returned and came joyfully to see us. They had been acquitted after a confinement of nine weeks. One, however, still remained behind. I was requested to write to Captain Chenery on his behalf; I did so, and the captain sent my note into the court, where it was to be decided whether Pat Lyons should remain a prisoner or return home a free man. When it was perceived that the note came from a female, it was treated with contempt; "Women did not care what they said, and it was from a woman." On further inspection they observed the date; "Quakers tell truth, and it was from a Quaker" – and accordingly Pat was liberated.

Martial law continued to be observed in Athy; Hugh Cullen, of Prospect, was made a prisoner, and carried from his fields to encounter this formidable power. Ephraim Boake saw the threatened destruction of his neighbour, the industrious father of a large family, whom he did not believe to have been guilty of any violence. Ephraim's body and mind were not rendered inactive by age; for, seconded by the representations of the kind–hearted Captain Palmer, he went to Dublin and exerted his influence with his friend Agar, Archbishop of Cashel, by whose means he obtained from Lord Castlereagh, whose brother, Colonel Stewart, commanded in Athy and that district, an order to stop proceedings by court martial.[80] His messenger hastened from Dublin on his errand of mercy; the uplifted sword was stayed, and, though long detained a prisoner, Hugh Cullen was not irrevocably torn from his family. His brother Paul, a fine young man, had been condemned by a court martial a little while before. His poor father attended the trial; when he returned, the family anxiously enquired, "What news?" "Good news," replied the parent, sadly. "My child is to die, and he is willing to die!"

Late one evening, as we leaned over the bridge, we saw a gentleman and lady watering their horses at the river, attended by servants fully armed. They wore mourning habits, and though young and newly married, looked very serious and sorrowful. Their chastened appearance, their armed servants, the stillness of the air scarcely broken by a sound, rendered the scene very impressive. We very rarely saw any of the gentry; when we did, they were generally dressed in deep black; for what family had not lost a member? Mourning was the language – mourning was the dress of the country.

Some of Ephraim Boake's relatives who resided at Baltinglass, fearing an attack upon that town, sought safety under his roof. But that night a party came to Boakefield, demanding arms. They were told there were none; they wanted the family to swear to this, but did not insist on it; and, on being refused admittance, said they would not break the door. They asked for whiskey and a newspaper. This was in Sixth–month (June), and was the beginning of our troubles in this way. It did not make much impression on our minds, but our pensive tranquillity was not long to last. About two months after this, in the dead of the night, a demand for wine was made at my mother's door, by persons who represented themselves as travellers, and excused themselves by reason of the inclemency of the weather. They asked for two bottles, which were handed to them from a window, and on going away they said, "Not one word of this in the morning."

In the Eighth–month (August) we heard of the French having landed at Killala, but in so small a force as not to cause any great alarm. It proved, however, that an able general was necessary to stop their progress, joined as they were by many of the country people. This able general was found in the good Cornwallis, who succeeded Lord Camden in the government of Ireland, and who held out the olive–branch, and sheathed the avenging sword whenever it was possible. He discouraged the distinctions of party, and when the Lord Mayor of Dublin appeared before him, wearing an orange cockade, he enquired the meaning of it, and on being told it was a badge of loyalty, said, "I did not know till now that the first magistrate was suspected." When he overheard some of his officers disputing about a bed, on their march to meet the French, it is reported of this gallant veteran that he said, "Gentlemen, any of you are welcome to my bed; a little clean straw behind the door will satisfy me."

At our fair it was pleasant to see so many people alive, and to behold the joy with which they greeted one another. Soldiers moved amongst them to prevent unlawful confabulations, and a reformation soon ensued at those places, by the people being dispersed early, and not permitted to assemble in drinking, and, as a matter of course, in fighting parties.

The days were now shortening. Another demand for wine in a larger quantity, and enforced in a more peremptory manner than before, was made at my mother's; and on the same night a person climbed over the rails of my brother's yard, and unbolted the gate for others, seeking more wine. This was the only attack made on my brother, and his subsequent escapes were surprising and unexpected to the family. The mail-coach was burnt; horses were taken out of the fields; and one beautiful moonlight night a desperate band plundered several houses about Narraghmore. Glassealy House was burned to the ground. The master of this mansion, T. J. Rawson, and his family were fortunately in Athy. He had been very active in bringing the disaffected to punishment, and was consequently obnoxious to them, and exposed to their resentment.

Alas! these banditti did not stop at plundering and destroying property. That fine night was obscured by murder – a murder which brought upon the country a greater stain than any other act had done. Hannah Manders, a protestant, who held a farm and was well liked by her neighbours, with her sister, her nephew, and a maid-servant, were all murdered. Another servant snatched up a little child, whose father had fallen at the time of the rising, and who was sheltered and protected there by the kind-hearted mistress, and ran away to conceal herself and it. They lay hidden in a lime-kiln, and the little creature, though quite awake, kept a profound silence, while the poor servant trembled lest it should cry out. The farm-house, late the seat of peace and plenty and benevolence, was burned to the ground. This savage deed caused general horror and detestation. It was thought that some incautious words which the servant had uttered after a visit from marauders might have been the cause of this cruel act; but nothing could extenuate the crime.

Not long after this the depredations seriously began at Ballitore. Those whose offences had debarred them from the privilege of protections were outcasts from society, and had no apparent means of subsistence save by rapine. They sheltered themselves in the County of Wicklow mountains, and from thence made nightly excursions for food, money and clothes, levying their black mail on the timid and the peaceful, while the lengthening nights favoured their designs.[81] Holt, who was their general, was said to be a brave and merciful man. Their first visit to Ballitore as avowed robbers was to Mary and Anne Doyle. My husband and I had spent the evening with Maria Johnson. We returned impressed with that tender feeling of compassion and sympathy which the sense of her injuries created, while the silence of the night and the gloom of the trees mingled awe with our regret. It was early in the Tenth-month (October). The clock was about striking ten when we called at Mary and Anne's door, being accustomed never to pass without calling on these dear friends, particularly now that for the protection of my mother we lived at the Retreat.[82] Four men were lurking near the door, and entered when it was opened for us. We saw that they were armed. My husband went to alarm the neighbours, and get assistance; for one unarmed man could do nothing. They would not let him return, for which I felt thankful, as single–handed he could only expect to be sacrificed, and he could get no assistance.

I remained with my friends, saw them robbed of their money and goods, and a pistol presented to Mary Doyle's breast, though I thought I saw the man uncock it first. He was of her own name, Doyle, a very handsome man, and affected to speak broken English. One fellow stood at the shop–door, repeatedly calling, as to some one without, "All's well;" sometimes adding, "All's devilish well."

When their work was done they liberated my husband, and we remained with our poor friends most of the night, although I often looked towards the Retreat, and thought of my poor helpless mother and our tender little children. When we went thither we found the house in confusion; the robbers had not long left it. They took several articles of value of my mother's, my sister's, and ours; and made my mother's man–servant accompany them to the apartment where our children lay in their beds. They asked our little Elizabeth where her father kept his money. She cried, and said she did not know. "I know," called out little Jane, "where my father keeps his money." "Where, honey?" "In his breeches pocket."

They broke open my husband's desk, and scattered his papers about the room; we missed none of them save three letters to me from Edmund Burke. The beauty of the pocket–book in which they were – a gift to me from his wife – no doubt caused it and them to be taken. I regretted my loss so much that I made a fruitless enquiry for them of the robbers on their next visit. It is probable these precious relics shared the fate of the guinea notes at Vinegar Hill, being used to light the pipes of the robbers.

They took a great deal of clothes, and broke the furniture, apparently to get at the contents, for they took a looking–glass off a chest of drawers, and laid it carefully aside. Perhaps, also, they recollected the superstitious notion that breaking a mirror brings bad luck to the breaker. In bursting open a wardrobe with the handle of a pistol, the charge exploded, and the ball passed through the bedstead in which lay little Jane. The room filled with smoke; the children screamed; the frightened servants ran in; and the robbers, also alarmed, hastened to see if the child was killed. She smiled in their faces, and told them not to be so frightened, for she was not hurt.

My dear mother appeared to be but little disturbed by this or the other scenes she had passed through; yet it is probable they accelerated her mental decay. We took the precaution of removing the whole family to sleep the following night at my brother's; but, though most welcome to continue there, we preferred returning to our own home as soon as we had it arranged after the attack, not believing a message from the audacious visitors that they would be with us again before next morning.

We richly enjoyed the satisfaction that morning brought us of a passing look at our dear Tom Eyre, of whom we had lost sight for some years. He was travelling post, disguised in a round hat and great–coat over his regimentals. Afraid of endangering our safety by openly calling upon us, he had looked anxiously around as the carriage passed along the high road. At length he saw my husband and my brother in a field conversing together. He sent his servant for them, and my husband sent directly for me. I found him leaning on each of them, and was struck with the great alteration in his dear countenance. He looked extremely ill, and was then labouring under an attack of gout.

He said he had been twice in the West Indies since he had seen us. His health had suffered from fatigue, and the hardships he had undergone when encountering the French in Connaught had given it the finishing blow. He said that in this last expedition it was evident that they passed through an enemy's country, though their brave commander, Cornwallis, would not seem to observe it, and, where paper money was refused, paid down gold. Tom, now Lieutenant–colonel Eyre, had the command of the French prisoners to Dublin. His wife was in England, for he said Ireland was no place for a woman now. He looked with longing eyes, filled with tears, upon the valley where he had sported in his childhood, lamenting that he could not see my dear mother, who had been one of his faithful guardians. He remounted his chaise, was soon out of sight, and we never saw him more.

As I sat at my work about eight o'clock that evening, my mind reverting mournfully yet sweetly to the past, the robbers knocked at the door. To the enquiry, "Who is there?" the answer was returned, "A friend;" and two enemies entered, who demanded our watches, and then asked for money. One of them sat down, the muzzle of his blunderbuss turned towards me. I desired him to turn it away, and he did so. Doyle was one of them; – his countenance was changing, – becoming darkened by guilt. They asked me to go with them to our desk for money. I requested they would not awake the children, and they immediately spoke low. Finding I had very little money, one pretended to struggle with the other for the blunderbuss to shoot me; I was not afraid, except that by their awkward handling the piece might accidentally go off. I had on these occasions very little fear, but I had also very little presence of mind. I was willing to give the robbers anything they demanded to get them away, and had no dexterity in preserving property. After ineffectual threats to procure more money, they wished me good night, and went again to Mary and Anne Doyle's; breaking their windows, robbing them, and striking dear Mary.

An impulse of general alarm caused many of the inhabitants to leave the village; some went to Dublin, and some to Athy. My husband took my mother, myself, and our two children to Carlow. Our poor neighbours looked sad, and wept at seeing "the old mistress" leave Ballitore under such circumstances. My husband returned next day, and very reluctantly I consented that we should stay at Carlow for a while, for fear is strengthened by flight from danger, and I was much less at ease at Carlow than at home, which I felt to be my right place. My thoughts dwelt also with poor Mary and Anne, but to them my husband was a protector. I became dreadfully terrified with the idea that Carlow would be attacked, especially one night when I was awakened by the sound of a horn, not recollecting that it only announced a mail–coach. Oh! the terror that blast on the horn gave me!

We now heard of the murder of William Hume of Humewood. Mary Lecky of Kilnock and her family were at Carlow, being expelled from her home by robbery and rough treatment. Elizabeth Lecky of Ballykealy was also there, although a message had been sent to her that she should not be molested. Still the treatment inflicted on the equally beloved inhabitants of Kilnock made her tremble for her own large family.

On our return to Ballitore, where "the old mistress" was received with heartfelt gladness, we bade adieu to the sweet Retreat and settled in our own habitation, which though a smaller and much less commodious house, had the advantage of the close vicinity of our dear Mary and Anne Doyle, from whom we wished no more to separate, and to whom every fresh trouble more strongly united us. We felt ourselves like weak trees supporting one another against the storm. My mother lived with us. It was now the fall of the year, but we could no longer look forward with comfort to the warm firesides and social evenings which we had often thought, whilst enjoying them, made winter the pleasantest season of the year.[83] We anticipated with too much certainty the dread and the dangers of that which now approached, and scarcely dared to look beyond it. In fact, all about us was gloom.

I went one afternoon to the Retreat; the house was locked, and the family who took care of it had gone out. I entered at a window; the withered leaves entered with me, and the winds whistled through the empty rooms, once the warm nests of domestic delights. I went into the garden; the autumnal blasts had strewn it with leaves, which mournfully rustled under my feet, for no hand, as formerly, had swept them away. In the gardener's house lay poor John Fleming in malignant fever; as I approached it, I heard his father addressing him in an anguished tone of voice. When I reached the door and enquired for him, the poor man answered, "He died two hours before day! I had no one with me to send for the priest, so I prayed that God would do His will with him." I thought that this might have been an acceptable prayer, poured forth in the bitterness of an afflicted heart which had no human aid to look to. For him, poor youth, there was much to hope; he was a young man of uncommon mind, and of a very serious turn. He was much attached to the cause of the insurgents; but he said during his illness that he hoped he had not much to answer for, as he had never wronged anyone of a shilling, and had never been present at the killing of a human being.[84]

Shortly after our return from Carlow an attack on Boakefield terrified us more than one on ourselves could have done. We heard for nearly two hours repeated discharges of shot, – then saw flames ascending. A dreary silence followed, broken at length by the noise of the robbers, and by a shot which they fired as they entered the village. We sat in fearful expectation of an attack upon ourselves, and could scarcely believe it when they passed us by; yet our anxiety for our neighbours' fate prevented our enjoying our own escape, and we longed for morning. When it came, our worst fears were put to flight. No one at Boakefield had been injured, though on each refusal to admit them the banditti fired a volley with the regularity of disciplined men. Those within endeavoured to keep in positions where they could not be reached by the bullets, twelve of which penetrated the hall-door; the windows were shattered, and several pieces of furniture damaged. A servant escaped out of the back of the house and ran off to Timolin, where a party of the army was stationed, to request their aid; they had been, however, advised "to leave the devoted hole to itself," and they took the advice. Soon afterwards this servant's life was attempted. The robbers at length got in at the back window; one of them, who appeared to be the commander, cried out, "I know my doom, but we are starving. I am Captain Smith, and I scarce care what I do. Why would you not let us in? Are any of you hurt?" He was answered that they had taken his band for the gang of robbers which were infesting the neighbourhood. "We are no robbers," said he, "and yet what else can you call us?" They did not take much out of the house, or offer any violence to the family, but made strict search for men who had been there, one of whom was actually hidden in the garret at the time. They desired the men to go out and save the stable, which they had set on fire; and then retired. Captain Smith and his band were soon after taken up and lodged in Baltinglass gaol.[85]

A cheering circumstance diversified these gloomy scenes. Robert Baxter, our early and beloved friend, who we believed had been for some years numbered with the dead, again appeared in Ballitore. He was now an officer in the Cavan militia, and called to see us on his route. His countenance was glowing with rapturous joy at the sight of his old friends and the well–remembered vale, and then shaded with regret at the havoc which time and war had made amongst the friends and the shades which he loved. His stay was very short; he introduced me to his wife as "Molly Shackleton," and made us kiss in the street; then he rushed off without his hat to see our children, and was particularly struck with the beauty of our little Jane. That dear child had a great dread of military men ever since the fearful day which the children called "Bloody First–day;" and she used to say to me, "I love every body in the world, but I don't love the soldiers, because they killed the doctor, and he was a pleasant man!" I was therefore astonished to see her clasp Robert Baxter fondly round the neck and cling to him, though he was dressed in full regimentals, as if by sympathy she acknowledged and loved her mother's friend.[86]

A general rebuilding of the ruined houses now took place, but even this work was in a great measure carried on by plunder. The stately trees of Ballitore were often missed in the morning, and we could hear at night the sound of their being felled and the creaking of the cars which took them away. Desolation threatened in various shapes – the darkness of the winter nights was illumined by the fires of the houses burnt by the insurgents, and fatal was their vengeance. One man whom they thought they had killed and had thrown into a ditch, pulling down part of the bank upon him, was not fatally injured, struggled out of his grave, ran naked to Baltinglass, and convicted his intended murderers. A large burial moved through Ballitore with a kind of indignant solemnity. It was that of a young man who had been hanged, and whose father, on his son's being apprehended, put an end to his own life. Such were the tragedies with which we were surrounded, and with which we had grown shockingly familiar.

Thus were we circumstanced when a sore domestic calamity seemed to fill up the measure of our sufferings. We thought we had a little respite from our foes, and we were once more assembled in peace around Mary and Anne's fireside, when our dear little Jane was trusted by me with a wax taper to go up stairs alone. The staircase was short, and her grandmother was in her own room with her attendant. I was not used to be so incautious, and the thought crossed my mind, "Is it safe?" A distinct voice seemed to reply, "The child is so steady;" and all recollection of her left me till I heard her shrieks. Then the truth flashed upon me, and I accused myself of having murdered my child! She had gone into another room than her grandmother's, and had laid down the taper; it caught her clothes, and the flames were not easily extinguished. A kind of convulsion stiffened her for a moment; the burns though extensive were but skin–deep, and those around us assured us she was in no danger. Alas, we were not aware that the fright she got had stopped the circulation of the blood. O! Why were we not aware of it? Let this be remembered by others, and may no one else experience the distress caused by our error.

The dear child soon ceased to complain of pain, kissed all those about her, and was cheerful, yet all night was thirsty, wakeful, and cold, with but little pulse. In the morning her whole form and sweet countenance underwent a momentary revolution which I cannot describe. We had sent to Athy for a doctor, but he said nothing could be done. Meantime, unconscious that she was leaving us, the dear innocent got her book and her work into her bed, and repeated her little verses, spoke with her usual courtesy to all around her, and, happy in her short life, closed her eyes never more to open them, just twenty–four hours after the accident happened. We who had lost our darling child of four years old felt deeply the deprivation, and struggled hard to submit to the will of Him who gives and takes away.

My grief was aggravated by self–accusation. I beheld my little cherub lie as in a placid sleep, her bloom not quite gone. I listened to those who desired me to reflect on the many fathers of families who lay buried in ditches, slaughtered in the prime of manhood and of usefulness; and to the widow who with tears reminded me that I had still my husband! I reflected how, a brief time ago, his precious life had seemed near departing, and I strove to extract consolation from the genuine sympathy bestowed by our friends; yet I thought no sympathy reached my heart so fully as once when I raised my eyes from contemplating the lovely remains of my child, and met those of a poor neighbour woman fastened upon me in silence, large tears streaming down her cheeks, her countenance filled with the deepest concern. She was a coarse–featured, strong, rough woman, and had forborne any expression by words of what she felt.

Our Jane was borne from our sight; the grave closed upon her for ever; her little playfellows bedecked it with flowers, and wept for their lost companion, while their schoolmistress and her husband mourned as for a favourite grandchild. Even in this season of universal dismay the loss of this dear child was very generally deplored; she was so beautiful, so engaging, so beloved – not like a thing of earth. So ended the year 1798. Oh! Year of woe!

That year, that eventful year, which to me began with the fulness of joy, I saw depart laden with deep and piercing sorrow. Thus trouble takes its rounds; but "shall we receive good at the hand of the Lord, and shall we not also receive evil?"

We were almost prepared to congratulate our precious child on her escape, and to think that her timid nature might have been terrified into imbecility, when, shortly after her death, the robbers paid us another visit, breaking in the windows in the solemn midnight, and scaring us out of our quiet slumbers to behold armed men in our very chambers. They discovered what we strove to conceal, for their search was very strict, and they took whatever suited their purposes; but withal treated us with civility and respect. They had been at other houses, and had just robbed a pedlar of goods to a large amount. Mary Doyle, whose face, even in that hour of terror, reminded me of the fine white marble figures I had seen in Westminster Abbey, pale, serious, smooth, and handsome, ventured to expostulate; but a false alarm that the soldiers were coming had more effect. We heard our little Elizabeth praying, as Ajax had once prayed, that the Lord would please to send us daylight.

Hearing that some of our plundered property had been found, and was in the custody of Squire Ryves of Rathsallagh till it should be claimed, Mary Doyle and I went thither. The way appeared long, lonely, and drear. The large old mansion of Rathsallagh exhibited a melancholy picture. Its neglected appearance, barricadoed windows, the absence of the female part of the family, and the presence of a military guard, made us think our own situation preferable, as we were permitted to enjoy domestic comfort. Some of our things were here, and while the squire restored them to us, he smiled, and warned us of our danger of being robbed again. He foretold but too truly, though for a while we heard only distant alarms, such as of the mail–coach and travellers having been robbed. Snowy weather, we thought, kept the plunderers from us, from apprehension lest the track of their feet should betray their haunts. The snow, however, melted, and a widow neighbour became the object of their pillage. She had charge of the post–office, so they got some money there.

A few nights after this they made a general inroad on the village, entering almost every house except my brother's. They had, in the course of their visits, got themselves intoxicated, and in that state beset our house. My husband told them he would open the door, and requested them not to break the windows; but they did break them, and, entering, ordered him fiercely to prepare to go with them. He refused, saying, "Do what you will to me here; I will not leave my family." "Ten of us were shot and hanged in Baltinglass." "I had no hand in hanging or shooting you." He had but a few shillings; they refused them, and enquired what o'clock it was. He told them he had been robbed of his watch. At this they took offence: "Do you call us robbers? We are no robbers; we only want a little money; we want no watch. Did you ask him for a watch?" They grew more and more furious, and struck at him with a hanger, which cut into the wainscot partition. They raised a gun at him, which he pushed aside. They presented a pistol; it burned priming.

My firm belief that they did not really intend murder preserved me in more composure than I could have thought; for there were six armed men threatening one unarmed and defenceless. But now the clatter of arms, the cries of three women who stood on the staircase, and the threats of those wicked men would have overcome me, had I not just then seen my husband escape from their hands.

The next moment was again terrible. Anne Doyle came in, holding her head with both hands, and saying in a tremulous voice that she believed she was killed. A ruffian had struck her with the butt–end of his pistol, and had wounded her head in two places. I saw a stroke aimed at the back of Mary Doyle's head, and averted it with my outstretched arm. She lamented aloud, and accused the robbers of having murdered her sister; not silenced by their offered blows, and their threats that they would kill her if she would not be quiet. At last one cried out, "Hush, for God's sake!" "Don't mention that name;" returned Mary, "He has nothing to do with such wickedness." They appeared to be struck with the solemnity and distress with which she spoke, their countenances fell, and their accents became those of compassion. One man, who had his face hidden by a handkerchief, took her hand tenderly, and exclaimed, "Surely you do not think it was I hurt her?" They went away soon after.

The next day an old woman came to enquire for Anne Doyle, and hinted that when the robbers thought we were rested they intended to pay us another visit; but before night a party of the Clare militia came in to protect the inhabitants. We could now sleep in our beds without fear of disturbance, yet deeply regretted that we owed this security not to confidence, but to force repelling force. The excesses of the military were not forgotten, and they did not appear to be cordially received by the lower class of people. The country was far from being settled; it was like the working of the sea after a storm. On the window–stools of the upper storeys of many gentlemen's houses were collected large stones, placed there to assist in repelling the attacks of robbers. Travelling carriages were escorted by military guards, and the mail–coach was guarded by two or more powerfully armed men.

To our particular feelings the public commotion was some relief, as it partially drew our thoughts into another channel than the contemplation of our affliction, and strengthened our hope that it was in mercy our darling child was called away. The marks of the flames which had caused her destruction and of the blood which flowed from our dear Anne's wounds, together stained the wainscoat; which also bore the mark of the hanger aimed at my husband. These were easily obliterated, but the remembrance must last with life. I now perceived that my memory, which had been uncommonly good, was much impaired, and I imputed it to the series of repeated shocks which my mind had sustained. Such shocks had deprived many of health and some of reason, and we who were spared both had additional cause for thankfulness.

One day we saw two prisoners brought in who had robbed a gentleman in open daylight on the high road; the soldiers got the alarm, and quickly apprehended them. In a few days their lives were ended by martial law in Carlow. The soldiers having been withdrawn from Timolin, Pat Lalor's house was robbed, his daughter beaten, and he himself barely escaped with his life. One evening the village was alarmed by a soldier having shot another man. Two of the "Ancient Britons," who had been sent on an express, entered a carman's stage–house, where were also some Kilkenny carriers. One of the dragoons forgetting he had changed horses with his comrade, and knowing that his own pistol was not charged, snapped the pistol he held in his hand in jest at one of the carriers; it was loaded with death, and the young man instantly lay on the floor a bloody corpse; the soldier, standing over him, wringing his hands, exclaimed, "Oh, what have I done!" He was tried and acquitted, much to the dissatisfaction of the country–people.

Several robbers were at this time shot or imprisoned. Amongst the latter was Doyle; he was in great danger, but he escaped death. We believed, notwithstanding, that the inclination for plunder still continued, for the day the Dumfries fencibles left Ballitore, several men of suspicious aspect appeared in the village, and our lower class of neighbours seemed to exult in the departure of the military, and to be crest–fallen when another regiment came. It was on a fine day, and while the market was being held, that we saw two men yet living pass through the village, escorted by a strong military guard; but on the same car were their coffins.[87] One had been convicted for burning the courthouse at Narraghmore, the other for the murder of Hannah Manders, and they were to suffer death at the places where their crimes had been committed. One of the men hung his head weeping, the other looked about as if stupified by terror. The march of the soldiers was slow and solemn, and the people in the market seemed afraid to notice the prisoners.

Hugh Cullen now returned to his family from a long imprisonment, and, attended by his glad father, called to see his neighbours, who welcomed him back to life and liberty.[88]

One of the curiosities of our village, our old neighbour Finlay McClane, after a severe conflict with death, yielded at last, having just completed his 110th year, and possessing his mental faculties to the end.[89]

The sad account reached us about this time of the death of our dear Tom Eyre. He was on his way to Clogheen, where his regiment was quartered, and my sister Grubb and he anticipated much pleasure in each other's society. His journey was arrested at Kilkenny by an attack of gout in the stomach, which speedily put an end to his life. At these tidings I mourned for him with sisterly sorrow, and wept bitter, unavailing tears, while retracing the pleasant scenes of childhood.

I did not say in the right place how spring, though remarkably late this year, at length clothed the face of nature in more than wonted beauty. But, alas, it could not bring to our minds the sensations of gladness which it had formerly conveyed. Our hearts dwelt on the recollection that our slaughtered neighbours, our murdered friend, and our departed child had been enjoying life and health with us when last the fields were green.

CHAPTER X.
1799.

Destruction of trees in Ballitore. – Return of Sally Shackleton from her travels in the ministry. – Arrival of Captain Smith and his accomplished family. – Sudden death of Ephraim Boake. – Hard times. – Outrages and robbery continue. – Betsy Barrington. – An army officer becomes a "convinced Friend." – Thomas Bewley and his sisters settle in the village. – Dolly Finn's second marriage. – The Smiths leave Ireland. – A picturesque funeral. – Peaceful times return. – Strange whim of a dying peer. – The Medlicotts. – Agrarian murder. – The Union. – The Bishop of Meath. – Death of Mary Bewley. – Ballitore Inn opened. – Melesina St. George. – John Christy settles at Irishtown. – His naval visitor. – Vain sports and places of diversion. – Dissolution of Ballitore school. – Pensive reflections. 151 to 166

AND now another calamity, as I deemed it, befel Ballitore. Incensed at the loss of so much of his timber, and having already sold Brownstown grove and other plantations, William Bayly advertised the trees of Ballitore to be sold by auction – those trees so carefully preserved by his grandfather and father.[90] But he had never sported in his youth beneath these shades, watched the successive budding of the beech, the ash, and the elm, and remarked their beautiful diversity of foliage. He had never mourned over their falling leaves, nor admired the exquisite incrustations of their leafless branches, sparkling in the cheering sunshine of a frosty winter's day.

My husband and John Thomas were the purchasers, and they strove to spare what they could, consistently with prudence. The six stately beeches at the meeting-house, and an arching shade over the approach from the high road, and at the other entrances to the village, were spared; insomuch that those who had never seen Ballitore embowered as it once had been considered, it still very shady. Though my own family reaped some advantage by this purchase, and though I was certain that if the purchase had fallen into other hands our village would have been completely dismantled, I could not conquer my regrets.

The meeting-house grove fell; so did that huge beech of great circumference which bore on its bark the initials of favourite nymphs and swains of several generations. The trees leading to Fuller's Court no longer overarched the way, or afforded a habitation for the little warblers on a summer's morning, or for the rooks whose cawings broke the stillness of the evening. I dreamed of the devoted trees, and I wept for their downfall. Yet perhaps to the circumstance which I so much deplored I owe the health and life of some of my friends; and how little would the presence of my beloved trees have consoled me, if beneath their shade I had been destined to lament the death of some dear friend cut off by one of those putrid fevers which so often visited Ballitore before their fall admitted a freer circulation of air.

After a prolonged absence of two years and a half, travelling in England, Scotland, Wales, the Isle of Man, and Guernsey, on a religious visit, our dear sister Sally Shackleton returned home, and her return diffused universal joy. Her presence chased many a cloud from our minds, and cheered the poor, who hailed with delight their unwearied friend, and thought all would go well now that "Miss Sally was come home." Her own heart heaved with contending emotions. Her wish to be again with her own family was attained, but the changed aspect of things distressed her. Her native shades were disfigured by the axe, her friend Doctor Johnson was laid in an untimely grave, her little niece in another, and her venerable mother reduced to imbecility. But her spirit soon recovered its calmness, and we were enabled to rejoice once more together.

The Essex fencibles were now ordered away, and were replaced by the 22nd Dragoons, Captain Smith commanding. He was a man of middle age, and his countenance and manner bespoke the high respectability of his character. Within a few years he had experienced a great reverse of fortune. He had enjoyed large possessions, and his wife had brought him £50,000. He unfortunately engaged in a bank, which failed, leaving him in comparative poverty. This occasioned his entering the army. His beautiful seat in England was sold far below its value. He loved the scene his taste had embellished, and, having taken a place at some distance, found a melancholy pleasure in viewing it through a telescope. His reverse of fortune became still more distressing when he was ordered to Ireland during the rebellion. He was engaged in the battle of Ballinahinch, where his humane feelings suffered deeply; and though he did his duty as an officer, he withheld his hand from shedding blood.

His excellent wife accompanied him to Ireland. They brought to Ballitore three fine daughters, Bess, Kitty, and Juliet; their little boy Louis, about nine years old; and their daughter-in-law Louise, who was pleasing and affable, with an animated and engaging countenance. Juliet Smith, the mother, was tall, slender, and stately, her face interesting, and her smile sweet. Her eldest daughter, Bess, lower in stature, was pretty, her eyes blue, her complexion fair, and her fine hair of a light brown. Kitty's figure and face were striking, with much expression in her fine black eyes. Juliet was delicate, and seemed to have outgrown her strength. Bess we thought partook of her worthy father's reserve – we knew not then of the treasures of intellect and goodness which lay beneath that modest and retiring exterior. Kitty resembled her mother in lively frankness. They all drew from nature with much taste. Kitty's acquirements in language were confined to French and Italian; her sister Juliet added to these a knowledge of Latin; but Bess had learned twelve languages with little assistance, and thirsted after universal knowledge.

The mother of these lovely girls was their friend and companion. She was an uncommonly gifted woman; and had experienced divine support when so many temporal comforts had been taken away. They were now moving in a lower sphere of life than that to which they were entitled; but to us they appeared to move in a high one. They kept a coach and several saddle horses; and dressed richly, yet with modest elegance. The mother always wore a riding habit. The young women took long walks into the surrounding country; they were very dexterous with the needle, and very charitable. Kitty's pretty fingers never looked so pretty, I thought, as when employed making a frieze suit for a poor little orphan whom they fed and clothed, and for whose schooling they paid.

Our friend Ephraim Boake had seen his 76th summer. The attachment between him and his neighbours increased as the time seemed to approach which must separate them; that time, however, we hoped was yet far distant, and the green old age of the venerable man strengthened this hope. One fine morning Ephraim walked down to his sheep–pond, near to the house, with the intention of washing his head there, as he had often done before. It was no wonder that his limbs, stiffened with age, should fail as he stooped to the fatal water, and occasion the lamented catastrophe which closed his long life. In about half an hour his body was found still floating, his hat and towel near, and his dog beside them. A messenger was sent for me, saying that Mr. Boake had fallen into the water, but not stating that the accident was fatal. I hastened to Boakefield, which I had nearly reached before I heard that its old master was no more. That dwelling was now a scene of distress. In the kitchen sat several men with dejected countenances, – in the parlour lay his wet clothes, and on his own bed lay the remains of dear Ephraim, looking as if asleep. His daughter (Jane Thomas) and her husband lay one at each side of him, endeavouring to restore the vital warmth, while attendants were rubbing him with flannels wrung out of hot spirits, and clapping and fomenting his limbs. With the assistance of the women I got the fumes of tobacco into his chest, and the vein which had been opened, but did not bleed, began to flow. I note this to encourage the trial of this means, though in this instance the faint hope raised by the flow of blood soon faded away, and the symptoms of death became more and more evident.

His daughter's anguish was inexpressible; she would not for a moment leave her father; or relax in the ineffectual search for life, but for twelve hours clung to the body, which growing colder and colder chilled her own frame into death–like frigidity. The chamber windows on one side looked out on the lawn spotted over with the unconscious sheep; on the other to the garden, newly dressed under the inspection of him who would never see it more. The contrast was striking between those peaceful objects and the distress within. I felt qualified to sympathize in this distress, for my own wound was torn open afresh. The stroke of untimely death had deprived his attached daughter of a fond parent, and me of a lovely child; well might we weep together.

The situation of the people had now strong claims upon humanity. Perhaps the waste of war and the neglect of cultivation in consequence were the original causes of the scarcity which was now so severely felt by the poor. Provisions were purchased by subscription and sold to them at low prices. The broth in which meat had been boiled was made into soup, and distributed to the crowds of children who surrounded our doors, and whose parents would once have shrunk from beggary. Potatoes were thirteen pence per stone.[91] My husband had a large stock of this necessary food, which enabled him to join largely in the public contribution, and also to feed his workmen in our kitchen without feeling the increase of expense so much as he might otherwise have done. When the spring work was completed, and he was about to discharge his workmen, the distress to which his doing so would expose them touched him so deeply, that he planned how he could continue to employ them. He had some land at Mount Blake which had been so trespassed on during and since the rebellion, that it was rendered totally unprofitable for farming purposes. He thought of building upon it; and accordingly the first stone of Ballitore Inn was laid; and, as the foundation was laid in charity, I hope it will ever prosper. The poor people laboured with grateful and cheerful diligence, and a pretty little house was soon raised, which proved suitable for the object in view.

Despite the presence of a military force, outrages and robberies still frequently occurred, and kept us in a state of perpetual alarm and anxiety. When these midnight robbers attacked a house in the country, they usually set fire to it if they met with any resistance; so that many of the farmers around were houseless, and were wont to come into our village at night. Some robbers were shot by the military; one of these had my watch in his pocket, but I did not regain it. Indeed it would not have been acceptable to me, stained with blood as I should have thought it – remembering also how its well–known hands had marked the time for its sinful possessor to use in deeds of desperation. We saw the dead bodies of these robbers go by on a car, partly covered with hay, and in the evening again passing from the barrack, on a bier covered with a sheet. Captain Smith highly disapproved of the rash act which his soldiers had committed.

In 1788, Betsy Pike spent a few weeks with us. She was then a very young girl, and greatly endeared herself to us by her amiable manners, her pleasing person, her good understanding, and happy disposition; and time did not belie these fair promises. In 1795, Joseph Barrington was so highly favoured as to obtain her hand. In 1797, they came for a time to Ballitore, Joseph being then ill in consumption. In those precarious times the cotton business in which he was engaged proved unsuccessful; his fairest hopes were crushed; his respectable parents were involved in the ruin of the house; and the young man sank under his misfortunes. His wife nursed him with the tenderest care, and fondly caught at every ray of hope. She had a little before resigned to the grave her infant child; yet, being blessed with a hopeful mind which sweetened the bitter cup, she bore calmly the distresses which she deeply felt. They took a pretty little house in Carlow, and opened a small shop; Joseph, ill as he was, industriously and ingeniously employing himself. He died in Carlow on the 25th of Fourth–month, 1798, his lonely widow remaining in her dwelling in placid sorrow, while war and the rumours of war raged around her. In 1800, she came to reside in Ballitore. She took Jonathan Haughton's old house, improved it and opened a shop there. We gladly welcomed Betsy Barrington as an inhabitant of our valley.

Dudley Colcough paid us a visit this year. When we saw him last he was a showy young officer, the beauty of his person rendered more conspicuous by his military attire. We were therefore surprised to see the gay youth transformed on a sudden, as it appeared to us, into a very orthodox Friend. He had sacrificed too much for us to doubt his sincerity, for he had by this step disobliged his father, whose only son he was. He told us he had been convinced of the truth of our principles by reading Barclay's Apology, which had accidentally fallen in his way at his quarters. One circumstance which he told me long after this period I may here introduce. Being the son of a man of fortune, young, inexperienced, and at a distance from those most interested in his welfare, his fellow–officers endeavoured to allure him to gamble. He consented reluctantly, and won half–a–guinea from one of them; instead of being elated with his success, his mind revolted at gaining by such means, and he insisted on restoring the half–guinea, which, of course, prevented any further solicitations to play.

My sister Sally took the Mill–house from my brother, and removed thither with my mother, Molly Hudson, and Mary Dickenson. My dear mother's increasing debility was gradual but sure.

Thomas Bewley, his wife, and his sisters Mary and Susan, left Dublin and came to reside in Ballitore. Thomas took from my husband the house in the Burrow which stood at the nearest angle to our yard. This he converted into a very neat habitation, made a tan-yard adjoining, and planted a nice garden. His sisters purchased from my brother part of the lime-kiln field, and Juliet Smith assisted them in planning a most desirable little dwelling in the cottage style. The situation took in the most beautiful view in the valley. I laid the first stone, and my long-beloved Mary and I rejoiced that to the tie of friendship was added the bond of neighbourhood. I was elated: perhaps too much so.

Poor Dolly Finn struggled to rear her young family of two sons and two daughters in this season of famine, and I believe it was maternal tenderness more than any other consideration which induced her to accept an offer of marriage from Pat Byrne, for her murdered Owen never seemed to lose his place in her heart. Her second husband was a mason, in good repute for sobriety, industry, and ingenuity; he was a widower; and his eldest son, about twelve years old, was an intelligent lad, and manifested much respect and affection for his step-mother. On the death of his father, who was cut off by a malignant fever in less than two years, he set out to seek his fortune, with the good wishes and recommendations of his friends.

About this time we opened a little school for poor children in Ballitore. There were several superintendants for a while, but at length the whole trouble devolved on Betsy Shackleton. Though so young she was competent to the task, and communicated her ingenuity in needlework to many of the pupils, while she sharpened her own talents by exercise. Bess Lennon was the school-mistress. The family removing from the house and other circumstances caused the decline of this little institution.

Juliet Smith, though prejudiced in favour of many of the inhabitants of Ireland, greatly disliked the country as a place of residence; which was not to be wondered at, considering that she knew it only in its unsettled and stormy state. She was desirous to fix her residence in the north of England. My brother applied to Thomas Wilkinson to direct their choice, and thus introduced those uncommon characters to each other. The zeal with which Thomas Wilkinson undertook and executed this commission impressed Captain Smith's family with the happy certainty of having obtained a friend previous to their arrival among strangers. They left Ballitore sincerely regretted; but their departure did not break the bonds of our friendship.

Thomas and Fanny Bewley moved into their new house. Through their pretty garden, which displayed the taste and skill of its fair mistress, we were admitted to their sister's cottage – advancing from the garden along a shady walk at one side of the pond which bounded my brother's garden, and crossing it by a picturesque wooden bridge. The cottage was surrounded by its tasteful little garden, and the perfect neatness within could not detach the eyes from the delightful landscape without. A drawing of the cottage by Juliet Smith decorated one of the rooms, and under it she had transcribed these lines: –

> Enough has Heaven indulged of joy below
> To tempt our tarriance in this loved retreat;
> Enough has Heaven ordained of useful woe
> To make us languish for a happier seat.

Mary Bewley delighted in the country and in all its occupations. She was settled exactly to her mind, and acknowledged that all her wishes as to temporals were fulfilled, even to the possession of a tortoise-shell cat. This comfort was soon interrupted by Susan taking a fever, which caused great alarm on her account; but she recovered, and all looked bright again.

My brother's mill was robbed of a good deal of its contents, and it was discovered that the person suspected of having robbed the post-bag some years before was a party concerned. No attempt, however, was made by my brother to bring him to justice, as the forfeiture of life might have followed conviction.

This summer, like the foregoing one, was remarkably hot and dry, and scarcity was still felt. We discovered that William Lennon's family had been twenty-four hours without food; and we were angry as well as grieved that pride should lead them to conceal their distress. A plentiful harvest crowned the year, and demanded gratitude; but the minds of the people were not yet settled. Mick Brennan and another young man having been made prisoners by the yeomen, and attempting to escape, were shot by them. Boakefield house was also again attacked, or rather entered, by four armed men, who confined the family in one room, while they plundered the house of property to the value of about fifty pounds.

Here let me describe the funeral of a youth in our village, as the ceremonies with which it was attended are now nearly extinct. Two youths of his own age, his companions and schoolfellows, walked first, with white hat-bands and scarfs, bearing between them an ornamented cross. Two more followed, one with the garland to plant on his early grave, the other with a basket of flowers to scatter over it. Then came twenty-four couple of young men and maidens, each couple holding a white handkerchief between them, the youths wearing white hat-bands and scarfs, and carrying ornamented wands, the girls dressed all in pure white. These simple tributes to departed worth and youth, rarely as they are to be met with in these days, were extremely touching.

Now that we rested once more, as it were, under our own vines and our own fig-trees, I felt as if Ballitore was itself again. In so narrow a circle as ours a tender bond of affection becomes twined with the tie of neighbourhood, which adds exceedingly to its strength. We can imagine a state of society in which even the temporary absence of a neighbour causes a shade of gloom, and his return a ray of sunshine; where the sickness or misfortune of one is felt by sympathy through the whole body; where the shopkeepers live in unaffected harmony, and lend and borrow goods for the wants of their customers, instead of taking advantage of the scarcity of any particular article. All this we can imagine to be possible, and perhaps to be practised, in other places. In Ballitore it is the spirit of the place, and no wondering thought is ever bestowed upon it.

Our neighbour, Lord Aldborough, having fallen into ill health, to cheer the scene planned to assemble around him at Belan a large party of young people of both sexes; and – whether in jest or earnest I know not – proposed that if these nymphs and swains should incline towards each other, they should be immediately joined in the bonds of Hymen. Before the appointed festive day the earl was so ill as to lay all these plans aside, and in a short time he breathed his last.

Thomas Kelly, the son of Judge Kelly, living near Athy, held religious meetings occasionally in Ballitore. This excellent man early in life devoted himself to religious duties, and with stability and sincerity trod the narrow path, choosing a wife of his own stamp, of the Tighe family in the county of Wexford.

This year Sarah Medlicott came to reside in our neighbourhood. Her husband was a man of ample fortune, but a poor miser, and unworthy of such a wife. She weathered through some years of her life with this ill–suited companion, from whom at length she separated, and supported her family in gentility on a very moderate income, submitting to many privations for the sake of independence, and resolving to contract no debts. Her three daughters, Susanna, Sally, and Isabella, came with her, also her friend Mary Costello, a person of delicate health, but possessed of uncommon talents and worth; her paintings and her pictures in needlework were admirable. This family at first occupied the glebe house at Timolin, but soon left it for Willowbrook.

A dreadful circumstance occurred at this time in our neighbourhood. The farm at the Nine–tree hill, which had belonged to the Duffy family, was the scene of this tragedy. The Duffy's had been ejected for non–payment of rent; and Toomy, who got the land after them, paid them a handsome sum of money on placing Higginbotham in possession. Kit Duffy beheld a stranger thrive on the spot where his ancestors had thriven, with feelings whose malignity no kindness (and much was shown him) could soften. He procured an associate, and while walking in apparent amity with Higginbotham, the two fell upon the unsuspecting man and beat his brains out. They escaped the hands of justice, and even continued some time in the country, boasting with savage ferocity of the deed, and of their intent to commit other acts of violence. I believe they afterwards went to America. Oh! How I lamented that our sweet Nine–tree hill was the scene of such crimes, and that such blood-stained beings were my countrymen.

Scarcity of food now amounted to famine. The potato-pits were nightly robbed, and the weeds of the fields were made to serve for food; but a fine winter proved that Providence cares for the poor, in not sending cold and hunger together.

And now our politicians began to speak much of "the Union"- both for and against it. I was not qualified to judge of the merits of the subject. I longed only for peace and quiet, and to behold once more our fields cultivated and our poor fed. It was amusing to hear the country-folk discussing the great political question of the day; they seemed to think that parliament was a great book which had been removed from Dublin to England. At length peace was proclaimed. The blessed word was chalked on the mail-coach, and bore the report through the kingdom, animating some hearts with joy, and depressing others with disappointment. When the definitive treaty of peace was signed, there were bonfires and firing of guns and illuminations, even in humble Ballitore.[92]

The bishop of Meath called at Ballitore, the spot so much beloved by his dear friend Edmund Burke, and was much delighted with our village. I did not see him; but my husband had a good deal of conversation with him, and showed him my manuscript book of verses and Burke's letters to me, and I afterwards had a most friendly letter from him. Soon after there appeared in the *Dublin Evening Post* an account of the bishop's visit to Ballitore, speaking of our village in terms of high admiration.

A very close trial was near us. Our beloved Mary Bewley was taken ill, and sank rapidly. The 11th of the Fifth-month, 1802, was her last day of life. She had been my close friend for nineteen years, and I had hoped we should pass our old age near one another, and that she would have long enjoyed that situation so answerable to her wishes. The truth awfully impressed my mind, "We are not to have our heaven here." The meekness, humility, and integrity of her character made the change not to be regretted on her account; but her sister Susan, her companion from infancy, mourned her loss. Her serene countenance meanwhile concealed the anguish which preyed on her life. She lived much alone in her little cottage, save that she sometimes had one of our daughters or a niece of her own to stay with her. Her conversation was profitable and pleasant to them, and she strove not to sadden their minds with the gloom which overspread her own. I believe her thoughts were constantly reverting to her lost sister. At one time she suddenly grasped my hands, and exclaimed, "It is now two-and-twenty months; and I wonder how I have lived so long!" and burst into tears. An illness, caused, I believe, by her sorrow, soon ensued, and she felt that it would surely prove fatal. In her heart she truly uttered, "Thy will be done!" and she beheld the prospect of death undismayed. Her pure, calm, and firm mind rested on the help from above in perfect tranquillity.

The inn on the high–road from Dublin to Cork was completed, and was let to Thomas Glaizebrook. It soon acquired a goodly reputation. One night in Fourth–month this year the house was uncommonly full of guests – Friends travelling to the yearly meeting in Dublin, gentry going to the Curragh races, and officers on their march. As we were retiring to rest, a messenger came down from the landlord to say that a lady had arrived late, that the house was full to overflowing, and there was no room for her to take refreshment in; that she sat on the settle in the kitchen, reading, waiting till she could obtain an apartment; and that, being much fatigued, she would be glad of the meanest bed in the house. Could we be so kind as to assist our tenant in this strait? My husband went up at once for her, and brought her down in a carriage; when we found from her attendants that she was a person of consequence. She retired to rest, after expressing grateful thanks, and we thought she would pass away with the morrow; but not so. Her servants told us that the Ballybarney estate in the neighbourhood belonged to her, and that she had appointed her agent to meet her at Ballitore inn, proposing to take her tenants from under the "middlemen" to her own protection. They also told us she had been for ten years the widow of a colonel, and had one son, fourteen years old.

I had seen but little of her the night before; when she entered my parlour next day, I was greatly struck with her personal appearance. My heart entirely acquits me of having been influenced by what I had heard of her rank and fortune. Far more prepossessing than these were the soft lustre of her beautiful black eyes, and the sweetness of her fascinating smile. Her dress was simply elegant, and her fine dark hair, dressed according to the existing fashion, in rows of curls over one another in front, appeared to me as becoming as it was new. These particulars are not important to others, but to me they are inexpressibly dear, because they recall the first impression made on me by this most charming woman, who afterwards honoured me with her friendship.

Melesina St. George spent two weeks in our house, having asked permission to remain with us rather than return to the inn. Providence had given her talents and dispositions calculated to promote the improvement and happiness of all around her, while her meekness and humility prevented the restraint of her superiority being felt, without taking from the dignity of her character. I was surprised and affected when I beheld her, on one occasion, seated on one of the kitchen chairs in the scullery, for coolness, hearing a company of little children of her tenants sing out their lessons to her. I wished for her picture drawn in this situation, and for its companion I should choose one of Edmund Burke assisting my mother to make pills for the poor.[93] It was with difficulty I prevailed on her to bring her little scholars into our parlour, because, she said, she would not bring them into her own. Admiring her method of instruction, I told her she would make an excellent schoolmistress. She modestly replied, with her sweet smile, "Not an excellent one;" but added that she had no dislike to the employment, and had contemplated it as a means of subsistence when the rebellion threatened to deprive her of her property.

She came again to Ballitore, and had apartments at the inn, where she entertained us with kind and polite attention, and amused her leisure by taking pen and ink sketches of the views from thence, not having her pencils with her. She afterwards sent me a volume of her own poetry, entitled, "Mary Queen of Scots, an historical ballad, and other Poems." It had been printed in London for private circulation, and was full of pathos and beauty.

From this period our friendship became confirmed in strong enduring bonds, and we constantly corresponded. She gratified me by employing me on her charitable affairs, and I paid visits to her tenants at Ballybarney, who declared themselves happy and thriving since she took them under her own care, and their prayers for her and their praise of her were freely poured forth. One of these tenants, whose absurdly consequential deportment was accounted for by his being "a dealer," told me he prayed every night for "the lady, and for Mr. Allen, No. 22, Upper Bridge–street," showing me at the same time an invoice of goods, for which he said he was in debt to Mr. Allen. This was a boast, for he had honestly paid for the goods; and why he thought being in debt added to his consequence seems strange, yet so it was.

On one of these occasions we contemplated an interesting scene. A lovely baby of four months old lay asleep in the cradle, while the fond father, Mick Dillon, with paternal pride wanted to take him up to show him to us; and when we forbade this, he turned the cradle to the light to give us a full view of his reposing cherub. The mother of the child died soon after its birth, and left six children with her husband. He put the infant out to nurse, but thinking that it was not done justice to, brought it home, and took charge of it, submitting to the loss of rest, and performing feminine offices with careful tenderness. We were affected by the contrast of these employments with the figure and countenance of the rough, strong, labouring man, and when we foretold that the boy would repay these present cares by the support and comfort he would give to his father's age, the man's conscious smiles expressed his belief in our prediction. I wrote to my friend Melesina an account of this singular circumstance, and she desired me to make the child a present of a complete suit from a store of baby linen and child–bed linen which she had committed to my care, to lend to her tenantry when poverty obliged them to require its use.[94] I made up the parcel with great pleasure, and having sent for the father, advanced joyfully with it in my hand, but was surprised to see no corresponding emotion in his countenance. His little nurseling was dead, having been carried off suddenly by whooping cough.

I thought if all proprietors of estates followed this lady's example, there would be no need of a revolution of government to ensure the happiness and reform the manners of the people. Her tenants longed to see her among them, but they longed in vain; their dear lady had availed herself of the peace to make an excursion to the Continent, where she married Richard Trench, an Irish gentleman, with whom she shared the fate of all the English travellers who were in France at the recommencement of hostilities. They were made prisoners, and the mother was thus separated from her son, who was then pursuing his studies in England, and afterwards went to India with his uncle, General Craddock.

The inn was a means of procuring us some valuable acquaintances and agreeable adventures *en passant*. The Bishop of Meath's account of Ballitore had interested several in our favour; amongst these was a family who spent one First–day at the inn, having a scruple to travel on that day; they were a clergyman from Bandon, whose name was Gorman, his wife, and two children. Having heard of their being there, we invited them down to tea, and were much pleased with them, while they appeared to be equally pleased with us.[95] My old schoolfellow Gilbert Kilbee had given them some of my verses, and the gentleman thought he could repeat my "Hunted Doe." Tears started into his eyes when he read Edmund Burke's last letter to me. His wife was daughter to Thomas Burke, my grandfather's pupil lately deceased, and a burst of filial sorrow overpowered her when she read her father's name in the school list.

Sarah Medlicott removed to reside at Fuller's–court and I rejoiced to see the abode of my infancy assume a more elegant appearance than ever it had done before. My aunt Fuller's flower–garden was annexed to Sarah Medlicott's house, and I passed through the glass sash–door once more. It was a long time since I had reviewed these beloved scenes of my infancy, longer known to me than any other place, and compared with which the other end of the village seems modern. I wandered about the garden late on a soft summer's evening recognising many an object, and while I looked towards the place of the yew–bowers, where the quicken, mingling its red berries with the green of other trees, had often attracted our attention from the sash–door of my aunt's parlour, I felt indescribable sensations, which I could only express by tears. My fondness for "the days of other times" afforded some amusement to those who could not as yet understand it.

Another friendship it was my favoured lot to form at about this time. Pleasant to my heart is the recollection, though mingled with a deep sadness, like the songs of Ossian! A young Scotchman, named John Christy, took the farm of Irishtown within three miles of Ballitore. It soon assumed a different aspect, the verdure of its fields displaying the superior cultivation bestowed on it. The new methods of husbandry which this young man introduced were of great benefit to other farmers; while his worth and talents, though accompanied by much diffidence, rendered him a very agreeable neighbour. There came on a visit to him his friend and countryman, William Ramage, a lieutenant in the navy. His countenance was striking, for, with its manly beauty, good sense, and vivacity, was combined such an expression of goodness of heart as made one love to look upon him; his manners and conversation were in unison with his person; the accomplishments of the scholar and the politeness of the gentleman were mingled with the frankness, ingenuousness, and simplicity of the sailor.

It was, indeed, a little singular that a handsome and lively young man should, without any breach of goodbreeding, retire from a party of fine young girls, on an excursion to the waterfall of Poula–Phouca, and silently seat himself before the waterfall to sketch the scene. I will do the young girls the justice to add, that so far from being mortified at the handsome stranger treating them as he would treat their mothers, they respected and admired him the more for being so completely devoid of male coquetry; nor would their respect and admiration have been diminished had they known that the real state of his heart would have precluded the possibility of a successful attack upon it.

We saw but little of him, though he spent some months with his friend, rendering him every assistance in his power in his new undertaking, and cheering his solitude with his society. He also ornamented the parlour at Irishtown by painting a border of roses round the ceiling instead of a cornice. The voice of war called him from this retreat; he went on board the "Hibernia," which was then lying at Cove and was commanded by Lord Gardiner, and left his friend much afflicted at the parting – a stranger in a strange land. However, he shortly expected his sister to visit him, and in the following year the report of her coming caused a stir amongst us.

A flood made us prisoners in our upper rooms, while our nephew Garret Leadbeater administered amply to our necessities by bringing provisions from the inn, which he handed to us from horseback, and, presenting us with a branch, reminded us of Noah's dove.

This spring a novel sight was exhibited here. On the hill to the east was a horse–race, tents were erected, and a great number of spectators assembled. The races held for a week. Several years ago an attempt to introduce cock–fights was made, and a cock–pit was built on old O'Hara's premises. These cruel sports were witnessed by many who esteemed themselves of the better class; but the circumstance that a stranger who attended them died of fever, and that a carpenter who was employed in connection with them died in consequence of a broken leg which he got in the work, put a stop to this business more completely than all the remonstrances of the sober neighbours had been able to do. Thus superstition effected what humanity was unable to do; and as "ill–luck" had stamped the amusement, the cock–pit was appropriated to a different purpose. Similar circumstances prevented a repetition of the horse–race.

For many years past my brother had entertained strong objections to the study of those authors which treat in seducing language of the illusions of love and the trade of war; and he published an advertisement declining to include such works in his course of education; thus relinquishing the credit and profit of preparing lads for college. During the year of the rebellion the school was further reduced, many of his pupils being taken home by their parents on account of the disturbed state of the times; and in 1801, declining to receive any more pupils, though many were still pressed upon him, he removed to reside at the Mill and superintend the buisiness there, leaving part of his family at the old mansion. In the present year the school was closed, to my great regret.

My brother's family removed to Griesebank, and the school–house was set to Sarah Medlicott; but though I esteemed her and her family, I never could enjoy their company in that house with the relish I did in any other, for I had been enthusiastically attached to the school. It had been our honourable means of livelihood, my earliest ideas were blended with it, and almost every recollection of my childhood was connected with what belonged to it. I had not imagined I should outlive the school, and when I visited the present amiable possessors of the dwelling, and waited till the "once ever–open door" was opened to me, I looked up at the stars, and said to myself "These are the stars which I have looked upon with the merry group who sported in this court;" and the hope sprang up that perhaps I should again see them shine on such another group.

My dear mother departed this life the 23rd of Third–month, 1804. Our beloved and venerable parent glided from us by degrees almost imperceptible. She was reduced to a state of helpless infancy. Still the serenity of innocence gilded her setting day, and surely we ought to rejoice that her pure spirit was released without seeming to experience the pangs of death! But my sister Sally, whose constant care she had been for three years, mourned long and deeply, and sobs from the old servants interrupted the silence at her grave.

Agnes Christy came to her brother's dwelling without letting him know that she had landed in Ireland, lest he should leave his harvest to escort her. She came by the canal, and met a group of Quaker females in the boat, whose enjoyment of one another's society she contrasted with her own loneliness. They were struck with her countenance and accent and solicited her acquaintance, while she was as much pleased with their kind attention to her, which gave her a favourable impression of our land. Several of my friends went to pay their respects to the stranger. I was not amongst these early visitors, knowing myself to be ill–qualified to press forward to the notice of a fine young woman who might chance to be a fine lady also.

The visitors represented her to be perfectly easy and unaffected in her manners; and they judged from the elegance of her carriage that she must have moved in polished society. This intimidated me still more, while she, as she afterwards told me, wished to know me and wondered I was not amongst those who called upon her. At length I met this "foreign wonder," and fell in love at first sight with my bonnie lassie Agnes Christy. She was tall and graceful, her countenance remarkably ingenuous and sweet, with fine dark hair, deep blue eyes, and beautiful teeth. She soon came to see me, and we talked of Ossian and Burns; at every interview our souls flowed forth more and more to each other, till at length they mingled in a united stream.

> Mysterious are His ways, whose power
> Brings forth that unexpected hour,
> When souls that never met before
> Shall meet, unite, and part no more!

It was singular that she should choose me for her friend in preference to those more her equals in age. She was the only daughter of aged parents, and her younger brother had gone to India as a physician. They were now without a child at home, having resigned their Agnes for her brother John's advantage, for she excelled in domestic management as well as in more elegant acquirements.

Her understanding was solid and her taste judicious, her delicacy unaffected and her humility exemplary. There was unstudied elegance and simplicity in her manners and conversation, which were very engaging, and her talents had been cultivated by a liberal education. Her heart was feelingly alive to distress, and numerous were her secret acts of benevolence. A most affectionate daughter and sister, her mind was divided between her duties, and she doubted the propriety of sometimes enjoying herself with us, believing she ought not to desert her post with her brother except to return to her dear infirm mother. Her company was much sought after, and her graces attracted admirers; but she quietly kept them at a distance, and the artless gravity of her deportment in mixed companies caused her often to be compared to a married woman. I believe she sought to know what was right for her to do, and to adhere to it, and that she found this the safe guide through many perplexities.

Dolly Finn, for so she was still called, was most seasonably assisted by a donation of ten pounds, sent to me for her by Frances Smith, the lady of William Smith, M. P. for Norwich, whose exertions for the abolition of the slave trade and the emancipation of the Roman Catholics will be long remembered. Thomas Wilkinson's acquaintance with this worthy couple had introduced my "Ruined Cottage" to them, and poor Dora's sufferings touched their feeling hearts. This donation was to assist in clothing and educating her children; it was sent annually for several years, and was of essential service; it co–operated with while it encouraged the exertions of the poor widow for the support of her young family.

The Bishop of Meath, his wife, and daughter were again at Ballitore inn. They called on me at the village, were very kind and polite, and I felt much gratified by their company and conversation, especially as Edmund Burke was the principal subject of the discourse. The bishop told me that he was shocked when he first saw him after the death of his son, there was such a shrinking and relaxation in his fine manly frame; and he supposed his heart was broken by that and by other troubles of a more public nature. The son, though a man of talent, was much inferior to his father, yet that great man scarcely did any thing in his private or public business without consulting his son, and this I look upon as one among the many proofs of the humility which adorned him. The bishop's daughter, a pleasing young girl, had been born in the castle in which the poet Chaucer had lived, and was thence called by Edmund Burke "The fair maid of Donnington."

The summer of 1805 I began my experiment of preserving bees by keeping them in a wooden house, in hives with flat wooden tops, in which apertures are made; through these the bees ascend into glasses, which when they are filled are taken away, and replaced by empty ones. With great delight to myself and my surrounding friends I placed the first hive in its new abode.

Our dear Susan Bewley now became much worse. Inflammation set in, and, though suffering under aggravated pains, she seized an interval of comparative ease to walk with her brother and sister through their gardens to their house, pleasantly as she was wont when she expected to return. But now she had taken a last farewell of her sweet little home, and made this arrangement to spare her brother and sister unnecessary trouble, and to die with them. Her sister–in–law Mary Bewley and my sister Sally got to Ballitore just in time to witness her unshaken patience under great bodily suffering, and the quiet close of her virtuous life. She died in the Ninth–month. How did the cottage seem to mourn its mistress! The leaves lay in heaps on the walks; the withered flowers were not cut down; the windows were closed; all was silent and lonely.

CHAPTER XI.
1806.

Marriage of James White and Lydia Shackleton. – Ballitore School re–opened. – Lorenzo Dow. – John Pim of London. – Michael Kearney. – Patrick Rogers. – A friend of the Burke family. – A widowed mother. – Happy lovers. – First vacation in Ballitore school. – A Danish mound. – More old Ballitore boys. – The Le Fanu family. – A heavenly vision. – A good Samaritan. – Harrington of Grangecon. – Mrs. Trench visits Ballybarney. – The jubilee. – A straw–plaiting school established. – How Maria Edgeworth did *not* visit Ballitore. – Spread of education. – Spontaneous combustion. – The Bonhams settle in the village. – Death of Lydia White. 167 to 179

TIME went on, and our good opinion of our Scottish neighbours continued to increase. John Christy possessed much good sense, intelligence, and literary information, and his fascinating sister became more and more dear to us as her character unfolded; especially to me, to whom she granted her confidence, which she did not do till our friendship was long and firmly established. We had occasionally spoken of her young countryman, the lieutenant in the navy, and I regarded him as her long known friend; but, when I found that he had stronger claims upon her heart, I rejoiced at the union of two such kindred minds, while I lamented that unpitying war should keep them separated. It was not vanity which caused my young friend to intrust me with this great secret. Her delicacy shrank from the idea of her attachment becoming a subject of conversation, for

Proud was her leal heart, and modest her nature.

Yet, distant from her own dear mother, her heart wanted to repose its various anxieties upon a female breast, and I trust her choice, however deficient it might be in many respects, was not wanting in sincere affection.

This year, 1806, was memorable by the marriage of James White to our Lydia Shackleton. They were married the 14th of the Ninth–month. James became tenant for the old schoolhouse and adjoining land, and my heart swelled with a double satisfaction on the union of my amiable and lovely niece with so worthy and accomplished a person, and on the prospect of the re–opening of Ballitore school. In 1807 I saw the school revived – my wish was accomplished. Strange perversity! why was I sad? Why did the idea of those "to the dust gone down," and of the scenes for ever passed away, (like the Jews who wept over the new Temple, while they recollected the old) rise like a mist over the present fair prospect?

Two sons of Samuel Haughton of Carlow were the last boarders received by my brother before he closed his school; and the revived establishment found its first pupil in James, another of his sons. The school opened on Lydia White's birth–day, on which she completed her twentieth year. I spent the evening there, as did my favourites Agnes Christy and Betsy Shackleton. Our neighbourhood became more animated, and the revival of the school promised to attract more inhabitants to it.

Lorenzo Dow from America held a meeting in Ballitore. Several meetings of Methodists were held here at this time, sometimes in the street. Our beloved Ebenezer Shackleton returned to his native village, and after some time he and his brother George became their father's tenants for the Mill.

We received some welcome visitors this summer, among whom was our friend John Pim of London. He took a survey of Ballitore, recognising the people, the places, and even the furniture which he had known in his early days, and delighting us with that happy mixture of good sense and simplicity which engages the affection and mends the heart. He is a minister, and before he left Ireland this time I heard him in Dublin meeting deliver a short, sweet testimony, humble and lively like his own mind.

Michael Kearney, elder brother to the present Bishop of Ossory, stopped at the inn when travelling, and walked to Griesebank to see my brother, who sent for me to partake of the gratification of seeing our dear parents' early friend. I was quite a child when I had last seen him at my father's house, but I remember that he and my mother were much attached to him, and spoke of him as a man of great wit, learning, and modesty. Alas! I felt surprised and sorry to see the hand of age upon him; he must be eighty years of age, but the fine sense, the delicate flow of unoffending wit, and the amiable modesty of his character continued to charm. He lamented the change in Ballitore, expressed himself much pleased with my description, which my father had given him, and spoke of old school–fellows. Edmund Burke, he said, left school a year after he came here. Burke was above him at school and at college, and took kind notice of him, and invited him to spend some days with him at Beaconsfield. Dick Burke, Edmund's brother, was his school–fellow, class–fellow, bed–fellow, and friend. My father's portrait was brought to him; it was touching to see him recognising the features of his buried friend. I think he said he had outlived all his cotemporaries.[97] I could have wept and embraced the good old man! I did neither; but I indulged in pensive contemplation of life passing away, of talents gliding down the stream of time, and of the devouring grave, which sooner or later must receive us all.

Patrick Rogers, an old friend and former school-boy, visited Ballitore. We had an intellectual feast recalling old times and dear old characters, and he told me an old secret; which was that when Thomas Wray came to school – he was six or seven and twenty – he was attached to a young woman whose brother was in the army, that she rejected him, and thereupon Thomas came to school at Ballitore to study such branches of mathematics as would qualify him also for the army. I recollected our idea that Thomas Wray was in love, and his saying "Fanny" was the prettiest name for a woman. Thomas Wray met this brother at Naas for the purpose of fighting a duel, but, instead of fighting, the matter concluded amicably. The lover returned home to the north, married his Fanny, and is father of a fine family. On meeting Patrick Rogers he spoke rapturously of their beloved Ballitore, and of the suppers which, after a day spent in fulfilling their different duties, assembled the master, mistress, their children, the parlour boarders, house-keeper, and ushers round the cheerful table, where wit, friendship, and free-dom gilded the parting hour. We talked till we could almost fancy ourselves young again, when Rogers' grave look dissolved the illusion, while he observed that our happiest days were past; but I told him I hoped not, and that in our children we shall live them over again. We look back upon the pleasant path of early life from a distance which preserves the beautiful out-line, while it conceals the little irregularities and difficulties of the way; while perhaps the path in which we now walk may in reality be preferable to any we have trod before. It is well at all events to endeavour to think so. He told me a singular circumstance which took place when he was a boy. There were found in Narraghmore wood two falcons, with little bells on their necks, on which was engraved "Buccleugh." Squire Keatinge sent them back to their ducal owner in Scotland.

An elderly gentlewoman, by name Hamilton, sent down a message from the inn to request I would go up to her that we might talk together of Edmund Burke, with whom she reckoned herself well acquainted. When on a visit to a gay family in London, instead of accompanying her hosts to places of amusement, she preferred spending her evenings with the Burke family, who did not find these amusements necessary for their comfort hav-ing in their well-furnished minds and domestic society a fund of superior gratification. She told me that when William Burke, their distant relation but near friend, returned from India, after a residence of some years, his hair and complexion were so changed that the family of Edmund Burke did not know him; and when he discovered himself, his friend Edmund fainted away.

Poor Dolly Finn's afflictions had not ceased. A young officer quartered

here suffered himself to be irritated by a cur assaulting his dog. He shot the cur and took its owner, James Finn, prisoner, to the great terror of the poor man's widowed mother, who too well remembered the despotism of military power. That power was, however, now limited, and when the young man attacked the peaceable Quakers with threats and insults in consequence of their taking part with the oppressed, he soon found he had overshot his mark. A complaint was preferred against him, a court of enquiry was held here by superior officers, and the young man appeared in danger of losing his commission, though he humbled himself as low as he had been high before. Poor James Finn might exult in the victory of right over might, but his day was soon closed! A young woman to whom he was attached took ill of a fever; James visited her, and spent several hours beside her sick bed. She recovered – but her lover took the disease and died. The anguish of despair impressed the mother's countenance; trembling and pale, and without the relief of tears, she spoke of the filial and fraternal affection of her son, just twenty years of age, "whose voice whistling or singing she must hear no more!" Her former wound was opened, and she mourned afresh her murdered husband when his son was laid beside him.

Three summers my friend Agnes Christy passed with her brother; she then felt it to be her duty to return to her parents, before another northern winter should visit their aged frames.[98] She was to spend a while with me before she left Ireland, and we intended to explore together some of the beauties of its scenery. This plan was frustrated, and we could not regret that it was so. Her lover had been presented by his friend, Lord St. Vincent, with a captain's commission. The generous young man expressed his fear of standing in the way of some of the earl's friends. "I was desired," said the old admiral, "to give it to the most deserving, and I give it to you." Before the new–made captain had been appointed to his ship, a change of ministry took place, and Lord St. Vincent resigned. The lover was then at liberty to hasten to his mistress, and he lost no time in doing so.

She was at her house when a messenger from her brother came to tell of his arrival. I partook of her secret agitations – known only to myself; and when she let her veil fall over her face and set out for her brother's, I thought of Rebecca meeting Isaac. It was more than two years since he had seen her; he then got leave of absence, and spent a few days with her and her brother. Her commands were still laid upon him to appear only as her friend; he strove to obey, but his expressive countenance was often on the point of betraying him. With me there needed no restraint; and, seated between them, I delivered myself up to the satisfaction of beholding their well–earned happiness.

The open–hearted sailor delighted to tell me of the beginning of his love. He had early chosen a sea–faring life, and when quite a boy had met with extraordinary escapes and trials. He returned from a detention in France to witness the death of his eldest sister, whom he tenderly loved, and who had stood in the place of his long–lost mother. He first saw Agnes when she was thirteen, while he was three years older. He could point out the spot in which she stood, while the unconscious girl, trying on a new beaver hat, looked round on the company for approbation, and, glancing her innocent eyes on him, took him captive.

> This sacred love, deep–rooted, from his soul
> No danger tore!

He indulged himself in seeking her company at her father's house; but great were his disappointment and dismay, when, after having spent five days in writing a love–letter, it was rejected with modest dignity, which, adding respect to love, more firmly riveted his chains. He had not, however, lost the title of friend, and her presence solaced him on his return from his various voyages.

So time passed on, he still cherishing his ardent passion, when every fond hope was destroyed by hearing that Agnes was about to be married; and he heard it in such a manner that he had no doubt of its truth. In the vehemence of his disappointment he left his peaceable occupation in a merchant ship, and went on board a man–of–war, too often rashly exposing a life which he did not value, and for years not daring to enquire aught of his lost love.

At length he heard by accident that she was still unmarried; hope animated his exertions; he soon rose to the rank of lieutenant; and then, and not till then, he renewed his suit with all the timidity of love, but she forbade his writing in any tenderer strain than that of friendship. They met in London after several years' separation, and were mutually struck with the improvement those years had made in each other. The young sailor wished to declare "viva voce" the sentiments he entertained for her; but when opportunity offered, the delicacy of true affection took away the power of expression. He was not, however, always unable to plead his cause, nor did he plead in vain. Circumstances intervened to prevent a speedy union, and Agnes suffered not the gentle firmness of her mind to yield to the the solicitations of her lover, who sorely murmured at the delay.

The obstacles being now removed or fast removing, their sun beamed more brightly, emerging from the clouds; and, as if to add a brighter ray, Agnes's mother arrived unexpectedly at Irishtown. Now did my friend seem to enjoy a full cup of happiness, and her countenance was irradiated by the joy of her heart. Soon the mother, daughter, and lover returned to Scotland. In the following spring they were married; and never again did I behold this dear friend.

After this parting, I spent six weeks in Dublin, getting a volume of my verses printed. It was the longest separation I ever had from my husband and children; and, though my friends were exceedingly kind, I longed to return to my own sphere again. I had, however, the great pleasure of seeing my friend Melesina Trench. She and her husband had, by repeated solicitations, obtained their liberty. Their passage from Rotterdam to England was in stormy weather and very dangerous, but they rejoiced to tread once more a land of liberty.

The school increased rapidly, and Ballitore got its old look again; the boys' gardens, long neglected, encompassing the back court, displayed taste and industry once more: the ball bounded in the ball–alley, the marbles rolled, and the tops spun. Eight of the bigger boys joined for a while in the compilation of a manuscript newspaper: a taste for poetry occasionally appeared; and I felt that schoolboys were in all ages the same kind of beings.

A vacation of one month was given this summer, the first ever given in Ballitore school; we were lonely without the boys, and without their master and mistress, who took that opportunity to visit their friends in Cork. The popularity of the Belfast Magazine so wrought upon the active minds of some of our young people, as to induce them to compile a manuscript magazine every month, to which most of the young and occasionally some of the old contributed, and several extracts were made from this compilation for the Belfast Magazine.

On the top of Max's Hill to the east of Ballitore was discovered, under a flag of immense size, a little sepulchre enclosed by flags, and containing a skeleton; it was not long enough to admit the body to lie at full length. On examining the bones, Dr. Bell believed that they were those of a youth, and that this was one of the burial places of Danish kings.

I was commissioned by Melesina Trench with the distribution of premiums to her poor tenantry in Ballybarney, to encourage the cultivation of their gardens. The premiums were – one guinea and a half to the best, one guinea to the second, and half a guinea to the third. My husband and John Christy were the judges. While they pursued their examination, I had a very agreeable companion in paying my visits to the cottages, for Philip Stacpole, an old pupil, had accompanied us from Ballitore. I had not seen him since he left school in 1777. The pretty slim youth was lost in the portly man, but his smile and the sweet expression of his eyes were preserved. His recollections of Ballitore and his relations of past events were highly interesting.

I received this summer another very agreeable surprise. I did not recognize the large man for whom I opened our hall–door till he told his name, nor did he recollect me till I smiled. It was Robert Baxter, and right glad were we to meet again. He and his wife stayed with us part of two days. He spent some hours reading the first volume of my "Annals" to his wife. Robert appeared unconscious of the flight of time, while he retraced the characters and circumstances which had so interested him in that year which he called the happiest of his life; and sometimes he laughed and sometimes he cried over them. His manner preserved that ingenuousness and simplicity which marked his youthful character, while an extensive knowledge of the world is added to his good sense and literary acquirements. His wife is an amiable, sensible woman; and I believe they both wish to leave the bustling military scene and settle down in domestic comfort. Their emotion at parting deprived them of the power of bidding us farewell.

In the summer of 1808 a family came to reside in the neighbourhood of Ballitore, and we frequently saw them driving through the village. The father, though advanced in years, was active and animated. He was exceedingly attentive to his three young daughters, whose characters might be guessed at by the apparently trifling circumstance of dress. Theirs was plain and simple, but elegant and genteel, bespeaking the cultivated mind. Their countenances and manners attracted me, and I longed for a nearer acquaintance; but as their line of life appeared to run differently from mine, I feared lest urging it might be deemed an intrusion.

Their father was Peter Le Fanu, the rector of Dunlavin, a man very eminent in his clerical character. Mary and Anne Doyle were frequent in their praises of this family, whose purchases at their shop were in general clothes for the poor, and whose humanity and affability engaged the admiration of these penetrating observers. But they were particularly interested by the clergyman's nephew, William P. Le Fanu, whose medical skill and benevolence began to be much spoken of in the neighbourhood.

I was reading one day the quarto edition of Marmion, then just published, which had been sent to me by the Bishop of Meath, when W. P. Le Fanu rode up to the parlour window where I was sitting, and, after apologizing for troubling me about a poor sick neighbour, to whom I had administered, and who had referred him to me, he entered into a disquisition on the merits of the poem. One needed not to hear him long to be convinced of the superiority of his genius, taste, and judgment, nor to look long in his face without feeling his unaffected politeness and good breeding. I was encouraged by his character and by his mission to me, and also by having heard of his skill in diseases of the eye, to ask his advice for a poor neighbour; and this gave me an opportunity of remarking his tenderness and good–nature, of which I soon had a still more convincing proof, when I myself had the benefit of his skill and kindness.

I was taken ill with a feverish attack, which I fancied that I and my female coadjutors were able to manage, and, after a struggle of three or four days, I believed myself well enough to receive company in my chamber. Of one of my visitors I inquired concerning this family, whose recent appearance had excited the curiosity of the neighbourhood. I was informed that the clergyman's father was a native of France, a man of high respectability, who had become a banker in Dublin on his emigration. The nephew had been educated for the bar; but, being possessed of an ample fortune, had renounced the law, and applied himself to the study of medicine, solely for benevolent purposes.

When I retired to rest that evening, I could find none; my fever had returned with added force, and my imagination was harassed with confused ideas of this family, while I tossed from side to side, in vain endeavouring to think of something else. At length the approach of morning brought a refreshing slumber, and in my dreams I saw my dear Sam Eyre, of whom I had dreamt but once before since his death. He appeared to be about the age at which he had died, twenty–two, his figure singularly elegant, and the beauty of his countenance mingled with an expression which inspired a sentiment amounting to awe. He was clothed down to his feet in a robe of linen exquisitely white and fine, over which he wore a dark dress without sleeves. I thought it might be a dress peculiar to India. We conversed, and he left me with a promise to return. I awoke, and felt as if I had been in company with an angel. My mind dwelt upon the vision, and I queried could our spirits, attached as they had been by the bond of infantile friendship, still hold communion with each other? Or did it foretell a more mature bond of friendship to bind me to another pure and elevated mind?

No doctor had resided in the village since the murder of our poor friend Doctor Johnson; but my new acquaintance, the student of law and medicine, heard of my illness, and came to visit me. He prescribed for me, and his judicious care arrested the progress of the fever, and I believe was, under Providence, the means of preserving me from a serious illness. Our friendship, thus founded on benevolence and gratitude, rapidly increased, and a close intimacy with all the family was the consequence. By the advice, encouragement, and assistance of this valuable friend, I was induced again to venture forth as an author, and to publish my "Anecdotes from real life for Children."

When the family returned to Dublin for the winter, we corresponded by letter. At the commencement of this correspondence, he thus marked the ground on which we were to proceed:- "Candour, plainness, simplicity, and open dealing are the bullion that has a universal and everlasting value. Politeness may stamp it into medals, and worldly–mindedness alloy it into the base metal which passes current in the world; but there is a superior coin into which honest minds convert it, and which honest minds alone should receive and pay." He left his patients in my care; and his letters generally began with minute enquiries and directions concerning them, and then expanded into sentiments of religion, morality, literature, and taste.

In summer the Le Fanu family returned to the rectory. The reverend gentleman possessed a vivacity which bespoke his French extraction, united to great good sense and benevolence; and he was a truly pleasant companion. Having lost his wife some years before, he superintended the education of his daughters himself, and his attentive care was repaid by their talents and virtues. The eldest daughter was a good classical scholar; her sisters also were highly accomplished, and sketched with much taste. They voluntarily furnished me with designs, from which engravings were made for my little book. Their simplicity, modesty, and graceful ingenuousness softened the lustre of their cultivated talents; and the sincere desire of their hearts was to be good themselves and to do good to others. Their only brother was at school, and we saw little of him. They had a cousin-german on a visit with them, a lively and most engaging girl, half-sister to my friend. She was niece to Richard Brinsley Sheridan. Another of their visitors was Everina Wollstonecraft, sister to the famous Mary, herself a woman of talent, and very pleasant in conversation.

The medical skill of my friend William Le Fanu attracted such crowds, that I was told by one of his rustic patients that "the biggest market that was ever seen in Ballitore was not to be compared to it;" that "a fair could not be missed out of it." I have seen him pale, languid, and exhausted after a levee of patients, who succeeded each other for several hours; but he would not complain of fatigue, declaring that it was the heat of the weather that oppressed him. We were very desirous of his company; but on those three days, appointed for charity in every week, this luxury was denied us. The voice of pain, sickness, and distress had chief power to allure him, though he was qualified beyond most others to give and receive the pleasures of social intercourse. His conversation, flowing from the springs of unaffected piety, solid sense, and refined taste, often sported in that playfulness which belongs to a pure conscience and an innocent heart; and the longer we knew him the more we prized his friendship.

He had a charity school opened at Dunlavin, which rapidly flourished under the superintendence of this worthy family. He stirred us up to a like charity here; for his constant aim was to do good. It was a great trial to us when Peter Le Fanu and his charming family left our neighbourhood, on his obtaining the parish of Saint Bride in Dublin. Sorely we missed them; and even the delightful letters of my friend William could not console me for the loss of his society. Encouraged by him, I was tempted to publish my Cottage Dialogues. He approved of their tendency, and was most anxious that all should exert their talents in whatever way was best adapted to advance the improvement of the Irish character, and increase the comforts of our poor people.

The beginning of this summer was hot and dry; and as usual the Irish farmer repined for the want of rain, which came abundantly when the harvest should be got in. The wheat suffered from mildew and from a small fly.

Henry Harrington, professedly a man of taste, built at Grangecon a fine picture–gallery, one hundred feet in length, which he filled with paintings. I believe he had enough, not hung, to furnish another. The beautiful situation of his dwelling, and his well–planted grounds, with the triumphs of art to which they led, made it a very desirable entertainment for strangers who were introduced there.

The cottagers of Ballybarney were favoured this autumn with a sight of their beloved lady, which diffused universal joy amongst them. In addition to the premiums for gardens, she had ordered a guinea to be given to the mistress of the cleanest house. She took me with her to Ballybarney, and her kindness in crossing a difficult stile, to please one of her tenants by looking at his garden, spoke more to the heart than the finest turned speech of the most refined sentimentalist could have done. She and her husband were not a little pleased with the improvement in the appearance of their village; their parental attentions continued to increase towards it, and I had still the pleasure of being the agent of their charity.

The jubilee which celebrated the fiftieth anniversary of George the Third's reign extended to Ballitore; loyal shots were fired, and a feu–de–joie being formed of a lighted furze–bush hung in a willow which bends over the river, the reflection in the water was very beautiful. The mail–coach passing from Dublin was brilliantly adorned with illuminations, which gratified those spectators who lost a night's rest to indulge their curiosity. Young Bruen of Carlow celebrated the jubilee by paying the debts of those confined for small sums in the jail of that town.

George Shackleton returned to us from Allonby, much pleased with the natural manners and simplicity of its inhabitants, and delighted with the refinement added to these in Thomas Wilkinson's conversation. It was in the year 1781 that Mary Mellor introduced me to the knowledge of Thomas Wilkinson, and on her return to Ballitore brought me a poetical address from him, to which I replied; and from that time our prose correspondence has continued, and our friendship has increased till it has become firmly established, though we have never seen each other's face. Thomas's genius owes nothing to the cultivation of school–learning, and his compositions both in verse and prose are full of originality. He is beloved and esteemed in a high degree by many persons of exalted rank and genius, and is looked up to by his neighbours as a man of sound judgment; yet he is not carried away from the foundations of humility. He is deeply interested in the welfare of his own religious society, in which he holds the station of elder.

Betsy Shackleton, having learned to plait straw, taught the art to several poor children, and introduced a little manufacture. She also assembled her plaiters twice a week, and taught them reading, writing, and ciphering, one of her sisters or one of our daughters assisting.

The Bishop of Meath suggested for my dialogues of the Irish peasantry the title of "Cottage Dialogues;" and his family kindly introduced the manuscript to Richard Lovell Edgeworth and his gifted daughter, who not only approved of its original tendency, but recommended it to their own bookseller in London as a work of entertainment; and Maria Edgeworth, whose writings reflect such a lustre on her sex, her country, and this age, with generous warmth patronized my humble efforts by accompanying them with a preface and notes to the English edition. I had several letters from Maria Edgeworth, whose handwriting (as if she were decreed to excel in everything) is exceedingly beautiful.

We this year made another valuable acquaintance, in a somewhat amusing manner. I was sitting in meeting on a week–day, when the door was opened by one of our servants, and I was called out. Exceedingly surprised and somewhat alarmed, I went out, and was told that a lady who was on a journey had called, and wished particularly to see me. Our servant had met my niece Betsy Shackleton on the way, and thus accosted her: "Oh, Miss Betsy, what shall I do? I'm going to call my mistress out of meeting, and I'm ashamed out of my life." "Why is my aunt to be called?" said Betsy. "Oh, because Miss Maria Edgeworth is come, and she wants the mistress." Away posted Betsy, and I found her and my daughter Elizabeth in high chat with the stranger, who was a woman in the prime of life, of a light, active figure. The small–pox had made ravages on a sweet face, but the brightness of her blue eyes, the benevolence of her smile, and the peculiar vivacity and intelligence of her countenance were beautiful.

She informed us that her name was Bonham, that her husband had lately come into possession of estates near Ballitore, and that it was probable they would soon spend some time in the neighbourhood. She was exceedingly anxious to establish schools here, and had called upon us to enquire the probability of their success. We were greatly pleased with her, notwithstanding the mistake her first appearance had caused. Our little daughter had been reading "Rosamond," "The Cherry Orchard," &c., and her imagination was so full of the idea of their author that she imagined the stranger must be Maria Edgeworth.[99]

We did not welcome the new year with joyous hearts, for our fears too justly foreboded that, before its close, we should be deprived of our dear Lydia White, who was the joy and pride of her family. To her a tender and most excellent husband looked for the sweet companion of his journey through life, and she was admirably fitted to train up her child in the way in which she should go; her steady consideration for the poor was a blessing to them, and her frequent offices of good neighbourhood were gratefully confided in; she conscientiously discharged her duty to the pupils, and her cheerful, contented, and placid temper made all her household happy. There were sometimes bright gleams which encouraged hope when a new medicine appeared to abate the symptoms, but these were succeeded by a darker sky. The sweet sufferer herself was for a long time free from apprehension of her danger; she bore her afflictions with that patience with which she was remarkably endowed, and was often, as was natural to her, innocently cheerful and witty.

Thomas Doyle, the son of Winifred Doyle, who sat for the portrait of "Rose" in the "Cottage Dialogues," had been instructed in Dublin in Joseph Lancaster's method, and became teacher of a daily school which was now opened in Ballitore. The committee held for the purpose of getting up the school was summoned by John and Margaret Bonham, now residing for a short time in our village, who themselves subscribed liberally. Margaret Bonham proposed a separate school for girls, and we readily obtained subscriptions for this purpose. A house was taken adjoining the boys' school, and a communication made between them, though the entrances were separate. The children of farmers and shopkeepers paid sixpence per week, of working tradesmen fourpence, and of labourers twopence, to be paid every Second-day morning. Mistress, monitors, and visitors were appointed; both schools filled very fast; and Margaret Bonham had the pleasure of seeing them established before she left Ballitore.

Soon after these dear friends left us, we were shocked at hearing of an accident which might have altogether deprived us of them. They lodged in Frederick-street, Dublin; the owner of the house kept a spirit warehouse adjoining a back parlour in which his wife was accustomed to sit, and where she used to remain up after the family had retired to rest. This time her servant was uneasy at her staying so long, and went down to see what detained her. On entering the room the servant perceived a black figure seated in the chair. She shrieked aloud; the family assembled, and found the unfortunate mistress of the house still in her chair, but quite dead, burnt to a cinder, and entirely black. There was no candle in the room; a coal was near her foot; but it was thought she was destroyed by internal fire. Had there been any blaze, the contiguity of the spirits would in all probability have caused a conflagration from which none of those in the upper apartments could have escaped.

Deep woe awaited us. This spring our darling Lydia White died, in the twenty-fifth year of her age. But He who ordained this trial graciously supported us under it. There is no other support. Vain is the help of man; and that we have a sure Comforter in the day of trouble must not be forgotten when our prospects are fair; else how can we look up with confidence? Our sweet Lydia was gone. The soft verdure of spring was spread over her grave, and the moon shone brightly upon it. Her uncommon perfections rose to our minds, at once afflicting and consoling us. Her consideration for others, especially the poor, was evinced in so many ways that it would be vain to endeavour to enumerate them. If she reared a kitten for a cabin, she gave it what she called a suitable education for its future lot, feeding it as it would be likely to be fed. Such apparent trifles are not in reality trifles; they display the character. It was on a sweet vernal afternoon that she was buried; how quiet, save the low voice of sorrow! and how the little children wept! The funeral was solemn, and attended by about a thousand people. But I must not linger thus beside her grave. Sweetest, dearest spirit, farewell!

CHAPTER XII.
1811.

Thomas Wray a "handsome Quaker."– Departure and return of Susy O'Hara. – A prisoner of war. – The rich woman of Ballybarney. – A new rector. – Notices of Burke and Beaconsfield. – The school library. – Arrival of the Grattan family, and anecdotes of Thomas Wilkinson. – The Duke of Leinster visits the village. – Death of Pat Rogers in an English prison. – A charitable fund established. – The great snow. – Tale of Carlow Castle. – Visit of Judge Day. – News of the proclamation of peace. – William Robinson, the new usher. – Joyful return of Joseph Williams from a French prison. – Results of the war. – A luminous arch. – Fearful storm and fall of a great ivy tree in the school garden. – Charitable bequests of the Keatinge family. – Illness and death of William Robinson. – Juvenile Magazine. – Visit from some of the Edgeworth family. – Misfortunes of Betty Curran. – Death of Deborah Wilson. – Hard times after the war. – A studious invalid. – Happy end of a Chancery suit. – Fever in the school. – Death of Samuel Grubb. 180 to 194

EBENEZER SHACKLETON became tenant to Maria Johnson for the farm at Fuller's–court, on a perpetual lease, so that the great grandson of John Barcroft now cultivated the fields which his ancestor had purchased. Ebenezer, being at Maria Johnson's residence near Bray, was introduced to one of her neighbours, whom, before they knew his name, the family distinguished by the name of "the handsome Quaker;" being a comely man, and wearing a broad-brimmed hat. They afterwards found that he was Thomas Wray, living happily with his Fanny and his fine family amidst these beautiful scenes, and still remembering Ballitore. Ebenezer was introduced. Thomas bowed politely to the stranger. His name was mentioned, "Shackleton." "Mr. Shackleton!" he seized both his hands – "you are the grandson of my old master! – I loved your grandfather next to my own father," and then all that friendship, remembrance, and hospitality could give were poured upon Ebenezer, whose heart was touched by this tribute to the worth of one whom he scarcely recollected.

Our old neighbour Susy O'Hara took leave of us with tears and blessings. Her son William, who lives in Cork, prevailed upon her to agree to spend the remnant of her days with him, promising to send her remains to be interred here. We had not long mourned for our loss when the car returned on which Susy had travelled, sitting on her bed; and the neighbours were surprised to hear that Susy was shortly to follow in the coach. Ballitore, in which she had lived fifty years, had such fast hold of her heart, that, "dragging at each remove a lengthening chain," she found she could not live with comfort elsewhere.

Isaac Williams inhabited the house near the bridge, which Joshua Webster had quitted. His wife Margaret delighted in cultivating her little garden beside the river. She laboured at it with her own hands, and it repaid her labours by its fertility and beauty. It also called off her mind a little from the painful reflection that her beloved son Joseph was languishing, in the opening bloom of youth, in a French prison. He had been shipwrecked on the coast of France, being a sailor on board a merchant ship, and was saved from death to be made a prisoner. They had received but one letter from him. He had undergone great hardships in travelling long journeys on foot, and in other ways, but his letter evinced feeling and resignation.

Ally Johnson, an old inhabitant of Ballybarney, having lost her sight, was allowed a shilling a week by Melesina Trench, and was led to me once a month to receive it. Her benefactress suggested knitting, and I got wool spun, and taught her to knit petticoats. Never had I so apt a pupil, and a source of employment was opened to her in which she took great delight. What she earned by this, added to her pension, made her comparatively a rich woman. She possessed true riches in a contented, cheerful temper, and a grateful heart. When the stock of wool was nearly exhausted, old Ally's health began to fail, and before a fresh supply was manufactured her thread of life was spun. She died peacefully, assured that her kind lady would defray the expenses of her funeral, or, as she expressed it, "would bury her;" and it was so.

Latham Coddington succeeded the late James Young in the care of the parish of Timolin. He resided at the glebe with his family. He is a well-informed, sensible gentleman, his wife is accomplished and handsome, and they have a beautiful group of children. Anne Coddington's mother, (widow of Colonel Bellingham,) a fine old gentlewoman, and her sister, wife of Colonel Walsh, were sometimes there. Colonel Walsh was exceedingly kind to me, noticing me for the sake of dear Edmund Burke, with whom he was acquainted. He sent me a volume of "Maxims" extracted from the writings of that illustrious man, and he told me that the last time he saw Edmund he was in his park, and the children of French emigrants whom he protected at a school passed in review before him. He was then so weak and depressed, that Colonel Walsh was not allowed to speak to him, but stood at his back. The colonel dwelt upon his amiable qualities, and remarked that his reception of strangers was most engaging. Captain

Nagle, whom I saw at Edmund Burke's in 1784, is now Sir Edmund Nagle and an admiral; Walker King is Bishop of Rochester, and William Burke died lately, blind.[100] Jane Burke, who has little use of her limbs, is confined to the breakfast parlour, but in tolerable health. She possesses the house during her life, a gentleman having purchased the estate.

Not long after learning these particulars, we heard of the death of Jane Burke at the age of seventy–six; and, some time after, Beaconsfield was destroyed by fire. That house, the scene of so much domestic happiness and social enjoyment, became a smoking ruin, as if all trace of that excellent family was to be removed from the earth.

Hannah Haughton and Anna Taverner left their dwelling in Ballitore, and removed to Freepark; whereupon James White took their house from my brother, and added it to his own.[101] The parlour was converted into a library, to which the boys have free access, and in which several of them delight to spend their leisure. James White's sister Sally, a very agreeable young woman, now became one of his family, to which her society and assistance were no little advantage.

Death, whose scythe mows down rich and poor, swept poor Fardy Lennon from the earth. Fardy had served four generations of our family, seemed to consider us still children, and addressed us, even when asking favours, in somewhat of a tone of authority, scarcely thanking us for what he considered as his right; and this was the case with the old servants of the family in general. The young people were sometimes amused and sometimes hurt at apparent disrespect to those whom they deemed entitled to respect; but we, who knew that this manner sprung from the tenderness with which they recollected our childhood, viewed it differently. It was a piteous sight to behold the bitter tears coursing one another down the wrinkled cheeks of this aged man, the morning of our lamented Lydia White's death, whom Fardy, when she was a child digging her little garden beside him, used to call his fellow–workman.

There came to Ballitore a family of the name of Grattan, to live at the Retreat. Richard Grattan, formerly a captain in the Kildare militia, was a pleasant, cheerful gentleman of considerable talents and a cultivated mind, with manners at once frank and polite. His wife, a very handsome woman, sensible, agreeable, and most careful of her children, proved, on intimate acquaintance, a noble character.

A brother of Captain Grattan's came to visit him, and they introduced him to me as a friend of Thomas Wilkinson's. I was agreeably surprised to find that he was the person whom Thomas Wilkinson had mentioned to me, in a letter written in 1786, as "a very amiable young man of the name of Grattan." He loved to speak of Thomas Wilkinson, who, he says, is a *statesman,* which means in Cumberland phrase one who owns the fee–simple of his land, but works on it himself: if he did not labour with his own hands, he would be an *estated man*. Our visitor told us that in the evening Thomas comes home, goes into his room, doffs his clog shoes, washes himself, and meets his friends at tea with hospitable politeness. He had lately been much engaged in opposing the enclosure of a common called Yanwath Moor. In the height of the debate one of his opponents made him trustee to his will; and such is the universal confidence in his upright character, that when the decision to enclose the common was come to, against his judgment, Thomas was placed at the head of the committee which was appointed to see that it was properly done.[102]

The Duke of Leinster, having been appointed by the Farming Society for the County of Kildare to visit along with other gentlemen our Lancasterian schools, called here.[103] He is a young man of genteel figure, agreeable countenance, and easy manners. Much interest is excited by the first nobleman in our land now entering into public life, and sincere desires are awakened that he may act so as to promote his own happiness and the happiness of the many whose comforts are so dependant on him.

In this year died our old friend Pat Rogers. The earnings of his life had been swept away by the bankruptcy of others, but he had health, talents, and an independent mind, and hoped to retrieve what he had lost; at least to leave his children a competence. In order to accomplish this, he went to London to settle accounts with the assignee of the bankrupt, and receive a balance due to him. This man, under pretence that Pat Rogers was the debtor, threw him into prison, and endeavoured by confinement to compel him to comply with the unjust demand. Pat resisted, assured that the laws of his country would soon liberate him; but the humiliation, grief, and confinement which he suffered combined to liberate him more speedily.[104] He died in prison, far from his home, his friends, and his children. That he should thus close his exemplary life was a close trial to those who loved him; his dear wife escaped that trial, and perhaps their spirits now rejoice together even in that event which appears to us so afflicting. His son got a situation in a bank; and his daughter, delicate in health and sore wounded in mind, was supported by that hidden strength which is never sought for in vain.

A fund for the assistance of poor housekeepers was raised amongst us, at the recommendation of Margaret Bonham, and was liberally assisted by her. A monthly committee, held at the same time as that for conducting the affairs of the Lancasterian school, directed this bounty, which to some was handed in money weekly, and to others given in provisions, as the case required. The clothing fund received an increase by a yearly donation of ten pounds from Sarah Medlicott; and these charities, collected in small sums, winding, like modest fertilizing streams, a silent course through the abodes of poverty, conveyed gladness to many a heart.[105] In about twelve months, by weekly subscriptions and some donations, £23 14*s.* 3*d.* was collected, with which were purchased twenty-seven blankets and ninety-one articles of clothing, which were distributed among fifty-one necessitous persons. The uncommon distress of the season caused many claims to be made upon those who had anything to spare.

On the 10th of First-month (January), there fell incessant and heavy showers of snow during the afternoon, and next morning the doors and windows were choked up. The snow was with difficulty cleared away from them, and footways were dug to allow people to go about their home business. The drifts were so great as nearly to bury the cabins under them, and in many places rose high above the hedges. It was a night of great dismay. Our excellent Winny Doyle had nearly perished on her road home from Birdtown. A woman was found on the morning of the 11th nearly exhausted, supporting herself by an elder-tree bough which overhung the drift into which she had plunged; some lads who were looking for sheep, and found her thus, took her to their mother, who laid her in a warm bed, and went into the bed beside her.[106] This act of humanity restored the frozen guest, but cost the kind hostess her life. Many affecting accounts reached us of persons lost on that fatal night.

An intense frost hardened the snow, and travelling was impracticable to the north of Ballitore, except on foot. With infinite difficulty a hearse arrived at Ballitore inn, conveying the body of a gentlewoman who had died at Kilkenny.[107] Her two sons of the name of Whitestone, one an ironmonger in Kennedy's-lane, accompanied the remains, which they intended to inter in Dublin. After staying nearly a week at the inn, they left the body locked up there, and set out on foot for Dublin. Two weeks after they returned, and, resigning the idea of taking the body further, laid their mother in the burial-ground at Timolin, about a mile from Ballitore.

Imprisoned as we now were, we were quite shut out from hearing how the surrounding world went on. The posts were stopped. Occasionally mail-guards brought hither and committed to our charge for the night the southern mails. The Cashel mail, borne by a horseman and followed by another sounding a horn, galloped through Ballitore, as being more passable than the usual road. Some days after this the mail passed in a more stately manner – in a coach and six! for Robert Grubb, a public spirited man, exerted his influence successfully to have the roads opened, and at length our long fast for news was broken, and I could not forbear thinking of Baron Munchausen's frozen words restored to sound by thaw.[108] We were a week without the post-bags coming in, and they came irregularly for some time. Then there reached us many accounts of the deaths of ancient people; amongst these was Michael Kearney, the worthy and learned cotemporary and friend of my father.[109] The 15th of the First–month the thermometer was twenty degrees below the freezing point, and it was a month before the snow disappeared. I expected a fruitful and warm summer to succeed this season of remarkable severity: but my friend James White entertained a different expectation, from the chill of the frost which had so deeply penetrated the bosom of the earth. His conjecture, more consonant to reason, proved to be the right one, for we had an uncommonly cold summer.

Though not in our immediate neighbourhood, we lamented the fall of great part of the castle of Carlow on the 13th of Second–month (February). Doctor Middleton, lately come thither, rented it, and expended some thousands in attempting to make that noble pile not only a habitable but a magnificent abode. He made excavations under part of the foundation, and planned a garden over arches which were to form the vaulted roofs of kitchens; so that a poor mechanic remarked that he was making a Babel. His design bespoke great taste, but failed in the execution, probably from a want of judgment or care in the workmen. Providentially it was on the first day of the week that the two towers which had been undermined fell; they fell so near a cabin that the wife had not power to follow her husband, who had snatched up the child and ran out. Terror held her motionless, till she saw the ruin stop within a foot of her house, when, dropping on her knees, she returned thanks to her great Preserver.

On his way to the assizes for our county, Judge Day called at Ballitore school to see the children of one of his friends. He was very affable, and at parting wished James White success, and James wished him "a pair of white gloves," which the judge is entitled to if no sentence of death is passed by him, and which Judge Day obtained at this time.

It was the 13th of the Fourth–month (April), on a morning breathing the sweetness of spring and the promise of summer, that William Leadbeater awakened me saying, as he entered the room, "It is all over! – the war is at an end!" His glad voice had the expression of grateful joy. Methought the eastern sky beamed with brightened hues, that the trees waved fresher verdure, and that heaven and earth rejoiced. Wherever we turned cheerful countenances congratulated one another, for those who were so happy as to have no relative exposed to the miseries of war felt a reflected joy from others who were relieved from anxiety for the fate of their friends.

Our neighbours, Isaac and Margaret Williams and their daughter Jane, were now animated with hope of embracing once more their long lost Joseph, whom they fondly expected, day by day, with increasing solicitude. While thus listening to every step, their anxious eyes continually directed to passing objects, a young man presented himself at the door: he appeared to have arrived by the coach. Jane Williams rushed out of the parlour, and had almost caught the stranger in her arms before she perceived he was indeed a stranger, and not her brother. She retired almost fainting, and her mother came forward to apologize for her daughter's agitation, and to point out to the young man James White's house, for which he inquired.

The stranger's name was William Robinson. He was a native of Gilford in the county of Down.[110] His parents died when he was about eighteen, and the care of three children, a brother and two sisters, devolved upon him. Providence had gifted him with an excellent understanding, a taste for literature, much application and industry. He became the master of a free–school, he taught the children of gentlemen at their houses, he copied wills, leases, &c., and thus maintained his little family, educating them himself, till his brother was advantageously apprenticed. James White, being in want of an usher of the established church, had been in treaty with this youth, whose worth and talents were well known to and strongly recommended by his friends in the north.[111] His coming had been delayed by the state of his health, which was injured by exertions for independence too unremitting for his delicate constitution to support; and on his arrival here the hectic glow of his complexion and the brightness of his eyes awakened apprehensions on his account. At the same time his pleasing exterior, tall in person and expressive in countenance, his manners agreeable, modest, yet unembarrassed and easy, added painful regret to these forebodings.

The virtues and accomplishments of the new usher soon increased the interest his first appearance had inspired. His conversation was full of good sense, tinctured with that pleasantry which springs from a lively imagination and a pure heart. The religious feeling with which his mind was imbued appeared more in his excellent example than in words. He had a poetical talent, and he drew from nature with taste and accuracy.[112] His view of Ballitore, taken from an upper window in my brother's house, does justice to the delicacy and fidelity of his pencil, and he had acquired the immortalizing art without instruction or assistance from others.

I have digressed from the story of the liberated captive. The account of his landing at Plymouth, rejoicing to be in a free country once more – then a letter from him with the Wexford postmark, which I opened for his mother, whose trembling hand could not break the seal – the day fixed for him to come to Ballitore, – all followed each other in rapid and joyous succession, putting to flight the shadows of suspense and fear. But they did not entirely chase away that indescribable anxiety which precedes the fulfilment of the dearest earthly wish, convincing us that there is a *plus ultra*, and that nothing of this world alone can, or ought, fully to satisfy the immortal soul. Yet I am sure the affectionate feeling hearts of this household were penetrated with humble gratitude and a sense of the favour granted in the restoration of this beloved youth.

The day appointed for Joseph Williams's return came at length. It was a fine summer's day, and his father and sister went to Sallins to meet him. His mother often appeared at her door, sending many a look up the road, "with all the longing of a mother." The hearts and eyes of her neighbours sympathized with her. Our post of observation was the low wall over the river at the bottom of our garden. The sound of wheels was heard, and then appeared the jaunting–car which had gone for him. We saw Margaret Williams turn suddenly into the house – perhaps her feelings had overpowered her. Alas! it was the feeling of disappointment, and another look revealed the cause – Joseph was not there! The boat had passed Sallins before his father reached it, and of course the young stranger had gone on to Athy: thither the father and sister hastened in a chaise, and about ten o'clock at night wheels were again heard. We ran to the door; the exulting voice of Jane Williams hailed us, "We have him!"

All who were out of doors pursued the carriage, and some had the happiness of seeing the youth spring out of it into his mother's arms. What an intrusion on the sacredness of such a meeting! Thus thought Mary Doyle, myself, and my daughter Elizabeth, even while an impulse which seemed at once involuntary and irresistible impelled us forward also, and we felt ashamed to find ourselves at Isaac Williams's door. Margaret and Jane espied us, and would have us in. The neat parlour, even neater than usual, a clean cloth spread upon the table, a blazing fire to take off the chill of the night air, of travelling, and of agitated feelings, the looks of unalloyed rapture beaming around us, – all conveyed to our hearts that most delightful sensation which arises from contemplating the happiness of others, increased by the knowledge that thousands were restored to like happiness. "Joseph is yet alive!" exclaimed the glad mother. "Look at him," said the admiring sister, "what a fine tall fellow he is!" He had grown taller since they parted, had a good, candid, and expressive countenance, agreeable manners, and was a sensible and industrious young man. He had deprived himself of part of his food while a prisoner, to pay for grammatical instruction in the French language. He was the active friend of his fellow–prisoners, and frequently assisted them by representing their cases to the charitable. Though he suffered much hardship, he spoke well of the French, and of their treatment of their prisoners of war, and assured us that the army was still much attached to Buonaparte.

The sword being now sheathed, several officers pitched their tents in peaceful Ballitore. How many pleasures did peace bring in her train, both by observation and report! Even before the preliminaries were entirely settled, the French and English interchanged visits. No personal enmity had existed, and they gladly embraced as brethren. Prisoners were restored to liberty and to home – of this we had seen one delightful picture.

The sudden fall on the produce of land, which caused pecuniary inconvenience to farmers, was scarcely to be placed on the reverse of the medal; for it had a reverse – the tears of those who mourned for "fathers, brothers, lovers lost!" flowed with increased bitterness from contrasting their situations with others. A disembodied militia and disbanded soldiers were thrown upon the country, many of them a dead weight, with idle habits; many a pest, with vicious ones. Accustomed to turbulence and plunder, some of these were suspected of deeds of violence and rapine. However, it was hoped that things would find their own level, and the quiet streams of peace fertilize the land through which they circled, and that those wretched beings who returned with the loss of health and limbs, or, still worse, of virtue, would feel their agitated spirits partaking of the calm now afforded.

An extraordinary exhibition claimed our attention. On the night of the 11th of Ninth–month (September), – a luminous arch from west to north stretched across the sky. It continued a considerable time before it faded away; but throughout the night "the blaze of meteors," which Thomson describes in his appropriate lines, attracted some curious eyes which preferred to the sweets of repose the gratification of gazing on these wonders.

Near the close of this year there arose such a storm as no one here remembered ever to have seen. It began on the 16th of Twelfth–month (December), early in the morning, and was felt all over the island.[113] Slates and thatch poured down or flew off the houses; trees were torn up or broken; yet little serious damage was done here.

In this storm one of the ivy trees that covered the piers of the gate at the entrance of the school–garden was blown down. The berries from which these trees grew had been sown by James McConnaughty on the day that my sister Sally was born. The naked pier discloses a neat top of cut-stone, which with its fellow – still covered with ivy – was given to my mother by her friend and neighbour Joseph Wills when the piers were built. The gift has now become visible, while the giver and receiver are seen no more.

Early in the year 1815 the remains of Antonia Grace Keatinge, the eldest daughter of Colonel and Lady Martha Keatinge, were brought from Montpelier, to be laid in their family vault at Narraghmore. She was twenty–three years of age, of a most amiable character, and remarkably benevolent – as the letters which I have received from her, relative to the charitable bequest of one of her sisters, can testify. The colonel added the interest of £500 more, in memory of another deceased daughter; and Antonia's legacy was now added to theirs. These bequests are recorded on tablets in the church of Narraghmore.

The assistance of William Robinson was a valuable acquisition to the school; but it did not long possess this advantage. He had suffered from a disease in his foot, which grew better; but he had not been long at Ballitore when it became rapidly worse; and he frequently said he believed he should not live long. He went to Dublin to consult the doctors and to see his sisters; all the medical men who saw his foot were of opinion that the case was hopeless.

He preserved his usual cheerfulness, except when quite overpowered by pain or sickness; and still entertained his friends by his anecdotes and playful sallies of wit. His gentle manners, his good humour and patience rendered him very dear to the family where his lot was cast. He required but little attendance, and he received it with gratitude. For about four months before he died he was confined entirely to his room, lying on the bed, under the care of Dr. Davis, whose skill and humanity were unremittingly exerted to mitigate his sufferings, though they could not restore him to health.

Sensible that he should never be able to resume the duties of his situation, he recommended James White to supply his place by the late-returned youth, Joseph Williams, whose good conduct and desire to improve himself he had observed. The advice was taken, and William Robinson then proposed to leave the house, lest the residence of an invalid in the family might injure the school. But this, his friends assured him, could not be the case, as his distemper was not contagious, and his room was detached from the other apartments; besides, they would not give up the pleasure of his society, nor consent to consign him to other hands. This determination was comfortable to him, for he loved this family, though his independent mind was not willing to encroach on their kindness. He proposed to pay for his board; but this would not be accepted, and he was made welcome as to the house of a brother. The schoolboys delighted in visiting him, and while he was able to receive them he was seldom alone in their playhours. He amused himself with learning French, and reading.

Thus passed eight or ten weeks, but his complaints gained ground, and he was no longer able to entertain himself with reading, or with the company of young people. Though he was daily growing worse, he would not allow his friends to be alarmed about him, till he perceived plainly that there was not much more time to spare. His brother had paid him a visit in the beginning of his illness, and had left him with the hope of his recovery, but now he was summoned to his death-bed. Their meeting was extremely affecting. The day after his brother's arrival he employed him to regulate his papers, desiring all those of a frivolous nature to be burned.

On one occasion, after enumerating his sufferings to a friend who sat beside him, he said, "As the poor body is suffering so much, it would be almost desirable that all was over." His friend replied "that it was well to be resigned however the disease might terminate." "Yes," answered William, "and I feel a good deal of satisfaction in waiting for the event. I have been supported beyond my expectation." At another time he said, "I feel sinking fast under my sufferings, but I have long made up my mind to hope in the happiness of eternity, and to rely on my blessed Redeemer: I thank God I have no distress of mind."

Richard Shackleton spoke to him about his French studies. "I am going," he observed, "where there is no confusion of tongues; where there is a universal language."

"I trust," said he, one day, "that I have been delivered from many evils. I have often enjoyed the Divine presence. For several years I have had great enjoyment of the world, and I have seen the image of the Lord, the great God, impressed upon all his works. One thing gave me some uneasiness, and that was my own insignificance amidst His great creation; but I recollected that He cares for the sparrows, and not one can fall to the ground without His knowledge."

He spoke much of the evidences of Christianity, but added that the speculations of the head do little to convince us. "You must renounce sin, you must do the will of God, and then your soul will become interested in His religion; even I, a poor, unworthy sinner, have often experienced great joy, and in silence and solitude, when I have been walking by myself, I have felt unutterable things."

About a week before his death, a young man came to see him, and read several pieces to him concerning the vanities of the world. One, who sat by, remarked that these subjects did not match William's present state, as she believed he had got beyond them. But the humble sufferer said he liked to hear anything that was good, and that he did not feel himself elevated above the smallest child. Speaking of one who had praised him, he said he could not bear it; he wished rather to be shown his errors, and directed to the Source of good. He spoke of a little society of methodists who used to meet at the house where he lodged in the North; he said they were a humble people, that he had often felt great sweetness amongst them, and was still much united to them. He spoke of the danger of a sect becoming fashionable, and of great repute in the world; also, of their possessing much wealth, or being greatly engrossed by business: that when he observed ostentation creep into a sect, he trembled for it, adding that amongst the methodists, protestants, quakers, and every society he knew of, there were some sincerely religious people, and there were also many who were slaves to the fashions of the world, and who cringed to the great.

On the 16th of First–month, the dear sufferer peacefully expired, his brother and friends standing round his bed; and the remains lay as in a placid sleep.

I entered James White's house a few minutes after this event had taken place. Many of the boys stood silently at the foot of the stairs which led to the apartment of death; some stood in groups, others sat in the windows, and a solemnity was spread over all, the more striking as contrasted with the gay spirits and active movements which were wont to enliven this house: tenderness and respect were mingled with their sorrow. They were not summoned to school that afternoon, but I believe there was not a quieter house in Ballitore. Joseph Williams had taken them, by two at a time, into the room where their late friend and instructor lay, just after his spirit departed.

William Robinson was interred in our graveyard by his brother's desire; the schoolboys and many of the inhabitants accompanying the remains in solemn silence.

One of the pupils now at the school was Thomas Fisher, a lad whose acquisitions were as remarkable as his modesty. For some time he printed with his pen a monthly collection of essays, called the "Juvenile Magazine," for the reading of which one penny was charged, except to the schoolboys, who paid a halfpenny; this money was applied to the education of poor children at the Lancasterian School. His father was so much pleased with this ingenious benevolence, that he got the magazine printed in Limerick, the profits of its sale being applied as above.

An account of the distribution of premiums for neat cottages awarded to some of our labourers was sent to the "Farmer's Journal," and procured us this autumn an agreeable surprise. One evening a young man and woman came to the post–office window, and inquired for a letter for Mr. Edgeworth; the name gave us a start, but we supposed there were other families of that name. A negative answer was returned; they smiled at each other, and the gentleman expressed a wish to see the cottage of "Rose." It had been mentioned, in the account of the premiums, that the character of Rose in "Cottage Dialogues" was drawn from Winifred Doyle. They were invited in, and proved to be Charles Sneyd Edgeworth, son to Richard Lovell Edgeworth and brother to Maria, with his wife. Next morning they visited Winifred Doyle, calling also at John Kelly's, Mary Casey's, and Fanny Lyons', who had also received prizes. They were pleased with all, but especially with Winny, whom they complimented with benevolent politeness, received by the worthy matron with graceful unembarrassed modesty. They also visited the Lancasterian School, which met their approbation.

Betty Curran was one of the successful candidates for a premium. She is daughter to Darby and Nancy Lennon, and has long been remarkable for the industry and ingenuity, which support her aged and infirm parents. She married Thomas Curran, a mason, who was exceedingly kind to her parents and affectionate to her. He made their little dwelling more comfortable, and parents and daughter united in rejoicing at their lot. One day, while repairing a lime–kiln, he was caught in rain; the ladder had been removed and no one was within hearing to relieve him; he was drenched with wet, and chilled with cold, and the consequence was a slow fever. The exertions of his wife and her anxiety on his account brought on the premature birth of two daughters. Her husband, who rose from his sick–bed to leave it for her accommodation, and endeavoured to work to provide for her, was soon obliged to submit to the increasing disease, and his father, from the county of Wicklow, came to take him home till he should recruit his health. One of the infants died, but the care of the other and her own weakness prevented his wife from accompanying him, save a short way, when they parted weeping, and he promised, if he found himself better, that she should soon hear from him. She did not hear so soon as she wished, and all her apprehensions were verified when his brother came with a horse for her. Her last baby was now dead, and she set out immediately. She found her beloved husband lying in the grasp of death; he knew her, welcomed her, and died in her arms. She staid till the dear remains were laid in earth, and then returned to her lonely home and her parents, who, sinking under their own grief, could do but little to comfort her. She brooded over her loss in sad silence; her looks had something of despair, and she has since told me that under Providence she believed she owed the preservation of her reason to the kind visits and consoling counsel of my sister Sally. It was long before I saw her smile; but she did smile when I gave her twenty shillings, sent by Margaret Bonham, and said, "Now I can buy a pig." The pig was bought, it throve, her attention was occupied, and gradually she entered upon more active employments. Grief had impaired her sight, and unfitted her for the use of her needle.

On the 21st of Third–month, 1815, our ancient friend, Deborah Wilson, died at her house in Carlow. She had been declining for a considerable time, and kept her bed three months. She was thirty–two years a widow, and exerted herself with great assiduity for the support and education of her nine children. She was guarded in her words and actions, and it has been testified that an unbecoming word was never known to escape her lips. Her exertions for the comfort of her family were successful. She had two daughters living with her and keeping a shop. She was a pattern of good housewifery, neat and frugal, generous, hospitable, and charitable. The divisions in our Society gave her much concern, and she bore her testimony against them. She died at the age of seventy–five, much regretted. Her remains were brought hither for interment.

The rumours of war had again disturbed our tranquillity. The restless ambition of Buonaparte had brought its own punishment upon the memorable field of Waterloo, which needs no such pen as mine. Its effects are thus sketched by my friend, writing from London: "We are here in the midst of the tears and the triumphs of a dear–bought victory." Peace was restored again, but this blessing was not hailed by all with thankful hearts. One of the many evils of war was the sudden increase of the farmer's wealth, owing to the increased price of provisions, and his consequent indulgence in unaccustomed luxuries. These consumed his wealth, the source of which was now greatly lessened; he dismissed many of his labourers; they pined unemployed amid the abundance of the harvest, and looked round in vain for assistance. Many who were once rich were so no longer; bankruptcies took place to an alarming extent, and all ranks agreed in feeling and lamenting the pressure of the times. Yet, compared with those countries which lay bleeding under the hand of war, we had little cause to complain of our lot.

Joshua Harvey left Ballitore to pursue his studies in Dublin, where he had opportunity of attending medical lectures. He left us as if to attend the Dublin meeting, and to return; thereby sparing ourselves and him the pain of a formal farewell, for a sincere regard subsisted between him and us.

Betsy Shackleton was hastened home from Dublin, on account of her sister Margaret's increased illness. She recovered from this attack, but was for a long time confined to her bed, and she was afterwards able to take exercise on the jaunting–car, and on horseback every day when her health and the weather permitted. For four years her continued indisposition had crushed the opening hopes of youth, and cut off this dear young creature from the active occupations suited to her age and cheerful temper; but she extracted enjoyment from what was attainable. Possessing a classical taste, and having a judicious instructor in her affectionate father, she made considerable proficiency in the Latin language. She often chose this reading in preference to English authors, in order that her thoughts might be more taken from her pain by the attention which a foreign language required. Her friends, old and young, loved her society and her sweet, sensible conversation, often mingled with wit and humour, and we sometimes flattered ourselves that she might be restored to health.

Meantime my brother and sister had another cause of anxiety hanging like a cloud over their beautiful abode, of which their quondam tenant, Peter Delany, threatened to deprive them. This unjust and litigious man, taking advantage of the unsettled time soon after the rebellion – during which he had been ejected for non-payment of rent – had made several attempts to substantiate a claim on the mill; and though he had been twice defeated at law, yet on his becoming a bankrupt he prevailed upon his assignees to file a bill in chancery against my brother. As he was provided with false witnesses, there were great apprehensions lest he should prevail. My brother and sister bore this state of suspense with great equanimity, and their daughters cheerfully formed plans for future humble life. The whole village was interested, and waited the event in anxious expectation. They saw with indignation Peter Delany wandering like an evil spirit about the little Eden, now gay with the bloom of summer, and marking it for his own.

At length the cause came on, and my brother went to Dublin. Peter Delany's miller, on whose evidence he chiefly depended, swore so strongly to every thing that he fairly outswore himself, and thus discovered the baseness of the transaction to the Chancellor, Lord Manners, who expressed his indignation in open court, and gave justice her due. A letter from my brother's attorney, received next morning, 24th of Sixth–month, conveyed to my husband the glad tidings. Long did the pleasant sound vibrate in my ears with which he broke my morning's sleep, as he shouted, "Glorious news! Delany is completely defeated!"

The news spread like wild–fire. Old James Kealy – forty years employed in the mill, whoever held it – being locked in, could not impart his feeling as he wished; therefore opening a window and thrusting out his arms he shouted to the passers–by with joyous solemnity, "Glory be to God! The master has gained!" Judy Coffee, the old female sexton, danced for joy, and a bonfire expressed the general rejoicing.

Ballitore was now cheerful, and nearly sixty boarders filled James White's school. But an alloy came to our enjoyments, and the visitation of illness again spread alarm. The parents of the schoolboys were immediately apprized of this, and many were removed from school; those who remained lodging in the village.

My brother–in–law, Samuel Grubb of Clonmel, after three years' lingering illness, was now rapidly declining, and died on the 9th of Eighth–month. His last words were, "My spirit is going where the wicked cease from troubling and where the weary are at rest." Most of his children were with him, and his sons, with affectionate tenderness, performed every office in their power for one of the best and most beloved of fathers.

My dear sister, nearly forty years his companion, was much shaken by this stroke, but her mind, resting on the Rock of ages, knew where to seek consolation. My dear brother Grubb was remarkable for his disinterested friendship. He counselled his friends in their business – and well qualified he was to do so – with as much earnestness and anxiety as if it was himself who was to profit by the means he pointed out. He left his family in very comfortable circumstances, most sincerely regretted by them, and by his neighbours and friends. He had beheld the slow but certain approach of death with calmness and resignation, humbly trusting in the mercy of his Redeemer, not in his own merits. He settled his outward affairs wisely, and gave orders concerning his funeral in such a manner as to avoid hurry and bustle in conveying the coffin into the graveyard. He was buried at Clonmel, and there was a very large and solemn funeral.

CHAPTER XIII.
1817.

ON the 22nd day of the Sixth–month this year, the first stone of George Shackleton's house at Griesemount was laid by his little niece Hannah White. Her father had written a date, &c. in Latin, which he wrapped in lead and put into a bottle, with coins of the present date, sealing it with the seal of Ballitore post–office. This was placed under the foundation–stone. When this bottle shall be opened, where shall we be who stood round to witness this pleasant ceremony? Our places shall know us no more!

About this time died our old neighbour Sally Kennedy, who, according to her own request, was interred in our graveyard. Thither were her remains conveyed enclosed in a grand coffin, in a stately hearse, ten carriages following, with mourners wearing scarfs and hat-bands – a parade ill-suited to the simple spot where she desired to be laid. She bequeathed £20 to the poor of Ballitore, which was expended on great-coats and cloaks for aged and infirm persons.

The truism that the scythe of death mows down impartially was sadly verified, when Eliza, daughter of our neighbour Richard Grattan, after undergoing much anxiety and fatigue in attending the younger part of the family in that fever which afflicted Ballitore this autumn, sank under it herself after nearly two weeks of a hopeless struggle. She died on the 20th of Tenth–month, sincerely regretted even by those who were only connected by the ties of neighbourhood. Most of the respectable inhabitants of the village attended her remains to Timolin, where they were laid. Abundance of tears were shed on this occasion, especially by the young maidens, cotemporaries of this lovely girl, whose age was about twenty–two.

The Ballybarney premiums for the best–kept house and garden were adjudged as usual this autumn, and we beheld with satisfaction the increasing beauty of the village. At the back of the schoolmaster's house was a shoot of woodbine, this year's growth, fifteen feet in length.

Our village blacksmith died lately. His industrious widow continues the business with the aid of a journey–man; but, prudent as well as industrious, she considered the danger of slanderous tongues, and therefore gave her daughter – a girl of sixteen – to her assistant, with board and lodging for a year as a dowry!

About six miles from Ballitore stands the Castle of Kilkea, belonging to the Fitzgerald family. It is a noble pile, and in good preservation. If the windows and chimney–piece in the principal room were not so modern, and the massy balustrades of the great stairs had been left the original colour of oak, and not disguised with white paint, it would have an effect more appropriate to the dignity of the building. There are a great number of rooms: in the large one before mentioned are two tablets, one bears the figure of an eagle, another a baboon, with this inscription:– "SIDIVPIET, *Crom–a–boo, 1573.*" The ancient kitchen, with its seven ovens, is in the lower part of the building, from which the ascent to the chief rooms is by stairs of solid oak. The entrance into this part is by a great door, studded with huge iron nails, and here are dark and dreary apartments, the whole recalling the idea of the feudal times.

On the 1st of the Third–month this year Betsy Shackleton left the school–house, where she had resided for five years, the increase of her sister Margaret's indisposition now requiring her presence at the Mill–house. Her departure caused sincere regret, and Hannah White's young heart began to experience sorrow, for this was a painful separation. But already exerting her powers of mind, which promised that admirable union of fortitude, feeling, and judgment once so conspicuous in her precious mother, she soon became reconciled, and spent most of her forenoons at the Mill, receiving her aunt's instructions; for from the dawn of intellect she had been her preceptress.

This year James White attended the London yearly meeting. The evening before he left his boys, he spoke to them in such a manner, showed such reliance on their honour, and bade them so affectionately farewell, that their conduct was sensibly influenced during his absence from them.

We had a visit of a few days from our dear friend Joshua Harvey, who this year went to Edinburgh to study physic. Our Jacob Harvey accompanied his cousins, Abraham and Mary Bell, to New York, where he is likely to spend some years. Affectionate and communicative as he is, his letters, frequent and full, afford much entertainment and delight to his friends.

Our dear, venerable cousin, Deborah Christy, died this year at the age of eighty–one. She was an excellent woman. She had chosen the good part early in life, and it was not taken from her. Left a widow in her youth, she devoted herself to her children, and found some consolation for the loss of their father in the affection and virtues of these beloved ones. Three of these she lost by death when they had pretty much grown up; but, borne above her sorrows by that which can alone support under such privations, she recovered the native calm cheerfulness of her temper, and made every one, but particularly young persons, happy about her.

A rumour was for some time afloat that on the 18th of Seventh–month this year the world should be burned, and several were terrified at the prediction. On that day our little world of Ballitore was suffering from an opposite cause, for we were driven to our upper apartments by a flood. This summer was wet and cold to a degree scarcely equalled by that of 1782. We could seldom let out our parlour fires; the fruits had not their usual flavour; the turf could not be manufactured in the bog; the corn ripened slowly, and when the time of reaping drew on, it had grown in the ear, and the appearance of vegetation from the uncut grain was indeed alarming. The priest not only permitted but recommended his flock to work in the fields on the first day of the week after service, in order to save the corn; and they did so for four First–days successively.[115]

The harvest was generally got in, though with great difficulty, because of the frequent rains and uncertain sunshine. Those who cut their wheat early had a pretty good, though a scanty crop; the rest was almost universally malty. In this season of dismay our patient peasantry forbore to murmur. "It is the will of God," they said, and worked on with pensive countenances. Their hope rested upon their staple diet, the potato crop. The oats, though less injured than the wheat, partook of the influence of the season, and much of that crop was malty also.

On the 10th of Eighth–month our beloved Margaret Shackleton exchanged her suffering state, I trust, for an entrance into that city the inhabitants whereof shall not say, "I am sick." Her funeral, in the fine summer afternoon, moving along the Mill–field, attended by her parents, brothers, sisters, relatives, friends, and neighbours, and expecially by many young women, was a most interesting sight. Her memory is sweet, and will be cherished with tender regret while we remain in that world which she has quitted in her twenty–third year The following reflections written by her were found after her decease:

"It is nearly five years since I could say I was very well. For my unpleasant feelings and the fretful, unkind manner which I have often shown since my complaints began, I can only hope for pardon in the mercy of Him who alone knows the heart, sees its temptations, sees its endeavours, marks the slightest inclination to right, and in His infinite goodness makes allowances for its weakness. What confidence should be placed in such an omniscient Being! If He allows our sufferings to be violent, or of long continuance, He will enable us to bear them, if we put our trust in Him. But alas, it is the want of this confidence, this faith, which produces fretfulness and a desire to be different from what we are.

Oh! if I could but think with thankfulness of the many alleviations there are to my sufferings which many people have not! But, instead of that, I am too much given to complain. May I be more patient. May I, at least, try to be so!

25th of Third–month, 1813."[116]

My dear and honoured friend, Melesina Trench, lost her only daughter at the engaging age of four years and three months; she was a most beautiful and amiable child. My friend's personal trials did not cause her to relax in her consideration for others. She applied the profits of the sale of her beautiful poems of "Ellen" and "Campaspe" to acts of benevolence, by assisting some charitable friends in England; and our poor people also partook of her bounty.

The 10th of Eleventh–month – the potato–digging not being yet begun by reason of the late harvest – was a day of dismay, for there was a hard frost, with every appearance of continuance. Sadness and alarm sat on many a brow, and famine seemed inevitable. Next day frost and fear had disappeared, and it was even acknowledged as a blessing from His hand who directs the course of the seasons, that this spur to exertion was given. No time was now lost. A fine, plentiful harvest of potatoes succeeded, and the dread of famine was removed.

This proved to be a mild winter. In the latter end of the Eleventh–month the gooseberry–trees were budding, and the cuckoo was heard by one of our neighbours. We heard that this extraordinary circumstance was remarked in other places also during the winter of this year.

I was greatly delighted at receiving a letter from the poet Crabbe. I had long wished to know whether his characters were drawn from real persons, and I wrote to him on that subject. As I knew not his residence, I had sent my letter to Melesina Trench to forward. It reached the bard safely, and obtained for me a most friendly reply, which caused a sensation throughout Ballitore. I was right in my conjecture that truth guided the pen of this admirable moral poet.

George Downes, a friend of Richard Shackleton, has occasionally paid short visits to Ballitore, pleasing us more and more at every visit.[117] This young man having strong literary tastes, pined and languished behind a woollen draper's counter. At length he was liberated, fitted himself for college, and is now eminent in literature, modest and unaffected in his manners, and has lately married an agreeable young woman, a native of Germany.

Hannah Field and Elizabeth Barker, Friends from America, visiting this meeting in the course of their religious services, were detained at the house of Betsy Barrington fully twelve days by Hannah Field's indisposition.[118] Their labours in public and in private, but most of all their sweet example of universal love, have, I hope, been blessings to many.

A letter was received by the committee for conducting our Lancasterian school, signed by some of the Roman Catholic inhabitants, requesting that the master might be permitted to teach the children of that persuasion their catechism in the school–room after school hours. To grant this request appeared to the committee an innovation on the prescribed rules, and it was firmly though civilly refused. Upon this, many who had never joined in our subscriptions made liberal contributions towards another school. They fitted up a house at Thoran for the boys, and built one for the girls, engaging Owen Finn, who had been educated in our school, as master.[119] The new school was presently filled, not by taking in those who were not already receiving instruction, but by emptying our school; the priest being active in the cause. Yet ours is still supported, and we hope will continue to stand.

On the 23rd of Second–month, about two o' clock in the morning, old Michael Neville, who was watching, with his dog, the loaded dray of his son, a carrier just come from Dublin, discovered by the growl of the dog that some one was near, and saw men concealing themselves behind a wall. He called to them, and threatened them with his pitchfork; they withdrew and fired. The shot giving the alarm, Edward Kelly called out "Robbers!" from his window; others repeated the cry, and several sallied out; but the ruffians departed, having fired another shot, and burst in one of Abby Widdows' parlour windows. Some of the neighbours staid up all the next night, and the following day resolutions were entered into to establish a nightly patrol of respectable inhabitants, some of whom were made special constables. When Lord Norbury and Baron George were on circuit, they were waited on by some members of this patriotic band, who were received by the great men very kindly. Lord Norbury said that if their example were followed, the value of such combinations would be very great; adding, that "while they stood by each other they would be invulnerable." He went to look at George Shackleton's new house, of which he expressed his approbation; frequently turning to view Balliltore, which indeed from that point is a most attractive object, he said he had long known "that unrivalled valley," and that it had maintained its comforts and respectability in a remarkable manner.

Joseph Humphreys introduced to us his friend Dr. Charles Edward Herbert Orpen, a native of Cork, whose indefatigable labours have established in Dublin a school for the deaf and dumb, to whose instruction he devotes himself. He is a well–looking young man, engaging in countenance and modest in manners, concealing rather than exhibiting the strength of his understanding and the play of his wit.

Our neighbour, Maurice Farmer, concluded on joining the patriot army in South America, and bade farewell to his beloved Ballitore – kneeling down and kissing the earth three times before he stepped into the coach which whirled him away to Dublin.

One day I was called upon by a gentlewoman whose countenance and manner bespoke her to be an old acquaintance, though I did not immediately recognise her; she told me that she was Maria Lennon, the widow of Surgeon Lennon, who once rented the Mill–house. It was nearly thirty years since I had seen her, then a graceful young woman. She related to me some of her adventures since she left Ballitore.[120] They lived for some time at Kilkenny, till her husband got the situation of surgeon to a regiment. They were afterwards stationed at Guernsey, and from thence went to Montreal in Canada. They had one daughter before they left Europe, and two were born in America. She describes the country as pleasant, the cold weather being alleviated by warm houses and a clear sky. The heat of the summer, however, is in proportion to the intense frost in winter; and one day that her husband had been much exposed to the sun, he complained of being unusually affected. His wife got the medical men of the place to visit him, but they made light of her fears, and he did so himself, desiring to be left alone, and saying he expected to be well in the morning. In the morning he was dead, having, no doubt, been killed by a sun–stroke.

His family, now deprived of his pay, were left in a strange country in great distress, but the compassion and generosity of the officers afforded them the means of support, most of which the widow applied to discharge debts contracted by her husband, whose beloved remains she would not leave in a foreign land with an aspersion on his memory. Then with her three children – two of them very young – she embarked for Europe. Her eldest girl, about twelve years old, assisted her mother materially on the voyage, performing offices less suited to her tender age than to her ardent and affectionate mind, which was ripe beyond her years. Arrived in London, Maria Lennon presented a petition, and obtained a pension for herself and children. Returning to her native country, she opened a school in Athy; from whence removing to Dublin, she received a small number of boarders, at one hundred pounds per annum each, herself paying masters. Here Henry Flood, who came to Ballitore school in 1778, saw her eldest daughter, about fifteen years of age, and was struck with her uncommon beauty. Two years afterwards he again saw her, improved in stature and loveliness, and advised her mother to take her to England, as no match in this country was worthy of her. However, he changed his opinion, and proposed for her himself. His proposal was accepted, when the young woman and her mother had ascertained that his family approved of his choice, for his rank and fortune were far beyond her expectations. Soon after his marriage, by the death of an elder brother, Henry came into possession of £25,000, and of the family estate, worth £5,000 per annum.[121]

Chance introduced us this year to the knowledge of a light shining in a dark place – Jane Darley, for twenty years a prisoner in the Four Courts Marshalsea. Her cousin, Moses Darley, came to Ballitore school in 1763. At ten years old Jane lost her mother, who was an heiress. Her father had a family by a former marriage, but she was the only child of the second. When she was seventeen her father died. She mostly spent her summers with her brother, the collector of Newry, at Arno's Vale, near Rostrevor. She was taught music and dancing, but her education was in more material respects greatly neglected. She was sensible of this, and improved her handwriting by copying any well written notes that she received, with as much care and assiduity as she would imitate a drawing; and taught herself to spell correctly by the diligent study of Johnson's Dictionary. These acquisitions were afterwards of the greatest use to herself and to others.

When Jane Darley came into possession of her property, she gave way to the liberality of her disposition, believing that her generosity was consistent with prudence. She rebuilt and engaged to let some houses, for which she was to receive fines; but before the contract was finished, the person employed to build them went to the Isle of Man, taking with him the keys of the houses. To recover these she was obliged too resort to law, but ere the case was decided she lost her houses by ejectment, and was in consequence thrown into prison. Her debts have long since been discharged, and she might now regain her liberty, but she has waited in the hope that some situation may be provided for her, in which to pass her latter days more comfortably than her present limited means would admit of. She is desirous to be matron to one of the public institutions; for her independent mind would disdain a sinecure. Her humanity and generosity occasionally beam beyond her prison–house; within its bounds she is a blessing. The exertions she made in her youth to acquire the free use of her pen have been an inexpressible advantage to her forlorn companions. Her merit is known to the Irish government, and her applications seldom fail of success. For herself she asks no favour – for her fellow–prisoners many, and they owe most of the alleviations of their situation to her representations on their behalf. Most of her time, even what should be allotted to sleep, is employed in writing letters to serve one or another. She is not discouraged from continuing these good offices by the base ingratitude which she has in several instances met with. Her disinterested benevolence depends not on her fellow–creatures for reward, yet she is beloved, admired, and revered; her advice is sought for; her decisions respected.

She has a little apartment to herself, which she keeps with great neatness; creeping flowering plants entwine the bars of her prison windows, and the walls are ornamented with her own drawings. She also indulges a poetic talent, and her mind seems to have risen by successful efforts against the subjugation of misfortune, through the assistance of Him who saw the sincerity of her heart, endued her with patience and fortitude, and made her an instrument of good to the forlorn captive. In a letter to me she says, "Time and retirement, injurious to the graces, have a contrary effect on our virtues, and to turn our misfortunes to our advantage is the truest philosophy. That I have done so is surely doubly fortunate to me, as it has indeed illumined the walls of my prison; perhaps in no other situation would I have acted so much to my credit and satisfaction, for the sunshiny path of life is not the one in which we gather most of our virtues." This worthy woman, now advancing to her seventieth year, is commonly known as the Queen of the Marshalsea. Sir Charles Morgan, the physician of the prison, and a man of gentleness and humanity, is the husband of our literary countrywoman, Lady Morgan, formerly Sidney Owenson.

On the 20th of Sixth–month, died in his forty–fourth year my friend William P. Le Fanu, to the inexpressible grief of his family and friends. He appeared to be worn out with his exertions in devising means of relief for the poor in this season of great distress. His own bodily sufferings he concealed till medical aid was of little avail; but two weeks before his death he was obliged to acknowledge and yield to the pressure of sickness, and even then his friends at a distance deceived themselves with strong hopes of his being restored to them; cherishing this illusion till the account of his death plunged us into grief. It is hard to attain to a state of resignation for the loss of so invaluable a friend.

On the night of the 23rd of Sixth–month, after a very hot day, we had an extraordinary appearance of lightning; the sky seeming to open, and to be entirely illumined to the eastward.[122] One of my daughters said it was like heaven opening to admit a pure spirit – we had the day before heard of William Le Fanu's death. While we surveyed this glorious show from the bridge, our ears were regaled with the rare song of a sweet bird which we called the Irish nightingale. The balmy air added to the combination of delights, but our hearts were too heavy to enjoy them.

What deaths we suffer ere we die!

The impression lately made by the death of dear Dr. Bell, my cotemporary, my school–fellow, and sincere friend, beloved and regretted by all who knew him, was renewed by the wound now inflicted, and thus sorrow is added to sorrow.

The rector of Narraghmore built a very handsome new glebe–house, and left the old one, which, however, remained for a good while standing. When I now saw it in a state of ruin, and being taken down, the pleasant hours which my dear father and the worthy Richard Beauchamp, the former rector, had spent there together, interchanging their liberal and instructive sentiments, rose to my recollection, and brought the cherished idea of him whose loss his family cannot cease to feel, and of that benevolent pair who were so beloved by all ranks around them. The name of Julia was once not unfrequent among the Narraghmore peasantry, who ventured to honour a child by the name of the general benefactress, assured that she would not be offended by the liberty.[123] Of later times the descendants of the Julias, partly from modesty, partly from ignorance, have sunk into Judys.

We must not repine at the loss of the old house and of the inhabitants who gave it value; for the new house contains a worthy family, whose exertions for the relief of the poor, in the seasons of distress, have made a deep impression on the hearts of the many who were relieved by or who witnessed their unwearied kindness.

The scarcity of firing, occasioned by the difficulty of saving turf last rainy season, caused such depredations that several were obliged to cut down their hedges in their own defence, to prevent their being entirely spoiled.

Our inoffensive neighbour, James M'Connochy, had spent several years in Ballitore, boarding at John Farmer's, walking abroad every fine day when health permitted, and paying morning visits, sometimes to one neighbour, and sometimes to another; cautious of interrupting family business, yet evidently expecting that attention that was indeed due to his courtesy. He had much of the courtesy of the old school, and also what was better, a kind heart and a tongue unpolluted by slander or detraction. His income was regulated by prudence and punctuality, and besides subscribing handsomely to our charitable funds, he gave much alms in secret. On the 15th of Eighth–month he walked through our fair, as well in health as for some time. He had long been infirm, and a longer indisposition than usual last winter had shaken him much. When he returned from the fair he was taken ill, and died next evening about ten o'clock, aged seventy–six, sincerely regretted by his neighbours. He had buried his wife and six children, and knew not of having a single relation in the world. He was interred on the 18th, in our plain way, in our little enclosure, according to his own desire.

His friend Thomas Johnson did not long survive James M'Connochy, whose funeral he had attended, and of whose will he was one of the executors. After his return to London, sitting alone one evening with his wife, he entered into many particulars respecting his affairs, advising her as to her future place of residence, should she be left a widow. Her tender spirit shrunk from this idea; he told her she need not be alarmed, as such advice might be necessary for her guidance. Not long after this conversation, after retiring to rest in usual health, he was awakened in the dead of the night by sudden illness; and before the doctor could arrive, he laid his head on his wife's bosom, and, uttering an affectionate exclamation, expired. The widow was overwhelmed with distress, and had not the relief of tears, but vented her anguish in shrieks of distraction; when a voice, intelligible to her mental ear, conveyed the awful command, "Be still, and know that I am God," and a light seemed to shine around her. Then her heart was comforted, and strengthened to bear with pious calmness this unexpected stroke.

A letter from Juliet Smith announced the death of her lovely daughter, Kitty Allan, who left five children with a disconsolate husband. She died the 14th of the Fifth-month, at Turin, where her remains were refused interment in the burying-ground; they were taken to Perignol, and laid among the original Waldenses – a community of about 20,000 protestants remaining in that quarter. Juliet adds, "During her stay at Nice she received the most kind attentions from some of the Barclays and Gurneys, members of your Society. I have always found that from such it only required to need kindness to receive it." Juliet Smith lost her accomplished and excellent daughter Elizabeth in 1806.

On the 21st of Tenth-month, 1817, died Maurice Farmer, who had left Ballitore to embark for South America. When taking leave of some of his London acquaintances, they wanted to detain him longer than he chose; and he, to alarm them into compliance with his wish, got on the window-stool, threatening to leap out. He lost his balance, fell from a great height, and was taken up and carried to the hospital which his brother Frederick attended. Frederick was summoned to a patient, and was grievously surprised and shocked to behold his unfortunate brother, his head, leg, and arm fractured, and in a state of delirium, from which he recovered before he died.

Early in Eleventh-month we welcomed back one of our daughters from a visit of several weeks in Dublin; but our joy was checked by the announcement of the tidings, "The Princess Charlotte and son are dead!" The account of her illness had reached us by that morning's post, and I had felt very anxious for her during the day. This unexpected termination of her life caused a revulsion in my feelings, which were all joyful when I saw my dear daughter; and I felt a kind of choking till relieved by tears. I had often pondered on the virtues of our promised future queen, and hoped much from them – hopes now, alas, destroyed by her untimely death.

We had enjoyed delightful autumnal weather, but a cold summer had defeated the promise of spring, and prevented the corn from arriving at perfection before the wintry frosts checked its growth; so plenty had not resumed her smile; and now the scourge of famine seemed followed by that of pestilence. The ravages which typhus–fever made in many parts of this nation were alarming and distressing. Our neighbourhood was favoured to escape better than most, but it did appear here. Dr. Davis bled the patient, and had him washed in cold or tepid water, and I think he lost not one to whom he was called in early in the complaint.

On the 12th of Second–month, 1818, James White and Mary Pike were married. This union gained universal approbation, and was proposed and considered with humble reference to Divine direction. My brother and sister walked into meeting before them, sat beside James, and signed his certificate as his parents – an interesting and affecting sight. At Betsy Barrington's a company of about thirty–four were assembled, and were entertained with hospitality, ease, and elegance.

Two days before the wedding, James Pim and Joseph Todhunter arrived post, express from Dublin, and presented to their former master a very handsome letter from James Haughton, enclosing the following address:–[124]

Dublin, 5th of Second–month, 1818.

JAMES WHITE,

Dear Master,

This accompanies a small piece of plate, of which we request thy acceptance. Should it be received with feelings correspondent to those with which it is offered, our wishes respecting it will be fully gratified. Nor can we believe that this token of our respect and love will be unacceptable to thee, in whom we ever found the friend and preceptor united. We avail ourselves of this opportunity to congratulate thee on thy approaching marriage, which we hope will be crowned by every enjoyment and felicity that can be attained here,

And subscribe ourselves,
with grateful attachment,
thy affectionate pupils,

JAMES HAUGHTON
JOSEPH TODHUNTER
THOMAS H. TODHUNTER
JAMES PIM, jun.
SAMUEL TOLERTON
THOMAS H. DEAVES
STEPHEN WINTHROP BLOOD
EDWARD MAGUIRE
THOMAS FISHER
JOHN TOLERTON
THOMAS GATCHELL
HENRY PIM
Absent, signed by proxy,
JOSHUA HARVEY

GEORGE PIM	WILLIAM T. HARVEY
WILLIAM HAUGHTON	JOHN HAUGHTON.

The names, beginning with "James Haughton," first boarder, range according to their standing at school. The gift was a large silver tea–pot, on one side of which was an engraving, designed by T. H. Todhunter, representing a telescope, globe, atlas, pen, closed books, and one volume open at the 47th problem of Euclid, with some mathematical instruments. The device was about an inch and a half high, and the following inscription was engraved on the other side:-

PRESENTED TO
JAMES WHITE, MASTER OF BALLITORE SCHOOL,
BY A FEW OF HIS LATE PUPILS,
AS A TOKEN OF THEIR AFFECTIONATE REMEMBRANCE,
12TH OF SECOND–MONTH, 1818.

To this were added a cream–ewer and sugar–bowl, into which William Todhunter, at present James White's pupil, dropped a pair of sugar–bows. Some of his Limerick pupils, disappointed at not having been informed of their schoolfellows' intention, sent, as their gift, a beautiful tea–equipage of white and gold china. There was such a round of social visiting on this happy occasion as we never remember before in Ballitore; and when that subsided, and things resumed their natural channel, their beloved master received visits from some of his former pupils.

An adult school was established here on First–day evenings; it was well attended, but some spelling–books having been sent from the Sunday–school Society, the extracts from Scripture gave offence to our Romish neighbours, and though an offer was made to lay the books aside, this condescension was not accepted: our school was prohibited, and another opened at Crookstown; yet ours, though crushed, was not destroyed, and gradually rose and overtopped opposition.

There came, on a visit to our neighbour Torrens, two fine young women of the name of Hart. They are an Irish family, but removed to England a few years ago. They have had great trouble. The father dislocated his shoulder, and it is thought in reducing it received an injury which caused his sudden death – while sitting at breakfast and apparently recovering from his hurt. His widow survived him about one year. Their brother, who was at sea, came to comfort his three sisters, and having arranged their affairs returned to his ship. While standing on deck, when the ship was being cleaned, a cannon rolled against him and killed him. Anne Hart, a beautiful young creature, and naturally as gay as beautiful, was about to marry, when her lover was summoned to Gibraltar to his sick father, and the marriage was deferred till his return. But he never returned. He died of the plague there, bequeathing to Anne one-half his fortune. His brother paid her a visit, conceived an affection for her sister, obtained her hand, and they all live together in sweet union.

Anna, the newly-married wife of William Forster, paid a religious visit to the meetings of Friends in Ireland. She joined our Society by convincement. Her rank in life was high, and she associated with the great. A few years ago she visited Ireland on a very different occasion – to attend the plays at Kilkenny. Her person and manners are graceful. She is sister to that worthy successor of Howard, Thomas Fowell Buxton, and, like him, advocates the cause of the prisoner. Anna Forster's companion was Priscilla Gurney, daughter to John Gurney of Norwich, and sister to Elizabeth Fry – whose name is dear to humanity, and whose efforts to reform the female prisoners in Newgate have been attended with wonderful success. Priscilla Gurney, though educated in our Society, had also moved in high life, and her uncommon beauty made her most attractive. She was one of those whose kind attentions were so soothing to poor Kitty Allan at Nice, and she spoke very sweetly of that amiable woman, for whom and for her afflicted husband she felt much interest. The dedication of these fine young women, Anna Forster and Priscilla Gurney, who have resigned so much more of pleasures and honours of this world than most have it in their power to do, affords a striking example; and the sweet serenity which seems to overshadow them encourages others to follow these humble travellers in the path in which alone peace will be the companion of the way.[125]

We had now a summer whose warmth and beauty even exceeded 1798, and this was accounted for by the breaking up of the ice at the North Pole, the accumulation of which was thought of later years to have affected our climate. Floating islands of ice have been met in the Atlantic; our friend, Jacob Harvey, was passed by two icebergs while on his voyage to New York, with his cousins Abraham and Mary Bell.

In the Fifth-month our sister Grubb paid a visit to her kindred in Ballitore; her friend Jane Jacob was with her; they were on their way to the north of Ireland, where they visited the meetings of Friends. On the 31st of that month my brother saw his four sisters surrounding his table once more! These were always pleasant meetings to us, but they are at an end, and we shall never meet again in this world!

George Downes was of our party, and James Henry, a fine youth, an enthusiastic admirer of the character of Elizabeth Smith; he was delighted to see the spot she had once inhabited.[126] They had been at meeting that day, I believe for the first time, and George Downes indulged me with this extract from his memorandum book:–

"From G. D.'s Itinerary for 1818, Sunday, May 31st:–

Mrs. Jacob knelt, and prayed with emotion in nearly the following words, – Omnipotent Lord God! who turnest the heart of man as a man turneth a water–course in his field – take away from some here present the heart of stone, and give them a heart of flesh, susceptible of the impression of thy divine finger!

Monday, June 1st.

I perched in a covert of trees at a sequestered farm and read the beautiful Italian poet Pindemonte. The opposition of the following prayer to that uttered by Mrs. Jacob yesterday struck me forcibly:–

O soggiorno fedel d'orsi e di lupi,
Dure vetuste rupi,
Del vestro aspro rigore
Date, vi prego, a un core
Che diero a me tenero troppo i Numi.

IN ENGLISH.

O faithful sojourn of bears and wolves,
Hard, ancient rocks,
Of your rigorous asperity
Give, I pray you, to a heart
Which the gods gave me too tender!"

My dear brother, Abraham Shackleton, was favoured with uncommon health all his life: he was remarkably temperate and remarkably active. For about a year he had declined the use of tea, sugar, or any thing which appeared to be connected with war, as he conceived commerce to be. He mostly breakfasted and supped on potatoes and milk. We regretted the loss of his company at the tea–table, and still more that he forbore from a refreshment which he was always accustomed to, and which he liked; and alarm mingled with this feeling, lest he should be injured in his health by such a change of diet at his advanced period of life. The valuable life of Anthony Benezet was thought to have been shortened by his leaving off the use of animal food. But who shall presume to call in question the tender scruples of virtuous men? If they fall in this field, they lay down their lives in an honourable cause. My brother now devoted his early morning mostly to throwing his thoughts on paper in the form of essays, which he wrote off at once, without previous copying or correction; nor did the elegance and strength of his style seem to need any improvement. He was wont after breakfast to mount his little mare Griselda, and to come to our house with his essay of the morning in his pocket, which he read to us; and often these pure and benevolent sentiments made our hearts and eyes overflow, while we wished that he was better understood by his best friends, seeing his generous, warm, and honest heart melting down more and more into that state referred to by his favourite Horace when he asks,

Dost thou become
Milder and better with advancing age?

The delight of this summer weather seemed to afford a novel enjoyment, we were so long unused to warm days and balmy nights. The heat of the summer caused my dear brother to throw aside his flannel vest; he soon felt the consequence of his imprudence, and after a few hours put it on again; but the mischief had been done. His lungs were attacked with an alarming inflammation, which, however, soon yielded to the means resorted to for his relief, and he was able to ride out among his congratulating friends, whose joy was alloyed by perceiving the continued oppression of his breathing.[127] Doctor Davis, to prevent water on the chest, which he was fearful might follow the inflammatory complaint, administered digitalis, which seemed to be of use; and though my dear brother was evidently shaken, and his strength did not return as might be expected, his patience and calm cheerfulness deceived us, and perhaps himself, for on the 18th of Seventh–month he reckoned himself fast recovering. But that day was succeeded by a night of great restlessness and suffering, and he never afterwards came down stairs.[128] During his illness he lay in his large, airy drawing–room, which opens by a sash door into the garden, which, I believe, he never more entered alive. How can I retrace the following days, when hope and fear struggled for mastery; when the tender ties of nature were rending our hearts; when, selfish that I was, I saw the deep anguish of the wife and children, and of my poor blind sister, who spent most of her days by his bedside, whilst I seemed to feel for no one but myself? We had always lived near together, and I never remember an unkind word having passed between us. But I will now borrow the aid of his dear daughter Betsy, and transcribe from her account of the last days of her beloved father the mournful yet consoling relation:–

Seventh–month. – On the 17th my father wrote an essay on duelling. On the 18th he wrote to his sister Grubb, and gave her a very good account of his health. He had been for many weeks alternately better and worse. He did not feel ill enough to keep his bed or his room, but he was not able to use his accustomed exertion without injury. He was patient, mild, and grateful for the most trivial attentions. One night, while in this uncertain state, he was heard to moan, and, being asked the cause, he said he was not ill, but that, feeling himself better, he was expressing his thankfulness to the Divine Being.

On the 21st of Seventh–month he seemed much affected. Being asked the cause, he grew very red, and much agitated; with difficulty, and sobbing, he said, "I have been thinking of thee all the morning, that thou hast chosen Mary's better part, which I hope will not be taken from thee". That evening he said, "I begin to feel the weariness of sickness." When we went to bed that night, he desired me to bring up three volumes of "Piety Promoted," that I might sometimes read to him. He contrasted these memoirs with the worthless productions which are frequently sent to Ballitore, alluding to some of the works of the modern poets whose fine talents are not consecrated, like Cowper's, to the best cause. He desired me to read the notices of John Aukland, Thomas Camm, and William Dewsbury. The following night he desired me to read of several other Friends, and also asked for the memorials of American Friends, several of which were read to him. He asked particularly for John Woolman, Anthony Benezet, and William Hunt.

On the 25th he was very weak and ill, and was kept mostly in the dark, but in the evening he desired the windows to be opened, saying he wanted to see the glory of nature. On the 26th some passages of Fenelon and Guion were read to him, to his satisfaction; he made some slight observation concerning their superstition, adding that it was no wonder. Several of the Psalms were read to him on the same day, which he appeared to feel much, and sometimes his eyes were full of tears.

On the 27th he was thought better. He observed that it was strange that he did not gain strength, seeing that the weather was fine, and that we said he had slept. He was answered that some people who were feverish were too weak to move without help. He then said, "Oh! I have no right to complain; Providence has been very good to me." His breathing growing worse, and weakness increasing, he suffered much from weariness, and used to move from his bed to an easy chair or sofa, or another bed; yet he did not appear sensible that his end was very near, but sometimes said that he expected soon to be better. On the 30th, Betsy Barrington came to see him, and said she would have come before but heard he was asleep. "Sleep!" said he, with energy; "sleep is one of the precious things belonging to health."

On the evening of the 31st he said to his wife that the lamp of life was almost out. When Doctor Davis called in, my father told him he thought he was fast approaching the period of his ancestors. The doctor acquiesced, and inquired if his mind was easy. He replied, "Quite so." That night his expressions all showed that he knew his awful state. He desired to see his will, got up, sat in the easy chair, and desired a table and writing–desk to be prepared for him quickly, "for," he added, "I am an expiring man." He put on his spectacles, read over his will, and dictated some alterations, expressing himself at long intervals and with great difficulty, but with the utmost clearness, mentioning his desire that the harmony of his happy family might continue, and also dictating that he was fully sensible of the infirmities and frailties of human nature. This was an extreme exertion, and he returned to his bed quite exhausted.

On the 1st of Eighth–month, at three in the afternoon, he expressed a great sense of his sufferings. He was asked had he any pain. – "No pain, but anxiety." "Anxiety about what?" He replied that he was ill at ease, adding, "When I am quite exhausted, I suppose I shall then die." His attendants were endeavouring to give him some relief by bathing his hands; he remarked how very bad he must be when the kindness of so many friends operated nothing to relieve him. Soon after this he was offered a preparation of laudanum, being told it might compose him; but he refused it, and took water in preference to anything. After this he did not appear to suffer so much. His hands were swelled, and we believed that the cessation of the circulation of the blood caused a kind of suffering which was indescribable; his breathing was also very laborious. "Human nature," said he, "cannot hold out long under such sufferings." His utterance became so imperfect towards evening that he could scarcely be understood.

He ceased to speak about midnight, and expired at two o'clock on the morning of the 2nd of Eighth–month, 1818, in his sixty–sixth year, which he would have completed had he lived to the 8th of Twelfth–month following.[129]

His excellent daughter has also furnished me with some interesting sketches of my dear brother's character, which may be fitly introduced here:–[130]

Some circumstances combining with a certain ferment which unsettled the opinions of many, both as to politics and religion, caused many Friends to express their disunity with some of the principles, or rather practices, of the Society. It is not for me to say who was right and who was wrong; I may, however, venture to say that I believe the differences between the leading members of the Society of Friends would never have amounted to a separation if there had been more of the spirit of meekness and long–suffering on both sides. I will speak only of my father. I believe he expressed his sentiments with too much heat and precipitation; and there was a want of allowance–making on the other side. His temper was naturally quick, his imagination fertile, and his understanding vigorous. Probably, with his talents and a most sincere and honest heart, he might have thrown light upon some subjects; and if he had remained in membership, I believe it would have contributed to his usefulness and happiness; but he was, in process of time, disowned by the Society. I believe it was unavoidable, according to rule; but I will console myself by believing that the Father of all the communities upon the earth did not disown him.

When I consider my father's conduct in his dealings with men, his strict justice, his disinterestedness, and his benevolence, I feel persuaded that his mind was set upon higher treasures than this earth affords. He had a most affectionate, tender, and warm heart; he could not endure to see a fellow–creature in affliction without attempting to give comfort. He was remarkably careless of the opinion of the world. If we only consider what is agreeable and elegant in society, we shall conclude that he was too careless in this respect. I hope that the sentiments he has expressed in conversation or on paper will one day have their use, though not palatable at the present time; and, granting that some of his sentiments were erroneous, I imagine their error was more observable because they were out of the common track of error. A man of good repute in the world, a really well–disposed, sensible, benevolent man – I will even say a religious man, that is, a lover of religion – will without compunction drink ten times as much strong drink as he ought; he injures himself, sets his children and servants a bad example, and encourages his company to partake with him. His error is so common that he seldom or never thinks that it is an error; neither, for the same reason, do his neighbours say he is in error.[131] It is thus also in politics and in war: great and grievous are the errors; but politicians are blinded by interest, by custom, or by the apparent necessity of the case. Warriors are blinded in the same manner; yet the error of their ways overwhelms the world with calamities and horrors. It was thus with slave–holders and with slave–robbers; the enemies of the slave–trade were at first considered unreasonable, inconsiderate, eccentric disturbers of the necessary customs which had obtained from time immemorial.

Far different were the errors of my dear father; they were like shooting beyond the mark – excess of benevolence, excess of candour and sincerity. Excesses are always inconvenient and sometimes injurious, but they are calculated to turn or attract the attention of those who are in contrary extremes, or to arouse the stupid and indolent.

My father had great talents and many acquirements. He was a good classical scholar, and at different periods of his life had studied many sciences with his wonted ardour. I have heard him speak of mathematical truths with great admiration. He delighted in astronomy, and latterly he was much engaged in the study of botany. His style of writing was correct, free, and energetic, in verse as well as prose. He was a declared and warm enemy to war, and to everything connected with it. In the latter part of his life he was much engaged in writing on this subject, and testifying his abhorrence of it by every means in his power.

His countenance was intelligent and animated, his figure light and well–proportioned. He was uncommonly active; at the age of sixty–five he was more agile than most men twenty years younger. He enjoyed remarkably good health, till two months before he died. He generally rose before five o'clock, and often before four, or even three. He delighted in beholding the rising sun; every extraordinary appearance in nature was a feast for him. During thunder and lightning he always walked out to enjoy the sublimity of the spectacle. I believe he hardly knew what fear was.

As the recollection of the controversy between him and the Society faded away, he became more attached to Friends. It was his nature to forgive and forget; and we may also suppose that, making his observations upon the consequences of the schism, he found no good had accrued, but that in many cases a spirit of free enquiry had degenerated into presumption, and that, in avoiding formality, some rushed into libertinism. He must have observed these facts; and the sincerity which animated his own mind caused him to acknowledge and revere religion wherever it was to be found.

On the 4th of Eighth-month the dear remains were laid in the grave. Perhaps so large a funeral had never before entered that little enclosure. Many from a distance attended. The day was very fine; the procession was silent and solemn. The widow stood beside the grave till the falling of the clay upon the coffin announced that all had ended. She was led away by her son Richard, with anguish in her looks, but no word expressed it. They are now separated, excellent, loving, and beloved as they were, after a union of nearly forty years. But she, who has always fulfilled her duties, feels her reward in the consciousness of her endeavours to act aright, even more than in the dutiful attentions of her children. Both she and they repress their own feelings, and comfort each other, and this, I believe, is an acceptable sacrifice.

James White, though a true mourner himself, feeling for the greater grief of the nearer connections, was assiduous to spare them by performing the necessary and painful offices which belonged to the sad occasion. Ebenezer Shackleton was the last of the family who resigned the hope of his father's recovery. He seemed, indeed, to cherish it till the last day; and then his health and spirits sank so much beneath the pressure of distress, that he could not pay to that beloved parent the last tribute of filial affection, but lay in a nervous fever from which he was long recovering.[132]

The weather this summer was finer than any since the year of the rebellion, and was even thought to exceed it. I never remember apples so abundant; the wheat harvest was most favourable. Nature smiled around us, but our hearts were sad. Where could we turn our eyes in our little valley, without meeting some memorial of him who was for ever removed from our sight, especially in his own sweet abode, so embellished by his taste?[133]

CHAPTER XIV.
1818.

Anecdote of Cowper's cousin, Lady Austin. – Fever in Ballitore. – Elizabeth Fry in Newgate. – Friends in Carlow attacked by the rabble. – John Pim of London. – Visit from *large* Phibbs. – An old Ballitore pupil attached in death. – Illness of the annalist and her happy recovery. – Benevolent activity of Margaret Bonham. – Theodore E. Suliot. – The "Ballitore Magazine." – Visit from the widow of Richard L. Edgeworth, and the elder son of Sir Walter Scott. – George and Wilhelmina Downes. – A tea party. – Moone house and its transformations. – Death of little Fanny Downes. – The story of Mary Mooney. – The foundlings of Ballintaggart. – Burying alive of Patt Mitchell's baby. – The queen's trial, and visit of George IV. to Ireland. – A deputation from Friends present an address. – Death of Molly Webster. – Ebb and flow of visitors. – Death of Anne Doyle. – Malicious burning at Ballintaggart. – Goldsmith's ideas of prison discipline verified. – Jacob Harvey returns from America. – An interview with the poet Crabbe. – Anecdote of Captain Clarke. – The prompter of R. L. Edgeworth's mechanical genius. – Death of the Bishop of Meath. – First balloon ascent from Ballitore. – Recollections of childhood in Fuller's Court. – Nancy McCabe. – A new manufacture started.[134]

214 to 229

MUNGO and Mary Bewley came to visit the house of mourning, and their company was pleasant. Mary told us that when her parents lived in or near Bristol, having a larger house than they needed, they proposed letting lodgings, which were taken by a widow gentlewoman and her sister, who were persons of uncommonly gifted minds and amiable manners. One of these was Cowper's friend, Lady Austin. She was very affable, and would have taken pains to perfect Mary in the French language, but the diffidence of the young maiden prevented her availing herself of this advantage. Lady Austin told her that, on going to join her husband in France, she advertised for a companion who could speak French. None offered so agreeable in other respects as a clergyman's daughter who was ignorant of the language; but this did not discourage Lady Austin, who taught her French on the journey. This young woman afterwards married a French gentleman, and is the person to whom Cowper addressed his "Epistle to a Lady in France."

Fever again appeared in Ballitore, and carried off many of our poor neighbours. Committees were held, and considerations how this foe might best be expelled engaged the minds of the inhabitants. Application being made to a committee in Dublin, fifty pounds were granted from government for the relief of the sick. Much pains were taken to arrest the progress of this calamity. Doctor Cheyne was employed to examine the state of the hospitals throughout the kingdom, and in the course of his enquiries visited Ballitore. He introduced himself to our Doctor Davis, with whom he had previously had some written communication leading him to wish for a personal interview. There was no hospital here, but the strong recommendations to cleanliness and fresh air superseded the necessity of one. Printed advices and warnings were distributed, and a resolution was signed by the principal employers not to give work to those who were inattentive to these injunctions. The whey and gruel supplied by the fund were distributed at the doors of the infected houses; glazed window-sashes for cottages were sold to the poor at a cheap rate, and in some cases given away. Doctor Davis was indefatigable, and was twice taken ill himself during this period of great fatigue to body and mind; yet he accepted no remuneration except for drugs.

George Downes and his wife came to visit their infant daughter Fanny, who is nursed in Ballitore. We congratulated that excellent young man on his union with a kindred spirit. Wilhelmina Sophia Downes is a native of Lubeck; she speaks and writes English well, but like a foreigner; she is a lover of literature, and has written good poetry in her own language. They have also a little boy, their first-born.

James Forbes, lately returned from England, came to visit his cousin Hannah Boake. He told us of his visit to Newgate with Elizabeth Fry, who read a portion of the Bible to the female prisoners without comment, but encouraged others to speak, when a clergyman present addressed the audience on the subject of reformation. The poor women listened with great attention, dissolved in tears. He dined with a company of forty at the house of Thomas Fowell Buxton, who has written so admirably on prison discipline, and is married to a sister of Elizabeth Fry. There was much conferring on the subject of prisons, and plans were handed about to be inspected.

Our quarterly meeting was held as usual in Carlow at the close of the year. The last sitting was by candlelight, and a rude rabble took advantage of the darkness of the passage to assault the women as they came out, throwing dirt on us, kicking some, and sticking pins into others. But they had cause to rue this frolic, which the townspeople highly resented. One of the rioters was imprisoned for a while, the priest from the altar condemned the outrage, and English as well as Irish newspapers noticed it.

John Pim of London paid a visit on a religious account to this nation in company with Benjamin White, an American friend whose father had been engaged in a like service in the year 1760. John Pim moves in an atmosphere of love, and seemed peculiarly imbued with this celestial feeling while in Ballitore, where in his youth his tender mind had its good impressions deepened, and where he had found in Richard and Elizabeth Shackleton a nursing father and mother. Oh how did his affectionate heart overflow with the sweetest recollections! Nature and grace united to pour them upon him, and he seemed to bear us along with him on this pure and crystal tide.

A stranger, a tall, genteel, elderly man, with a lively little wife, walked into our parlour; the gentleman introduced himself as an old scholar, by the name of Phibbs. Now, in the year 1774, I wrote a verse on the murder of a cat, and introduced "large Phibbs and Toby" therein. Why Richard Phibbs obtained the appellation of "large" I know not, but this I know, and ought then to have known, that a nickname was a grievous offence. I incurred the displeasure of nearly the whole school. One boy, indeed, whom I handled roughly enough for not taking the cat's part, took mine against a host, at the head of which was "large Phibbs," whose resentment, though not expressed to myself, I dreaded so, that, being pleased when the otherwise unoffending youth left school, I cherished the hope of never seeing him again; and now the ancient feeling returned with the name, to which, as a dernier resort, I replied, "Toby?" "No, Richard," said he; adding, "I am *large* Phibbs," and repeating the unfortunate stanza.[135] I felt myself redden with the remains of remembered dread, but it was the last flash of that fire, and it became extinguished in good-humoured mirth. He was pleased to hear that Moll Whelan, now Mary Casey, was living, visited her, and made her a present, telling her he was glad to see her, and hoped they would meet in heaven.[136]

John Duckett of Philipstown died of a lingering illness at an advanced age. He cherished hopes of life for a long time, but when they expired, "Bury me," said he, "as near my old master as you can." His "old master" was Richard Shackleton.

This spring the remarkable mildness of the weather encouraged an early vegetation. We felt some uneasiness at seeing our apple-blossoms assailed by a little black fly, and strove to banish the intruder by making fires under the trees; however, though far less abundant than last year, the garden produce was not to be complained of. In the Fifth-month the potato promised to be most luxuriant, till the nights of the 27th and 28th brought frost which blasted the early blossoms, and blighted the hopes which the farmer and the poor had cherished from them.

We had the company of John Kirkham, an English ministering Friend, at our meeting, where his warning of the uncertainty of time was so strong as apparently to foretel that the close of it was near to some of the assembly.[137] My sister Grubb was led in the same line soon after, when she came to pay a visit to her kindred in Ballitore, and to sympathize with us in our mutual loss. She feared that she would, while amongst us, endure a wound of like nature, for I was dangerously ill. Having enjoyed all my life a state of health which was seldom and slightly interrupted, I was better able to struggle for life, though surprised at the state of weakness to which my distemper, two bleedings, a blister, and powerful medicines reduced me. It was forty–eight years since I had been bled before. When I was assisted from my own chamber to the drawing–room, my sensations were those which I hope long gratefully and pleasantly to remember. I was delivered from extreme bodily pain; I was surrounded by my affectionate family. I looked out of the window – summer glowed in all its beauty; the garden was gay with flowers, and fruits and blossoms mingled together on an apple–tree; the room was light and airy, and a pot of mignonette in the window diffused a soft fragrance. Wealth could not purchase, I thought, more comforts than I enjoyed, and I hope I was thankful. Yet through all the attentions and comforts which I experienced the idea of my beloved brother would come pensively over my mind. I seemed to look around for his endearing sympathy, his instructive and delightful converse, which I had often found so soothing in sickness and in sorrow. Never can I forget the time when, at ten years old, I had the ague, nor his visits every evening to draw a picture for me in a little book which he had made for the purpose.[138] That book, preserved with care and often looked at with great enjoyment, I am now afraid to open.

The Bonham family, having returned from their northern tour, became our neighbours, and kept up a friendly social intercourse with us; yet I believe John Bonham's feeling heart found a vacuum which could not be filled here, in the loss of my dear brother, whose tastes and benevolence so coincided with his own. Margaret Bonham appears to value life and all its comforts only as it gives her power to do good. The activity of her nature urges or drags on those who are of feebler force. Disregarding weather, she walks about in pattens, or rides on horseback with a servant walking beside her, inspecting the situation of the poor, and thoughtful to assist them by promoting that independence which springs from industry. She encouraged us to raise a fund, by subscribing one penny per week to purchase wool and flax to employ the very poor, herself subscribing largely. Our schools were a principal object of her attention, and her penetration soon discovered where defects lay and how they should be remedied. She visited the schools at Abbeyleix, taking in her train Harriet Le Fanu, Betsy and Mary Shackleton, Lydia Jane Leadbeater, and James White.[139] That true nobleman, Lord De Vesci, patronizes and promotes these schools, one of which is for the children of the wealthy, who pay one hundred guineas annually; several teachers are employed, and the science of gymnastics makes a part of their education. Curiosity has been found so troublesome at this school, that it is not easy to gain admittance, though James White was invited to spend a day there, which he afterwards did, much to his satisfaction. To see *this* school was not Margaret Bonham's object; it was that for the poor drew her to Abbeyleix, where one hundred and twenty children are taught on the plan of Pestalozzi, and where their time is fully occupied, their attention constantly engaged, and their faculties kept active; showing the excellence of a system which enables them to calculate with such admirable facility and precision, while their eyes sparkle with intelligence and their cheeks glow with animation.

The year 1820 began in frost and snow, which lasted nearly six weeks.[140] The weather was for most part of the time pleasant, and the sunbeams showed to advantage the beautiful incrustations with which the frost invested every branch and spray. We could turn our small milk–pans upside down in the dairy, without fearing to lose a drop of the contents, and iced cream was served to us daily.

Theodore Eugene Suliot, a native of Paris, now became for a time an inhabitant of Ballitore, his services being secured by James White as his assistant in the school. He had spent four years at Glasgow university, and obtained the distinction of Master of Arts.

Captain Grattan's son Henry, assisted by Richard Davis Webb, commenced the "Ballitore Magazine," and, on his leaving his native land to join his brother in New York, Theodore Eugene Suliot supplied his place as editor.[141] To the first number was prefixed an appropriate and affectionate dedication to James White. These fruits of early talent, many of which displayed excellent moral sentiments, afforded delight to some readers; while others looked on them with a less indulgent eye, fearing that more important matters might be neglected for such flights of fancy. Genius is modest, sensitive, and easily discouraged; the opinion of the graver readers prevailed, and the little work was discontinued. These volumes were afterwards published.

The widow of Richard Lovell Edgeworth, with her young daughter and little son, being on a journey, walked down from the inn to see me. She is a very pleasing woman, possessing that simplicity and ease of manner which so frequently attend a superior mind.

The 18th regiment of Hussars halted at Ballitore on their march, and a soldier called for a newspaper directed to Cornet Walter Scott.[142] We inquired if he was the poet's son. "He *is* the poet's son," was the reply; and my husband sent a request to him that if he came down to the village he would call upon us. His polite acquiescence was soon followed by himself in person. My husband apologized for the liberty he had taken, by telling him that I had once been favoured with a letter from his father. The youth is tall and finely formed, with an interesting and sweet countenance. He was dressed in a blue uniform, and wore a belt glittering with silver, which crossed over one shoulder. This embroidered belt, his youth, and the graces of his person strongly recalled to my mind the "Fortunes of Nigel." His manners were easy and modest. He professed to be much pleased with Ireland, spoke with interest of its old castles, and wished his father could see this country. His father was, he thought, the author of "Waverley" and the succession of tales that followed that work. No other gentleman, he believed, had had such opportunities of knowing the manners of Scotland.[143] In Sir Walter's youth, when he got two or three guineas, he lived among the peasantry till they were spent, and thus acquired a thorough knowledge of them. His father's lameness, he heard, was occasioned by cutting an eye–tooth, the nerve being destroyed in consequence. He smiled at a description of his father which was read to him from a letter of Thomas Fisher, and said it was correct; remarking that the heaviness of Sir Walter's countenance is dispelled by its animated expression when he engages in conversation.[144] He told us, among other things, that his father never saw Melrose by moonlight.

Our friend George Downes, having been attacked with a cough and spitting of blood, was ordered by Dr. Perceval to the north of Germany. Before he undertook so long a journey, he made trial of the air of Ballitore, spending about a week in the Cottage, accompanied by his excellent Wilhelmina. We were alarmed on his account, and much as we loved his society, we did not wish him to defer trying the means recommended. To Germany they went. It was his wife's native land, and she had the gratification of introducing her husband to her family and friends, and of perceiving how soon he won their love and admiration, not more by the lustre of his talents than by the simplicity of his manners and the sincerity of his heart.

On the 26th of Seventh–month James White's boys borrowed the untenanted Cottage from their master, and invited some of their friends to a party there. I esteemed it an honour to be one of those invited. Their beloved master and mistress, with Sally and Hannah White, were the foremost guests in rank and affection. Happy change of time and manners, when perfect love casteth out fear! Fifteen boys, including Theodore E. Suliot, were our hosts. They were dressed in their best, and their countenances were radiant with delight.[145] After our repast at a plentiful and well arranged tea–table, we took a walk to the river side, enjoying the calm of a sweet summer's evening; and on returning to the Cottage parlour found the table again spread, and a variety of fruits were handed round with cordial and pressing attention. There was no affectation of kindness; it emanated from warm, unpractised hearts, from which the fresh bloom of candid youth was not rubbed off by contact with the world. The sensations of their seniors were very delightful; to me, the oldest of the company, they were perhaps as much so as to those whose perceptions were more lively, and not the less so for the tender recollections which mingled with them. Oh! how did the idea of the associates of my youth float before my mind, bringing in succession the remembrance of many whose childhood promised as fair for length of days as my own, but who have long since entered into another state of being.

The scenery around Ballitore has undergone the changes incident to time. Many of the trees surrounding Counsellor Ashe's tomb, on a hill near Moone, have been cut down. Moone House, the residence of the late Samuel Yeates, has become a ruin, though built with a view to durability. It was the object of my admiration in my childhood, when I journeyed so far [two miles] from Ballitore. The little boat on the water fronting the hall–door; the leaden statues of Harlequin and Columbine, of Doctor Faustus and the Devil, placed on low walls on either side of the house; the adjoining ruins of Moone Abbey; the tower used as a pigeon–house – all made it appear to me a most desirable abode. Alas, the change! Tom Watts, attached to the Yeates family, told me with much concern that none of the house was left standing "except a bit of the roof." Samuel Yeates bequeathed the house to his widow, the land to his son by his first wife. They are opposed to each other. The widow having refused the offer of her stepson to purchase the house, he took means, by building a wall against the back–door, to prevent her living in or letting it, and consequently it fell to decay. She then made a present of it to one of her old servants, who is now selling the materials. Harlequin and Columbine have long since deserted a place no longer the abode of mirth; Doctor Faustus stands noseless in Boakefield yard; we do not enquire where the other personage has retired to, but turn our eyes from the scene of desolation.

On the first day of 1821, at a quarterly meeting in Carlow, Betsy Barrington spoke as a minister in the women's meeting.[146] She is worthy to fill this office, and has long been a preacher in life and conversation.

Sometimes we escape the waves which threaten to swallow us up; at other times we are nearly overwhelmed beneath them. They beat hard upon the bark which held much of George Downes's treasure, when he lost his beautiful little daughter by the carelessness of her nurse, who, going from her cabin (in the fields between Ballitore and Willowbrook), left Fanny in care of her own little boy, and with so little fire as she thought secured the children from danger.[147] But a spark sufficed to do the business. Betsy Barrington took the nurse and child to her own house, where every attention was paid, and the sufferings of the dear babe perhaps alleviated. She lived about eighteen hours after the accident. Her parents were about getting her home, as she was nearly three years old. They came the day after her death, and had her laid in our graveyard. They felt this grievous affliction with all its aggravations, but they bore it like Christians; they sent their forgiveness to the nurse, with a present beside her wages, but requested that they might not see her. The poor woman seemed as if she could scarcely survive the calamity, and with her family left Ballitore soon after. Sadness was spread over the village, and my husband's and my own wound was opened by a sorrow so like our own.[148] After George Downes returned to the duties of the school where he assists, a boy was reciting his lesson to him, where Demosthenes was censured for his intemperate joy on the downfall of Philip, as it was the seventh day after his own daughter's death. The lad evaded this by saying, "a domestic calamity." I wish I knew the name of that kindhearted youth, whose delicate and quick perception gives such a fair hope for his future character.

An attack on Ballintaggart farm, held by John Fahy under John Bonham, by which an outhouse and four head of young cattle were burnt, caused a revival of our Ballitore patrol. These guardians of the peace were soon superseded by the police, who were stationed here, at Timolin, and at Narraghmore. Their major was the son of James Napper Tandy, who was my peaceable grandfather's pupil, and was afterwards so conspicuous in the disturbances of 1798.[149]

Some years ago a basket–woman died here, leaving her little daughter, Mary Mooney, unprotected. Mary Davis and Sarah Leadbeater, children themselves, took the child into their care, and raised a subscription which boarded, clothed, and schooled her, till Fanny Bewley took her to assist her servant. Afterwards she lived with Thomas Barrington, and grew tall and handsome. From thence she went to Waterford, where she fell into a consumption, and the kind family in which she was a servant, after having done much for her recovery, yielded to her desire of returning to this place. She could not claim a home, she was an illegitimate child, and her father had a family born in wedlock. To his house she went; he was a farmer in struggling circumstances, and was then from home. She was admitted, but could not expect to be welcome to her father's wife, though one of the daughters shewed tenderness to her. Betsy Barrington got her removed hither and placed with Fanny Lyons, who accommodated her very comfortably. Her wages paid for her lodging, and Betsy Barrington and Mary White supported her till her death. Mary Davis and Sarah Leadbeater having a portion of the money collected for her in their hands, on the establishment of the savings' bank here this year, placed it therein, and this afforded wherewithal to answer the expenses of her interment.[150] Young, beautiful, inclined to be vain, and unprotected by a parent, we acknowledge that a providential care had been extended in life and in death over this fair blossom, which was cropped before a blight had fallen upon it.

A schoolhouse had been built at Ballintaggart, judiciously planned by Margaret Bonham, and conducted under her own and her sister's inspection. This excellent woman has exerted her influence with the governors of the Foundling Hospital, to rescue the orphan children in her neighbourhood from situations unfavourable to mind and body. She has placed them in decent cottages, under the care of respectable peasant matrons, where they may acquire habits of order and industry. She obtains for these women the allowance for their board, clothing, and schooling. They are obliged to send them to school, herself and her sister taking care that they are done justice to, and at a suitable time they are apprenticed to protestant masters.[151] Two of these children were overheard conversing: "I would not speak to my mother if I met her," said one little girl: "I might have been drowned or smothered only for the Foundling Hospital," said the other.

On Whit–Sunday a child was born to Pat Mitchell, a labourer. It is said that the child born on that day is fated to kill or be killed. To avert this doom a little grave was made, and the infant laid therein, with clay lightly sprinkled on it and sods supported by twigs covering the whole. Thus was the child buried, and at its resurrection deemed to be freed from the malediction.

Ballitore, secluded as it is, is not unheedful of public transactions. The death of our good old king last year, and the death of the wonderful Bonaparte,

> Who left a name at which the world grew pale
> To point a moral or adorn a tale,

were events of no ordinary occurrence. And now we sympathized with the unfortunate Queen Caroline, and respected the intrepidity with which she faced her enemies, not knowing that the agitation of her feelings obliged her to undergo the operation of cupping to prevent apoplexy. We rejoiced at her victory, yet we could not deplore her death, as her future prospects gave little expectation of comfort in this life. Nor did we turn our eyes from pictures of joy. The coronation of George IV. was celebrated in Ballitore by only two illuminated houses – Captain Clarke's, late of the Royal Veterans, now on half–pay, and a pensioner's, his neighbour. General illuminations, however, welcomed the landing of the monarch in Ireland. All houses, except those of Friends, united in such a show as never before had enlightened the valley.[152] Even a transparency was sported, and festoons of flowers whose bloom was heightened by the lustre of the light. Why should not Ballitore partake of the general enthusiasm which the visit of the king to our island called forth? Every circumstance attending his landing conveyed an interest. The gracious condescension of his manners – nay, more than condescension – hearty cordiality, so acceptable to the Irish, so much in unison with their own character, won the warm hearts of a people disposed to love and desirous to be loved. "He is a big man," says one countryman to another. "If his body was as big again," replied his companion, "it would not be big enough for his heart." All ranks pressed onward to grasp the royal hand, freely extended to them all; and one poor man who partook of that honour swore loudly that he would never again wash his favoured hand. Countless throngs hastened to the metropolis, to look upon their king; and Ballitore, smit with like longing, poured out its inhabitants to meet him on the Curragh of Kildare. The first day appointed for his appearance there was a day of constant rain; yet thousands – some in carriages, come on cars, some on horseback, some on foot – from different roads, attracted to one spot, assembled on the mighty plain. The stand–house – rebuilt it was said in three weeks, at the cost of three thousand pounds – was prepared for the royal visitant, who, I believe, would not have willingly caused the disappointment of that day; but it was said the gentlemen of the club, not being quite ready for his reception, prayed him to defer his coming to another day, which also proved wet; yet he came. Those who ventured in the wet, or some of them, were gratified by the sight of their monarch; while others, who arrived too late, were tantalized by the knowledge that they were on the Curragh with him, and by the shouting in the distance as he moved off.

Young Collins, one of the deaf and dumb pupils at Claremont, addressed the king by letter, styling him, "Dear George." The king was pleased, and expressed himself so in a reply which enclosed ten guineas, and desired Collins to be a good boy.

Addresses poured upon the king, nor were our Society wanting in this mark of respect. James Forbes and several other Friends were appointed to present one from them. Their hats were taken off, and they were invited to advance into the presence of the king. The address was read by James Forbes and given to the king, who read his answer deliberately, and pronounced with emphasis those words which noticed the loyalty and good conduct of the Society.[153] It was then proposed to the Friends to kiss the royal hand; but the monarch, mindful of their conscientious scruples, said, "Oh, no, no," in a kind accent, and his reception was very gracious. They withdrew backward for a little while, when the king, turning away, permitted them to resume their natural movement.

On the 27th of Ninth–month, 1822, Molly Webster departed this life in her ninetieth year.[154] She was long in a declining state, and her life was, I believe, prolonged by the cares and comforts bestowed upon her by her daughter. Her former scholars heartily regretted the loss of the beloved friend of their childhood.

We remarked that Ballitore is seldom, if ever, without visitors, and seldom with all its inhabitants at home. This ingress and egress of society tends to expand the social affections, and serves as a guard against the narrowness which a secluded life is in danger of contracting. Ballitore needs this intercourse, for the dwellers of the village are so attached to and so vain of one another, that it is necessary they should become acquainted with the good qualities of other people.

We now resigned all those hopes with which we had flattered ourselves of Anne Doyle's recovery. She was unable to leave her bed, too weak to hold conversation with her friends, and her knowledge of her sister's feelings prevented her expressing in her hearing much of her own; but one night she spoke much to her cousin Lucretia Wright, and she sent messages of love to a sister in Canada, and to many of her friends by name, expressing the affection with which her heart overflowed, and giving counsel of excellent import.[155] Afterwards she desired her cousin not to speak of what she had been saying; thus preserving to the last the exceeding modesty and diffidence which were such very remarkable features in her character. With a strict sense of propriety and quick discernment, she was one of the last to remark on the faults of others, choosing rather, in a Christian spirit, to reprove them in privacy. I never knew any person more free from the vices of tale-bearing and detraction. She possessed a noble independence of mind, which induced her to consider her own accommodation and comfort as of no importance if they interfered with her social duties, among the first of which she valued integrity. Indeed her sister and she were ever highly valued for their honourable dealings, arising from dispositions naturally generous, kind, and considerate to all around them. I had known, valued, and loved Anne Doyle for thirty years, and, having passed twenty-five of them under the same roof, I had the opportunity of knowing her better, and consequently of valuing and loving her more.[156] But now came the separation from us – from that sister whose life seemed to be bound up in her life, and whose tender, unremitting cares for six years were probably the means of prolonging her existence. On the 9th of Third-month her pure spirit left the emaciated frame; an expression of that placid sweetness which calmed her weary hours remaining on the pale countenance.[157]

William Griffith, who is employed to inspect schools and prisons, spent two days in our neighbourhood. He tells us that Goldsmith's plan of prison discipline, as described in the "Vicar of Wakefield," is now adopted. Thus what has been looked upon as impracticable and romantic may, when matured by good sense and humanity, in time prevail over long established error. Therefore let the benevolent persevere in their line of duty.

At the time of our yearly meeting Jacob Harvey arrived from the United States. I met him first in Dame-street, walking between his glad father and mother. Instead of the youth who this time seven years, with his tall, slender form, and shining ringlets shading his lovely countenance, was about to take his departure, here was presented to our view the stout, comely figure and face, still retaining its sweet expression combined with the grace of manhood. His heart was as warm as ever, and his former love of anecdote, of which his store is much enlarged, was a source of delight to his auditors. We rejoiced over him with trembling, when we considered how near he had been to taking his passage in the Albion, that "fatal bark" which was lost about the time of his landing, and in which perished many who were probably as dear to their connections as he is to his own.[158]

Our neighbour, Captain Thomas Clarke, lost his good wife after a tedious illness. This calamity almost overcame him with grief. He expressed his regret and his respect for the deceased in his own peculiar manner, requesting the attendance of the police from Athy to accompany her remains, and to fire a volley over her grave, as he wished her to be "buried with military honours." But the appointed day proved so wet that he would not permit his beloved wife to be brought out in the rain. The police had to be sent back, and next morning she was interred, the military honours having to be dispensed with, save that one shot was discharged from his own old firelock. It seemed a little to console him when he told me that his Eleanor had lain four days in state, accompanied by all the splendour he could procure. His sorrow, though expressed with singularity bordering on the ludicrous, was sincere and deep, and his loss of a helpmate embittered his closing days.[159]

Our young friend, John James Lecky, indulging his classical taste, set out in the year 1820 on a tour to the continent. When in England on his return he visited the poet Crabbe at Trowbridge, of which place he is rector. His house, surrounded by trees, is cut off from the town by a high wall, and seems as though quite in the country.[160] He describes the person of the poet as rather tall, a little bent; and adds, "Thought and activity are very visible in his countenance; his mind seems to possess all the energy of youth, though his body is evidently losing it. His crown is bald, and the few hairs he has on his temples and back of his head are well charged with powder. He talks fluently; he likes to argue a point with you, and he does it so well, so acutely and clearly, that it is pleasant to argue with him. From his look and manner now, I guess that sensibility has been the character of his life. Everyone about him seems anxious to serve him, and his family appear strongly attached to him. He told me he never had any ear for music. In answer to my surprise at this, he laboured with much earnestness to convince me that an ear for music and a taste for harmony of verses were quite distinct, and did not of necessity go together. He told me he was born at Aldborough, a seaport village on the coast of Suffolk, and remained there till he was three or four and twenty; he was then introduced to his patrons, who were the means of bringing him forward in the world, and, by their means, about this time got a living near Belvoir Castle, in Leicestershire, where he remained till about six years ago, when he removed to the living of Trowbridge. From the time he first left Aldborough he never visited it till this summer, and I am sure, from the way he spoke of it, that the scene of his birth and youth 'had its attraction still.' It has lately, from being a poor village, become the resort of visitors at watering seasons, and he said he found it like an old friend in a new coat. He told me it was from his residence in this town that he had his knowledge of seafaring men and manners. He said writing paid him very well, and money was a great inducement to write. 'Yes,' said he, 'and fame too, but the nearer we get to that state where money will be of no use, the less it is to be regarded.' He said the 'Tales of the Hall' deserve and have had a greater popularity, than any other of his works; that the 'Smugglers and Poachers' was an imaginary tale, and was suggested to him by a conversation with Sir Samuel Romilly, in which Sir Samuel reprobated the evils which arise from the law as it now stands on these points. He said he intended moving for some amendment [in the Game Law], and thought a popular writer might found a story with a good moral on the mischiefs resulting from it. 'Lady Barbara and the Ghost' Crabbe has told just as he heard it. He told me he is oftener at a loss for incidents than for characters; that few of his stories are real, nor are they entirely made out; but that he has been in the habit of putting parts of different stories and incidents together, till he makes out what pleases him. He seldom takes anything out of books, but all from what he sees and hears. Now I was not so impertinent as to ask him all these questions, but when I was alone with him in his study, he told me most of what I have written without my asking him. I was greatly struck with his unassuming manner; he will hear you with as much attention, and show as much deference to what you say, as if he was your inferior. He goes to bed at twelve, rises at nine, and from breakfast till four, his dinner–hour, he is alone in his study, – from that hour till twelve he devotes to intercourse with his family, &c. Though his second son, John Crabbe, is his curate, yet he himself preaches every week. The church is just at his gate – a fine old Gothic building – built, as he told me, when labour was a penny a–day."

We have been reading with very great pleasure the Memoirs of Richard Lovell Edgeworth; the first volume written by himself, the second by his daughter Maria. While he was yet a child he imbibed the love of mechanics from an acquaintance with a gentleman of the name of Deane. The name struck on my recollection, and on referring to my little record of the year 1780, I found the following account of a visit to him:–

"William Taylor and Dr. Forsayeth told us of an orrery made by an old gentleman named Deane in Granby Row, and took us to see it. When we came to the house, William Taylor and the doctor introduced us (my father and a bevy of young damsels) to the old gentleman, who was sitting in his study at a curious reading–desk, which turned round and brought him the books fixed in it. There were glass–cases for books, with double shelves, one shelf attached to the glass–door for smaller, and the other inside for larger books. He shewed and explained to us the orrery, made by his own hands, and was very kind and obliging. He belongs to the law, and only employs his leisure hours at this work. He never, he said, enjoyed his life so much as when he was thus employed." This orrery was made after the plan of that of which a plate is given in Ferguson's Astronomy. The modern orrery is of a different form.

That dear friend whom I never saw, and whom I shall now never see, Abigail Roberts, died the 15th of this year.[161] Our friendship seemed not to need personal interviews; it was fond and sincere, and I shall greatly miss her valuable communications. Her young friend, Thomas Noble Cole, conveyed to me this information. He was her neighbour, and she was much attached to the youth, who was bound to her by grateful affection.

My kind friend the Bishop of Meath had been for some time in a declining state of health. His death was announced at different times in the papers, and he himself read one of these reports to his family at the breakfast table. The inevitable hour came at last; and in the second month of this year the benevolent, the amiable Thomas Lewis O'Beirne expired. A letter from his daughter informed me of this event.

This year a novel object was exhibited in Ballitore, a balloon, made with great care and ingenuity by Henry Allen. His brother Richard came from Dublin to assist in the business of setting it off. Nearly the whole of the village population assembled in and about Betsy Barrington's house. It was a time of anxiety to all, I believe, while the balloon was filling, especially to the modest scientific youths on whom so much responsibility rested. It was filled; the hand of Robert Lecky of Cork was taken off from it; and the first balloon that ever mounted through the shades of Ballitore rose majestically and sailed along the blue ether, when

"A shout that rent the golden stars ensued."

George O'Connor stopped neither to hail nor admire, but pursued the soaring wonder, and brought it in triumph back. It had descended near the moat of Ardscull, and was so little injured that it made another excursion with equal success; but on a third occasion it was lost.

On the 14th of Eighth–month in this year George Shackleton and Hannah Fisher were married in Limerick.

Our old neighbour and long tried friend, Abigail Widdows, owed much of the comfort of comparative health to the unwearied attentions of her daughter, for Rebecca was one of the best and most affectionate of children. Alas, now all her cares were put in requisition to alleviate the tediousness and distressing illness which confined her mother nearly five months to the bed of pain and restlessness, which were borne by the poor sufferer with a good degree of patience and resignation. Abigail Widdows was left a widow at three and twenty. She had a well–stocked shop and the tailoring business of the school, and was an object to which many a young farmer might have aspired, did not her conduct forbid any chance of success. She was a pleasant woman, but discreet withal, and her behaviour to the young men who boarded with her was guarded by prudence and decorum.

My sister Lydia and I felt the evening of our day darkened by the departure for England of our dear Ebenezer and Deborah. Sweet Fuller's Court must be left, when it had obtained beauties which I could not have believed it in the power even of its tasteful possessor to have bestowed upon it. My mind reverted to matters of ancient date. I thought I knew the identical spot in the parlour where I made the joyful discovery that I could read. I recollected my sensations of fear when for the fist time descending the remarkably easy staircase. The sash-door opening into the garden – the wall–like hedge – the ancient yews and hollies – the tall trees beyond the garden – the arch over the gate which entered it – all brought back the scenes of early childhood, when I, a little solitary, freely admitted into those walks alone, my imagination heated by classical stories, adorned my hat as well as I could, and aimed at personating Dido. These recollections were the passing clouds, but the settled gloom was the exile of those whose presence could dispel the passing clouds. The last look I cast upon Fuller's–Court I beheld the clear kitchen coal–fire shining through the bright window, since which time, now nearly three years, I have not been inside the gate of the little enclosure. Smitten with grief, I felt satisfaction that so many years of my life had gone by.

> Oh, mortals, blind to fate, who little know
> To bear high fortune or endure the low,
> The time may come

when I should be glad to have years added to my stock, to enable me to enjoy blessings for which I hope I feel a degree of thankfulness. "In patience possess your souls." Leave all to the Wisdom which orders aright, and in due time it will be made manifest that we cannot do better than submit quietly to the appointments of Providence.

Nancy McCabe had pulled down her good–looking cabin at Ballybarney, and built a smaller. Women appear to be chief actors here, the husbands sometimes engaging in distant jobs of work, and generally, I believe, returning to a comfortable home. To the remonstrances made to Nancy on her enterprise, she opposed the recital of misfortunes which had occurred in the former abode: "Was not my son smothered in his blood before he could say, Mother?" [He was supposed to have burst a blood–vessel.] "Was not my child, that was fit for the Duke of Leinster, scalded to death in a pot of potato water? Is not my eldest son almost a cripple with a swelled knee?" But what seemed to decide her operations was a dream into which were introduced fairies and a white lady. She might have brought forward a better excuse in the frequency of fever in that house, the mud walls of which may have received and retained the infection. A few rows of well–grown larches committed to her care obtained from her the title of "a grove." Her garden is surrounded by such trees, mixed with laburnums, – "The laburns, you know, that throw their yellow blossoms about." Why should not the same idea be presented to Cowper and to Nancy McCabe?

An association to encourage a little manufacture was formed here as in other places. Subscriptions were raised to purchase wool and flax, the spinning of which was chiefly paid for by articles of clothing. The terms were low on which the poor women were employed, but something was earned when nothing better offered, and it was found a useful resource.

THE END.

APPENDIX.

BALLITORE SCHOOL LIST,

From the opening of the School by Abraham Shackleton, on the 1st of Third month, 1726, to the arrival of the last boarders at James White's School, on the 15th of Eighth–month, 1836.

Year	Month	Day	
1726			
	3	1	John Fuller, Henry
			Richard Braddock
			Thomas Braddock
			Charles Braddock
			Samuel Watson
		2	John Watson
			Samuel Watson
		5	James Hutchinson
			Richard Sealy
		6	Thomas Duckett, John
			William Duckett, John
			John Duckett, John
			Abraham Duckett, John
			Jonas Duckett
			Solomon Watson
		9	Robert Parke
			Thomas Parke
		12	Thomas Wilcocks
		17	Barker Thacker
		20	Abraham Fuller
	4	1	Jacob Fuller
		2	Edward Fawcett
			Robert Pemberton
			John Pemberton
		6	John Coppock
			Thomas Weston
	4	17	Anthony Henderson
		20	Oliver Simmons
	5	5	John Lapham
		17	John Nicholson
	7	14	Barcroft Pim
	8	1	Samuel Strangman
		19	Edward Eustace
	9	28	Richard Harrison
	11	4	Alexander Shelly
	12	16	Daniel Reynolds
		20	Joseph Nuttall
	1	6	James Fitzgerald
1727			
	3	1	Samuel Watson, Solomon
		2	Abel Harris
		23	John Dawson
		30	William Lecky

Year	Month	Day	
	4	19	Thomas Pim
	5	27	Joshua Clibborn, Joshua
	6	5	Jonathan Nicholson
	7	16	Joshua Kinnier
		18	John Hickinbottom
	8	11	Francis Randal
			George Randal
	9	6	George Boles
1728			
	9	6	Jonathan Boles
	11	18	Amos Rooke
	12	14	Bancroft Fuller
	2	1	John Watson
		6	Joshua Clibborn, Abraham
			Henry Robinson
	3	27	John Pim, Joshua
	4	25	Samuel Neale
	5	15	John Clayton
			Robert Williams
	6	12	Amos Strettell
	8	8	Charles Motley
	12	2	Walter Mason
1729			
			James Mason
			James Pettigrew
	2	4	Thomas Boake
			Ephraim Boake
			Thomas Herritage
	3	26	James Hoope
			Joseph Strettell
	4	22	George Bewley
	5	14	Joseph Medcalf
	6	22	Joshua Hoope
	11	6	Thomas Robinson
		13	Samuel Fayle
		23	William Gregg
	12	29	William Porter
	1	23	Harrington McCarthy
1730			
	2	16	John Higginbottom
		21	George Newenham
	4	13	Peasley Harrington

Year	Month	Day	Name
	5	27	Joseph Gunson
			Josiah Gunson
	7	24	Stephen Fitzgerald
	8	9	Joseph Eves
		12	Samuel Pim
			John Fletcher
	9	23	Walter Fletcher
	10	12	George Hutchinson
	12	12	John Camak
			William Camak
		26	John Chayter
1731			
	1	29	John Barclay
	2	1	Jonathan Fletcher
		14	Thomas Bewley, Mungo
	3	5	Jonathan Watson
	4	6	Joseph Fade Goff
	7	11	Roger Webb
	8	14	Henry Harvey
	1	9	Peter Eves
			Francis Peasley, Peter
1732			
	5	17	Amos Strettell, jun.
			Robert Morris
		31	John Clibborn
	6	2	Thomas McMurtrie
			Henry McMurtrie
		31	William Freeman
	7	23	Warren Henderson
			Thomas Henderson
	8	15	Richard Pearce
1733			
	3	22	Robert Rooke
	4	4	Robert Strettell
			Abel Rooke
	5	16	Samuel Morris
	6	5	Henry Pemberton, Henry
		24	Richard Roach
	7	5	Walter Borrowes
	8	5	Timothy Handcock
	1	8	George Newett
1734			
	1	29	George Best
	3	6	John Winnett
			Clement Winnett
			Charles Winnett
			Henry Winnett
	3	15	William Bridges
		24	Thomas Burton
			Joseph Fuller, Samuel
		29	Richard Brocklesby
	4	6	Henry Carter
	6	5	John Steel
		17	William Busby
		24	Henry Graham
	7	2	Jacob Handcock
		25	John Newett
	8	2	George Penrose, William
		5	John Turner
		22	John Allen
	11	7	Joshua Allen
		16	Stephen Palfrey
		27	George Gardiner
	1	10	Francis Medcalf
		12	John Inman
1735			
	1	27	Robert Dillon
		29	John Fletcher
	2	14	Richard Goff
	3	21	Ambrose Medcalf
	4	2	Thomas Short
		6	Newcomen Herbert
		11	William McMurtrie
		23	Henry Ashe
	5	28	John Cullen
	6	9	Ebenezer Pike
	7	1	Thomas Pearce
	10	1	Thomas Strettell
		22	John Deaves
	1	4	John Bayly
1736			
	3	4	Edward Kenney
	4	1	James Robinson
		14	William Richardson
	5	15	Matthew Smith
	6	28	James Dulamon
	9	11	Henry Knowles
		17	Thomas Camak
	11	15	James Fanton
		22	Thomas Bushe
	1	2	John Waring
			Thomas Waring
1737			
	2	13	Peter Pennett
	3	2	James Sparrow
			Alexander Sparrow
		23	Robert Cheney
			Joshua Cheney
			John Cheney
	4	13	Zacharias Ache
		15	John Butler
	5	20	William Gamble
	7	1	Alexander Strong
	8	18	Joseph Taylor
			Edward Taylor
		25	William Dillon
			James Dillon
	10	19	Thomas Archbold
	11	10	James Clanchy
	12	1	John Charles Audebert
			Samuel Heamer
		9	Nathaniel Watson
	1	7	Joshua Strangman
		13	John Brown
			Thomas Brown

Year	Month	Day	
1738			
	2	10	James Robinson
			John Gelling
		17	John Waters
		19	Patrick Henderson
			John Henderson
	3	1	John Eves
		10	John Joubert
	4	3	John Slater
		12	Anthony Grayson
		23	Thomas Hutchinson
			John Hutchinson
		28	Thomas West
	5	5	Peter Beasley
	6	1	Richard Howes
		7	John Featherston
		19	Thomas Pearce
	7	13	Hilliard Hely
	8	30	William Hartnell
	9	3	William Hall
	11	27	John Thacker
			Charles Graydon
			John Graydon
	12	9	John Du Bedat
	1	1	Joseph Walpole
		5	Hamilton Low, Robert
1739			
	3	1	Trustrum Porter
		23	Matthew Medcalf
	4	18	Henry Cheney
	6	13	John Dillon
			Christopher Dillon
		15	James Duran
	7	7	Henry Russell, Eliza
	12	16	William English
	1	17	Joseph Pim
			Tobias Pim
1740			
	2	3	Robert Young
		7	Thomas Ayers
			Henry Deaves
	3	5	William Knight
	4	16	William Mason
	9	3	Alphonse Laporte
	12	31	John Russell
	1	1	John Lescure
		4	James Carroll
1741			
	2	8	Christopher Farlow
		20	William Taylor
	4	17	Matthew Bathurst
			William Bathurst
	5	26	Garrett Burke
			Edmund Burke
			Richard Burke
		28	Matthew Cullen
	6	6	Robert Pettigrew
		22	Henry Greenwood
	7	2	Cooper Penrose
			William Penrose
		6	Francis Beale
	8	10	Hutchinson Wheeler
	9	5	Annesley Hughes
		14	Johathan Haughton
	10	28	Francis Russell
	11	17	George McCannon
			John Murray
	12	14	William McCarty
	1	18	John Fonblanque
		23	John Nevins
1742			
	1	26	Edward Sands
	2	3	Mervyn Matthews
		12	John Jacob Taylor
		28	Josiah Jackson
			Samuel Jackson
	3	17	Robert Taylor
		24	Abraham Robinson
	5	8	John Jones, senior
		28	Edward Richardson
		29	Samuel Beale
	6	21	Clement Zouche
	7	18	Hercules Libert
	8	1	Nicholas Christian
		5	James Brown
		30	Joseph Deane
		13	Robert Dunckley
			George Dunckley
		24	John Freeman
			Euseby Stratford
			Francis Stratford
	12	15	James White
		28	Ralph Jackson
	1	3	Thomas Bennett
			William Bennett
		14	William Hartley
1743			
	3	10	Thomas Houlden
		24	William Cunningham
			James Rudd
		25	Philip Matty
	4	13	William Morgan
	5	4	Joshua Ridgeway, John
		14	James Wight
		28	Andrew Thomas
	6	3	Abraham Chaigneau
		15	William Harrington
	7	13	Daniel Allen
			Michael Kearney
		15	Daniel Barnard
	9	1	Richard Carden
		9	David Chaunders
		10	William Kennedy
		22	Robert Colvill
	11	13	Hercules Troy
		20	Lewis Aimée
		24	Richard Sherlock
			William Sherlock
			Thomas Sherlock

Year	Month	Day	
	12	13	Jacob Barrington
	1	2	James Villiers Walsh
		7	Richard Longfield
1744			
	2	1	Nathaniel Orpin
	3	20	William Mead
	4	14	Robert Johnson
			Benjamin Johnson
		24	Caleb Chaunders
		25	William Mackenzie
	5	21	William Berkeley
	6	19	James Stephens
			James Dalzell
		23	Jonathan Connolly
		29	George Farran
		30	Robert Walpole
	7	10	Henry Pearce
			Maurice Rayner
	8	2	Daniel Donovan
		15	Robert Lovett
	10	7	Gregory O'Brien
	11	7	John Donovan
			Peter Donovan
		14	Thomas Harman
		24	Anthony Edwards
	1	4	James Faulkener
		11	George Robbins
1745			
	1	26	Thomas Pearson
			Samuel Pearson
	3	1	Joseph Sleigh
	4	10	Paul Abbot
	5	12	John Power
	6	13	Crofton Vandeleur
			William Coulthurst
		23	Christopher Marrett
		27	James Lecky, George
	8	10	John Geoghegan
		21	Edward Shee
		27	Isaac Willan
			Jacob Willan
		30	Caleb Crowther
	9	1	Robert Longfield
		6	James Green
	11	25	Nevill Forth
			Fennell White Warren
	1	14	John Maddock
1746			
	2	14	James Maddock
	3	4	John Jones, jun.
		11	Caleb Carden
		23	John Lecky, George
		26	Gilbert Eames
			Ralph Gates
			Francis Gates
	4	9	Edward Stephens
	5	11	Henry Harvey
		29	Richard Fleming
	6	19	Thomas Bewley, Daniel
			George Bewley, Richard
	9	28	Robert Lecky, John
1747			
	9	28	James Lecky, John
	1	4	Robert Favier
		9	John Fuller, Samuel
	1	24	Simon Barker
			William Barker
	2	6	John Hammon
		21	Samuel Kathrens
			George Kathrens
		23	Thomas Jackson, Thomas
		28	Thomas Butler
	3	6	Wright Pike
		17	Isaac Tyrrel De Zouche
		18	Ralph Barker
	4	2	John Hudson
		30	Thomas Morris
	5	30	Thomas Knowles
			Philip Lefanu
	7	18	John Leybourn
	8	29	William Bury
	11	16	William Phillips
	12	29	Edward Nowlan
			William Nowlan
1748			
	2	13	John Kavanagh
	3	5	Edward Morris
		6	Robert Fennell
			Joshua Fennell
			Richard Pike, Richard
	5	20	Robert Michell
			James Michell
	6	15	James Shee
		27	Edward Hunt
			Christopher Hewetson
	7	3	Thomas Penrose
		21	George Darcy
	8	10	Joshua Haughton
		17	Isaac Michell
	9	25	John Christy, Thomas
	10	18	William Reade
	12	6	Arthur Thompson
		14	James Delany
	1	28	Benjamin Ball, Benjamin
1749			
	2	3	James Morgan
			Robert Brunton
		10	William Ayers
		17	Thomas Green
	3	8	James Wall
			Pierce Wall
		9	Samuel Judge
		23	John Watson, John
		30	Forest Bourne
	4	5	James Napper Tandy
		18	Thomas Curtis
		22	John Hill
	5	4	Ebenezer Geale

Year	Month	Day	
		10	Henry Carroll
			Frederick Carroll
			Edward Carroll
	6	7	John Davis
		14	William Grove
		15	George Nixon
		16	Joseph Reade
		18	Peter Charrieir
		29	Thomas Dick
		30	James Dance
	7	9	William Hill
			George Hill
1750			
	1	19	Thomas Caulfield
	2	22	Thomas Ogle
	3	6	Green Despard
		8	Oliver Cromwell Wall
		14	Peter Banfield
		17	James Woolley
	4	6	John Penrose
		11	Thomas Bewley, Richard
			William Jackson
		13	Graydon Smith
		19	Nicholas Hughes
		23	John Duckett, Abraham
		29	Isaac Fletcher
	5	20	John Gethin
	7	15	Joseph Sandwith
	8	5	Thomas Woolley
	8	11	Samuel Taylor
	9	22	Sir Edmund Grymes
	10	16	Francis Peisley, Samuel
			Robert Hudson
	11	17	Robert Whitby
		21	William Pilsworth
	12	4	Thomas Yeates
		25	Robert Montgomery
		28	Edmund Armstrong
1751			
	1	29	Maximilian Favier
	2	26	Peter Judd
	3	8	William Drope
		14	Robert Wilson
		16	John Howell
		20	Henry Boake
	4	10	William Candler
			John Fellowes
	5	16	William Morgan
			Hamilton Morgan
		18	James Read
		21	John Lawrence
		23	John Chillcott
		26	George Betson
	6	9	John Conran
		13	Christopher Standring
		14	William Dexter
		15	St. George Molesworth
			Bouchier Molesworth
			Dunbar Doyle
			Charles Doyle

Year	Month	Day	
		23	Patrick Mahon
	7	5	Thomas Murray
		16	Benjamin Wills
		20	Robert Molesworth
	9	27	George Day
1752			
	3	6	William Howard
	3	10	John Barker
	4	17	George Widdrington
		20	Jonathan Pim
	4	20	Joseph Baker
	5	1	Henry Butler
		3	James Edwin
		19	Thomas Posgate
		20	Phillips Callbeck
	6	25	Simon Durand
	7	6	Jesse Ballnawes
		24	Samuel Cherry
	8	17	Peter Hebert
		26	Daniel Tracy
	9	23	Ralph Smyth
	12	4	Searles Jackson
1753			
	1	29	Thomas Haughton
	2	7	Christopher Colles
	3	26	John Briscoe
	4	5	John Pounden
		9	Timothy Sullivan
		16	Philip Sullivan
		30	Samuel Barry
	5	8	Richard Barry
		23	Robert Eccles
	6	20	Anthony Robinson
			Joseph Robinson
			Abraham Clibborn
			Clayton Bayly
		24	Richard Johnston
		30	David Terson
	7	12	Thomas Carleton Webb
		19	John Crosbie
		29	Richard Vincent
	8	13	Mark Anthony Perrier
		28	James Mariner
	9	3	William Garratt
		11	Francis Lucas
			Charles Lucas
		15	Richard Pounden
		24	Timothy Ryan
	11	8	John Ridgway
1754			
	3	25	Thomas Wrightson
	3	25	Aldborough Wrightson
	4	15	Isaac Haughton
			Benjamin Haughton
		22	Ponsonby Molesworth
	5	9	James Andrews
		12	Anthony Sedgwick
		23	James Malone
	6	6	Thomas Hatton

Year	Month	Day	
			John Hatton
		9	William McClear
		13	Rawdon Hauttonville
		24	Peter Charretié
		25	Hugh Pigknott
	6	30	George Golding
			John Eliot Turner
	7	1	Michael Howard
		4	John Despard
			Andrew Despard
		14	Lambert Wheeler
		15	Joseph Beard
	8	4	Benjamin Read
			William Read
		23	William Mahon
	9	13	Daniel Duff
	10	18	Mark Galbraith
	12	17	James Rice
1755			
	1	10	Benjamin Yeates
	3	15	Anthony Crebessac
		19	Domville Hartpole
	5	26	Joseph Calcutt
	6	1	Richard Eaton
		23	George Tandy
		28	Francis Turner
			Rawdon Stothard
	7	1	William Walsh
	8	1	William Green
		11	Nicholas Doyle
		18	William Stuart
		28	Edward Pickering
	9	3	Charles Custis
	9	5	George Sall
	10	17	Edward Ellison
			William Ellison
	11	17	Frederick Falkiner
	12	2	Robert Lecky, William

1756 – In this year Richard Shackleton became master of Ballitore School.

Year	Month	Day	
1756			
	1	23	Thomas Gregg
			William Chapman
	2	12	William North
		28	Thomas Buckley
	4	12	Benjamin Bloomfield
			Joseph Bloomfield
			John Bloomfield
			Henry Fuller
		19	George Turner
		27	John Watson, Saml. jun.
		29	Abraham Shackleton
	5	3	Edward Miles
		17	Thomas Pearson Smith
		19	Edward Kennedy
	6	9	Matthew Ryan
		14	William Molesworth
		17	James Eaton
		22	Stephen Read

Year	Month	Day	
	7	7	Philip Charretié
			Thomas Champion
		24	Lawrence Dowdall Curtin
	8	30	Edward Gray
	12	8	Chaworth Brabazon Hallows
1757			
	1	22	John Bertrand
	2	7	Henry Toler
			John Willington, James
		23	Thomas Sullivan
	3	30	James Sullivan
	4	5	William Colles
	5	2	Richard Wilson
		26	John Eyre
		31	Anthony Brabazon
	7	25	Henry Fortick Sheridan
	8	8	Joseph Albey
		24	Somerville Pope
		26	Edward Pierce Willington
		28	John Bayley, jun.
	9	1	William Ormsby
			Henry Ormsby
		6	John Thompson
		11	Handy Pemberton
	10	4	Francis May
		27	James Lecky, Robert
			John Lecky, Robert
1758			
	1	6	Samuel Watson, Sam. jun.
		23	Richard Webb
	2	20	Samuel Peisley
	3	2	Thomas Scott
		13	John Wilson, John
			Henry Eaton
		30	Benjamin Stratford
	4	10	Richard Geoghegan
	5	6	Morrough Browne
		17	James Henry
		22	Josiah Caulfield
	6	22	Edward Griffith
	8	1	Paul Hughes
		8	Poyntz Willington
		28	Francis Anderson Morris
	10	6	Thomas Ellison
			Bingham Ellison
			Robert Gildea
		14	William McLaughlin
1759			
	1	15	John Lynch
	2	5	James Trenor
			John Trenor
		18	Edmond Blood, Charles
			Samuel Cavanagh
	3	13	John Watson, John
			Robert Watson
			George Watson
		23	James Adams
			William Adams

Year	Month	Day	
	5	8	Charles Read
		29	Thomas Holliday
	7	12	Thomas Prentice
		17	Adam Ormsby
			Christopher Ormsby
			Thomas Elwood
	8	20	Henry Russell, Henry
	9	2	Daly Vero
	10	29	Samuel Pearson Haughton
			John Barcroft Haughton
		31	Robert Stratford
1760			
	3	3	John Pexton
		16	Richard Pike, William
	5	8	Robert Clayton Sankey
		19	Henry French
			William Lancaster
		27	John Alcock
	7	1	Edmond Blood, Thomas
		10	John Wheeler
			Thomas Beaumont
		12	Nathaniel Price
		22	Hamilton Lowe, James
	8	19	George Naylor
			James Naylor
	10	14	Samuel Darcey
1761			
	1	5	Thomas Emett
		7	Thomas Gaugain Landey
	3	12	Howard Parry
	4	12	Charles White
	5	1	Henry Humfries
		13	Samuel Neale, Samuel
	6	6	Isaac Simmons
			Thomas Simmons
		7	Henry Lapham
		17	Pierce Lett
		29	Busteed Ireland
	7	14	George Leckey
		23	George Cotter
	8	13	John Chamberlin
	11	9	Laurence Nicholas Zelius
	12	7	William Keatinge
		21	Svend Peter Stuberg
1762			
	1	14	John White
	2	2	James Garrett
	3	19	John Ratcliff
		22	James Duffey
			John Duffey
	4	13	Alexander Shelley, Alexr.
		25	James Abell
		28	Richard Abell
	5	6	James Bradshaw
			Robert Bradshaw
			William Toppin
			William Delap
	6	1	Robert Bayly
	7	2	Samuel Grubb
		3	Thomas Thacker
		4	Anthony Deaves, Henry
		14	Robert Johnson
	8	3	Thomas Duckett, Abraham
			Abraham Duckett, Abm.
	9	1	Newman Travers Curtin
		1	Samuel Adams Curtin
	9	14	John Robison
			Charles Robison
			William Gray
	11	21	Joshua Watson
1763			
	1	13	William Whelling
		31	John Haughton, Jonathan
	2	13	William Wright
		25	Francis Tighe
	4	14	Nicholas Barnes
		21	Stephen Gordon
		26	William Gregg, William
	4	26	George Gregg
			William Johnson
		28	Israel Read
	5	6	William Wheeler
		8	Matthew Young
		13	Timothy Bridge
		16	John Fuller, John
			Thomas Fuller
		23	Geo. Newenham, Geo.
			George Rainsford
	6	4	Richard Sullivan
		12	John Pim, Samuel
		14	John Neale
	7	17	Thomas Tailford
		18	Francis Freeman
			Caesar Freeman
	8	6	William Holmes
			Richard Holmes
		31	Michael Cahill
	9	22	Richard Sparrow
		25	Moses Darley
	10	11	Legh Hoskins Master
	12	3	William Carter
1764			
	1	15	Archibald Nevins
		27	Thomas Chaytor
	2	16	Joshua Ridgway, Henry
	3	11	William Walker
		14	Henry Rogers
	4	25	George Dibbs
	5	7	Thomas Eyre
			Samuel Eyre
	5	10	George McCally
		10	Henry Pemberton, John
		21	John Cheney, John
		21	Benjamin Ball, Robert
	6	11	Patrick Rogers
		28	Francis Johnson
	7	2	Patrick Freeman
		16	Robert Hume
			Clement Hume

Year	Month	Day	
		21	Edward Hodson
		24	Malby Brabazon
			William Brabazon
		27	John Robinson
		30	Robert Graham
			Dacre Graham
	8	11	Robert Hawford Boyd
		17	Richard Goff, Fade
	8	18	John Petticrew
			Joshua Petticrew
	9	19	John Hutchinson
		20	Francis Greenhow
			John Bewley
		24	Thomas Robinson
		27	Stanley Heyland
	11	9	Andrew Boles
	12	17	Murray Kathrens
			Samuel Kathrens
1765			
	4	15	Thomas Johnson
		19	Samuel Pim, Samuel
	5	10	Dominick Heyland
			Abraham Atkinson
	6	4	Robert Roe
		5	Loftus Robinson
			James Howis
		10	George Stewart
		21	John Scamaden
			William Malone
		26	Bealy Rogers Breton
	7	4	John Bonafons
		17	Denison Hume
		21	William Wallis
		24	George Brabazon
	8	5	John Haughton, John
	9	12	Richard Davis
	11	8	Paul Johnson
1766			
	1	20	Luke Lawlor
	2	12	Josiah Bryan
	4	20	Richard Jessop
			Joseph Fuller, Abraham
		24	Charles Cahill
		28	Henry Fred. Courtenay
	5	26	John Mosse
		28	John Pasley
		30	Thomas Evans
	6	6	James Walpole
		8	Robert Eyre
			Edward Eyre
		15	Thomas Conway
			William Conway
		21	Rupert Preston Vallancey
			John Congreve Booth
	9	1	Alexander Mitchell
		20	Michael Becher
	10	27	James Magrath
		13	William Rayner
	11	7	James Taylor

Year	Month	Day	
1767			
	1	18	Joseph Scott
		19	William Leonard
	2	25	Peter Clark
		28	Harman Black
	5	7	George Lloyd
		9	Peter Cambridge
		11	Samuel Andrews
		16	Mordecai Abbott
		24	Edmund Burroughs
	6	19	John Plowman
		23	William Cooper
		29	Richard Cotter
	7	6	John Mooney
		13	Daniel Mooney
		20	John Pim, John
			Thomas Pim
			William Pim
			Joseph Pike Pim
	8	27	Johsua Wilson
			Benjamin Wilson
	9	28	John Carroll
	11	11	Joseph Dudley
1768			
	1	12	Samuel Thornton
	2	29	William Grace
	3	31	George Edkins
	4	6	Samuel Elly
			William Jessop
	5	5	Jonathan Dudley
		9	William Woodward
		11	Charles Gore
			Richard Gore
		16	Joseph Sparrow
		23	William Steacey
			Thomas Cotter
	6	16	William Boardman
	7	13	Thomas Lhoyd
		25	William Pike
	8	14	Henry Ashworth
			Samuel Ashworth
	10	9	Robert Lloyd
	12	12	John Bayly
1769			
	1	3	Thos. Hutchinson, Thos.
		23	Henry Rochfort
	3	27	Simon Bradstreet
			Samuel Bradstreet
	4	1	Thomas Gribble
		8	Thomas Strangman
		26	Josiah Johnson
			James Evans
	5	19	Caesar Colclough
	6	26	Edward Currin
	7	5	John Deaves, Henry
		24	George St. George Robison
			William Robison
	8	14	Thomas McLaughlin
		27	Jno. Willington, Jonathan

Year	Month	Day	
	9	1	Thomas Wandesford
	11	3	William Lecky, William
		16	Nathaniel White
1770			
	3	11	Thomas Richard Hamilton
		14	Isaac Jackson
	5	1	Henry Harris
		27	Acheson Johnston Crozier
		30	Abraham Neale
			Samuel Penrose
		30	James Hutchinson, James
			William Hutchinson
	6	1	James Hutchinson, Thos.
		11	Jacob Fuller, Samuel
	7	24	John Barcroft
		30	William Reynolds
		31	John King
	8	1	Richard Jacob
			Isaac Jacob
		6	John Clibborn, George
	9	9	Thomas Hoope
	10	16	William Fielding
	11	17	Thomas Bell
		18	Thomas Knight Albey
	12	3	William Duckett, Abm.
1771			
	2	21	Martin Benton
	3	2	William Goff
	4	16	Eyre Massy
		20	Thomas Higgins
	5	28	James Prossor
	7	9	Barker Thacker, Barker
	8	22	John Barclay
	9	9	William Rea
	10	9	Peter Bell
			Morgan Byrne
1772			
	1	10	George Penrose, George
		14	Thomas Harris
	2	25	John Williams
	4	30	Burrows Erwin
			Thomas Jacob
	5	2	Edward Scriven
		9	Robert Turton
			James Nicholson
		14	John Holmes
		15	Moses Pim
		18	Benjamin Alloway
	6	15	William Duckett, Jonas
			James Jenkisson
		20	Joseph Knott
		23	Richard Wiley
		27	John Conway Hughes
	7	9	Thomas Duffey
	8	22	John Elsey
	9	9	James Whyte
			Christopher Whyte
		12	John Rea

Year	Month	Day	
	10	13	Thomas Rea
		17	Frederick Millikin
	12	6	James Skinner
1773			
	4	22	George Taggart
		24	Eyre Linde
		26	Joseph Haughton
		27	Eugene Sullivan
		28	William Dudley
	5	9	Charles Ayres
		10	William Hall
			John Hall
			Joseph Hall
		24	George Barcroft
		27	James Malone, Francis
		28	William Waring
	6	5	John Nicholson
		7	Thomas White
			Benjamin White
		8	Nicholas Chaytor
		19	Joseph Strangman
		22	Hosea Guinness
	7	7	George Stanley
			Richard Phibbs
			Toby Peyton Phibbs
		9	Joseph Thacker
	8	19	William Crowe
		21	Joseph Rawlins
		30	John Deaves, Ebenezer
			Anthony Deaves, Ebenezer
	9	2	George Massy
	10	7	David Sherrard
		9	Philip Stacpole
	11	15	William Mulock
1774			
	1	25	John St. Clair
		29	Joshua Beale
	3	22	Joshua Pilkington
			William Pilkington
	4	12	David Skinner
	5	3	John Farrell
		11	Francis Russell, John
		17	John Bennett
	6	4	George Magill
		21	George Hart
			John Hutchinson, James
	7	1	Samuel Pasley
		3	Robert Taggart
		6	John Peile
			Robert Peile
	8	8	John Thacker, John
		10	John Beale
		28	James Forbes
			John Robinson, John
	9	10	Gilbert Kilbee
			James Kilbee
			Alexander Henry
	10	24	Joshua Desvoeux
	11	4	James Kathrens
	12	13	John Mason

Year	Month	Day	
1775			
	1	2	Henry Fuller, Samuel
		8	John Goodwin
		10	Pim Nevins
		16	Richard Sherwood
		24	James Eustace
			Robert Eustace
	2	4	Laurence Cotton
	3	23	Sir Richd. Eyre Cox, Bart.
	5	17	Joshua Parvin
		22	James Seaton
		31	John Morris
	6	1	Richard Duckett
		10	George Mansergh
			Henry Leslie
	7	5	Charles Seaton
		9	Thomas Dalton
		10	James Coghill Hagarty
		28	Edward Power
	8	31	William Beale
	9	1	John Haughton, Joseph
	10	5	Robert Baxter
	12	4	Wm. Palliser Barrington
		16	Alexander Ewing
1776			
	2	15	Joseph Keen Dixon
	3	3	William Leslie
		4	Robert Donkin
		12	Matthew Mansergh
		24	Samuel Wily
	4	7	John Taylor
		15	Ephraim Hetherington
			Thomas Boake, Ephraim
		28	William Fitzgerald
		29	John Williams
	5	11	John Radcliff
		22	John Christy, John
	6	15	Robert Dowling
	9	11	Thomas Homan Mulock
	11	12	Thomas Kathrens
	12	8	John Brownrigg
1777			
	1	9	William Henry Lowther Crofton
		22	Charles Fleetwood
	2	5	Peter Widdows
	3	30	John Edkins
	4	12	Frederick Lee Conyngham
		14	James Fitzgerald
	5	7	William Leadbeater
		19	John Dawson, John
		24	William Irvine
	6	12	Aldworth Phaire
	7	7	John Wilson, Andrew
		21	James Hamilton
	8	1	Samuel Hodson
	9	5	Godfrey Byrne
		13	Leslie Battersby
		14	Richard Senior
		23	Richard Odlum

Year	Month	Day	
		29	Henry Purdon
	11	1	Frederick Cary
	12	11	Charles Rawdon
1778			
	1	8	Francis Hutchinson
	2	19	Robert Johnson, Robert
	4	4	Richard King
		10	Mark Toomey
		16	Benjamin Rochfort Read Bowen
		28	Thomas Smith
			George Percy Smith
		30	Jeremiah Hanks
			Joseph Hanks
	5	18	John Harpor
		24	Alexander Forbes
	6	23	Edmond Power
		25	William Alexander Conyngham
	7	10	William Massey
		22	Robert Sandford Palmer
	8	1	Joseph Lapham
		25	James Ferrall
	9	3	Robert Mottley
		21	Henry Flood
	10	23	Joseph Greenwood
	11	8	Samuel Strangman
		25	Edward Cooper
		26	Charles Coote

1779 – In this year Richard Shackleton's son, Abraham, became master of Ballitore School.

Year	Month	Day	
1779			
	1	21	John Conran, James
			William Conran
	1	22	Henry Bunbury
	2	6	Samuel Alexander
		24	William Wilson
	3	28	Hunt Walsh Johnson
	4	13	Edmund Murphy
	4	25	Anthony Lynch
		28	Abraham Abell
	5	19	Thomas Beale
	6	1	Richard Powell
		16	Trevor Fay
	7	5	Robert Nixon
		14	Thomas Bernard
	8	4	John Strettell
		13	James Abbott
		16	George Forster Dalton
	9	19	Richard Calcutt
		23	William Cooley
	10	19	Thomas Wilcoks, John
	11	6	James Frazer
		8	William Montgomery
	12	20	Weilly Malone
1780			
	1	4	Westby Percival
	2	14	Samuel Johnson
			Richard Johnson

Year	Month	Day	
		28	John Jackson
			Thomas Jackson, William
	7	17	Michael Lacky
	8	25	John Forbes
	10	31	Peter Alexander Leslie
1781			
	1	8	Robert Lacky
		17	Thomas McGwire
			Edward McGwire
		18	Edward Stephens
		19	John North
		21	Ashleigh Crofton
	2	5	Aaron Atkinson
	4	9	John Pim, Tobias
	5	2	John Vaughan
			George Vaughan
	8	23	John Borough Leslie
		28	Joseph McGwire
	10	4	Samuel Brooke
			John Brooke
1782			
	2	20	Francis Boyle Derenzy
	3	4	Peter Wilson
		18	Nicholas Cooper Morres
	5	20	Benjamin Wilson
			Thomas Wilson
	6	17	Robert Shaw
	7	1	Maurice Moran
			Philip Butler
		15	William Mooney
	8	25	John Baptist Cuvillie Shannon
	9	19	William Middleton
1783			
	2	1	John Perkins
	3	29	William Greene
			Arthur Greene
			Joseph Greene
		31	John Dunbar
			Dennis Delany
	4	13	Curtis Farran
		24	John Perkins O'Brien
		26	William Hawkins
	5	9	William Cartwright
			Samuel Long
		19	Samuel Dawson
	6	9	William Dowdall
		16	John Hudson
		23	Patrick Fenerty
		30	Thomas Butler
	8	13	Bernard Shaw
		20	Joseph Cooper
		25	William Farron
		28	Richard Evans
	9	9	John Watson
		13	Edward Featherstone
		29	Peter Smith
	10	27	Thomas Wilson
	12	6	Robert Hamilton
1784			
	1	13	John Seavers
		15	Robert Simmons
			Thomas Dowling
	3	4	John Peck
		31	George Ashe
	4	1	William Murray
			Alexander Murray
		12	John Fetherston
			Theobald Fetherston
	6	10	Charles Bernard
		28	William Rawson
			James Rawson
	9	4	Joseph Bernard
	10	4	Frederick Steele
		19	Skeffington Hamilton
	11	18	Thomas Steele
	12	1	Christopher Ussher
			John Ussher
1785			
	1	28	Thomas Pim, Jonathan
		30	Samuel Watson, John
	3	6	John Magrath
		7	Dudley Hartpole Colclough
		24	Joseph Welsh
	4	5	George Hartpole
		15	Richard Newton Bennett
		23	William Holmes, M.D.
		27	William Henry Turner
	5	7	Allen Adams
		15	John Bailie Ferrall
			William Bailie
		20	John Robinson, Anthony
		30	Samuel Wilson
	6	4	Hercules Campbell
		25	Emanuel Bayly
	8	24	Josiah Martin
		26	Pooley Smith
	9	3	Jonathan Sisson Cooper
		29	Samuel Penrose, Samuel
			George Randall Penrose
	10	24	George Armitt
1786			
	2	5	Simon Foote
	3	5	Richard Manders, Isaac
			Howe Greene Manders, Isaac
			John Manders, Joshua
			Thomas Manders, Joshua
		6	Richard Shackleton
		23	Francis Wemys
	5	15	Joseph Turner
	6	3	William Duckett White
			John White
		18	William Gold Patrickson
			Chr. Clarges Patrickson
	8	17	John Kennedy
	9	11	Hamlet Wade
		29	Molyneux Smith

Year	Month	Day	
	10	23	William Cole
1787			
	1	2	Richard Hudson
	2	26	James Welsh
	3	8	Anthony Pim
		12	John Brohan
		27	John Power
	4	12	Henry Magill
	6	19	William O'Hara
	7	2	Richard Yeates
	8	3	Abraham Grubb
		6	Sandwith Martin
			John Martin
		19	Peter Wilkinson
	9	18	Thomas Willan
	10	11	John Reilly
		15	John Couzens
	11	15	Abm. Devonshire Penrose
		21	Margaret Shackleton
	12	10	Benjamin Haughton, Sam.
			Issac Wilson
		16	Thomas Greer Grubb
		17	George Penrose Ridgway
1788			
	1	11	Samuel Robinson
		24	Edward Lucas
	2	7	Richard Leigh
	3	3	Robert Power
	4	24	Henry Grubb
			Robert Grubb
	5	8	Joseph Smithson
	7	17	Henry King
		21	William Heighington
	8	29	Richard King
	10	20	George Slamer Grant
	12	21	William Reilly
1789			
	4	19	James Wall
			Harrington Wall
	7	1	George Humfrey
		21	Henry Cole Johnson
	8	28	John Hornidge
			William Hornidge
	9	1	Alexander Cahill
	10	29	Joseph Harvey
1790			
	1	4	Jonathan Williamson
			Francis Williamson
		19	Maurice Farmer
	3	31	Thomas Nevins
	4	6	Henry Smithson
	5	17	Benjamin Haughton
			John Haughton
		21	Saunders Frayne
			Parsons Frayne
	6	15	James Reilly
	8	12	Solomon Watson
			William Watson

Year	Month	Day	
			Joshua Watson
	11	19	John Thomas Allinson
1791			
	3	28	Goodwin Warner
	4	27	Joseph Devonshire Fisher
			Joseph Fisher
	5	24	Thomas Kathrens
		31	William Penrose
			Thomas Courtenay
	6	4	Francis Davis
			John Sparrow
			Andrew Martin
		7	Richard Burchell
		9	Richard Grubb
		11	William Murphy
		13	George Robinson
	7	2	Thomas Williams
		15	Francis Penrose
		27	James White
	8	27	Jonathan Pim
			Anthony Robinson
	9	9	Linegar Rogers
	10	14	Henry Sandwith
		20	James Macklin
1792			
	3	2	Arthur Curtis
	5	28	Barcroft Wilson
	6	4	Luke Farnan
		11	Thomas Smithson
		12	Charles Dudley
			James Forbes
	7	6	William Corlett
		24	James Stewart
	8	20	Stephen Devereux
	9	1	Thomas Fayle
	11	28	John Deaves
1793			
	1	8	William Phelps
			James Phelps
	4	25	John Penrose
			William Dudley
		27	Samuel Penrose
			Joseph Penrose
	5	3	Benjamin Parvin Wynne
		9	Archibald Nevins
			Pim Nevins
	5	16	Thomas Reeves
	6	7	Robert Lecky
	8	5	John Bewley
			William Bewley
	9	13	Henry Haughton
	10	7	John Freeman
1794			
	3	6	Robert Watson
	4	2	Robert Goodbody
			Thomas Goodbody
	6	2	William Thacker
		14	George Peet, Edward
	7	12	William Garrett

Year	Month	Day	
			James Garrett
	8	16	John Russell
	9	24	Edward Peet
	10	31	James Fisher
	11	10	Robert Mansergh
	12	24	Reuben Harvey
1795			
	3	18	Samuel Grubb
	4	7	Joseph Dugdale
		24	George Firth
	5	22	Joshua Fayle
		26	Benjamin Gatchell
	6	20	Joseph Jacob
	7	6	Joseph Walpole
			William Walpole
		20	Joseph Wood
	8	25	John Pim
	9	16	John Knott
	10	5	Richard Garrett
1796			
	1	12	John Watson
	3	8	Penrose Nevins
		10	William Hoyland
		31	George Peet, Nathaniel
	4	8	George Phelps
	4	22	William Watson
	5	12	Joshua Hamilton Cox
			Richard Cox
	7	22	Robert Walpole
	8	6	Edward Carroll
		20	George Bewley, Mungo
	9	7	John Hancock
			Robert Hancock
		15	William Delap
		24	Thomas Power
	10	5	Thomas Chandlee
		27	John Usher
	11	21	Robert Mottley
1797			
	2	3	Thomas Montagu Black
	3	15	Robert Davis
	5	8	Abraham Spain
		22	Joshua Strangman Conran
	9	17	Devon Seymour Conway
			Henry Waters
	10	19	George McMahon
1798			
	4	1	Thomas White
		23	James Nicholson
			Joseph Nicholson
	9	1	James Bewley
		4	Edmund Mooney
1799			
	8	23	Samuel Phelps
	10	7	William Farmer
			John Farmer
		14	William Hancock
	11	5	Thomas Bond
1800			
	4	17	Henry Bond
	9	17	Jonathan Haughton, Ben.
1801			
	4	14	Samuel Haughton, Saml.
			Thomas Haughton, Saml.*

***Ballitore School was dissolved when Thomas Montagu Black left school.**

Ballitore School re-opened for Day Scholars under the joint direction of RICHARD SHACKLETON and MARY STEPHENS.

Year	Month	Day	
1802			
	11	22	Elizabeth Leadbeater
			Deborah Leadbeater
		23	Margaret Shackleton
	12	6	Mary Shackleton
		21	Lydia Shackleton
		27	Alexander Bewley
1803			
	1	3	John Paine
			Wentworth Paine
		19	Catharine Germain
			Catharine Walsh
	1	28	William Leadbeater
	2	4	Edward Pitts
		7	William Dunn
			Sarah Egan
		14	Catharine Nowlan
		25	Mary Paine
			Susanna Butler
	4	12	Robert Fitzgerald
	5	19	Anne Haughton
	5	23	Anne Brian
	6	1	Catharine Maher
	7	5	Mary Lee

JAMES WHITE re-opened Ballitore Boarding School.

Year	Month	Day	
1806			
	11	24	Richard Shackleton Leadbeater
			William Horan
		25	Edward Cullen
		27	James Farmer
			Frederick Farmer
	12	29	Francis Carter
1807			
	1	1	James Haughton, Samuel, **first boarder**
		5	Richard Butler
		7	William Hoysted
		22	James Maher

Year	Month	Day	
		26	Joseph Harvey
	2	23	Michael Conran
	3	1	John O'Neill
			Thomas O'Neill
		13	Samuel Clibborn
			Barclay Clibborn, Cooper
	3	28	Francis Peet
	4	4	Henry McManus
		17	Joseph Todhunter
			Thomas Harvey Todhunter
		18	Barclay Clibborn, James
			Thomas Greer Clibborn
		28	William Drury
			John Drury
			Henry Drury
	5	9	Jonathan Wright
		18	James Pim
			William Walpole
			Hugh Cullen
		23	John Pim
		24	George Courtenay
		27	Thomas Lawler
	6	5	Joseph Robinson
		9	John Towers
		27	William Goodbody
	7	1	Richard Jacob
			Thomas Greer Jacob
		2	Charles Stephens
		14	Jonathan Pim
			Joseph Wakefield Pim
		16	Richard Davis
		21	Robert Elly
			Samuel Rogers
	8	15	John Thacker
			William Thacker
	10	1	William Harvey
		4	William Henry Hutchinson
	11	7	George Penrose
			Joseph Penrose
		20	Richard Bewley
		24	William Fitzmaurice
			Robert Fitzmaurice
	12	14	Charles Coote
		17	Joseph Strangman
		29	John Haughton
1808			
	2	15	Edward Jones
	3	26	William Going
	5	5	Jacob Harvey
			James Mark
		10	Thomas Knott
	6	4	William Pim
		15	Thomas Stephens
	7	12	John Warren
			Richard Warren
		16	Thomas White Harris
	10	12	Joseph Wigglesworth
		24	Joseph Revel
		29	Edward Tracy

Year	Month	Day	
1809			
	1	21	John Manly
	3	1	William Robinson, John
		26	Samuel Tolerton
	4	10	William Risdall
	5	27	Francis Hanks
			William Hanks
	8	1	Samuel Eves
		15	James Fisher, Joseph
			Thomas Harvey
	9	4	John Archbold
		11	John Lawler
	10	2	Richard Colles
		9	John Bressingham
		10	William Greer
		29	William Tracy
	11	20	Edward Farmer
	12	4	John Jacob
1810			
	1	15	Morgan Maguire
			Edward Maguire
			Thomas Maguire
			Thomas Lenan
	3	10	John Broughan
	5	31	John Murphy
	6	1	Theophilus Jones Dixon
	8	1	William Coote
		11	Thomas Fisher
		12	William Todhunter
	9	3	Thomas Nagle
	11	9	Richd. Shackleton Rayner
	12	11	Thomas O'Brien
		15	Richard Eames
			Benjamin Eames
1811			
	1	7	John Hartwell
	2	14	John Robert Greer
	3	4	Michael Timmons
	8		John Fitzsimmons
			John Stratford Rodney
			Joseph Butler
			Thomas Dixon
	8	20	Matthew Lawler
	9	10	Samuel Neale
1812			
	1	23	Solomon Sproule
	4	12	Thomas Sturgeon
	5	12	Frederick Mooney
	6	3	James Byrne
	8	7	John Tolerton
		15	Thomas Gatchell
			John Dixon
		30	James Harvey
	10	3	Samuel Lapham
	11	1	Patrick Mooney
	12	26	Hancock Gregg
1813			
	1	17	George Lowman

Year	Month	Day	
	2	10	Michael Cullen
			Hugh Cullen
		11	William Deaves
			Thomas Deaves
			Joseph Harvey, Reuben
		21	John Kain
	3	11	Edward Read
		12	John Dillon
		22	Bernard Reilly
	4	6	John Grattan
			Henry Grattan
			Edward Grattan
			John Dempsey
			Nicholas Walsh
			Matthew Fay
			Daniel Menzies
		13	Michael Lloyd Apjohn
		21	Henry Baker
	5	10	Paul Cullen
		12	Joseph Barcroft
	6	13	John Franks
			Robert Marshall
	8	7	William Boake
		10	Jacob Wiggins
		24	Edward Gatchell
	9	24	Joshua Strangman
	10	26	Joseph Greer
	11	16	John Hughes
		29	Henry Pim
			Frederick Pim
1814			
	1	7	James Connell
			Thomas Connell
	2	12	David Taylor
	3	3	Jonathan Richardson
		19	Peter Lyon
		21	George Smith
	4	1	Wm. Robinson, Anthony
		3	Joseph Waring
		4	Edward Singleton
		15	George Morgan
			Henry Morgan
			Jeremiah Morgan
			Nicholas Baker
		27	Sandford Palmer
	5	19	George O'Connor
		31	Edward Newenham Hoare
	6	12	Arthur Gloster
		13	Stephen Winthrop Blood
		16	John Briarly
			Joshua Harvey
	8	9	Henry Wall
			Joshua Harvey, Reuben
			John Harvey
			Joshua Malcomson
		11	John O'Neill
		12	Ralph Smyth
		15	George Pim
			Jonathan Greenwood Pim
		16	Joseph Brown
		28	William Thom
			John Thom
	9	1	Edward Newenham
		8	William Haughton
	10	4	John Straton
			Robert Straton
		11	Nathan Gatchell
		17	Henry Thompson
			James Thompson
			Thomas Doyle
		29	Jonathan Pim
	11	2	John Rynd
	12	4	Thomas Robert Barton
1815			
	1	31	Joseph Metcalf
			Charles Metcalf
	3	14	Samuel Walker
	4	13	John Lecky Watson
	5	1	Joseph Doyle
		8	George White
			Edward White
		10	John Bell
			Samuel Lapham
	6	1	John Sprig
		15	William Chapman
	8	6	William Burke
		13	George Eagle
	10	11	Robert Parke
		29	Bernard Murray
	11	10	Joshua Abell
1816			
	2	2	Thomas Hancock Davis
	3	11	William Jackson
	4	1	Samuel Manliffe Wright
	5	12	John McCormic
	6	5	John Gale
	8	4	Henry White
		29	Wm. Thomas Brewster
	10	9	Samuel Allin
			John Allin
		13	Thomas Burton
	11	12	Lemuel Dunbar Barton
		13	Alexander Harper
1817			
	1	12	Thomas Allin
			Samuel Green
		14	Robert Ball
		27	Philip Walsh
			John C. Lloyd
	4	12	James Pim
	5	6	James Butterfield
		22	William Cooke
	6		James Dixon
		27	Richard Fitzsimmons
	7	14	John Meredith
			Thomas Meredith
		16	John Dixon
			Martin Ennis

Year	Month	Day	
	9	3	Francis Hennis
	12	30	Edward Haughton
1818			
	1	10	William Jenkins
		19	Thomas Simpson
			George Simpson
	2	7	Benj. Wilson Greenwood
	3	2	Manliff Barrington
	4	21	George Ashe
		28	Christopher Bagot
		29	John Garnett Coghlan
	5	17	William Carter
	6	1	Thomas Hyland
			William Hyland
			John Dawson
		2	James Pim
		10	Joseph White
			Henry Fowler
		15	William Ashe
		18	Thomas Calvert
		24	Nicholas Grattan
	7	13	Henry Donnelly
			Birmingham Donnelly
			Edward Irvine Donnelly
			Frederick Donnelly
		28	William Edmundson
	9	10	Samuel Hill
		21	James Glaizbrook
	10	8	Charles Fitzroy Neynoe
1819			
	2	1	Saunders Barton
		11	Henry Dawson
			Edward Dawson
		24	Richard Murray
	3	8	Stephen Wilson
			John Wilson
		9	Richard Going
	4	3	Gabriel Joseph Fisher
		19	Thomas Cronyn
	5	7	William Penrose Watson
		8	Thomas Webb
		10	George Gregg
	6	7	John Strangman
		18	John Stephens
		28	Richard Davis Webb
	7	4	Lawrence Maxton
		26	Joseph Allen
			Lewis Rawson
			Thomas Rawson
	8	2	John Miley
		28	William Brydges Neynoe
	9	23	Hill Hamilton
	10	1	Jeremiah Taylor Hunt
		10	Francis Davis
		27	John Hoysted Fenton
	11	3	Richard Bolton
			Richard Vesey
		11	Joshua Edmundson
			William Butler

Year	Month	Day	
1820			
	1	25	John O'Neill
	4	10	Thomas McCheane
	8	26	Edward Golding
		31	Francis Penrose Cherry
	9	16	James Robert Clarke
	10	2	Thomas William Boake
		4	John Stuart Murray
1821			
	1	10	Charles White
	2	21	John Kelly
	3	1	George Penrose Neale
			William Bourke
		12	Benjamin Cox
	9	4	Thos. Hancock Strangman
		11	William Alexander Helton
		18	John Carroll
		29	Edward Smith
	11	5	Robert Lecky
	12	8	John Conran
1822			
	1	19	Thomas Kelly
	2	4	Thomas Pim
		16	Matthew Biggs
	3	23	Thomas Pim Nevins
		25	Joseph Pim
	4	1	Edward Barton
	5	6	Joseph Gilmore
		7	Wilkins Goodwin
		14	Edward Cullen
	8	9	Joshua Grubb
			Jonathan Richardson
		26	Wight Pike
			William Hill Pike
	10	9	Henry Harrington Wall
	11	9	Robert Gilmore
			Edward Nicholson
			John Boake
			Samuel Boake
1823			
	1	1	Robert Malcomson
		10	James Crowe
			John Bell
	3	5	James Dickinson
		5	Jaffray Harvey
		7	Robert T. Hendrick
	5	4	John Langtry Bell
	6	10	Samuel Grubb
		8	Edward Harding
	8	16	Samuel Greer
		27	John Todhunter
			Joshua Edmundson Todhunter
		30	George Wynne
	9	8	William Hogg
		12	William Cherry
	10	8	Robert Crowe
			William Crowe

Year	Month	Day	
		9	William Harvey Pim
	12	5	Gifford Glascott
1824			
	1	7	Thomas Haughton White
	4	10	Thomas Browning
		12	John Williams
		18	George S. Barclay
		24	David Malcomson
	5	24	John Grubb Richardson
	6	10	William Henry Harvey
	7	3	Samuel Knott
	8	14	Robert V. Griffith
	9	4	Joseph White
	10	18	Henry Higginson Fitzsimmons
	12	10	David Browning
1825			
	1	26	Henry Goouch
	2	3	Giles Keane
		28	William Fayle
	3	1	William Cullen
			James Cullen
		26	Joseph Hatton
	4	4	John Thacker
	8	24	James Clibborn Hill
		29	John Classon
	9	3	Thomas Williams
			Obadiah Williams
		6	Richard Pim
			John Boake, returned boarder
		10	Thomas Pim
		13	Anthony Singleton
		16	Samuel Hanks
	10	1	Henry Williams
		22	Joshua Jackson
	11	3	James Henry Webb
	12	15	Richard Cherry
1826			
	1	5	Thomas Johnson
	2	7	Thomas Agmondisham Vesey
		8	Charles Miller
			William Rowley Miller
			Samuel Strangman
	8	10	Wakefield Pim
		18	John Greeves O'Brien
	9	9	Nathaniel Thompson
	10	6	Albert White
		28	Thomas Jackson
	11	26	Travers Arthur Golding
			Dupré Golding
1827			
	2	12	John Croker
	4	9	Silvester Kelly
	5	13	Edward Biggam
	9	7	Edward Davis
		10	Richard Langtry Bell

Year	Month	Day	
		12	Edward Strangman
	10	16	Thomas Martin
	11	17	Thomas Pim Goodbody
1828			
	1	13	John Simpson
	4	9	Joshua George Fennell
	8	7	Richard Pike
			James Nicholson Pike
		19	William Langtry Bell
		20	Joseph Grubb
			John Grubb
	10	16	Andrew Watson Mahony
		17	Johsua Pim
	11	4	Thomas Greer
		15	James Cooper
1829			
	3	25	Thomas Newberry Russell
	8	17	Alexander Allen
		20	William Pike
			George Langtry Bell
	9	2	James Pike
		5	Robert Grubb
		25	Abraham Grubb Davis
	10	9	Thomas Malcomson
	11	14	Henry Hoare
1830			
	4	23	Andrew James Newton
	8	9	William Uprichard
1831			
	1	11	Jas. Nicholson Richardson
			Henry Torrens
	8	16	James McCullagh
			Thomas Richardson
	10	10	Joseph Henry
			Thomas Chandlee
			Jehu Henry
1832			
	3	25	William Greer
	8	2	Charles West
		11	William K. Fayle
			William Robinson
			Joshua Eves
			Joseph Poole
			Theophilus Fielding Ashe
		13	Joshua Forbes Russell
		14	Charles A. Pim
			John T. Pim
			Henry William Holland
		17	James Clibborn
			Mark Flower
			Alfred Grubb
		26	William Atkinson
	11	1	Thomas White Waring
		30	Joseph Richardson
			William Richardson
1833			
	4		John Greer

Year	Month	Day	
			Louis F. Goodbody
	8		Joshua Fennell
			Thomas J. Fennell
			William Roche
	8	30	John T. White
			Arthur Gordon
	10		William H. Conran
	11	16	Joseph Carroll
			Joshua Carroll
1834			
			John Falls
			Robert Bell
			Richard Dowd
	11	3	Joseph Charles Harvey
		12	George Fennell
			Charles Fennell
1835*			
	3	6	Henry Fennell
		8	Roderick Miley
	5	30	Robert Dowd
	6	1	Thomas Conran
	8	7	Richard Davis Grubb
1836			
	2	20	Henry Cherry
		22	James H. Pim
	5	4	Robert Cooke
	8	27	Jonas Barclay
			William Barclay
			Henry Barclay
	8	15	William Harvey
			Reuben Harvey
			Thomas Harvey

*** 1855 in second edition.**

In many instances students listed in January appear to be included in the previous year, e.g. Jonathan Bowles, Amos Rooke and Barcroft Fuller are presumably from 1727, but are listed in 1728.

Possible misspellings are retained as in the original e.g. 1768 Thomas Lhoyd – later that year Robert Lloyd was enrolled and the previous year George Lloyd had been enrolled. 1784 Issac Wilson.

APPENDIX.

The original editor removed a description of the village in 1766 from Chapter One of the Annals of Ballitore and replaced it with Mary Leadbeater's poem, 'Ballitore,' which we felt obliged to reproduce here as it had been included in the printed volume. This appendix is a modern (2008) creation.

[The punctuation differs in the original editions, the version here is based on the 2nd edition]

BALLITORE.

(A poem by Mary Leadbeater, 1788)

Lo! rosy Summer now draws nigh,
And Spring resigns the weeping sky:
Slow she retires, and turns again,
As loath to leave the lovely plain;
While buxom Summer, bright and fair,
Comes sailing on the glowing air,
And joys in Griese's silver wave
Her loose ambrosial locks to lave.
Then come, my friend, and taste once more
The beauties of sweet Ballitore;
This charming spot, where joys abound,
By rising hills encompass'd round;
Fair hills, which rear the golden brow,
And smile upon the vale below.
   Let us begin, where fair and wide,
Grac'd with young elms on either side,
The lov'd Mill–avenue we tread,
Dear to the daughters of the shade.
As some fair virgin sits retir'd,
In lovely, lowly state admir'd,
Her beauties but in part reveal'd,
The rest in modest guise conceal'd;
So Ballitore from hence is seen,
Half hid in shades of deepest green.
Where'er one turns his raptur'd sight,
The beauteous landscape gives delight,
The verdant groves, the enamell'd meads,
The rising hills, and opening glades;
Neat houses here and there he sees
Dispers'd among the tufted trees;
The cultur'd fields with plenty blest,
In summer's pride the gardens drest,
The crystal streams, which gently flow,
Diffusing nurture as they go;
And Griese, that, with meandering glide,
Past the sweet village rolls its tide.

Our minds the pleasing prospect fills,
Environ'd by the distant hills;
Delightful hills, which gently rise,
And seem to kiss the bending skies.
Far as the eye can reach, we view
A tow'ring structure, fair and new;
Then a contrasted scene behold,
A castle ruinous and old.
Contemplative, in these we find
Fit objects for the musing mind;
So generations pass away,
Born, rising, hast'ning to decay.
Onward our saunt'ring steps we bend,
And now the little bridge ascend:–
How sweet to stand and gaze around,
And listen to the dashing sound
Of the white wave, which foams along,
Tumbling the rugged stones among!
There rears that house its modest head,
Where my blest hours of childhood fled:
Amidst these bow'rs so sweet and gay
Sally and I were wont to stray;
Nature's soft chain, with friendship twin'd,
Our sister hearts in one combin'd.
Here as a sheet of silver bright
The mill-pond charms the dazzled sight,
Deck'd with the sallow's hoary pride;
We walk admiring by its side.
We cross the dyke, the field we gain,
The fair Mill-field, a lovely plain:
But lovelier once, all gaily drest,
The cowslip gilding o'er her breast;
The ruthless plough her bosom tore,
The golden cowslip charms no more.
We come to Fuller's-court, the square
For widows fam'd and maidens fair.
Here my dame Fuller keeps her home,
And three fair daughters grace the dome;
Enter the portal when you will,
And all is neat and all is still.
There Julia's ever-open door,
Encompass'd by the smiling poor:
Or to the right direct thine eyes,–
The thread industrious Mary plies:
Though small her house, her heart is wide,
For Truth and Friendship there reside.
We pass the gate: how fair the sight!
The trees their bending heads unite;
In the blest cool we move along,
Regal'd with the wild warblers' song:
The village, through the arches green,
Is through a long perspective seen.

O'er the trim fence now cast thine eye,
The variegated landscape spy;
The sloping hill, upon whose side
The grove erects its sable pride.
Turn to the left; that structure tall
Encloses those within its wall
Who great by blood, but greater far
By manners and by virtues, are.
See in the grove that structure neat,
Here we for worship duly meet:
Oh, may we clothed in silence hear
The still small voice for ever near!
But, not to place and form confined,
The worship of the all–perfect Mind
Doth like the sun its beams impart,
And loves the temple of the heart.
How pleasant the surrounding grove
Where the gay students love to rove!
The stately fir with verdant head,
Dear to the Muse the beechen shade,
United form a calm retreat
From glowing summer's raging heat.
Here with soft breath the tuneful flute
To gentle Echo makes his suit,
Though not in strains so softly gay
As blooming Hall was wont to play.
Too venturous boy, where dost thou rove,
Far distant from this peaceful grove?
Beyond the vast Atlantic's wave
Dost thou the thundering battle brave?
Or, fainting, pale, and bleeding lie,
No tender parent weeping by?
Perhaps sad recollection strays
To former scenes and happier days,
To scenes which must return no more,
Thy flute, this grove, and Ballitore!
And now the School approaching near,
A humming noise salutes the ear;
The busy bees who sip the flowers
Which blossom in Parnassian bowers
Rich stores of honey thence convey–
The treasures of a future day.
The door unbarred, with mirth and glee
They rush and hail sweet Liberty.
Come, we'll attend the sprightly train
And view them sporting on the plain,
With rosy cheeks and laughing eyes
Each to his dear amusement hies.
This bids the bounding ball to fly;
That sends the feathered cork on high;
Some sling the stone with dext'rous throw,
And others bend the guiltless bow.

Those whip the whirling top, and these
The rolling marbles better please.
One in his captive linnet joys,
And one his pigeons' care employs:
These, straining every nerve on high,
Behold the kite in rapture fly;
The sweets of Nature those invite
Who, in their gardens gay, delight
To sow the tender seed in earth,
And careful watch the springing birth;
To see the flower its leaves unfold,
With crimson stained, and bright with gold;
Or on their mossy seats recline,
And duteous court the gentle Nine.
   Amongst the throng my darling Phaire
Comes singing on, devoid of care;
Belov'd of all; for o'er his head
Scarce six unspotted years have fled;
Sweeter than Spring's first blossom'd bough,
But, Skinner, not more sweet than thou–
Oh, fairest flower that grac'd our shade.
How soon did all thy glories fade!
   When Winter comes, it hath its charms;
E'en Winter's cold their bosoms warms;
Fearless they tempt the frozen tide,
And o'er the slippery surface glide;
Or with incessant pains and care
On high the snowy pillar rear,
Or in the hall at close of day,
While six fair tapers lend their ray,
They turn the instructive page, and find
A feast to feed the immortal mind.
Some trace the map with curious eye,
And point where different kingdoms lie;
Here those self-taught the pencil guide,
And imitate the garden's pride,
While these, with more exalted views,
Record the labours of the Muse.
   Say why each eye so bright appears,
Why every cheek contentment wears?
See where divine Hygeia stands,
And scatters blessings from her hands;
She o'er the cheek the roses spread,
And tinged the lip with brighter red,
Kindled the lightening of the eye,
And taught the nimble feet to fly.
Not all the jewels that adorn
The crown by Britain's monarch worn
Can equal or compare at all
With those that grace my father's hall.
   Scorn not these scenes which simply please;
Great Burke once led a life like these;

Though Britain's cause he now maintains,
He sported on these verdant plains;
Though now his numbers swell so strong,
Here tuned his Muse her infant song.
   Yet even these have ills to bear;
No state on earth is free from care.
Perhaps in playful transport tost
The ball or shuttlecock is lost;
The pigeons wander, linnet dies,
And sorrow dims the brightest eyes;
Or, when the kite sublimely sails,
Upborne by all the flying gales,
The cord is broken, down she flies,
And distant fields receive the prize.
Or when the gardens shine most bright,
(Alas how transient is delight!)
Some roving dog, in luckless hour,
Has trampled down the fairest flower;
Or filthy swine with brutal taste
Has laid the pride of Summer waste:
Or when they hope secure to glide,
Descending rain has marred their slide;
Their pillar, late so snowy-white,
Deformed and spoiled disgusts the sight.
   Lo! the poor invalid on high
From the sick chamber casts his eye,
Behold their sports with jealous pain,
And wishes for his health again.
   See all forlorn the new-come boy!
Tasteless to him each scene of joy:
How does he solitary roam,
And whine, and sigh, and think of home!
Some thoughtless lads deride the swain,
While others pitying soothe his pain;
Thus (while they wipe his tears away):
"Like thee we mourn'd: but now can say
No joys more sweet than here thou'lt find;
So give thy sorrows to the wind."
   Alas, what grief, should Vice invade
With backward steps this learned shade.
Or Folly, with unmeaning face,
Intrude into this happy place!
No longer are ye dear to fame,
But fall a prey to guilt and shame;
Your glory fades, and ye no more
Are deemed the pride of Ballitore.
But heav'n avert the fatal day
Which takes your innocence away!
   Learning's the growth of Ballitore;
With caution ope that close-shut door.
High in an antique chair of state
The village mistress keeps her seat;

Her little subjects standing by
Their horn–books and their samplers ply,
Watching with fear her awful nod,
And trembling at the lifted rod.
These piers were once the Burrow–gate;
(Beneath each pier is placed a seat
From whence the never–wearied eye
As far as Fuller's Court can spy;
The trees so green, the houses white
With mingled beauties charm the sight.)
The old, the gay, the grave, the young
Here to the village forum throng:
Here ragged politicians muse,
And tell the listening crowd the news.
On the new bridge, fast by, we stay,
And the Retreat's loved walls survey.
Before the door, a grateful view,
A verdant carpet nature threw,
With thousand colours gaily dyed,
All bright in summer's rosy pride:
Here the diseaséd poor repair
To tell my pitying aunt their care;
She hastens to relieve their woes,
Bids Famine feed, and Pain repose.
The road hence from our village leads,
Which trees adorn with bending heads;
So thick the twisting branches blend,
They hide the hill we must ascend.
So when the present bliss we know
We look not at the future woe.
This hill so steep when we descend,
Our feet with quickest motion bend;
But, when ascending, leave with pain
The beauties of this charming plain.
Still lingering on the bridge we stay
While the sun shoots his evening ray:
Wide spread the silver waters here,
Unruffled, calm, serene and clear;
But, straitened at the other side,
With gently–tinkling murmurs glide;
A darker gloom these waves arrays,
On those a brighter lustre plays.
And now the setting orb from high
Rolls down the blushing western sky;
Around he throws his parting fires,
And in a blaze of gold retires.
On every side we cast our eyes,
Behold, the fading landscape dies;
The glowing colours melt away,
And twilight dims the eye of day.
But yonder, see, arrayed in light
Mounts the pale empress of the night,

Walking in brightness through the shades.
Onward the host of heaven she leads,
Brighter she gains the etherial way,
And sheds around a milder day;
From high beholds her silver beam
Reflected in the lucid stream.
The stream, rejoiced so bright a guest
Should sleep upon his placid breast,
Would fain his gliding waters stay,
With her delightful locks to play.
   A solemn silence reigns around,
No busy footsteps beat the ground,
The moon no careful watch–dogs bay,
No breezes shake the bending spray,
No flute awakes the slumbering grove,
Where not a leaf is heard to move;
Scarce heard the distant dying sound,
Such solemn silence reigns around.
   Here ends our walk – and here, my friend,
The gay description I shall end;
These lines present no fancied view,
'Twas truth the faithful landscape drew.
Here from the busy world retired,
The fragrant air I first inspired,
And here may all my days be spent,
With innocence and sweet content;
With contemplation ever calm,
And friendship, life's most precious balm!
But where are all these blessings found,
Unless by thee, Religion, crowned?
O, be thou first to gain my breast,
And be it worthy of the guest!
Content and innocence appear,
Celestial maid, when thou art here;
Thou raisest Contemplation's eye,
To see the blest abodes on high:
Our friendships, formed by thee, endure;
'Tis thou who can'st our bliss secure:
Thou bid'st our passions all subside;
Be thou my guardian and my guide;
Then in this sweet sequestered shade,
More lovely by thy presence made,
Remote from envy, care, and strife,
Calm shall I pass my quiet life,
Taste purer joys when these are o'er,
And lay my bones in Ballitore!

BALLITORE & ITS INHABITANTS

SEVENTY YEARS AGO.

By BETSY SHACKLETON.

From Carney's-hills to Narraghmore,
From Moone to Inchiquire,
'Tis claffic ground round Ballitore,
Sin' auld lang syne.

Joseph Harvey.

DUBLIN:
PRINTED BY RICHARD D. WEBB AND SON.

1862.

Title page of original edition

PREFACE.

WHEN the editor of this little volume became a Ballitore schoolboy in June, 1819, he had just entered his fifteenth year, an age which is probably exceeded by no other period of life in the capacity for suffering or enjoyment.[162] He had lately been removed from a boarding school in a dull country town, situated in a flat, uninteresting district of Ireland. The superintendent of the establishment was coarse, sensual, hypocritical and cruel; the social arrangements of the place were cold and comfortless, the discipline was harsh, the house was like a barrack, the play–ground like a barrack–yard, and the mental diet scanty and unattractive. It was a deplorable place, and is fruitful in dismal recollections. Oh! what a change to Ballitore!

This village is embosomed in a beautiful valley, the little river Griese meandering through the fields, with wooded hills on either hand. One of these is called the Nine Tree Hill, and although not more than five hundred feet above the sea level, it commands a very extensive and lovely prospect of the plains of Kildare and Carlow, and the distant highlands of Wicklow, Kilkenny, and the Queen's County, including some of the loftiest elevations in Ireland, for example, Lugnaquilla, Thonalagee, Cadeen, Mount Leinster, Black Stairs, and Slieve Bloom.

The School–house was – and is, for the house still stands, though the school is no more – a venerable two–storied building, with a court–yard in front. Having been built at different periods within the last hundred and fifty years, it is full of all sorts of small rooms and labyrinthine passages, such as excite curiosity when first inspected, and cling to the memory through life. Behind the house was the playground, a fine cheerful open yard, ornamented with lofty poplars, and separated by a green painted railing from a large and beautiful garden and orchard.

The school was then well filled, and the master was James White, son–in–law to the second Abraham Shackleton. All who knew him can testify to the sweetness of his disposition, the vast range of his aquirements in philology, mathematics, and general knowledge, his prodigious memory, his remarkable modesty, and his entire freedom from pedantry or the ostentation of learning. Besides his rich intellectual endowments and the great scope of his attainments, he was generous, high–minded, and so kind–hearted, that many of his pupils, whose parents or guardians failed in keeping their engagements with him, continued still to experience his protecting care, and have acknowledged their life–long debt of gratitude to him. He always appealed to the higher feelings of his pupils, and endeavoured to lead rather than to compel them into the paths of learning. Corporal punishment he detested, and he considered that any advantage arising from the agency of emulation is more than counterbalanced by the spirit of envy, and the other bad passions which it is apt to excite in the breasts of disappointed candidates. The school was full of life, ease, and social enjoyment; for not only was there a free and friendly, yet respectful intercourse between the pupils, their master, and his wife and sister, but the boys had also this advantage, that in the village itself, which contained many families, – all living in competence, on the same social level, but with great simplicity and freedom from ostentation, – there were many open doors to such of them as had any claim from relationship or community of literary taste. In this last particular the Friends in Ballitore were noted above all others in Ireland. There was probably no living member of the sect who exceeded James White in the vast stores of his knowledge.

In an open part of the village, near the market–place, lived William Leadbeater, and in their little parlour his admirable wife might generally be found pursuing her literary avocations, yet always ready with cordial and polite courtesy to bear with the interruptions of visitors, whether rich or poor, old or young. With them lived their three gifted daughters.

At Fuller's–court resided Ebenezer Shackleton, whose first wife was the second daughter of Mary Leadbeater. He was a sagacious man, of a penetrating, original, many–sided intellect, generous in no common degree, disliking or despising mere profession, but doing as much good in secret as would have made an enviable reputation for a more ordinary individual.

Then there was Betsy Barrington's venerable old house, a very temple of comfort, kindness and hospitality, the resort of "Friends travelling in the ministry." Many of the old "Ballitore boys," of whom not a few are now beyond sixty, have delightful recollections of the cordial welcome, the snug little parlour, the well–spread tea table, the piles of alphabet cards, and the enjoyment they had in seeking their destiny in a time–worn copy of *Wither's Emblemes* (printed in 1635), in which their kind hostess took such innocent pride, and of which she told so many stories of predictions in its pages having been wonderfully fulfilled.

During our school days the Mill–house was the home of Lydia, the widow of Abraham Shackleton, and with her lived her sons Richard and George, and her daughters Betsy and Mary, of whom the younger son and daughter alone survive. Lydia Shackleton had been a beauty in her youth, and at an advanced age she retained a fair complexion, great dignity and ease of manner, active and industrious habits, a good memory, and correct and fluent language. She was one of the most lady–like women it has ever been our lot to meet. A native of Manchester, which she left when very young, she retained her English accent through life, and was fond of relating anecdotes of the home of her childhood. She was a descendant of Judge Fell, so often mentioned in *George Fox's Journal* as a protector of the persecuted Friends, and whose widow took for her second husband the founder of Quakerism. She also claimed as one of her ancestors the celebrated martyr Anne Askew, who perished at the stake in the reign of Henry the Eighth. Besides the families we have named, there were Thomas and Fanny Bewley, their young and beautiful daughter Lucy, Mary and Anne Doyle, Doctor Davis, and many others, who formed a somewhat numerous circle of intelligent and unaffected people, united by the ties of friendship, affection, and mutual esteem.

It was in this charming Ballitore, which, though sadly stripped of its former ornaments, still contains a community of Friends who live in the same ancient simplicity, that the writer became acquainted with Betsy Shackleton, the author of the following pages. She was then in her thirty–sixth year, having been born in 1783. The recollection is as fresh as if yesterday of her lively manners, expressive countenance, dark hair, dark eyes, fresh complexion, and sweet smile, her sympathizing disposition, and energetic and industrious habits. She was ever doing or contriving some good thing. Deeply and truly religious herself, she aimed rather to guide and instruct the tastes, habits, and judgment of her poor neighbours than to imbue them with her doctrinal opinions. She was diligent in her attendance at the poor–school, and took an active and zealous part in every effort for the benefit of those who required her sympathy and assistance. To her sick friends she was a willing nurse, to the suffering a sure sympathizer. She delighted in the unostentatious exercise of that power which none possess in such perfection as accomplished and sensible women, of purifying, elevating, and judiciously directing the tastes and habits of the youth who come within their influence. Having acute feelings with a delicate perception of poetic beauty and a strong sense of humour, she enjoyed with keen relish the writings of Pascal, and the finer passages of Burns and Cowper; and she reproduced with dramatic fidelity the idiomatic wit and drollery of the Irish peasantry, in a series of Dialogues which she wrote at the commencement of the temperance reformation, with a view to popularize her own views of the best means of promoting habits of cleanliness, order, and sobriety among our people. Many of these were printed in large numbers, and widely circulated.

Her domestic affections were intense, and were lavished with a vehemence which overwhelmed her with affliction, when, in 1811, her darling sister Lydia, first wife of James White, died of consumption after a lingering illness, in the twenty–fourth year of her age. This beloved relative was of a remarkably sweet and engaging disposition, and was truly "an angel in the house."[163] Betsy Shackleton lamented this loss most bitterly – and her grief – unlike that ordinarily felt for the death of relations or friends – continued with remarkable poignancy almost as long as life lasted. She attached herself to her sister's only surviving child with all the affection of the fondest mother, and after her niece's marriage, in 1832, her anxious affection was unsparingly bestowed upon her children.

The death in 1826 of her aunt Leadbeater, to whom she was tenderly attached, was also very severely felt by her, and it was to assuage by employment the anguish of this bereavement, that she shortly after wrote a little volume of "Recollections" of her venerated relative. A few copies only were privately printed for circulation amongst intimate friends; for, although correct in her delineation, she depicts a being so good, so guileless, and so free from the unamiable infirmities of humanity, that she would be naturally liable to the charge of exaggeration.

The "Recollections" suggested the composition of the following reminiscences of her own childhood. A copy of this little work, in the author's own handwriting, was presented by her to the editor more than a quarter of a century ago, and the recent publication of the charming "Annals of Ballitore" having induced him to search for it among his papers, he has been so struck by the vivid sketches of old times, the lively delineations of character, and the amusing incidents with which it abounds, that it occurred to him to publish a small edition, so that the pleasure of its perusal may be partaken by a larger circle than was practicable while it remained in its manuscript form.

Besides the insight it gives into the character of the writer, this little book is a contribution to that valuable class of literature which faithfully depicts the real workings of the infant mind. Betsy Shackleton was deeply sensible of the misery which children suffer from harshness and want of sympathy. She regarded with dislike approaching to horror the discipline to which they were sometimes subjected by the generation then passing away, and was most anxious to promote a kindlier and more considerate treatment of that which was rising around her.

From the remarkably sensitive and reflective character of her mind, it will be justly concluded that she was diffident and had an humble opinion of herself. This will be more fully seen from the following letter, which, a few hours before her death, she dictated to her niece, Hannah Suliot, for the satisfaction of her sister Mary, who was desirous to know the state of her mind.[164] While dictating it, she found great difficulty in speaking, and the last few words could hardly be understood.

"Dear sister Mary,

Thou wishes to know the state of my mind at this awful period. I have nothing to boast of and little to encourage. I hear a good deal of usefulness; but those acts are not fit to enter into the kingdom; they are mixed with earthly things – vanity and hypocrisy – so that I really believe that some actual sins that have been repented of are more acceptable in the

Divine sight than such proud virtues. How can He who is of too pure eyes to behold iniquity permit of beings clothed in such virtues to enter the kingdom? But there are precious promises that we shall be washed clean by the Redeemer. I am sometimes afraid that I address myself too familiarly to the great Creator; yet we are invited to come boldly to the throne of grace. At other times I am so struck with the insignificance of myself, and the inconceivable greatness of the Creator of the universe, that I wonder how I can suppose it possible that I can be noticed; but then we are assured that the very hairs of our head are numbered. Thus do I converse with myself of fears and hopes; but mercy is the pervading subject, and the close of all contemplations. Thy very affectionate sister."

Betsy Shackleton died of a lingering and painful illness on the 9th of March, 1843, in the sixtieth year of her age, and her remains rest in the Friends' burial ground on the hill side at Ballitore, where repose so many worthies, including her own ancestors for many generations.

CONTENTS.

BALLITORE & ITS INHABITANTS

SEVENTY YEARS AGO.

CHAPTER I.

The way to the village. – Aunt Fuller's dog Fox, and her very genteel daughter Debby. – Terrors at a funeral. – The handsomest woman in the world and her parrot. – Infant criticism on Quaker inconsistency. – A child's imaginations. – A farrier surgeon. – The meeting-house. – Notable members of the congregation. – Some particulars of Quaker costume. – The extreme difficulty of sitting still. – Molly Haughton. – Aunt Mellor's wonderful bonnet. – Grandfather Shackleton. – Adventure in the meeting-house. – Joshua Beale. – Bob Hudson. – Infant intolerance. – A village baker and her maid Poll Pepper. – The first Abraham Shackleton's first house in Ballitore. – Vicissitudes of aunt Mellor. – Beauty preserved without soap or water. – Joe Willis's house and garden in the golden days. – Johnny Gavin's splendid signboard. 262 to 270

I WILL go back to the utmost stretch of my memory, beginning at the Mill-house, where I now write. Captain Peaton lived here at that time. On our way to the village we walked close by the Mill-pond 'till we reached the corner of the Mill-field, and proceeded along a path by the hedge.[165]

My Aunt Fuller lived at Fuller's-court. Her dog Fox used to frighten me with his very shrill bark, which I thought resembled the voice of his mistress. I looked upon her daughter Debby as a person of very great gentility, because she wore high-coloured silk gowns which made a rustling noise as she walked into meeting. From tradition and from the happy verses handed down from the golden age, I learned that there had been an orchard in the mill-field, of which I never saw any vestige. I remember, however, the large trees which met at top over the road from Fuller's-court to Molly Haughton's neat cottage.[166] Molly was very neat; she also had a smart little dog. In 1789, Molly's husband, Joss Haughton, died. My grandmother took me to the funeral. I was very much frightened at the prospect, thinking we were either to go into the grave with the body, or up to the sky. My only consolation was the reflection that all the people would not go to the funeral unless they expected to come safe back, and therefore I had as good a chance of safety as the rest.

The next house was Bob Bayly's.[167] His wife I conceived to be the handsomest woman in the world.[168] At this house there was a parrot which I longed to see, as much as we can long for what we deem to be quite out of our reach; and such was the notion I had either of entering that house or of seeing the parrot, much less of hearing it speak.

Nearly opposite Bayly's was Hannah Haughton's.[169] I wondered that a plain Friend like Hannah who would not wear ribbons herself was satisfied to sell them, though I don't suppose I mentioned my surprise to any one. I believe children think very deeply without ever proposing their doubts. Perhaps in the present happy age for children the case may be different, for their thoughts and meaning are now sought out. In my time our inquiries were often thought impertinent. I am persuaded, however, that even now children do not communicate their best and finest thoughts, for many of them could not be uttered. This reminds me of the grandeur of some of my ideas when about four years of age. Pascal speaks of "the grandeur and the misery of man." They are often combined, and they were so with me, when I walked about the parlour wondering how I came into the world, how the parlour was made, how the ceiling was held up, how the world was created, the ground spread out, and the sky supported – still recurring to myself as I walked about between the earth and sky. Perhaps the original ideas of children come nearer to the Divine sublimity and simplicity of the Bible than all the philosophy of the learned. About this time I remember lying in bed grieving at the possibility of my father and mother dying; and sometimes I was tortured by the idea of men being hanged. The image of the condemned man coming out to execution was vividly before me, and the anguish of his mind. I pictured to myself the horrid spectacle of a field of battle; the contending armies moving towards each other, the cannon, the swords, the bloodshed, appeared to me in their unsophisticated reality, unhallowed by policy or custom. Such are the views of children. Cruelty and injustice appear to them in their naked deformity.

A row of poor cabins was separated from Hannah Haughton's by a gate, as at present. Mary Kelly, who was nearly supported by Hannah, lived in one of them. Ned Lennon, a farrier, lived in another. He bled Anna Taverner in his best style when his hand was steadied with whiskey.

The Meeting-house was on the other side of the road, as it is now, but there was no patten-room, nor any women's meeting-room.[170] The roof was supported by a pillar from which issued two great arms. These, I dare say, added to the solemnity of its appearance in our young eyes. The gallery ran the whole length of the building opposite to the entrance, so that there were fewer seats then than at present, but this deficiency was compensated by the side seats, where I believe every person had his or her own place. My aunt Fuller sat in the highest corner; next sat my grandmother, who was worthy to sit in the front of the meeting [*i.e.* in the gallery], but her weak eyes forbade her sitting opposite to the light. She wore a singular black bonnet composed of several pieces, having a pasteboard front, a crown like a hood, and a large cape. She always took this off in meeting, and appeared in a black hood, one of the symbols of a plain Friend. She wore a cloth cloak all the year round, with a little standing collar. She also wore a green tabinet apron, another symbol as characteristic as the black hood. Both of these were only worn in meetings and only by Friends who were most strict or in the highest estimation. Next to my grandmother sat Debby Wilson, who wore a soft silk cloak which I cannot forget because I longed so much that my screeching lutestring was like it, for I could not stir my hands without the whole meeting hearing my rustling. Next sat Madge Boake, Nelly Hudson, Abby Widdows, Molly Webster and Molly Hudson, all old or elderly, and sitting according to their degrees of rank. Under the gallery sat my mother, Abby Haughton, Anna Taverner, and my two aunts, Mary and Sally Shackleton.[171] The latter had lately begun to speak in meeting. Anna Taverner also spoke now and then with great elegance and feeling. Her delicacy and her English accent, no doubt, added to the charm of her sweet voice. All these last–mentioned Friends wore black hoods but not green aprons. I used, while in meeting, to long for a hot day in summer, not only for the charm of hot weather, the wonder it excites, the happy and languishing idleness and the brilliancy of nature, but that I might see what sort of clothes these black–hooded Friends would wear, and wherewithal I should be dressed myself. I remember the pleasure with which I viewed their little white silk or muslin handkerchiefs, their summer gloves and light gowns; but, above all, Anna Taverner's. I think I see her elegantly and feebly creeping into meeting, with a harebine gown of the most delicate shade and exquisitely neat.[172] All the rest of her habiliments were spotless, and put on with a peculiar grace, suiting her stooped and weakly but beautiful person. I was so blind as not to know 'till I was a big girl that she had a beautiful face. Anxiety and debility had given a sorrowful expression to her countenance. Through these I could see no beauty, and I even thought her unusually the reverse. Abby Haughton's smooth forehead and smiling mouth pleased my fancy, and she was really very pretty; so was my mother.

We, children, sat on a little seat at the head of the meeting, facing the gallery. I can associate little else but pain with my meetings. Being very impatient and restless, I found it impossible to sit still. I am persuaded that no Friend in the meeting laboured harder for stillness than I did, and I used to try to wish that meeting might not break up soon. All in vain; as soon as I came home, I was told of my misconduct. As I have experienced so much woe when a child from my behaviour in meetings, I am inclined to make great allowance for the restlessness of children at such a time. I suppose I should have been more still, had I been less watched by myself and others. Let any grown person be placed before his judges with orders to keep perfectly still, will he not feel his nose itching, his back aching, his curiosity burning to see objects behind him, and, in short, his whole body weary of remaining in the same position. It is a species of torture, and not of the lightest kind.

On the seat behind me sat Hannah Haughton, Jenny Boake, and other grown–up young Friends of our rank.

I forgot to mention Molly Haughton who sat on the side seat. She was a distant relation of Bob Bayly's, and wore a large black satin cloak. This had belonged to the late Susy Bayly, who had been brought up a Friend, and was one of the renowned family of the Strettells. I may as well acquaint the curious reader that Molly was a tall, straight woman, with long taper waist, large hips, and small head. Her old–fashioned cap was worn so as to expose her large forehead, and was tightly bound by a ribbon, which I verily believe compressed the part it surrounded. We know that the human form may be changed by pressure. Molly was a pleasant woman. When we visited her she generally welcomed us with a scolding for our long absence; but this was done in a good humoured way. "Oh ho," she would say, shading her eyes with her hand, "is thee come at last? It's time for thee. 'Tis good for sore eyes to see thee. We ought to nick the post, or spread rushes under thy feet. Well! what news? Did thee hear So–and–so was married? And, by all I hear, it was a poor match enough. They tell me she had a fine fortune, but there's no believing the half one hears." The price of provisions and fuel was generally discussed. We always found Molly well stored with news of every kind, and it was a pleasure to add to her stock, for she never heard anything with indifference. She was either surprized, or shocked, or glad, or sorry – just as we wished. The most indifferent of our jokes was complimented by the ready laugh, whilst the sympathetic sigh was as much at our command. If the subject were quite indifferent, even to Molly's taste, she would say, "Now does thee tell me so?" or "Is it possible?" or some such comfortable expression. We may smile at this, but it is one of the secrets of domestic happiness to be easily pleased with what we hear. How many sources of enjoyment are closed to the fastidious taste; and, moreover, our fastidiousness paralyzes the social powers of our companions.

Molly was a very neat, industrious, economical body. We entered her house by the kitchen, where the utensils were always shining and the maid sat at her spinning. In the parlour, which was furnished with bright oak chairs and tables, Molly sat at her knitting, with her feet on a stool, and a switch beside her on the surbase to beat the dog for barking at strangers.

While using the switch she accompanied the strokes with a few smart words, which served at once to scold the dog and welcome the guest. Tradition says that Polly Taylor – for this was Molly's maiden name – was a fine handsome girl, that she wore a magnificent stay hook, and that she performed extraordinary feats of agility.[173]

But to return to the Meeting–house. The more gay and dressy friends sat on the seat behind Jenny Boake. My aunt Mary Mellor, my mother's younger sister, was one of these. She wore a high–cauled bonnet, kept up by wire, and having a broadish ribbon round it. It was fastened by a very long pin, which my brother Ebenezer and I thought she drove into her head when she put the bonnet on. Her long hair was turned up in a peculiar style, which was considered dressy. She also wore a black silk cloak, and in winter a muff into which she sometimes put my little cold feet, when I have been so happy as to sit beside her in meeting; and not being a strict Friend, she allowed me more latitude in fidgetting than fell to my lot when I was near the elders.

On the back seat sat Becky Widdows, Lucy Webster, Hannah Webster, and some other young women who thought too humbly of themselves to sit up higher. Old Jenny Miles also sat on the lowest seat.

At the men's side my grandfather sat next the gallery steps, which were in the middle of the length of the room.[174] I recollect seeing him with his head leaning on his hand, his face down and the tears falling from his eyes. I knew that this was caused by devotional feeling, and I seemed to catch his fervor, for I wished to be like him, putting up rapturous petitions, making covenants with my heavenly Father, confessing my sins, and being so affected as to be unable to restrain my tears. Yet even after these devotional meetings, I have received my usual portion of reproof. Probably when the sparks which were kindled by myself or by something better had gone out, my natural carelessness and restlessness returned even with redoubled force. Such has been the case through the days and years of my mature life, so that I have learned to understand the confusion which follows the compassing ourselves about with sparks of our own kindling. My father and Ephraim Boake sat under the gallery also. I remember being affected at my father's tenderness in meeting. Ephraim Boake sometimes dropped a few words to us; so did my grandfather.

On the side seat sat Ben Haughton of Prospect, Joe Haughton, John Haughton, and Tom Boake.[175] Joss Webster sat low down. Dick Manders, Dick Miles and Johnny Gavin sat inside the door; they had lost their membership in the Society either by marrying out or by drunkenness.[176] The Ballitore school–boys occupied the forms which filled up the middle of the meeting–house. As these forms had no backs, they were a great hardship upon the gristly bones of youth.

We hung our cloaks upon the back of the women's lowest seat, there being no cloak–room, or patten–room.

The gallery was not used except when ministers from other meetings visited us. The front of it was closely boarded up, and the boarding was so high, that we, children, could see nothing of the preachers except the tops of their bonnets or hats, until they stood up to address the assembly. This circumstance increased my veneration for them and my impatience to hear them speak.

When I was about eleven years old, my father and mother went to the Dublin Yearly or Half–year's Meeting, leaving us under the care of Molly Haughton. One day, as she took us early to meeting, I gratified myself by sitting in every part of the house to which I was not accustomed. While I was in the gallery, in walked Tom Boake, a quiet sedate young man. I sank down upon the floor, and was so overwhelmed with fear and shame at being seen by him in such a place, that I could not bring myself to come down. There I sat during the whole meeting, afraid to breathe or stir. I had a wretched time of it, and plenty of leisure to make good resolutions. Oh! if ever I was delivered from such miserable bondage, how sober and steady I should be. Alas! my resolutions were something like Tam O'Shanter's pleasures,

> – like the snow falls in the river.
> A moment white, then melts for ever.

At long last the dreaded moment arrived for breaking up the meeting. Much as I suffered during the sitting, I trembled at every noise indicating the breaking up, and the disclosure of my imprudence. My heart was ready to jump out of its place when the Friends rose. I could see them through the chinks of the boards moving quietly away. I knew not whom to dread most. The Ducketts were so genteel, all dressed in silks, that they seemed the worst of all. At length I saw Molly Haughton talking to them at the door, and heard her mention my doings. The fear of being caught in the gallery now overcame every other feeling, and I crept down the steps, scarcely raising up my guilty head. The formidable Ducketts laughed at me, and I got home safe, only to plunge into some other scrape. I believe I had reached the climax of my mischievous exploits about that time. I remember little else but a succession of faults and fits of remorse, broken resolutions and fruitless repentance.

Joshua Beale of Cork spent some time at my father's, helping to make some alterations in the school, which for a time were deemed improvements. He said I was proud; I believe he was mistaken. I don't know what a child could be proud of, who was always on the stool of repentance, and who wished to be like anybody but herself.

At the other side of the way from the meeting–house lived Bob Hudson, a butcher, who sometimes was drunk, and sometimes came to meeting, according to the different states of his mind.

At the same side lived Tom Johnson who kept a large shop and sold drugs. His good wife Betty was my aunt Fuller's daughter, who married Tom, out of the Society. This fault was enough to prevent me from having anything to do with them, for I was very intolerant. Nevertheless, I played with their children at Molly Webster's school. I once even ventured to go home with them, but was frightened at myself for entering their parlour. They left Ballitore about the year 1794, when they saw a distant prospect of the rebellion. After some time they removed to London, and finally returned to live in Dublin, where all their children were married, and where two of them, with the father and mother, died. My aunt Fuller also removed to Dublin, and died there in 1799. Her daughter Debby died before her. They left behind them a great many silk gowns and quilted petticoats, and fine cotton stockings with clocks in them of Debby's knitting. My aunt also left behind her the sweet savour of having fed and clothed the poor, and paid her husband's debts. The cleanliness of her kitchen is also spoken of to this day.

In the centre of the village was a row of very middling houses, where pretty good ones, built by my uncle Leadbeater, now stand. John Wilson, a shoemaker, inhabited one of them; he was a sort of a Friend, and married Betty Widdows, the faithful servant of Deborah Carleton. Another of these houses was occupied by Judy Horan, a baker. She was a widow, who reared her two little boys with care, encouraging them to work in a small garden that she might keep them out of the street. One of them is now (1826) a respectable priest, with whom she lives. Poll Pepper, her attached servant, attended the oven, ran many miles for barm, (for there was no made barm in those times) and carried loads of bread, scolding or petting the children meantime. It was said that she had been cured of the dropsy by eating raw oatmeal. She was blind the latter part of her life, and for some time before she died was supported by the neighbours.

It was in the next house to this that my grandfather was born in 1726.[177] I suppose my great grandfather lived there before he took the present School–house; and after he took it the boys continued to go to school in his old dwelling, and did so, I believe, for half a century.

About the year 1795 my aunt Mary Kathrens (formerly Mellor) and her husband came from Dublin to live in that house. She had married out of our Society. The first time I happened to be near her and her husband, as we were going to meeting, I walked at the other side of the way, so great was my zeal against transgressors. Her husband was very sickly and fretful whilst she was cheerful and full of hope. They were poor, but she had a pleasure in exerting herself. She kept the post–office, took in needle work, and dealt in various matters, though she had no shop. She had two children – Mary, who was very shy, and James, a noble creature, with black eyes and an arch smile. My uncle Katherns died of consumption in 1796. My aunt did all she could to ameliorate his sufferings, and when he was gone, she consoled herself with the reflection that she had done her duty, and that his sufferings were ended. She lived in Ballitore till after the rebellion of 1798, when she returned to Dublin, where her fine son died of the small–pox. After some years she married Henry Chambers, who soon became sickly. She nursed him tenderly till he died. She subsequently laboured under a succession of heavy trials; pecuniary difficulties came thick upon her, but her fortitude and good humour supported her. We see few wrinkles upon her pleasant countenance, and now at the age of seventy she appears little more than fifty.

Next door to my aunt Mellor lived a pair named O'Hara, with a large family of sons. That house, which is still standing, was originally built for an inn. Of Susy O'Hara, who had been a beauty, it was said that she never washed her face, but rubbed it with flannel and flour. They had one daughter, also named Susy, who was very pretty, and died young of consumption. The first time I heard of the hectic flush was in her case.

Then came Paddy Murphy's house with steps up to the hall door. We only heard of the beauty of the house, when it formerly belonged to Ben Wills.[178] It always wore a reduced aspect in our degenerate days. We used to hear that in the golden days gone by were to be seen Joe Wills's beds of tulips, his fish-pond, his trees, his walks, and all that could charm the eye. I cannot conceive how that little spot of ground between the street and the river could contain such an elysium as my father and my aunts used to describe, and which I only remember as an ugly common, till Dempsey built his house at the corner.

Then came Johnny Gavin, a shoemaker. The front of his house was adorned with a splendid sign, on which was painted a gentleman with a bright blue coat drawing on a boot. Johnny was a strange–looking man, who strutted about with a conceited air. His daughter was a belle, and his father a degenerate Friend.

Paddy Gannon lived at the corner of the street, and kept a public house, as did many others after him at that same corner. His wife was a fine-looking woman. They were several years without children, and afterwards had plenty; but they had little reason to rejoice in any of them, except one hump–backed daughter, who was very ingenious and industrious. Like many other publicans, these poor people finally sank into abject poverty.

Next to these lived Paul Brennan, a tailor. He had a beautiful wife who died in her prime, and it was said that Paul tore his hair with grief.

The Borough was a collection of miserable cabins, which were arranged into narrow lanes, on the site occupied by the present Market–house and the ground behind it. Tom Murray blowing his bellows at a miserable forge is present to my recollection. He was weak and thin, and loved good eating; his wife Biddy was strong and industrious, and tried to keep him in order. They both died of fever in the same week, in 1818. Their son settled at a distance. Molly, their only daughter, lived many years, to remind us of her languid, helpless father.

Jem Lyons' house stood alone in the Borough. He was our grave–digger for many years, but was at last laid in the grave himself. His wife, Bet Lyons, was a conspicuous character in my grandmother's kitchen.

CHAPTER II.

Molly Webster, the incomparable village school–mistress. – Joss Webster, the wool–comber – and their excellent daughter, Lucy Allmint. – Ned Miles. – Abby Widdows, and her fortunes in trade and in architecture. – Her daughter Becky. – Betty Malone. – Peggy and Nancy Brett. – Bill Lennon, the enterprising butcher. – Nurse Lennon's reminiscences of old times, and of Edmund Burke
271 to 279

BUT the house in the Borough which I best remember was Molly Webster's. She was for many years an eminent personage in our village, as school–mistress, doctress, and interpreter of dreams. Some said she also had the gift of fortune–telling, but I never was witness to its exercise. I believe there never was a better school–mistress. Those who remember her, make many invidious comparisons between the schools of the present days and Molly Webster's. Indeed I fully believe that Bell, or Lancaster, or Owen Finn never taught children to read in so short a time as my teacher. Nor was she severe. She certainly kept a little birch rod always beside her, which she sometimes held in threatening posture; and some rare times she inflicted its smart upon the skin of a plebeian. I never remember feeling it on mine, nor even the brass thimble with which she tapped the head of a dunce. In teaching the alphabet she patiently went on from + (criss–cross) to the final Zed, which she called *izzard*. She said A and the pupil said A; she said B and the pupil said B. If she was in a pleasant humour, and the pupil was very young or very good or very pretty, she would make the impression more delightful as well as more lasting by saying A was an apple–pie, B bit it, C cut it; or C for cat, D for dog, or for Debby; T with a hat on, round O, crooked S, Q in the corner, and so forth. But all these incitements to beguile us into the road to learning would never have succeeded without steady perseverance. She was also wont to hold out encouraging language, such as "Sweet girl" – "Lovely, fine boy!" My sister Margaret she called "the lily of the valley" – my brother Richard "the rose of Sharon." She also talked of gilt books, the favour of our parents, one of her husband's cackajay apples, a new laid egg, and so forth. These, indeed, might make us love our school, but it was the patience, the perseverance, which taught us to read. She was no less expert in teaching girls to work. I remember contemplating her powers while she was settling my work, with a feeling I could not describe. She appeared to me to be a sort of creator. She led us through all the gradations of hemming, and sewing, and running, and felling, and stitching, 'till we were fit to work a sampler. That was the highest of our ambitions, except it might be to work flowers upon a pocket. We soon learned the marking stitch; then to make letters; then little stiff sprigs; then great flaunting flowers such as never grew. The mistress knew the various stitches which an accomplished girl ought to learn – double cross stitch, hem stitch, queen stitch, Irish stitch, chain stitch, oielet holes, &c. Indeed we had an unbounded opinion of her knowledge and capacity.

A number of impressions of seals hung in a frame at her back. She sat near a window. Many books lay in the window-seat. I believe a Bible was one of them – the Universal Spelling Book, the Pennsylvanian Spelling Book, Reading Made Easy, and no doubt many of the little books which were then given to good children, such as Cinderella, Sinbad the Sailor, Tom Thumb, The House that Jack Built, &c. Bags of old samplers hung near her. A bed was in one corner of the room, and a large box of apples at the foot of the bed; for her husband, Joss Webster, dealt in apples besides being a wool-comber. A chest of drawers stood near the bed, and I think they generally lay more or less open, for the hen laid in one of them, and the cat kittened in the other. I believe I never thought of this being untidy, but, on the contrary, a very great perfection; and indeed only what I would wish, if I had a house and a chest of drawers. I thought the mistress happy to have such tame hens and cats.

People with sore fingers, the scrofula, consumption, coughs, pains, aches, sick children, or any other calamity came to the mistress for relief. She was never at a loss – a handful of rue, a handful of elder, a handful of vervain, ditto marsh-mallows, twenty snails – all pounded, and put down in a cruiskeen with a pound of lard or fresh butter. Let it *simper* all day. Strain it, and rub the part affected for nine nights. Poultices of herbs, decoctions, and infusions were all prescribed in their turn, and often succeeded. These prescriptions by no means interfered with the business of the school. They were at her tongue's end, and sometimes we saw frightful sores and heard talk of others yet more dreadful.

The mistress sometimes amused us even in school with wonderful stories. If she saw us biting off our threads, she would tell us of a beautiful young girl who did so. At length she became very ill, and grew worse and worse 'till she died, was opened, and a large ball of thread was found in her stomach. This story made an indelible impression. There was another story to frighten us from sighing. Stealing and lying were of course followed by terrific consequences. Molly was a useful woman in her day, but I suppose her terrors and superstitions would hardly do for the present age of refinement.

Another remarkable trait in the character of this illustrious person was her extreme want of neatness in her house. Nothing but her consummate skill in teaching could have induced my mother to send us to such a dirty place; but it was extraordinary to behold the perfect propriety of her dress when she went out visiting. Her stiff camlet gown was taken out of its folds, her milk white apron, her cap and border were all perfectly neat, and her conduct and conversation were fit for any company. She was frequently invited to drink tea at all our parents' houses, and her scholars were always glad to see her, and eagerly listened to all she said. I never remember her husband bearing her company on these visits, but he was a more diligent attender of meetings than his wife. He remembered the hard frost in 1739, and took his father's cattle to water at that time.

Joss Webster, her husband, carried on his trade of wool–combing, and there he treated his pets to potatoes roasted in his comb–pot. The like of these I never tasted, so sweet and hot, and given out of his greasy hand to "the best girl in forty shillings." He generally wore his shirt sleeves tucked up to his shoulders. He had a venerable countenance adorned by fine grey hair; and an inflexible temper – but I remember nothing of it.

The pair had no son, and two of their daughters married out of the Society. Lucy alone remained to help them. Sometimes she went to service, and gave them almost all her earnings; or if they appeared to want her at home, she stayed with them. She passionately loved her father, and was very affectionate to her mother. She lived as servant both with my grandmother Shackleton and with my mother, and was most faithful, affectionate, and irritable. When I was a child, she and I sometimes fought not only with our tongues but with our hands.

Joss and Molly Webster removed to Athy for some years, and then returned to Ballitore, but not to the Borough, which had been destroyed in the rebellion. Several people had attempted to supply Molly's place as village school–mistress, but no one succeeded. They wanted a certain something which to this day, it is said, has not been supplied. On their return from Athy the old couple settled in the house next the bridge, where Molly resumed her throne and Joss his comb–pot, much to the satisfaction and benefit of the village. But they were grown old and feeble; Molly seldom went out; Lucy was now at service near Carlow, and it was with no small joy, tempered with a degree of incredulity, that Molly heard of her daughter's hand being solicited by a rich tallow chandler aged about seventy. This report was happily confirmed, and after some time they were married. I believe Lucy was then about forty. They were married in Ballitore and the wedding dinner was given by Fanny Bewley.

It was said by the neighbours that Lucy was now rewarded for all her filial attentions; but I believe her chief enjoyment was in the prospect of being able to help her parents more than ever. As they grew more feeble, she persuaded her husband, Billy Allment, to invite them to his house, and there she dutifully attended the three old people. Her father and husband died within one week, and her mother was most tenderly cherished for many years 'till she died of old age. Lucy now gives vent to her inexhaustible kindness, good nature, and generosity in providing for her sister's children.

Ned Miles' house also composed a part of the Borough. I believe he had been reduced from affluence or very easy circumstances to the low state in which I remember him as a shoemaker. His wife Betty became childish, and I was much frightened on hearing her doating expressions.

Beyond the Borough and towards the bridge was the house of Abby Widdows, which was built by herself. She also made the ground of her garden, which had been covered by the river. She was not a little proud of this achievement. Abby held about the same rank in the village as Molly Webster, but she aimed at much higher things.

Hers was a singular character, very goodnatured, passionate, proud, enterprising, industrious, and weak. Her accounts and her language were confusion beyond all comprehension or interpretation or disentanglement. Yet Abby was a worthy woman, and I believe she was more clear in her views of heavenly virtue than of justice between man and man, of policy, or of the need of sacrificing our own pleasures or fancies to the claims of circumstances. In early times when she was a young widow she had a course of successes, and was consequently thought to be a clever woman. She succeeded so well in the business of tailor, which she carried on by the assistance of journeymen, that she embarked in the shoemaking line, kept a shop, built a range of cabins (which was known as Abby's Row), and had a set of wretched tenants. But at length she got out of her depth, and was obliged to call a meeting of her creditors, who treated her with great lenity. So far from being ashamed of this misfortune, she always spoke of it as a very respectable era in the course of her mercantile career. Her creditors were shopkeepers, but she always gave them the title of merchants or "marchants." Yet it was told of Abby that when first engaged in business, she one night lost her rest because she owed fourpence. This delicate feeling must have soon worn away by repeated rubbing, or the poor woman could not have dragged on her existence.

Her son Peter was one of my father's assistants' in the school, and being deeply in love with Jenny Boake, the boys nicknamed him "Peter Boake." In process of time he went to America, where he still lives. Her daughter Becky lived as servant in our family; she afterwards went to Dublin, to Suir Island, and to Cork, living at service in a Friend's family in each place.

At length poor Abby's affairs becoming more and more embarrassed, she was reduced to sell some of her encumbering property; but she was always angry with her deliverers. She gave up housekeeping on her own account, and lived as housekeeper to my father. She was a very important person in the kitchen, took her meals in the parlour, and slept in a large room in the midst of her own furniture. She and I had many tiffs, but I listened to the story of her misfortunes with respect and sympathy, and became a party in her displeasure with those who took her house from her.

She left us in 1797, went to live with my grandmother Shackleton, who was then in a state of dotage, and built a good house for herself during that service. It was destroyed during the Rebellion, for which she was indemnified by government. She then refitted it, went to live there with her daughter, and kept the village post–office for a short time; but all was confusion – letters, dockets, and accounts. She kept shop, sold earthenware, baked bread and cakes, and always found it difficult to make ends meet. My grandmother and my aunt Sally lived with her for a short time, till the former died in 1804. She then had a succession of lodgers, both old and young – men, women, and children. At length came my aunt Chandlee, who remained in her house seven years, and died there of a tedious illness in 1823. Abby died shortly after, at an advanced age.[179]

Becky carried on a part of her mother's business very quietly and respectably, fell into ill health, and died the last day of 1825. Though very unpretending, and far from conspicuous in any way, yet she is much missed, and we recal with pleasure and regret the time when her mother sat in her arm–chair by a great stone–coal fire, knitting as fast as her fingers could move, and cordially receiving her frequent visitors, whom she was wont to entertain with a relation of her confused affairs. The guests usually rose up from their seats as wise as they sat down, except that their ideas were more indistinct. It used to be said if Abby only possessed a door case, she would build a cabin to match it. She was formed for high life, which appeared in her manner of issuing orders, in talking of her tenantry, of her houses and lands, in her carelessness of money, and in the easy grace with which she sat in her own parlour. Oh Penury! how many noble souls dost thou sink and cramp, how many extended views dost thou limit, how many generous purposes does thou defeat!

Opposite the house which Abby Widdows inhabited in old times, and where my uncle Leadbeater now lives, stood a row of houses belonging to Betty Malone, Bill Lennon, and Paddy Dempsey. Betty Malone was a widow when I first knew her, with two daughters, Susy and Peggy. They were an ambiguous sort of Friends. The departed husband was, I suppose, born in membership, and was probably disowned for marrying Betty, though the smallness of her cap always made me take her for a Friend. Her daughter Susy was a fine–looking girl, and remarkably neat. She was deranged when I first knew her, and died of consumption. Peggy also had been very pretty. One day she went out of meeting, as it were to stop the bleeding of her nose; but in reality to elope with James Brett. This pair had a daughter named Nancy, who was sent to school by her father, and became as accomplished as she was amiable and sensible, but a cloud of sorrow overcast her countenance. Nancy was always respected, and I believe her friends redoubled their attentions to her when she needed them most. Her natural taste for drawing having been cultivated at school, she drew a little view of the bridge and the central part of Ballitore, which is very correct, and was much valued by my aunt Leadbeater, to whom she presented it, and who hung it over her chimney–piece. Nancy at length fell into delicate health, and was carefully attended. She recovered for a time, and was then suddenly seized with inflammation, of which she died in a few days, much lamented by her relations and friends.

In the next house to Betty Malone, but of inferior degree, lived Bill Lennon, whose wife was my nurse. The house was built with the help of her wages, and against her better judgment. It was too large for their means, and was always a clog upon their exertions. Bill was a butcher; he was a man of considerable talents, a good accountant, a politician, and was gifted with no common eloquence. Above all, he had a spirit of enterprise capable of raising him to the highest mercantile rank if he had had the opportunity of exercising it. His trade of butcher, however, in the small village of Ballitore, prevented him from rushing into any great extremes; but he was unfortunate to the utmost of his ability. He was always in debt, but always furnished with resources to keep out of jail, and to carry on the business. He seldom paid his rent; but his agreeable company and advice were so necessary to his landlord that they were not only on good terms but were particularly intimate. Their politics agreed, and their eloquence was very much of the same stamp. Their friendship was still farther confirmed by the excellent yarn stockings which my nurse knit for the great man, by the clothes she washed and mended for him during his stay in the country, and by the care which she took to have his umbrella ready if a shower came on. The most powerful monarch stands in need of such accommodation, whether they be in the shape of coaches or umbrellas, of yarn stockings or of costly ermine. Deprive a king of his washerwoman, and see what a poor figure he will make upon his throne.

Benjamin Wills, the landlord of Bill Lennon, and of many other tenants of more or less note in Ballitore, was a person of great consequence amongst us. His presence or absence made a vast difference. The very expectation of Mr. Wills coming down produced no small sensation in the breasts of the villagers, but in none more than in that of Bill Lennon, whose extravagance and thoughtlessness were increased by the frequent presents made by his wife's rich relations on the Curragh of Kildare – the fleeces of wool, the sacks of oatmeal, potatoes, and various other provisions which the good old farmers thought they never missed. A woman's going out to nurse is often destructive of domestic comfort, and an entire breaking up of domestic economy. Those who have extravagant husbands are particularly tempted to try that resource, and they are the very women who ought to stay at home.

My poor nurse was so unfortunate as to have the charge of three of our family in succession. As I was the first, she was most partial to me, and to this day she relates my wise and amusing sayings, and speaks of the time when she was nursing me as the height of her prosperity and happiness. My father's school, by her account, was then too full to admit another scholar. The garden was so beautiful that one might suppose, from her description, that, like Calypso's, "an eternal spring embroidered her isle." She speaks of the flowers as if they were always in blow, as if the fruit was always on the trees, and larger and in greater perfection than the degenerate fruit of the present day. The schoolboys were all pleasant; their parents all rich and generous; the kitchen full of servants, all in high spirits; worthy, honest Friends constantly coming to the meetings; swarms of beggars fed at our doors; loads of beef and mutton brought from the butchers; the Four–tree Field was greener than ever it was since; the inhabitants of the village were cheerful and innocent; there were no impositions; no striving who could get most business; no taking houses or lands over poor people's heads; or, if such a cruel circumstance ever occurred, the tyrants never had luck after. Even the Fates were just in those days. Then she spoke of "the old master" – my grandfather Richard Shackleton – how pleasant he was! how full of his jokes! how he scolded her for not going over the water (the phrase we had for crossing the bridge to the Retreat) often enough. How he did not know his own cows, but desired them to be put in pound when he saw them wandering about the village, thinking they belonged to some careless fellow. And "the old mistress" – how sober and discreet she was, and so respectful to my mother's nurse. And there was Nanny McConnaughty, the housekeeper at the Retreat, who asked my nurse to drink tea with her in the pantry. And there was the widow Fuller, who always gave her cake and wine – none of your home–made wines, but real foreign wine. And there was good–natured Mrs. Haughton (cousin Betty, my mother's housekeeper), who brought up my nurse's supper *herself*, and insisted on her eating it. To be sure she was a little passionate, but it was over in a minute, and "the best sort of people are always so." And there was Miss Peggy Abraham, who used to sit for hours with her in the nursery, telling her about England. In short, by my nurse's account, Ballitore was a paradise when she was young and blooming. But it must not be thought that I heard of her beauty from herself. I could only gather it from the most distant hints, such as comparisons between the real beauties of those days, and "what they now call pretty girls" – from remarks upon her present poor looks, and her assertion that she had once a pretty clear skin and complexion. She was, however, very handsome, and had hands fit for a duchess. She remembers Edmund Burke, says he was a fine, large, pleasant, comfortable–looking man, and very familiar. She did not like him the worse for praising the beauty of my elbow, which owed all its beauty to my being a fat little child when he saw it.

William Gill, the old steward, was also a favorite with nurse. When she had done nursing us, she returned to her home, where she experienced a succession and a variety of troubles – death of children, loss of property, the illness of herself, her husband, and children, her eldest daughter marrying to disoblige her, and lastly the unpromising conduct of her son, who was foolishly indulged by his mother and as foolishly treated with severity by his father.

I ought not to forget that in my childish days my nurse gave me twopence every fair day, and sometimes accompanied this gift with a present of black cherries. At length I thought myself to big to accept my nurse's money, and refused it. I believe she did not afterwards press it upon me. At that time I had no doubt but that when I should grow up, I could and would relieve her from all her difficulties, little knowing how prudence and selfishness grow with one's growth; and as little how difficult it is to do good, and peculiarly so to such a family as that of my nurse, who had the most mistaken ideas of independence, or spirited conduct; for they thought they had "a high spirit." They were indeed very easily offended, and particularly so with such of their creditors as were urgent for payment. Yet I believe this disposition, when it took a right course, preserved them in a state of mind far above all the little pilfering ways which are too common among the poor. The dishonesty of Bill was that of the merchant who borrows money which he is uncertain of being able to repay. His poor wife was very particular to pay little debts incurred by herself, but she thought it a poor mean thing to demand money from her son or her husband.

Bill became dropsical, and died in 1816. The house, the trade, the difficulties, and the high spirit all now fell to his son John, who married an industrious good young girl. His landlord forgave him several years' rent, and paid him a sum of money to leave the house. For several years it did not look likely that John would provide comfortably for his family; neither his wife nor his mother could conceal from the public that he was indolent and inclined to drink. Whether his reformation was effected by the care and advice of a good wife, or by his own wise reflections, or both together, we cannot say; but the truth is that John Lennon is now not only the best butcher in the village, but a sober, industrious, and obliging man. His mother is comforted in her old age. She lives with us, yet is always wishing to be on a floor of her own, always lamenting the hard times, the degeneracy of every thing both in nature and in morals, the mixture of pride and meanness in the "quality" now–a–days and the misery of the poor. She makes frequent inquiries every session of parliament about the probability of Catholic emancipation being conceded, but she says she does not expect it. She is angry at the Union, which deprived us of our Irish parliament; angry at the informer Reynolds, who betrayed his countrymen in 1798; and hates the Orangemen, though not because they are Protestants, for she likes the nobility and gentry. Some years before her husband died, she lived at the Ballitore Inn, where she made great acquaintance with travellers of rank, and always remarked that if they were not upstarts, but real quality, they were humble and polite, and treated her with proper respect. Whilst a servant or a person of low degree demanded the best of everything, a gentleman was content with what was convenient; he would give up his room to a lady, and would put up with one of an inferior description. A duke or a lord would eat a potato and lie upon chairs sooner than give her any trouble. She had indeed met with some solitary exceptions, but she always found that they were newly–created peers or peeresses, who had not learned how to behave themselves.

So much for my poor nurse, whose virtues only required to be thrown into a better light than was her hard fate, and whose errors were drawn forth and exposed by the same unfortunate circumstances. The same may be said of her husband, if not of her son.

I have little to say of Paddy Dempsey. He was shot in the mill–field by the Suffolk Fencibles who guarded the Mill House, which was a barrack in 1798. His wife, Poll Dempsey, survived him many years. She was a baker, and when unable to bake on a large scale, she made pikelets and carried them about the village. Her son Christy is now a man of considerable consequence at the sign of The Three Birds and the Sheaf of Wheat.

CHAPTER III.

AS we move towards the bridge, we arrive at the little house where Molly Webster lived when her daughter Lucy was married. We learn from the people of an earlier generation that Harry Fletcher once resided there, and kept it remarkably neat; that he played the flute more sweetly than ever it was played in Ballitore; and that he was the best painter that ever painted my father's house. Isaac and Margaret Williams inhabited that cottage for some years, and also kept it very neat. Their garden as seen from the bridge was beautiful. A pyrocanthus grew up the end of the house; a bower was seen at a distance close to the edge of the river, and a frilled window–curtain secured their daughter's chamber from the public gaze. If Harry Fletcher had thus adorned his dwelling, and if we had only heard of it from the old people, we should have thought it almost like enchantment. My reason tells me that Harry's improvements never exceeded Margaret's, but my imagination is in favour of Harry. Probably Jane Williams's voice was as sweet as Harry's flute, but having only heard of the music of Orpheus and of Fletcher, I knew no difference between them.

That little house still stands, and is now inhabited by the first "fancy tailor" who ever settled in Ballitore. Alas, what will Ballitore come to? What has become of that charming simplicity so often described as one of its peculiar attributes? Is the last vestige of it gone with my precious aunt Leadbeater? What shall be given in exchange for this invaluable gem? Let us try to preserve it if the least particle still remains. Learning, industry, politeness, truth and sincerity are all good – some of them excellent; but we cannot do without Simplicity, with her open brow, her soft voice, and gentle smile. She is sister to that "Good Matron" which my aunt has so sweetly described, and distinguished from the more steadfast and reasonable personage, Philanthropy.

We are now standing upon the bridge, gazing on that river – that winding Griese which fills us with pleasing and melancholy associations. It reminds me of my happy childhood, when I rowed a boat from the mill through all the weedy difficulties 'till we shot under the arch of this bridge, and past the shallows 'till we reached the little creek at the end of our shrubbery. Oh! happy days, when *she* helped me to row who now lies mouldering in that graveyard which I see from this bridge. It is now more than fifteen years since I followed that dear body to the silent grave, cut off as she was in the bloom of beauty and of happiness. Oh! that my grovelling thoughts could follow her to her blissful seat on high. How many have followed her, but that first invasion of my happiness is still the most grievous. Will Time never blunt the point of that sorrow?[180]

The view of our river must always recall my beloved aunt Leadbeater to my mind – sweetly and softly recall her, as softly as the winding and the murmuring of that stream. I think of her wandering on its banks, and celebrating its beauties in the days of her youth. I think of her enjoying it and living beside it through her whole life, even to old age. I think of her leaning over her garden wall, her mind filled with poetic images, and overflowing with benevolence and friendship. As I stood beside her, she pointed out to me Harry Fletcher's house, the Retreat, and all the little scene. The pleasure of being with her, of sitting with her in the house or in her bower, of walking with her in her garden, of listening to her, of sharing her overflowing sympathy, was so easily obtained that I did not prize it enough. It is like a charming vision that has passed away. Those blessings which are most necessary to our existence are least prized by us. My aunt's company seemed as necessary as the air or the water, and her benefits were as plentifully showered upon us. But there is a Source which can never be dried up or taken from us. There still remain bread and water to nourish and comfort us, if we could wholly resign that which is taken from us by Divine appointment.

Now comes the Retreat, which I long yet dread to approach. Of my own family I cannot speak with indifference – perhaps not with impartiality; and now that many of them are laid in the grave, any pleasure I may have in describing them must be of a melancholy kind. I remember the Retreat almost as long as the house in which I was born. When we were children, we often spent the day there. The idea of neatness and exactness is connected with the Retreat and with my grandmother. We entered a neat little paved yard, and then a very small hall or passage. At the right hand was the kitchen, and on the left was the parlour, which was covered with oil–cloth. I remember the patting of my aunt's feet on the floor. Near the door was a little closet. I forget its contents. Then the fire–place, with a low straight brass fender. A green, wooden–bottomed chair stood at one side, and my grandmother sat in a common arm–chair on the other side, a window at her right hand, and a clock behind her. Two windows looked into the garden. Between them stood a table, and on that table a very small bright brass hand–bell, which I longed to ring but dared not touch. I think a mahogany cheese–board was also a piece of the parlour furniture, and stood in the middle of that table. In the corner of the room next the door going to the garden was a bookcase. I was particularly pleased with those books. Many of them were for children, and my aunt Leadbeater either directed my choice or handed me what I asked for. I was not fastidious. If the book was for children, I was content. In another corner was a corner–cupboard, with a leaf which was let down at dinner time for a sideboard. My grandfather Shackleton had a peculiarly shaped chair. The back rose from two sides and one corner appeared between his knees. A velvet cap also hung up, to be ready for him when he took off his hat. I believe the parlour was white-washed. The fireside was adorned by a favourite cat, called Minny, who was famous for opening the parlour–door. I believe the simple latch was visible to both men and cats, although the handle was a civilized brass one. There was a hall between the two parlours, through which we went to the garden. In this hall was a little pewter cistern and tiled sink, where I delighted in washing my hands. The best stairs went out of this hall, and were so polished with dry rubbing that they were dangerous to walk upon. My grandmother's cloak and garden–bonnet hung upon the banisters. The back–parlour was the scene of my grandfather's evening devotions. He retired there regularly every evening for a considerable time, and his family thought they observed the traces of his employment upon his countenance. In the back parlour was a bed, where Nanny McConnaughty died. I don't know whether there was always a bed in that room, but I know that my grandfather's desk was there, and that there was another corner cupboard which contained the finest of the china. On ascending the stairs we see several greenhouse plants in the lobby, which separated the two best rooms. In one of them Job Scott died. We go through the other to a little closet or passage, where my aunt Mary had a small bookcase with wire doors. From thence we enter my grandmother's room, of which I have gloomy and heavy recollections. The bed, and the drawers, and even the powder–boxes seemed to me to be dark and heavy. A closet was off this room, where I believe my aunts slept. The common way down stairs from thence was by a back stairs that ended in the kitchen. There were rooms higher up, where I suppose Molly Hudson and the servants slept. I thought the kitchen was remarkably neat and pleasant. When I now reflect on it, I think it must have been greatly crowded, but the impression upon my mind is cheerful and agreeable. A cupboard behind the door contained more than all the preserves that I could conceive. If my mother wanted any nice thing that she had not, I thought of course my grandmother had it in that cupboard. A mangle stood at the windows; a high–backed seat stood by the kitchen fire, and extended itself into the middle of the floor. Over the fire–place hung a variety of kitchen utensils, all bright and in good order, which Biddy Cody cleaned once a week. She was not one of the servants, but a poor woman who wanted help, and was very feeble. She also distilled herbs, and when a child I had a foreboding that when Biddy should die we should have no more peppermint water, and such like. So it proved. We now depend upon essences which are too dear to give to the poor. Formerly we had great jars of distilled waters, which were good for every complaint.

There was a little pantry off my grandmother's kitchen, of which I have very pleasant ideas. It was there I was first allowed to assist in making cakes – that is, to cut them out with a glass tumbler. A fowl–yard and hen–house were at the back of the house, and these provided plenty of eggs.

Everything at the Retreat seemed to me so secure and so proper, that I thought my aunts very happy. Even the birds' nests were as they ought to be, and were not robbed. In short, I thought everything at the Retreat nicer and better than what we had at my father's.

Molly Hudson was a person of great note in the house. My grandfather had invited her to stay a while there, when her brother's house was burnt. She accepted the invitation, and lived with them as long as the family remained together. As she had been by trade a dressmaker, she cut out the gowns of the family and helped to make them. She was very pleasant and accommodating, often paid a visit to my aunt Chandlee, who lived at Athy, and took care of my sister Margaret in Wicklow. I remember asking her how old she was. She answered twenty, which seemed to me a great age, but I believe she was above sixty at that time. She died in 1812, aged eighty–six.

My grandmother's garden was very neat, and in my eyes had the same air of perfection and security which I had not observed anywhere else. The hedges were clipt, the auriculas stood in the blowhouse, or out of it, as was most proper; the hyacinth and tulip roots were duly taken up, and rubbed, and spread out, and hung up in paper bags, and as duly put down again to bloom and fade; the saffron crocus was pulled and dried; and the caraway seeds and all the herbs – everything was done with due care and consideration. The little walk from the blowhouse to the field which ran parallel to the road was overshadowed with variegated shrubs and trees. A grass plot nicely shorn was opposite the parlour windows. A flower knot was adjacent, but I forget the exact position. A clipt hedge separated this pleasure–ground from the kitchen garden. Fine apple–trees grew among the cabbages. A bower of framework covered with green creepers was a most attractive spot, and gave an additional charm to the garden. I believe this was my aunt Mary's bower. I remember her sitting there at her work, whilst her little materials lay on a spider–table beside her. This I thought was as it should be, and if I were grown up, I would always sit at my work in a garden.

We walked on from that bower to the garden–house, where Dick Manders kept his tools. A narrow serpentine walk led us to the dwelling–house, between little yew–trees or junipers nicely clipt into long oval shapes. The garden extended a long way behind the house, and it was there that we feasted upon the small fruits. Two sides of it were fenced by neatly clipt hedges, and close to the hedge was a smooth grass walk forming a little terrace, from which there were sloping beds of strawberries; and at intervals grassy steps, which delighted me for many reasons; one of them was that we had not the like in our garden; another, that I could run up and down them with ease ; and a third, that like all the other walks they were smooth and short as velvet. At the other side of this part of the garden was a wall covered with fruit trees. I remember when very young walking round the garden with my grandmother. She walked with an ivory–headed staff, either to support her, or to point out to Dick Manders what was to be done, or to knock little pieces of stone or clay off the grass. I also remember her pointing out to me her variegated trees and shrubs, which grew at one side of the flower–garden. I thought these walks very tiresome.

After my aunt Mary became, in 1791, my aunt Leadbeater, she continued to live some years with her parents at the Retreat, and her little daughter Elizabeth was a great pet in the house. It is said that she could read a few words at three years old, and I believe she read fluently at four.

My grandfather died in 1792, at Mountmellick, of a violent fever. Many Friends accompanied the funeral to Ballitore. I remember the neighbours coming in to sit with my mother soon after his death, and lamenting his loss as if he could not be done without. It was expected that my grandmother would sink under the affliction, but it is now believed that her faculties had begun to decline about that time, and that she was thus spared the acute suffering which must have been caused by such a privation. My grandfather was lamented by people of all denominations, as well as by his family, his neighbours, and distant friends. He was very fond of me, and it was thought he helped to spoil me. He was of a most sociable disposition; his talents were bright; his understanding strong, comprehensive, and highly cultivated; and while his wit was sparkling, it seldom caused pain to others. I can well believe how much he must have been missed out of the village, particularly as he had resigned his business to my father, and troubled himself little about the concerns of his farm or household, leaving all that to "the mistress," as he called my grandmother, so that he had little to interrupt his social enjoyments. Nor was he idle, for he had a very extensive correspondence, attended all the Friends' meetings with which he was specially connected and many others besides, and was often named upon religious appointments in the service of the Society of which he was a prominent and highly respected member.

His company was an ever new delight. His return from his visits to England or to various parts of Ireland was always hailed with joy. He called to see all his friends, and spoke cordially to the poor neighbours whom he met in the street.

My grandmother, although of a more sedate and orderly disposition, was also much beloved by her friends and neighbours, and, though so different from her husband, was quite a companion to him. She had a sensible and well-cultivated mind, a great knowledge of history, and a good taste in general reading; and, above all, they were closely united in religious fellowship.

When my father was from home, my grandfather attended a good deal to the school. I believe he visited my mother daily. I have a faint remembrance of the animation with which he entered our parlour, of the cheerfulness he created, and of running for his arm-chair, and mounting upon it with my arms about his neck. He often kicked up riots among us, and then ran away to tell my grandmother what he had done; upon which she gravely reprimanded him, and pitied my poor mother for being disturbed, and the children for being teazed.

I cannot remember very much about my aunts Mary and Sally at that early period, for I was only nine years old at the time. I knew that my aunt Mary wrote verses, and was very industrious at her sewing and knitting, and that she induced me to be industrious by setting herself a task along with me. My aunt Sally spoke in meeting; always came to visit my mother when she was unwell; used to cut our hair; was very droll, and visited the poor.

It was when I grew older that I became more attached to both my aunts. There were certain peculiarities in my aunt Mary which always pleased me, and are now hallowed by her death. She liked to drink cold water out of a tin porringer, I believe from her associating it with the kindness of her father's pupils or old servants, who thus quenched her thirst in her childhood. She liked hard eggs, and usually prolonged the pleasure of eating them by adding crumbs of bread. She roasted her oysters and added crumbs, with butter and pepper, her eyes glistening with pleasure while preparing this feast. If this pleasure was anything like that of an epicure, we more than forgave it; we loved it and sympathized with it, because she handed round these nice little morsels to all of us with so much kindness and affection. No species of enjoyment was too little for her. She would roast the head of a snipe in a candle, and cook cheese in the same way, and then hand them to us in like manner, while we amused ourselves by expressing our detestation of the smoky morsel, which she took in good part, as she did all our freedom and our criticism. When we asked her a question that it was not right to answer, she would begin the lines: –

"The secrets of thy friends do not disclose,
Lest by so doing thou resemble those
Whose ears are leaking vessels, which contain
Nothing; but what's pour'd in runs out again
Straight at the mouth," &c.

and a great deal more from her favourite poem, *The Maiden's Best Adorning*. We stopped our ears, but she went on to the end. We all laughed, and meanwhile she kept her secret inviolable. She was the best listener I ever knew. I believe she was never absent or inattentive. She looked as though she were drinking in with pleasure all we had to say. Yet she was not gazing upon your face, nor uttering little unmeaning sounds of approbation. She went on with her work, or even with her writing, while we talked or read to her, but her whole countenance showed that she was attentive and lost nothing.

In 1793, Job Scott died of small–pox at the Retreat. He had visited Ballitore very frequently before he took ill. On these occasions he took particular notice of me – I do not know why, except that he saw or felt that I loved him, and was touched by his preaching. At one time, when my aunt Mary and he took me with them to Castledermot, he told us the names of all his children. They were Oziel, Lydia, Sarah, Mary, James, and Ruth. Oziel has since died. Lydia and James are, I have been informed, bright and literary people. His wife, whose name was Eunice Anthony, died some years before he left home. I wrote down all the little stories he told me about them in a diary which my aunt taught me to keep, and which one of the school–boys burned some time after, when we had a quarrel. When Job was going to the half year's meeting, he stopped at our house, sent for me out of meeting, and took me with him to Dublin. This he did with my father's permission; but as my mother knew nothing of the matter 'till I was on my way to Dublin, I had no clothes but those I wore, and she thought it necessary to send some after me. Job then returned to Ballitore, took the small–pox, and died. He was attended on his death–bed by my father, my aunts Mary and Sally, Doctor Paul Johnson, and Anne Tuke of York. My aunt Mary, seeing so many about him, was backward in visiting him; but he liked her company, and sometimes wondered that she was not more with him. The notes kept by her and my father respecting his illness were thrown in the background, or destroyed by those who stood higher in their own opinion. He died the 22nd of Eleventh–month, 1793. I saw him once while on his death–bed.[181]

I will now leave that abode of peace called the Retreat. It was really a retreat from worldly cares to my grandfather; but my grandmother seemed to me to be always busy, anxious, and overdone – "hampered" was her word. They were seldom without company, either paying them a visit, or travelling to and from the various Friends' meetings that were held in different places. According to my aunt Leadbeater's journals, their friends' visits always delighted them. Nothing appears in her accounts but sociability, joy at meeting, and sorrow at parting. I suppose my aunt Sally, in her reminiscences of those times, lets us behind the scenes. Sheets, bolster–cases, and pillow–cases had to be aired; fires had to be made; beef steaks and mutton chops had to be dressed; geese, ducks, and chickens had to be killed; big tables to be laid out; head, foot, and side dishes to be provided. Sometimes company arrived on a washing day, or a wet drying day. This was inexpressibly teasing and "hampering." My grandfather laughed at all these things, which only elicited flashes of his pleasant wit. My aunt Leadbeater lent a hand of help, and was fatigued and incommoded like other flesh and blood; but her angelic mind forgot all that was disagreeable, and restored itself in the beams of friendship. She would accept of assistance from her friends, and all was right.

The avenue from the Retreat to the high road was overshadowed with trees before the rebellion. Nelly Hudson lived at the foot of the hill; Jack, her husband, had leave to live there too; but he was either not thought of, or was deemed an incumbrance, if not a nuisance. Yet he was a quiet, civil, tall man, and had formerly been handsome; but the poor fellow had an unfortunate liking for strong drink, which hurt his character, weakened his intellects, and reddened his eyes so as to destroy his beauty. John, the eldest of their large family, was usher to my father; he was in love with Betty Wilson. He once told one of the school–boys that he would not show him how to do his sum, "if he cried his eyes out" – a harsh speech which called forth my sympathy towards the boy to a painful degree. The present is a far happier age for children, for they are not expected to perform impossibilities. Yet Roger Ascham two hundred and fifty years ago, and John Locke early in the last century, had the sense to know that the true way to make children like learning or anything else, is to make it agreeable to them. This seems a truism at the present day, yet we still speak of it as a new discovery.

Madge or Margaret Hudson was the eldest daughter of Jack and Nelly. She was considered a pretty girl, though she had a cocked nose. But she had black eyes, red cheeks, a small mouth, red lips, and white teeth. She was as dressy as she could afford to be, and withal very notable. She married a north countryman, lived in plenty in the north for many years, and then went to America.

Sally, the next daughter, was also considered handsome. She dressed more unlike a Quaker than her sister, was often visited and advised about her inconsistencies, which the poor girl did not understand, although her mother boxed her ears to make her comprehend our principles. She was very industrious. Her brother Richard gave her a little fortune, and she married her sister's brother-in-law, who was so diligent at business that he had not time to come to Ballitore to be married. Therefore Sally considerately went to him. They also lived very comfortably in the north of Ireland, and then went to America, where she soon died. Both she and her sister became religiously strict Presbyterians, though they never could understand Quaker refinements. I believe their worthy and industrious mother, who still lives, is much in the same predicament; but she does not trouble her head about such things, and thinks we should all keep to the profession we were born in.

Her second son Richard was a good little boy, and gave his mother the first shilling he ever possessed. He served his time to a woollen draper in Dublin, afterwards went into business for himself, had a golden sheep over his door in Westmoreland-street, paid the rent of a better house for his mother, married a fine looking girl, drove into his native village in his own gig to show his wife, and lived a few years in apparent prosperity. His family were all exalted. Our friend George Downes, when a lad, helped to attend his shop. But alas! it was a bubble, and it burst. Poor Richard felt his misfortune so deeply, that he became subject to epileptic fits, which sometimes maddened him and always weakened his intellects. His wife and children went to her father, and poor Richard spent the remainder of his days with his mother in Ballitore. She was poor, but she never thought him a burden, though her nights were generally disturbed by his frightful malady. No affection is more strong, more invincible, more enduring than that of a mother. When more disturbed in his mind than usual he has often wandered away for many days, leaving his mother in the utmost distress till he was found. George Downes used to make it a point to pay him a respectful visit, when he came to Ballitore to regale himself with his intellectual friends; for he did not shun the humbling sight of the ruins of intellect. Richard Hudson dragged on his existence till the year 1825, and had one hundred fits within the last twenty-four hours of his life. His mother deeply lamented her son. When I spoke as if I thought his death must be a relief to her, she did not join in with me, or seem to like the notion.

Her third daughter, Jane, was sent to the Friends' Provincial-school at Mountmellick, in the hope of making a Friend of her; but it was in vain. I know of no advantage she gained there, except that she learned to work neatly with small stitches, instead of her mother's rapid mantua-making flourishes. She came home, left off the little Provincial-school bonnet, gradually ceased attending Friends' meetings, and then went to church. I believe her mother was secretly so well pleased with the good matches which her two elder daughters had made, who became more steady and religious after they had completely left us and our meetings, that she did not wish to prevent Jane from taking the same course. Jane married John Atkinson, a respectable man, who lived in Ballitore till he died. He left two nice little girls and a boy, who are all well brought up by their mother. They all live with old Nelly, and are employed in mantua–making, quilt–making, spinning, knitting, and doing everything that could be wanting in such a little family. Ellen Atkinson is the nice mistress of the Lancasterian school.

Molly, Nelly's fourth daughter, is of a strong large make, suitable for the heavy work of the house, and seems to have a mind and taste comformable to her outward appearance. I never heard that any one troubled his head as to her "way of thinking." She makes patch–work quilts, is a great spinner, and seems likely to lead a single life.

Abby, the youngest of Nelly's children, was considered handsome. As she grew up, she became very dressy. As she was born after her father was disowned, she was at liberty to make her bonnet any shape she liked, and to wear as many ribbons as she pleased. She had many admirers, but they were dismissed from various causes, and she is still unmarried, her beauty rather faded. She inherits her mother's taste for mantua-making.

While I am speaking of this family, I may as well mention that Nelly broke her leg a few years ago, Dr. Davis was called in. As she was an old woman, the leg recovered but slowly. A bone-setter was called in, who succeeded no better. She wished that he should consult with Dr. Davis, who told him that he would not consult with a person "not of his own profession." The bone–setter afterwards mentioned this circumstance, and said that Dr. Davis refused to talk to any one "who was not a Quaker." In spite of etiquette and cross purposes, poor Nelly got well, and now stumps about at the age of eighty.

During the great snow of 1814 it was reported that Jack Hudson, Nelly's husband, was dead. My brother Richard and I then lived with James White at Ballitore school, and Jack's residence was next door. Richard and I talked over his negative virtues – what a quiet man he was – how he was the last of his family (that is, of the original stock of Hudsons) – how he told me, the last time I met him, that he was as weak as egg broth; and we made some grave reflections upon the uncertainty of life – how Jack was as well as we were the evening before – and how little we knew what would happen to ourselves before the next evening. We expressed our uneasiness at the difficulty there would be of carrying poor Jack to the graveyard through the snow. At length, Richard said he would go in and see the family. He knocked at the door. John Atkinson, a relative of the deceased man, opened it, whistling. "Thee does well to keep up thy spirits," said Richard. "Why?" said John. "So poor Jack is gone!" said Richard. "No, indeed, he is eating his supper of rashers of bacon. Will you come in, and take share?" For joy that Jack was alive, Richard accepted the invitation, and then came in and related his adventure to me. I admit that it seemed rather flat to us that all our reflections and faint praises and lamentations went for nothing. We learned that Jack had fainted in the morning, and this gave rise to the report of his death.

Nelly Hudson was the last hostess and caretaker of several old people. Molly Hudson, who lived at the Retreat, ended her days with Nelly in 1812. Jenny Darcy, a sister of Ephraim Boake, who had been a beauty, and whose picture hangs in Jane Thomas's parlour, also died while under her care. Sally Neville, a poor Friend from Athy, boarded with her for several months, and died there on the 29th of Sixth–month, 1827, a day memorable for the funeral of my beloved aunt Mary Leadbeater. Sally was troublesome to herself and others, owing to an odd temper, and a very untoward set of children whom it is needless to describe, both because they were not inhabitants of Ballitore, and because they are instances of the ill effects of being surrounded from infancy by unfavourable circumstances. No doubt Robert Owen and Spurzheim would cast their mantles of charity over their errors, whether organic or occasioned by education.

CHAPTER IV.

Murder of Mark Lyons. – Denny Lyons' long courtship, and its happy conclusion. – Maurice Lyons, the carpenter. – Hannah Kealy, and her delicate attention to blind aunt Sally Shackleton. – An austere family. – Apparition of John Dunn. – View from the head of the Mill Avenue. – Retrospect. – The school-house. – The parlour. – A little girl's fancies. – Playing "meeting." – "Laughing at heaven." – Ballitore post-office seventy years ago. – The study. – The writer's literary favorites, John Woolman's Journal, Thomas Ellwood, Piety Promoted, the Spectator, Robinson Crusoe, Pilgrim's Progress, Gulliver's Travels, etc. – The lodge. – The dairy. – The dining-hall. – The air-pump, the electrifying machine, the solar microscope, and the telescope. – Views from the Nine-Tree-Hill. – The exquisite sense of enjoyment in youth. 291 to 300

OPPOSITE the cabin inhabited by Nelly Hudson in my childhood lived Mark Lyons and his large family. Mark was an inoffensive man. At the time of the rebellion of 1798 he was very old and feeble. On the fatal morning of the 27th of Fifth-month [May] he took refuge in our graveyard. Perhaps he looked upon it as a sanctuary; but no asylum is secure from the ravages of civil war. A soldier gave a rapid glance into the burial-ground, spied the unresisting victim in a corner, drew his trigger, and shot him dead. But I will not mix up any more of the horrors of the rebellion with these recollections, which I am gathering for my own amusement.

Mark's eldest son, Denny Lyons, was an ingenious carpenter and a handsome quiet man. He commenced a courtship with Fanny Flood when they were both young. She was servant to Hannah Haughton, and kept the kitchen remarkably neat. In this she was much assisted by Denny's handy work. He put up shelves, drove nails, kept hinges in order, made a salt-box so small that it was the wonder of all who saw it, and a thousand other little conveniences which were prompted by inventive love. Fanny in return regaled her lover with a nice cup of tea and a plate of toast beside a comfortable fire. Denny grew fat, and being of an easy disposition and enjoying so much comfort in his single state, he suffered year after year to roll over his head, without delivering Fanny from the pangs of suspense. The lines of age were also making their inroads upon Fanny's countenance, and, to add to her misfortunes, Denny's mother was bitterly hostile to the match, and some even said that she left her curse with him if he married Fanny. Twenty long years were thus trifled away. During this period Fanny had spent some golden evenings, but their brightness only served to deepen the gloom of others. One would suppose that Denny had been held back by some unseen power which at length ceased its influence, for in spite of his mother's influence, the fair one's wrinkles, and his own increasing coldness and laziness, they were married, to the great surprise of the neighbours and the inexpressible joy of Fanny. I ascribe this happy conclusion to Fanny's good humour and neatness, which Denny thought would make him comfortable; and so it proved, for their house was most attractive. Fanny always looked joyful. Denny continued to supply her with household conveniences; her old mistress helped to furnish the dressers, and ornaments of curled shavings were suspended from various parts of the house as emblems of the owner's trade. After some happy years spent together, Denny fell into ill health; all the cares of his wife and the skilful attention of Dr. Davis could not restore him, and he died in 1821.

Maurice, the youngest brother, is also a carpenter, and resides in his brother's house. He has a large family, and expresses himself with considerable fluency. We seldom enter Maurice's gate and walk up that green lane, except when bearing our departed friends to the silent grave. We are told that our graveyard was formerly embowered in trees; but they were cut down before my time, except a few solitary stunted firs.

As we walk up the village to the high road we pass Maurice Lyons, ascend the hill, and at our right hand find Hannah Kealy's. She has a husband whose name is Mat, but the house is generally known by the wife's name, an error which we frequently fall into in Ballitore; I do not know why. I remember nothing of this couple till 1798, when their home was burned. Their present dwelling is very comfortable. The gable–end faces the road. An elder hedge stands in front of the door, and would quite interrupt the view of the village, but that my aunt Sally persuaded Hannah to cut a vista through it, which gives them one of the prettiest of our views, embracing the village, the bridge, the river, the adjoining fields, the road animated by the inhabitants moving to and fro with their dogs and cows, horses and cars, whilst the hills of Prospect and Mullaghmast bound the landscape. Hannah Kealy takes care to keep the vista closely clipt, "lest Miss Sally should hear of it; for the poor thing cant see it now," – for Hannah lived at one time with my aunt, who has been quite blind for many years.

The family of Dunns – John, James, Betty, and Mary, – have lived, as long as I remember, in a small cabin on the left hand side of the road as we walk towards the Mill Avenue. They were all unmarried, and seemingly of very stern tempers. John was more kind to his sisters than James. He was a tall, bony, strong looking man, giving out his opinions with a loud, firm voice, as if they were incontrovertible. I believe the dislike of both brothers to our sex was equal. John died a few years ago of a tedious illness. James still lives, and is a great Scripturian. He deals out Scripture phrases at a great rate, and preaches patience to his sisters when in violent pain or grief, or oppressed by poverty. He never pronounces a soothing expression, and even tells his dying sister that all her pains are too little. He gains a poor livelihood by making little chairs, tables, stools, and boxes, which are either bespoken or are carried by him to the neighbouring fairs. He picked up the craft by his own genius, and has made chairs for the use of their own house, which combine the properties of both chair and table, the back of the table being made to turn down. Nevertheless he is a stern and disobliging brother, and keeps his own little store of provision separate from that of his sisters.

Betty, the eldest sister, has ever since I knew her had a very large quantity of grey hair, which she told me had been beautiful when she was young. She also told me that she had been very handsome, and had many lovers. It is often said that she boasted of "never having kissed man's lips, barring her brother John's." But I suppose there have been very few of these salutations among this austere family.

Soon after John's death, his sisters said they heard a noise in the cabin at night, and that, looking out of their bed, they beheld their departed brother sitting on a stool at the fire. He nodded as if he had something particular on his mind. They said, "What brings you there, John?" He made no reply, but gave a long look up, on which they concluded that he owed some money in the village. They enquired in all the shops, but did not find that he owed anything. He continued his visits 'till Betty's leg was badly hurt, and then disappeared. Betty was a very formal person, made long speeches, and professed to dislike or disdain all mankind. She had a tedious illness, and died in 1826, leaving Mary and her cross brother to live together. Mary was the least eminent person in the family; nevertheless she also made pompous speeches. The whole family had a turn for biblical knowledge, and were ready to make religious reflections upon every subject. They were Roman Catholics.

Ballitore Inn and the adjoining row of houses were not built 'till later times than those to which these recollections refer, and therefore they shall pass unnoticed by me at present. The Kealys' houses at the opposite side of the road are of older date. James and Nelly Kealy were the oldest of the family that I knew. James was a miller to our family 'till a short time before his death. He was a quiet, respectable man. His wife was more talkative and entertaining. She lived servant with my grandmother, and I believe her wedding dinner was given by her mistress. When I was a child, she used to sift oatmeal at our house every year. I liked to be with her, listening to the old stories and learning to sift. This old couple had several children, mostly engaged in the milling business. Their only daughter was married to a north countryman.

We now stand at the top of the Mill avenue, which was planted at each side with elm–trees by my great–grandfather himself. The Mill House stands at the foot of the avenue, green hills rising behind it, and the Griese winding through the valley, between its verdant banks. The village looks particularly pleasing from this point of view, for we perceive no ruined tenements, nor the fronts of poor–looking houses, nor the wretched cabins which are seen at the other end of the village. We are reminded of nothing but comfort and cleanliness when we observe Betsy Barrington's whitewashed house, enclosed in her pretty garden, with other little dwellings half hid among the trees. All looks like the abode of happiness, and peace, and love. Such are the ideas which always feed my imagination when I look down upon Ballitore from the top of the Mill Avenue, or from many other points along the high road; and particularly so when I am returning home after a long absence.

I have very little recollection of the Mill when I was a child. My father rebuilt it in 1790, when my uncle Leadbeater and he were in partnership. Joss Haughton from Carlow was their clerk. He had a good wife with a sorrowful countenance. I believe children greatly dislike the appearance of sorrow. I never think of that woman without compassion, though I have been told she was not particularly unhappy. She had a sister with her who had red hair, and wore a bib and apron, and a frock of an old–fashioned shape. They lived part of their time in a small house attached to the mill, and the remainder in part of Abby Widdows' house. As the milling business was bad at that time, my father and uncle dissolved the partnership. Joss Haughton returned to whence he came, and my father set the mill to Peter Delany, a genteel, plausible young man, whose father was wealthy. He made money, and was doing very well 'till the rebellion of 1798 drew near. There I leave him. He occupied the Mill House where we now live, and which was much smaller than it is at present.

I have now walked in imagination round by the Mill, as I remember that little circle in my early years, and have noticed many of the families who resided within it. I have gone over the Mill–field and down the street into the village; penetrated into the recesses of the Borough; past over the Bridge to the Retreat; passed rapidly by, yet casting a mournful glance at the graveyard; have ascended the hill, and looked down from the high–road upon my beloved Ballitore; have fancied that the Griese resembles that happy stream in Calypso's Isle, which returned upon its steps, "et sembloient ne pouvoir quitter ses bords enchantés." I have taken the whole round, and have not ventured to view that one house which interests me more than any place upon earth – the house where I was born, where my father was born and all his children – where I experienced my first and purest joys, and my first and most bitter sorrows. I have shrunk from the description, as I should shrink from viewing it if I returned to Ballitore after a long absence. Nothing seems to me so mournful as to return to our native place, which we left in our youth, and to find ourselves grown old and most of our companions dead. It is with a degree of this feeling that I now approach that old building. When I was young, the wall of the court–yard in front was lower than it is now, and was surmounted by rails a little way at each side of the entrance. The front of the house had very much the same appearance as at present. There was a large bow–window in the corner, near the kitchen window, and it was used for a green–house. The floor decayed, and it was taken down. A low wall and rails separated a little strip of a yard next the kitchen from the main yard, and kept the immensity of beggars from the kitchen window; and it was so natural to me to hear of beggars standing at the rails, that rails seemed to me to be made for beggars to stand by. The pump, as well as the brew–house, was visible through these rails.

We enter the hall door – which way shall we go? Joy and sorrow await me everywhere. Let us turn to the left. We enter the little parlour, alias a little hall; but it was a parlour a hundred years ago. In the window seat stood an immense bell, which I could scarcely lift. It was rung for the boys to go to school and such like purposes, and appeared to require no small strength to swing backwards and forwards. The flags of this hall were the newest and the most level in the house, which made it a desirable place either to whip a top or to play Scotch hop. On the other hand its vicinity to the parlour was objectionable. The parlour opened from this little hall. At the left hand side was a table with a mahogany tray upon it. Then came the cupboard. The top shelves were decorated with the best china, quite out of my reach. Not so the under shelves, for I was obliged to dust them, which was a great burden to me after the novelty was over. I used also to reckon the silver spoons, and to put by the tea things after breakfast and tea. I remember, while carrying these things along the floor, feeling my mind quite oppressed at the idea of ever, ever putting by these things. It seemed a most sorrowful and wearisome prospect that I should every day of my life have to go through this routine. Indeed I had such a dislike to every other employment as well as this, except when novelty lent its charm, that I used to be pleased at any commotion or alteration which rendered it unnecessary for me to go through my usual track. For this reason I liked to hear of the French coming; whitewashing, painting, making listing carpets, my mother going abroad, &c., were all agreeable to me. But, above all, I delighted in going from home, and was equally glad to come back again. In the under cupboard were decanters of wine, tea, sugar, and our little porringers. The closet which now opens from the corner of the parlour was of modern invention. A cherry–tree table stood near that corner. Then an oak arm–chair with leathern bottom. Then the fire–place with its tall chimney–piece; the white spots of the Kilkenny marble are still in my memory. In these spots I pictured to my imagination a lion in his den, a sugar tongs, my aunt Mary with her hair down, and her skirts sticking out, like one of the figures in *Gay's Fables*, a little bird, and so forth. The marble was framed in wood. A broad piece was at top, on which were pasted maps of Europe, Asia, Africa, and America, marked with the names of the boys who drew them – Trevor, Fay, Turner, &c. I thought Brazil was the most distant part of the world, and therefore in my waking dreams I always travelled to Brazil, across all the quarters of the globe which I saw between that and Ireland. I suppose we had a low fender – certainly no hearth rug, for they were not heard of at that time. If our hearth was black, and our curb polished bright enough to be dangerous to stand upon, we thought we were very genteel. My mother sat always at the side of the fire next the window. A little round table stood beside her, and four substantial walnut chairs stood between the fireplace and the window. The old windows with their massy frames and seats still remain; but the shutters are now inside, formerly they were outside, and were bolted within. The windows were opened and shut for that purpose with a thundering noise. My mother's little clumsy work–box, given her by her grandmother in Manchester, stood in one of the windows, and the youngest of us usually sat upon it. Upon a large table between the windows stood my father's desk. It was regarded as a very great curiosity, because it folded up, like all the portable desks now made; but it was then a modern invention, was considered very convenient, and was shown to every one who came to the house. I can just remember a green cloth covering the table, but my father became uneasy at having his table dressed, while so many people were naked, and he cut them up into garments. In the corner near the Library was our baby–house, made by Tim Lyons the carpenter, and painted by my father. The roof appeared to be slated, the walls brick, the panes of glass black, and the frames white. The steps up to the hall–door were also painted, and the door was secured by a puzzling lock, which could be opened if you placed the letters thus, TITUS. I was long before I knew the secret. The baby–house consisted of four rooms, a bed–room, a drawing–room with the floor painted in stripes, a kitchen, and a parlour. The furniture was appropriate. My sister Margaret had a doll dressed like a very precise Friend, with black hood, cape, gown, &c.; but my father did not like it, which surprized me. The study–door comes next, then another large heavy chair, then the old cabinet which still stands there, but is mounted on a higher frame than heretofore. Formerly its feet or supporters were four round solid balls, about as big as a man's head. They were worm–eaten. Under the cabinet my father kept his camera obscura. When a child, I was afraid to look under it. Probably some nurse had frightened me about it. Another chair stood between the cabinet and the parlour–door. I don't like that chair, for boys in disgrace often sat upon it. "Go sit behind the door," is a painful sound to me. The parlour was covered with a listing carpet, manufactured by ourselves, assisted by the schoolboys, and everyone who happened to come in. The warp was nailed upon the floor, and the weft was worked with wooden needles. While a carpet was making the parlour was all in confusion; it was a time of delightful variety and idleness, and everyone was pleasant. As I am no longer a kitten, but a grave old cat, I should now think a carpet–making time a time of no comfort or enjoyment. Confusion is no longer agreeable; idleness has lost its charm. But to return to our parlour. A large map of Africa hung over the table next the door; a map of Europe at the other side of the cupboard; opposite the parlour–door hung a map of the Roman Empire, and opposite the study–door was a chronological and biographical chart. I remember William Penn was entered as a statesman, George Fox as a divine, and that I was a little proud of this. Our little chairs and stools stood by the windows.

As there was a ledge under the window, wide enough for us to sit upon it with our feet upon the window stool, we made use of this elevation as a preachers' gallery when we had play meetings among ourselves. I generally preached. My nurse relates that she once laughed at me, and I said "Nurse Lennon was laughing at Heaven." Many of our plays were of this kind. We built up our chairs atop of each other, and went riding to Castledermot meeting. Amongst my many and endless misdemeanours, I used to climb up the side of the cabinet, and sit on the top of it. This was a sad example to set to the younger ones. At that time my father kept the Ballitore post–office, in the upper part of this cabinet, and four small cells only were required for the purpose. On one of these was printed "Dead letters," and "Newspapers" over another. Various curiosities were kept in the drawers; a little door in the middle enclosed some private drawers, and was itself a vehicle of concealment. The lower drawers were devoted to domestic purposes; one of these, which contained pieces of cloth, &c. for mending the boys' clothes, was often rummaged and consulted upon by my mother and the tailor.

Let us now enter the Library, or Study, as we always called it. My father kept it in exact order. I could tell the learned names printed over the different classes of books, but I prefer reminding myself of them as they appeared to my own view. The first division to the left hand was headed Theology. It was there I found John Woolman's divine Journal, which I read through; the beginning of the journal, which concerned his youthful days, his errors, repentance, and reformation, was of course the most interesting and the oftenest read, but I neglected the essays at the end. *Thomas Ellwood's Journal* was regarded as an entertaining book. It was delightful to read of him without his hat, running "a fair course" through the fields, and his father chasing after him – then the hat was restored, and then retaken – all the boxing, and cuffs, and persecutions which befel the poor young man in his father's house were highly diverting. His sister's kindness was a pleasant relief. Then there was the "mountier cap," the scarcity of money, the twenty shillings lent him by his father, the imprisonment, the bed under the table in the bow window – Gulielma Maria Springett – how he defended her from an attack of ruffians – all was delightful, 'till he was married to some orderly body; and then I stopped, and have been ever since intending to finish it when I should acquire an orderly taste – but I have not yet put my intention into execution. *"Piety Promoted, or Dying Sayings of the People called Quakers,"* was also to be found in that corner – a precious book, fit for all ages and I believe all tastes. We must all die, and we therefore feel an interest in the state of mind in which our fellow–creatures leave the world. *Select Lives of Foreigners* was also a great favorite of mine, and I was interested by the Journals of Thomas Chalkley, and George Fox; but I never read them quite through, much less over and over again, as was my practice with favorite books.

The next division was Physics, which I did not care for – nor for Mathematics – or Philology, except that I found Dictionaries under that head. When we turn the corner of the room the two volumes of *Pine's Horace* were conspicuous, with an urn of Derbyshire spar standing between them, and on each side of it a bottle containing some strange animal preserved in spirits. I forget where I found my favourite volumes of History, the *Spectator, Robinson Crusoe, Pilgrim's Progress, Sandford and Merton, Telemanchus,* or delightful *Gulliver's Travels* – how I thought myself too happy as I read them, swallowing the story down like stolen waters. I do not know why my grandfather did not like me to read *Robinson Crusoe,* but I read no farther than to that part in which his perplexities, difficulties, and dangers, and solitude were at an end. I read *Pascal's Thoughts* as a school book, translating it from the French, but I did not then know that it contained a mine of wisdom and instruction. In the last division there were some concealments of forbidden books, which I did not fail to discover, but I forget what they were. A table stood near the window, upon which stood a box containing curiosities, my father's desk, and an air–pump. Two globes stood on the floor, under a loose shelf were some large fossils, and various ornaments, maps and scientific articles, hung round the room wherever there was space for them. A press contained letters from my father's correspondents, all sorted and labelled. Keys, labelled also, hung near the door, and a number of walking sticks stood in one corner. My father sat very much in this little room, which was seldom used by anyone else.

Let us return to the hall. A large bin for oats stood opposite to the hall door. A little room at the foot of the stairs was called the Lodge, because William Gill, the old steward, lodged there. He died when I was a child, and the room was afterwards used for a shoe–closet, but was still called the Lodge. Another closet was afterwards devoted to the same purpose, but still retained the same name; and when we came to live at the Mill House, we unconsciously called our shoe–house the Lodge.

Walking through a narrow passage towards the back yard, the pleasant, cool, and lightsome dairy was on the right hand, and at the end of the passage was the laundry, where Betty Brady the washerwoman told us long and entertaining stories.

On returning to the hall, we pass the lodge and enter the boarded hall, where the boys' boxes were kept. It was also one of the many places used either for play or study. I forgot to say that there was a stone sink behind the hall door where the boys washed themselves, and where the servants washed them twice a week. So powerful is habit, it never entered into our heads that there was any impropriety in this public situation.

Passing through the boarded hall, we enter the Dining Hall, where were two long tables. At the upper end of the room was a fire place, in which was kept an immense fire in winter. I have a cheerful idea of this room, though I hardly know why. My mother sat at the head of one table at dinner, and my father at the foot. The ushers presided over the other table. The boy's bird cages hung up and down the room. We girls dared to look at them when the boys were in school. We played a good deal in the dining hall, at those times running over the tables and forms. In the evening it looked very pleasant to see the room lighted with six candles, the boys reading or doing what they pleased, my father sitting amongst them, his favorites asking him questions – for he had favorites, though he might not acknowledge it, and in matters of moment where justice was concerned, I have no doubt he was impartial. But it is impossible for us not to observe one child, or one man, or woman to be more amiable or engaging than another; and if we observe it, we must love them better; and if we love them better, we must either manifest our affection or restrain it. My father was not a man who could easily conceal his feelings. He frequently showed the boys experiments with the air–pump and the electrifying machine, and we were generally admitted on these occasions. I do not think I ever listened to one of the lectures which accompanied these experiments, 'till I had first gained some instruction for myself by my own free will; and as to lectures on the globe, I only longed for them to be over. In this room my father showed us the magic lantern also, which was inexpressibly amusing. Loud laughter was not enough to express our wonder and delight. The solar microscope also gave us great pleasure; we were all astonishment when we saw the gigantic mites contending with each other, and not less so as to behold a flea as large as a lobster, or a cutting of my father's beard magnified to the size of a thick transparent tube. As to our telescope, it was not very large, nor powerful, but

I shall never receive as much pleasure from Herschel's, if I ever see it, as from that small one of my father's. How delightful to plant it upon the Nine Tree Hill, and to be able to reckon the panes of glass in a house so distant that we scarcely discerned whether it had windows or not! or to see the owner of the house walking in or out of it, and his children playing on the lawn, and discover upon a distant hill men, cows, or horses, which were not perceptible to the naked eye! The first view of such things produces a young delight which never can be equalled. The next happiest day to that on which we experience any species of pleasure for the first time ourselves, is that on which we witness the same enjoyments in a young person whom we love.

THE END.

ENDNOTES.

ORIGINAL 1862 (2nd Ed.) EDITOR'S NOTES IN BOLD 'THE ANNALS OF BALLITORE' and 'BALLITORE & ITS INHABITANTS SEVENTY YEARS AGO'.

1. Line different in 1st Edition p. 3 – 'He died about a year after his wife, to who he was so devotedly attached that after her decease he was never seen to smile, and his hair, which was previously black, rapidly became as white as snow.'
2. **In 1841, by P. Kennedy, Anglesea-street, Dublin** (Note not included in 1st Edition); instead of duodecimo, 1st ed. says '... was subsequently published in one volume...'
3. Term 'Kildare Place' omitted in 1st ed.
4. Title of Chapter 1 in 1st ed. – THE ANNALS OF BALLITORE, SINCE THE YEAR 1766; BEING MARY LEADBEATER'S HISTORY OF HER OWN TIMES AND OF HER NATIVE VILLAGE.
5. 1st ed. '... autumnal scene ...'
6. It is at this point in the text that the original editor removed the description of the village and replaced it with Mary Leadbeater's poem, 'Ballitore,' – in the words of the editor, '(The general description of the village of Ballitore as it appeared in the year 1766, which here follows in the author's manuscript, is now so inapplicable that it is thought best to omit the few pages it occupies in the "Annals" and to substitute, with some omissions, a poem written by her in the year 1778, which will recall to many of the readers of these volumes some of the beloved scenes and sports of their childhood.)'
   With the help of Christopher Moriarty we have now re-inserted the intended description of the village and the poem has been retained as an Appendix to the work. The transcription was made by Christopher Moriarty from the National Library microfilm copy of the original manuscript and we thank them for their permission to reproduce it here. It is taken from the, Ballytore Papers P1091 – Page 16 of both printed 1862 editions it begins on page 4 of the manuscript. Note there is only one paragraph break in the manuscript.
7. This marks the end of the 'missing' text or restored pages and is followed by page 27 of the printed edition.
8. This actual map, an orginal Map of Dublin in 1728, by Charles Brooking, was donated to the Library by Richard Chinn as a legacy of his late mother and now proudly hangs once more in Ballitore, in the Community Library and Museum, in Mary Leadbeater's House.
9. Tullalost in both eds. but actually Tullylost near Rathangan.
10. 1st ed. '... in as far as she could ...' – missing word 'had' from this line also – '...and an uncommon...'
11. 1st ed. '... cannot account for.'
12. 'fomented' as appears in 2nd ed. The line in 1st ed. – 'It was thought interest fermented family dissensions.'
13. 1st ed. 'She had the happy art of nourishing confidence with restraint.'
14. 1st ed. '... when we were ...'; 2nd ed. '... when wew ere'
15. 1st ed. 'county' rather than 'country'
16. Word 'his' missing in 1st ed. '... resigned into the hands of son ...'
17. Silent written as 'silen' with't' missing in 1st ed.
18. 1st ed. – '... her for wife his son ...' – missing word 'to'
19. 1st ed. '... a person remarked on his complaisance not very kindly ...'
20. 1st ed. '... the boys – the bustle ...' boys' rather than 'the days'
21. No quotation marks in 1st ed.
22. 1st ed. '... asked ...' rather than inquired
23. 1st ed. '... whe n on a suddenl ...'
24. The second half of this paragraph from 'Poor little Newman...punishment enough.' does not appear in the 1st ed., which in turn has an effect on page numbering and Chapter III ends in 1st. ed. at p.90.
25. Some of contents missing from 1st. ed. – Aldborough Wrightson's grave.– Heroism of Arabella Forbes. – Tom Eyre rebuked by a blockhead. ... (and) ... Molly Hudson begins a twenty years' visit to the Retreat. – A convict rescued from "the Duke of the World."– A tender-hearted Judge ....'
26. **No wonder. Whatever the claims of Purver's translation to correctness, it is strangely deficient in the pathos and beauty of the authorized version. – *Editor.*** 1st ed. has two asterisks – a 2nd at end of paragraph. Footnote in 1st ed. does not ascribe the note to the 'Editor.'
27. Writtens as is – 2nd ed. has full stop inside bracket –.") both editions have quotation marks within.
28. 1st ed. full stop outside square bracket
29. This paragraph was follwed in the 1st ed. by the paragraph beginning with, 'On the 7th of Fifth-month, 1777, William Leadbeater came to school.' – see next note.
30. This whole paragraph is out of position and appears earlier in the 1st ed. after the paragraph about the bone setter which ended with the boy being expelled from school and finishing his career '... in a state

of abject beggary.' The editor of the 2nd ed. has placed it in chronological order after Margaret's marriage in 1776.

31. 1st ed. does not include the next two paragraphs but continues with, 'On the 22nd of Twelfth–month, 1778, in anticipation of my brother's marriage ...'
32. The omission of these preceding two paragraphs and their subsequent reintroduction in the 2nd ed. makes us wonder about the decisions and the editors themselves?
33. **William Colles was the proprietor of the marble mills at Kilkenny.**
34. **The second Richard Shackleton, the subject of these verses, spent the whole of his long life, with brief intervals, in his native village, where he died in the summer of 1860, in the eighty–first year of his age. A devoted student of four great poets, to whose chefs–d'oeuvre he chiefly confined his studies, his friend George Downes on one occasion addressed him thus: "Richard, you know Virgil, but you don't know Latin; you know Ariosto, but you don't know Italian; you know La Fontaine, but you don't know French; and you know Milton, but you don't know English."** This note is not in the 1st ed. and the first stanza has a break/space after 'In close union humankind.' thus dividing it into two. Next two paragraphs (2 complete pages of 2nd ed.) do not appear in the 1st ed.
35. Preceding two paragraphs not in 1st ed. possibly as they are of little consequence to the 'Leadbeater' narrative or maybe they might have been thought to be a little risqué.
36. 1st ed. does not add '...with perfect truth,–'
37. 1st ed. 'I have often applied to him these lines:–'
38. 1st ed. the preceding two lines are as one separated by a semi–colon '... Civil War;" as the American war ...'
39. Next three paragraphs (3 pages in 2nd ed.) omitted from 1st ed.
40. Once again the descriptions of the death of the boys and the story about Forbes wooden leg may have been incidental and may be the reason they were omitted from 1st ed.
41. 1st ed. – '... parole.'
42. 1st ed. – '... as fair and as sweet as the daisy, and as innocent," formed a combination to refresh his mind, wearied with the ardors of the torrid zone.'
43. 1st ed. '... he was captain of foot ...' leaving out 'a'
44. 1st ed. probably more correctly a capital E for Essay on the Sublime and Beautiful
45. Often in the 2nd ed. a quotation may only have quotation marks at the end as here but I have added others. In 1st ed. every line of a quotation might have quotation marks.
46. Retreat not in italics in 1st ed.
47. 1st ed. '...believe he told...'
48. 1st ed. Bayley
49. ibid.
50. 1st ed. this last part as a quote – ... "he would like to go to heaven, if he were sure of meeting his father and mother there."
51. 1st ed. Inverts the lines which begin 'My father, for the life of him...and he said so.' and instead it reads – "With these arms we have visited" This was so extremely apropos to the snuff–box, that my father, could not, for the life of him, restrain his wit on the occasion. But though my father's wit was thus sportive, his good nature could repair its transgressions.
52. 1st ed. 'After eight years residence amongst us he died, regretted by all who had enjoyed his friendship.'
53. 'Visit to Ballitore of Benjamin Rotch...' simply written in 1st ed. as 'Visit from an American gentleman.' Regarding the death of Edmund Burke the line 'Letter from him to the author, dictated during his last illness' does not appear in Chapter VII contents in 1st ed. Neither does 'Spread of Republicanism Principles'
54. **This excellent matron was the prototype of Rose, in Mary Leadbeater's "Cottage Dialogues."**
55. **Thomas Wilkinson was a native of Cumberland, a poet, and a member of the Society of Friends, with whom the author of the "Annals of Ballitore" frequently corresponded, although they were never personally acquainted. Wilkinson was a neighbour of Wordsworth, who refers to him in the following stanzas addressed "To the Spade of a Friend, an Agriculturist": –**

Spade! with which Wilkinson hath tilled his lands,
And shaped those pleasant walks by Emont's side,
Thou art a tool of honour in my hands
I press thee through the yielding soil with pride.

Rare master has it been thy lot to know;
Long hast thou served a man to reason true
Whose life combines the best of high and low,
The labouring many and the resting few;

Health, meekness, ardour, quietness secure,
And industry of body and of mind;
And elegant enjoyments, that are pure
As nature is; – too pure to be refined.

Here often hast thou heard the poet sing
In concord with his river murmuring by
Or in some silent field, while timid spring
Is yet uncheered by other minstrelsy.

Who shall inherit thee when death has laid
Low in the darksome cell thine own dear lord?
That man will have a trophy, humble spade
A trophy nobler than a conqueror's sword.

56. This is closed with full stop at '... painful to record.' – separate sentence in 1st ed.
57. 1st ed. '... elder brother ...'
58. 1st ed. '... and maintaining her authority ...'
59. 1st ed. 'This couple, the offspring of farmers ...'
60. In the list of pupils at Ballitore we often see a treble–barrelled name e.g. 1746 Robert Lecky, John – After some discussion with Christopher Moriarty at the Friend's Historical Library, we believe this to mean the father's name as demonstrated here in the text.
61. 1st ed. '... married a named Chambers, with whom she removed to Dublin.' words 'person' and 'reside in' missing.
62. 1st ed. 'James White left Ballitore, and left behind him ...'
63. 1st ed. '... I had received a kind answer to my enquiry after his health, dictated by him and signed by his hand, which left little room to expect his continuance on earth.' Follwing letter and postscript not included in 1st ed. simply followed by last 3 paragraphs beginning. 'This summer a bonfire...'
64. 1st ed. '... election for the County Kildare ...'
65. 1st ed. '... constituted part of the inhabitants ...'
66. 2nd ed. '...more delightfully ..., misspelled 'mroe'
67. 1st ed. '... and looked long and wistfully, with almost human affection in his eyes at his master.'
68. 1st ed. 'Bayley'
69. 1st ed. depredations written 'deprecations'
70. 1st ed. – this is not a complete sentence but punctuated here with a semi-colon and continued as part of one long sentence.
71. ibid.
72. 1st ed. '... purpose being defeated ... its detention there persuaded ...'
73. 1st ed. 'We laid our beds ...'
74. 1st ed. '... when the soldiers came, they should be placed, the insurgents said, in the front ...'
75. 1st ed. 'Bayley's'
76. 1st ed. '... whose young daughter, who had participated ... widow, now shared her joy ... nature. This young creature, still a child was endued with uncommon courage and prudence in this time of trial.'
77. This line not in 1st ed.
78. 1st ed. '... and returned towards the graveyard with it, till a boy met us who had been sent to fetch it; therefore the body had been washed, wrapped in its shroud, and laid in the coffin before we got there.
79. 1st ed. '... about half way between this and Athy, and there the insurgents were informed that ...'
80. 1st ed. 'Ephraim's body and mind were not rendered inactive by age., He went to Dublin and exerted his influence with his friend Agar, Archbishop of Cashel, by whose means he obtained an order to stop proceedings by court martial from Lord Castlereagh, whose brother, Colonel Stewart, commanded in Athy and that district.
81. 1st ed. 'County Wicklow mountains'
82. 1st ed. '... particularly now that we lived at the Retreat, for the protection of my mother.'
83. 1st ed. '... often thought, whilst enjoying, made winter ...' 'them' missing.
84. 1st ed. '... the insurgents; but said during his illness ...' 'he' missing.
85. 1st and 2nd ed. written goal but obviously should be gaol.
86. 1st ed. '... Robert Baxter fondly round his neck ...'
87. 1st ed. '... that we saw pass through the village, escorted by a strong military guard two men yet living; ...'
88. **Hugh Cullen was father to Paul Cullen, the present Roman Catholic Archbishop of Dublin, 1862.** 1st ed. says 1861; suggests the editor completed the work in that year but it was printed in 1862.
89. 1st ed. '... mental faculties to the last.'
90. 1st ed. 'Bayley'
91. **In the famine year, 1847, potatoes were sold at two shillings and sixpence per stone in Dublin.**
92. 1st ed. '... and l illiminations ...' i.e. and L illuminations
93. This line not in 1st ed. 'I wished for her picture drawn in this situation, and for its companion I should choose one of Edmund Burke assisting my mother to make pills for the poor.'
94. 1st ed. '... suit from the store ...'
95. 1st ed. '... We heard of their being there, and invited them ... and they appeared to be equally ...'
96. 1st ed. '... however deficient in many respects ...'
97. 1st ed. 'contemporaries.'
98. 1st ed. '... her brother, when she felt ...'
99. 1st ed. "Rosamund"

100. 1st ed. '... Captain Nagle ... is now an admiral and Sir Edmund Nagle; ...'
101. 1st ed. '... and restored it to his own.'
102. 1st ed. '... that when the decision was made against his judgment for enclosing the common...'
103. 1st ed. '... county of Kildare ...'
104. 1st ed. '... but the humiliation which he suffered, grief, and confinement, ...'
105. 1st ed. '... donation from Sarah Medlicott of ten pounds; and these charities, collected in small sums, like modest fertilizing streams, winding a silent course through the abodes of poverty, convey gladness to many a heart.
106. 1st ed. '... A woman was found on the morning of the 11th, supporting herself by an elder–tree bough which overhung the drift into which she had plunged, nearly exhausted; some lads ...'
107. 1st ed. 'With infinite difficulty a hearse, conveying the body of a gentlewoman who had died at Kilkenny, arrived at Ballitore inn.'
108. 1st ed. '... long fast from news ...'
109. 1st ed. '...amongst these was the worthy and learned cotemporary and friend of my father, Michael Kearney.'
110. 1st ed. 'County of Down'
111. 1st ed. 'Established Church'
112. **The following sonnet was written by William Robinson:–**

TO M. VOLNEY, AUTHOR OF THE "RUINS OF EMPIRES."

Volney, thy scheme–all cheerless and unblest,
Which robs its votary of his guardian power,
Snatches the solace from affliction's hour,
And dims with clouds the sunshine of the breast;
Sweeps from the wretch dejected and distress'd
When dangers thicken and when tempests lour,
His refuge and his hope, his shield and tower,
And leaves him hopeless, helpless, and depress'd;
Casts his an orphan on the world of care
To drudge and toil, then drop from life and light
Into the gloomy gulf of dark despair,
Wrapt in eternal and oblivious night.
To thee I leave this cold and joyless plan,
And hail Religion as the friend of man!

Distress'd and depress'd written distrest and deprest in 1st ed.; also note begins – The following sonnet will be read by interest and then title and then on next line – By William Robinson in italics.

113. 1st ed. '... It was on the 16th of Twelfth–month (December), began early in the morning, ...'
114. 2nd ed. has Dr. E.C. Herbert Orpen but it was Dr. Charles Edward Herbert Orpen (see page 200) so it is correct in 1st ed. Dr. C. E. Herbert Orpen and has been corrected here; Difference also in last lines – 1st ed. – Last re–union of the children of Richard Shackleton. – Two sides of a truth – Illness and death – ...
115. 1st ed. '... endeavour to save ...' changed here to '... in order to save ...'
116. 1st ed. this date is given as 1816.
117. 1st ed. '... Richard Shackleton's ...'
118. 1st ed. '... friends ...' with a small 'f'
119 1st ed. previous two lines all one line separated by a comma '... another school, they fitted ...'
120. 1st ed. 'She related to me some of what had befallen her since she left Ballitore.'
121. 1st ed. 'Henry came into possession of the family estate, £5,000 per annum and £25,000.'
122. 1st ed. '... entirely illuminated to the eastward.'
123. 2nd ed. Mistake in first word – written 'Tha' but properly 'The' in 1st ed. and corrected here
124. 1st ed '... Haughton, inclosing this address– ...'
125. **The following lines were addressed on this occasion to Priscilla Gurney, by Mary Leadbeater:–**

TO PRISCILLA GURNEY.

Did such a mind beam through a homely face
Beauty were not required to lend a grace
Did such a face veil an unworthy mind,
Our partial eyes might be to errors blind.
Sweet, ministering spirit! with delight we see
Inward and outward graces joined in thee.

126. The following, including an extract from the diary of George Downes does not appear in the 2nd ed. The text resumes after the translation of the poem – 'My dear brother, Abraham Shakleton...'
127. 1st ed. '...relief, and he was soon able to ride out...'
128. 1st ed. '... suffering, and from that time he never came down stairs.'

129. 1st ed. 'He ceased to speak and move about twelve at night and expired at two...'
130. 1st ed. 'Some sketches of my dear brother's character drawn by the hand of his excellent daughter, may be fitly introduced here:–...'
Included in the 2nd ed. is a note on Betsy Shackelton – **As Betsy Shackleton is here mentioned for nearly the last time in these "Annals," it may interest the reader to learn a few further particulars respecting her. One of the most gifted of a gifted family, she had a keen insight into character and much ability in delineating it – an exquisite perception of poetical beauty, and of originality of thought. Her mind was highly cultivated; she was remarkable for sensibility, intensity of family affection, cordiality in friendship, active benevolence, and a ready sympathy with every effort for the benefit of her fellow–creatures. After the death of her aunt Leadbeater, to whom she was warmly attached, she wrote a small volume of "Recollections," which was privately printed, and although penned in glowing terms it is considered by competent judges a faithful portraiture of her venerated relative. She also left in manuscript another little work entitled "Ballitore and its Inhabitants Seventy Years ago," which is a proof of her retentive memory, her sense of humour, her reflective cast of mind, and her great power of minute and effective word–painting. Her sketches of costume and character and of a state of society which has now nearly passed away are extremely graphic and amusing, and would be found especially interesting to the members of the Society of Friends, portraying as they do, with great fidelity, a community of their worthy predecessors at a period when all the external peculiarities of Quakerism were maintained with the fullest appreciation of their importance. Betsy Shackleton died in the home of her childhood, the school–house, Ballitore, on the 9th of Third–month, 1843, in the sixtieth year of her age, – and her memory is still precious in the hearts of many by whom she was loved and respected.** This footnote is not in 1st ed.
131. 1st ed. '... neither do his neighbours say he is in error, for the same reason.'
132. **Ebenezer Shackleton died at Moone, near Ballitore, on the 29th of Third–month, 1856, in his seventy–second year. He was witty, outspoken, and largehearted, and was remarkable for a capacious intellect, extraordinary originality, and unaffected benevolence.** This footnote is not in 1st ed.
133. 1st ed. '... memorial of him for ever removed ...'
134. 1st ed. 'Anecodote of Captain Clarke' not included in Chapter contents and George IV written 'George the Fourth.'
135. 1st ed. names the 'One boy' – Williams, indeed, whom I handled ...'; also inverted line, '... when the youth otherwise unoffending, left school ...'
136. 1st ed. ' ... "Moll Whelan," now Mary Casey, was living saw her, ...'
137. 1st ed. 'Friend' with a small 'f' – '... an English ministering friend ...'
138. 1st ed. '... the ague, nor his visits to me every evening ...' Possibly the book now in the County Library Archives from which I took the image for the front cover.
139. 1st ed. '... Mary Shackleton, L. J. Leadbeater, and James White accompanying.'
140. 1st ed. 'This year began in frost ...'
141. 1st ed. 'Captain Grattan's son Henry, assisted by one of his schoolfellows, commenced ...' Richard Davis Webb is named in the 2nd ed. and is the printer and the editor of Betsy Shackelton's 'Ballitore & Its Inhabitants Seventy Years Ago,' as well as being the printer of 'The Leadbeater Papers.'
142. 1st ed. 'The 18th regiment of Hussars, on their march, halted at Ballitore ...'
143. 1st ed. '... the manners of the country.'
144. 1st ed. 'He smiled at a description of his father read to him from a letter of Thomas Fisher, and said it was a just description; remarking that the heaviness of his father's countenance...'
145. 1st ed. 'They were drest ...'
146. 1st ed. 'On the first day of this year ...'
147. 1st ed. does not contain the reference '... (in the fields between Ballitore and Willowbrook) ...'
148. 1st ed. '... opened by this sorrow so like our own.'
149. 1st ed. 'Their major was the son of James Napper Tandy, so conspicuous in the disturbances of 1798, and who was my peaceable grandfather's pupil.'
150. 1st ed. '... having something of the money ... Savings Bank ...'
151. 1st ed. – brackets '... (herself and her sister taking care that they are done justice to), ...'
152. 1st ed. 'All houses, except Friends', united in so dazzling a show as never ...'
153. 1st ed. '... and they were desired to advance into the presence ... The address ... pronounced those words with emphasis which noticed ...'
154. 1st ed. '... On the 27th of Ninth–month, Molly Webster ...'
155. 1st ed. 'She was unable to leave her bed; she was too weak ... Lucretia Wright, and sent messages of love to her sister in Canada, ... expressing the love with ...'
156. 1st ed. '... having passed twenty–five of these under the same roof ...'
157. **Mary Doyle survived this sister nearly twelve years, and died on the 6th of the Fourth–month, 1834. It was in reference to these near neighbours and beloved friends that Mary Leadbeater wrote the following lines, which are among the most characteristic that she ever penned:–**

MY NEIGHBOUR.

Who is it, while adown the tide
Of rolling Time our vessels glide,

I see fair sailing by my side?
My neighbour.

Scarce conscious that thou art so near,
Scarce conscious that thou art so dear,
Onward my quiet course I steer,
My neighbour.

But should the stroke of Death divide
The twisted bands so firmly tied,
Should absence tear thee from my side,
My neighbour.

How wide the vacuum I should feel,
How deep the wound, how hard to heal,
How oft to thee should memory steal,
My neighbour!

For while my heart o'erflows my eyes,
And countless acts of kindness rise,
For every act still more I prize
My neighbour.

If prest with grief, if worn with pain,
Patient thou hear'st while I complain,
And sweetly bid'st me hope again,
My neighbour.

And when distress and sickness fly,
And round me shines a brighter sky,
I read thy gratulating eye,
My neighbour.

I see thy hearth so bright and clear,
Thy cordial welcome greets mine ear,
And converse pleasant as thy cheer,
My neighbour.

To spread the mental feast is thine;
The sage's thought, the poet's line,
If thou possess them they are mine,
My neighbour.

Thou lead'st me to thy garden rare,
With me its treasures thou wilt share,
And wishest mine to bloom as fair,
My neighbour.

Needs not that each to other's mind
By tastes congenial should be join'd,
For stronger links our union bind,
My neighbour.

Thus still adown life's rolling tide
Together may our vessels glide,
And may we anchor side by side,
My neighbour.

25th of Eleventh-month, 1810.

This note is not included in the 1st ed.

158. 1st ed. '... perished many who were as dear to their connections as he is to his.'; Following paragraph not in 1st ed. Text resumes with, 'Our young friend John James Lecky ...'

159. **Poor Clarke, (commonly called Captain Clarke, although he used to style himself more modestly as "formerly lieutenant in the late 12th Royal *Vitherans,*") frequently made himself a laughing-stock by his harmless vanity. On one occasion he was inspecting a body of haymakers in his lawn, when he suddenly thought he would gratify them by a novel sight of martial display; he accordingly went into the house, arrayed himself in his old regimentals, cocked hat, sword, and all, and marched out with important strides amongst his labourers. "Do I look warlike?" quoth the captain. "You look like the very devil, captain," said one of the admiring spectators, with**

questionable flattery, greatly to the innocent delight of Clarke, who afterwards related the compliment to his friend Mary Doyle. This note and the paragraph it refers to are not in the 1st ed.

160. 1st ed. 'His house, surrounded by planting, and cut off from the town ...'

161. **Abigail Roberts resided during a very long life at Mountrath in the Queen's County, stirring rarely from home, after the quiet fashion of those days. She was a member of the Society of Friends, and having a share of poetical talent, an active correspondence was maintained between her and Mary Leadbeater which was only terminated by death. Although living little more than thirty miles apart, these two friends never had a personal interview. Beside a great variety of unpublished poems, Abigail Roberts was the writer of three excellent little books for the Kildare Place Education Society, namely "The Schoolmistress," "Tom Higgins," and the "Cottage Fireside," which have had a large circulation in Ireland.**

162. One of the pupils who erolled in June 1819 was Richard Davis Webb who helped edit the Ballitore Magazine and who actually printed this original work in 1862 after the publication fo the Annals of Ballitore.

163. **Betsy Shackleton wrote a short Memoir of her sister, from which we make the following extracts:- "She finished her course at the age of twenty-four: she was then a wife and a mother, and was like the guardian angel of all who came within her sphere. How did the unsparing consumption feed upon her spirits, as well as undermine her health! yet she resigned up her husband, her child, her friends, and the world, which had so many charms for her innocent, happy mind, to Him who made her. She enjoyed and possessed the world's good things as not enjoying or possessing them, for she was loose from the world, and not spotted by it. She skimmed lightly over the path allotted to her, scattering her benefits, and not looking behind her to admire or even think of the good she had done.**

She had from childhood an originality of genius and a sweetness of temper which rendered her entertaining and interesting to all who knew her, being entirely unaffected, unconscious of her virtues, her talents, or her beauty. Her features were regular, and her countenance lovely. She evinced remarkable fortitude on many occasions; indeed, whenever there was occasion for courage or presence of mind, she displayed them; yet her tenderness and sympathy for the afflictions and pains of others was exercised to so great a degree as sometimes to injure her health. She early displayed an independence of mind which taught her to wait upon herself, to invent improvements in anything she was employed about, and to despise ornament, or the grandeur that springs from wealth. To the poor she was ever kind and attentive, and would debar herself of gratifications, or even of necessaries, to assist them.

In 1806 she married James White, a man who could appreciate her uncommon qualities. Their virtues and talents were not lost upon each other. Simplicity and truth bound them together, and their sphere of usefulness was enlarged. Her first consideration in every situation of life was, "How can I be useful?" A few months before her first child was born, she read Euclid with much pleasure; this she chiefly did to give her thoughts an agreeable turn, as other women read novels in order to divert their minds.

I shall go no farther. I am not capable of raising my thoughts from earth to heaven, from the fleeting joys of this life to the eternal felicity prepared for the righteous. Though I am fully persuaded that her enjoyment is greater than it has entered into the heart of mortal man to conceive, yet my nature deplores that she should lose her earthly treasures – though I believe the revelation which describes all tears to be wiped away from their eyes in that blessed country, yet it seems to me that she weeps for her husband, for her child, and for us. When I see the garden flourish, and the sun paint this fair creation, I regret that her eye is dim, and that she is covered up with the heavy earth, forgetful that she basks in the divine rays of the majesty of her heavenly Father. Let me therefore cease to lament the ravages of the worm on the dear form. Let me consider it but as the shell of the immortal soul – a shell which was intended for corruption, to mingle with the dust."

164. **Daughter of her sister Lydia White, and wife of Theodore Eugene Suliot, of Franklin Mills, Ohio, United States, where she now resides with her family.**

165. **It took pretty nearly the same direction as the present road from the Mill to the village. Forty years ago there was a very pleasant open path across the Mill–field, which is now entirely enclosed by a wall and hedges.**

166. **This cottage stood midway between Fuller's–court and Ballitore House, on the same side of the road.**

167. **Now known as Ballitore House. Bayly, as an heir of the Strettells, the original founders of the Quaker colony at Ballitore, was the owner in fee of the principal part of the village.**

168. **If not "the handsomest woman in the world," Kitty Bayly, formerly Kitty Yates of Moone, was remarkable for her beauty. Before Bob Bayly married her, he had paid his addresses unsuccessfully to another celebrated beauty, who soon after married John Stratford, afterwards Earl of Aldborough. There is a tradition that the rivals and their lovely brides happening to meet at a ball, Bayly, who could never pronounce *th*, addressed Stratford as follows: – "Well, Jack, which of us has got *de* best of *de* bargain?" The future Lady Aldborough was more eminent for her personal beauty than for some more important qualities.**

169. **This was the house occupied for nearly fifty years by Betsy Barrington, whose admirable character, beaming countenance, and hospitable parlour were so well known to the visitors to Ballitore, and to so many of the schoolboys.**

170. Patten–room, a small room used for cloaks and umbrellas, and in which women left the pattens which were in former times commonly worn by them when they walked the streets in dirty weather.
171. Afterwards Mary Leadbeater. In the text the asterisk denoting the footnote appears after the relevant word not at the end of the line.
172. A thin, rather stiff woollen material for women's wear now no longer manufactured.
173. Molly Haughton died in 1818, aged eighty.
174. Richard Shackleton.
175. Afterwards "Joseph Haughton of Ferns," an elder in good esteem, and remarkable for the heroic meekness and moral courage with which he maintained the peaceful testimony of Friends, during the hottest time of the rebellion of 1798, in the county of Wexford. As an indication of his courageous firmness, it is related that on one occasion he happened to be riding homeward on a lonely road by moonlight, when, on passing the end of a lane which led to a graveyard, he heard a plaintive cry coming from thence. He rode up to the entrance, fastened his horse to a tree, and entered the cemetery. At length he came to an open grave which had been recently dug. Looking in, he saw two bright eyes, and found that the cries were those of a poor goat which had fallen in, and was unable to extricate itself. He helped the animal out, and rode home. There are thousands of stalwart men who would rather march to the cannon's mouth, than perform such a feat under such circumstances.
176. Bob Hudson and Johnny Gavin frequently got drunk together, and when tipsy were always careful to use "the plain language." It is related that on one of these occasions Johnny exclaimed, *"Oh! lapis, lapis calaminaris."* Bob inquired what that meant. Johnny quoted a text of Scripture by way of explanation, and Bob gravely remarked, "Johnny, thee is a very religious, good man."
177. We have it from the best surviving testimony that the house in which the first Abraham Shackleton opened school and where his son Richard was born, still stands, and is that which is now occupied by Owen Finn, a respectable shopkeeper, and son to Dolly Finn so frequently mentioned in the "Annals of Ballitore." William Leadbeater built the porch to keep the old house from falling, and he divided the large school-room, which occupied the ground floor, into the present shop and the apartments behind it. It is related that the boys used to watch out of the front window, for "the man with the wig," who came up from the School–house of later days (where the family and the boys boarded and slept) with word that "dinner was ready."
178. This house stood on the site of a range of buildings, one of which is now the post–office. Behind, "in the golden days," were a garden and orchard, and in front, stretching down to the river, the elysium described in the text.
179. In a letter from an old Ballitore schoolboy, enumerating the tender and amusing reminiscences called up by a perusal of the "Annals of Ballitore," the writer observes that he "must not omit Abby Widdows and her griddle and pikelets, with as much tea and sugar as we could consume (when money was plenty) for a tenpenny bit. One of my schoolfellows almost broke the bank one night by drinking sixteen cups, and thereby earned a nickname which I shall not mention to ears polite."
180. Referring to her married sister, Lydia White, previously referred to in the Preface.
181. Job Scott, a native of Providence, Rhode Island, was a very eminent minister in the Society of Friends. His "Journal" which was popular amongst them for nearly half a century, is written with remarkable clearness and power, and affords an excellent exposition of their doctrines, as held by the founders of the Society; the evangelical idea being frequently put forward, whilst the chief prominence is given to the doctrine of the "Inward Light." In the account of his last illness, published at the end of his "Journal," there is no reference to any of the Shackleton family as having ministered to him at that time. It is greatly to be regretted that the notes which they furnished were suppressed, on the part of the compiler, as they would have doubtless added to that freshness, variety, and human interest, the studied absence of which is one of the principal causes of the dryness that is such a marked defect in the greater number of the writings of Friends published in the last century, and which accounts for the comparative neglect into which they have fallen.

INDEX.